The Complete Homemaker

The Complete Homemaker

Marshall Cavendish London & New York

Edited by Isabel Moore

Published by
Marshall Cavendish Publications Limited
58 Old Compton Street
London W1V 5PA

© Marshall Cavendish Limited 1972-73-74-75-76

Parts of this material first published by
Marshall Cavendish Limited in the partworks
*Golden Homes, Supercook, Come Alive,
Fashionmaker* and in *Flowers and Plants in
the Home*

This volume first published 1976

Printed by Henri Proost, Turnhout, Belgium

ISBN 0 85685 159 0

Picture credits

Anthony Verlag: 77
Bryce Attwell: 208, 210
Barclays Bank: 253
Barnabys: 31(b)
Behr: 120
John Bethell: 42(t), 78
Steve Bicknell: 38, 106
Michael Boys: 33(c), 37(b), 86(t), 99(t)
J. P. Broad/R. McEvoy: 70/1
Brolac: 37(tl)
Camera Press: 31(t), 33(t), 94(r)
Heidede Carstensen/Jacques Hartz: 87/
Studio Geisler: 24(b) /Studio 2000: 21, 35(t)/
Studio die Wohnform: 29, 66, 67, 68, 76,
79, 122/3
John Cook/Whitecross Studios: 60
Clive Corless: 42(b)
Michael Dunne: 103
Alan Duns: 84/5, 86(b), 92, 96(b), 97(t), 128-31,
137, 138-40, 156/7, 166, 168/9, 173, 185, 195,
197, 214, 215, 216, 217, 220/1, 222, 231, 242,
244/5, 246, 255
Richard Einzig: 8
Leonardo Ferrante: 58
Roger Gain: 93
John Garrett: 182, 207
Melvin Grey: 206
Nelson Hargreaves: 10-17, 35(b), 80(b)
Jerry Harpur: 194
Intermeuble: 22/3
International Wool Secretariat: 46

Paul Kemp: 186, 193, 196, 199, 201, 203, 229,233
Don Last: 156/7
Max Logan: 230
Bill McLaughlin: 37(tr), 55, 93(t), 95, 96(r),
98(t), 101, 102, 104(inset), 108/9
Mayflower Studio: 248/9
David Meldrum: 228
Nigel Messett: 44, 48, 63, 74
Brian Morris: 73(t), 91(l), 94(l), 209
Grazia Neri: 20
Stanli Oppermann: 237
Paf International: 27 /Delu: 227, 236
The Picture Library: 251
Roger Phillips: 132-6, 142/3, 148/9, 150/1,
152/3, 159, 160/1, 162, 163, 167, 174/5, 177,
178/9, 180, 180/1, 181, 190, 191/2, 204/5, 211,
212/3, 218, 223, 224, 225, 226, 232, 234, 238
John Prizeman/Ideal Standard: 34
Paul Redman: 36, 124
Iain Reid: 235
Rufflette: 80(b)
Eddie Ryle Hodges: 73(b)
Sale Stone Senior: 97(b)
Red Saunders: 187
David Smith: 188, 189
Harry Smith: 108
Syndication International: 26, 28, 32(r), 51,
52, 61, 62, 80(tr), 83, 91(r), 98(b), 100
Transworld: 24(t), 88, 126, 240
Tubby: 56
Michael Wickam: 99(b)
Elizabeth Whiting: 30, 41, 80(tl), 121
Zefa: 18, 32(l), 104

Introduction

For the newly-wed, the about-to-be-wed or indeed any young couple, setting up home is one of the most exciting of adventures. But although it is — and should be — a marvellous experience, real problems can arise which may create anxieties, perhaps even mar the pleasure of the occasion.

The Complete Homemaker is specially designed to assist you in solving these problems, for it provides an enormous range of practical advice, hints and ideas that will turn your house or flat into a comfortable, unique home that is truly yours — and at a price you can afford. And nowadays when such essentials as decorating, furnishing and even eating can cost the earth, if you're not careful (and often even when you are), such assistance is absolutely necessary if you're to cut budgets while maintaining standards.

Like all good books, it begins at the beginning: choosing colour schemes, learning to decorate, even redesigning rooms to suit *you*; then there's a comprehensive selection of professional-looking soft furnishings to make — with all instructions clearly explained and lavishly illustrated so that you'll know exactly how your bedspreads, curtains or cushions will turn out. The section concludes with some individual finishing touches with pictures and flowers, plus lots of sensible, easy-to-undertake home repairs to keep your home well cared for.

Eating together will probably be one of the focal points of your new life, so it's vitally important, as the book recognizes, that you shop wisely, learn the basics of cookery and prepare meals for the two of you that are both tasty and economical. Entertaining, something that should be fun but often turns out to be downright traumatic for the inexperienced cook, is also dealt with at length. Included is a section on how to prepare and 'pace' yourself so that you can actually enjoy being with your guests, plus a whole series of delicious, carefully balanced menus guaranteed to turn you into the hostess of the year!

And last, but certainly not least, is a chapter of good advice on those seemingly peripheral problems that often turn out to be pretty central to any solid, caring marriage — like actually *getting* married (it's more complicated than you might think), finding out about mortgages and what they entail (plus a tell-at-a-glance monthly repayment chart) and how to save as much money as possible on income tax.

There's lots for everyone in *The Complete Homemaker*.

Contents

Section I Making your house a home

Section II Kitchen crafts

Making your house a home

Decorating

Learning to paint

It isn't for nothing that carpenters scathingly refer to paint as 'long putty'. Many a botched woodwork job has been rescued by first-class painting. Equally, a bad paint job will ruin the finest woodwork. And come the time that you want a project fit for exhibition – the 'I Did It Myself' show – it is infuriating to see it spoiled by a stray bristle, an ugly run, or worse. Yet careful separation, and the observance of a few rules, can make your next painting project the most successful yet.

Choosing a brush

A good brush is a good investment – not just in better mileage, but in helping to preserve your good temper. A cheap brush is often stiff, making it difficult to avoid ugly brush marks on the finished job. If the bristles are too thin to pick up a decent load of paint, you may be tempted to dig too deeply into the paint – the result will be a clogged-up brush which you cannot get clean. And a cheap brush will also shed an infuriating number of bristles – at least a couple of which you will not notice until your otherwise immaculate gloss paint coat has dried out.

To be good, a brush does not have to be the most expensive one in the shop. But its bristles will at least be plump (to pick up a sufficient paint load), soft to the touch (to avoid brush marks), and long (to apply the paint smoothly). The best brushes are those with natural bristle – hair of hog or boar. This bristle has naturally split ends, which provide a grip to hold the paint and help it go on smoothly. The bristles on a good brush taper slightly at the end.

General-purpose paint brushes range in width from 1.3 up to 10cm ($\frac{1}{2}$–4in). For most indoor gloss paint or varnish work a 5cm (2in) brush is easiest to handle, while a 2.5cm (1in) brush is used for detail work, such as drawer handles and narrow edges.

New brushes shed hairs, and often contain odd bits of bristle and factory dirt. To keep this rubbish out of your painting the brush should be 'flirted', that is, flicked against the hand, and then washed in warm, soapy water and rinsed in clean water. Lay it flat to dry out.

Most professional painters break in a new brush by using it for priming or undercoating. This allows them to deal with the odd stray bristle where it matters least. They also keep one set of brushes reserved permanently for white or pastel paints, since darker pigments left in the 'stock' (handle) may 'bleed' into lighter paintwork.

Materials required

For painting a whitewood Welsh dresser, the paint tools required are: 1. Paint kettle. 2. Brushes 5cm (2in) and 2.5cm (1in). 3. Glasspaper – grades 0 and 1. 4. A cellulose-based filler, such as Polyfilla. 5. Small sponge or duster for surface cleaning. 6. Patent shellac-based knotting for treating knots. 7. Thinners – for which to buy, see instructions on the paint tin. 8. Pva adhesive, which you will mix in a thin solution with the cellulose filler to 'raise the nap'. 9. A flexible scraper to apply this mixture'. Also, you need newspaper or dustsheets to protect the floor.

Wood preparation

Whitewood furniture is made from deal or pine. It sometimes shows knots, it often has the exposed endgrain of plywood showing, especially on door edges, and the timber itself is somewhat coarser than more expensive woods. But careful preparation will give it a uniformly smooth finish.

If the woodwork has any knots, these have to be treated to prevent

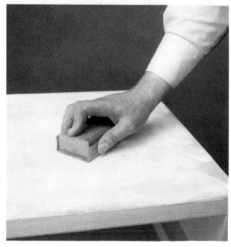

TOP *'Flirt' a new brush by flicking the bristles against your hand to remove loose hairs and debris.*

SECOND FROM TOP *Raise the nap by applying a slurry of filler and adhesive as thinly as possible.*

THIRD FROM TOP *Apply a stiff filler mixture with a flexible scraper to close up deeper cracks, pressing it firmly into the cracks to prevent it from falling out later, and carefully feathering it out over the edge to form a continuous, smooth surface for the paint.*

BOTTOM *Smooth the wood surface by sanding down lightly with glasspaper after the filling dries out.*

resin from 'bleeding' through the paintwork. Paint them with a thin coat of the shellac-based knotting, and leave it to dry.

Next raise the nap. Make a paste from 1 ounce (28gr) of the cellulose filler and the same volume of the pva adhesive, mixing with water to the consistency of cream. Apply it to the wood as thinly as possible with a scraper, working both with and across the grain. Work a small area at a time, as the filler hardens rapidly. When this has dried, rub down the surface with grade 0 glasspaper.

This treatment ensures that the surface of the wood is completely smooth. Whitewood tends to swell when moistened and so it is wise to raise any uneven fibres deliberately and sand them down before priming. The filler will also cover any small dents in the wood and close any tiny hair cracks that otherwise would not be obvious until they had been painted over. If any deep cracks are still visible, fill these with a stiff mixture of the cellulose filler and water, following the instructions on the packet. Give it at least an hour to dry – from a pale grey colour, it will turn white – before sanding down very lightly with grade 0 glasspaper.

Before you paint

The traditional three-coat indoor paint method consists of a lead-free primer, with undercoat and topcoat. Buy, if you can, from a store with a fast turnover of paint; pigment settles during storage, so the fresher the paint the easier it is to mix. If in doubt, stand the tin upside down for a day or so before using it, to help loosen settled pigment.

Prise off the lid by levering at several points around the rim, being careful to avoid distorting the tin. If the lid is not airtight, any remaining paint stored in the tin will form a skin. (Any skin in an old tin should be lifted out in one piece by running a stick around the edge; otherwise the skin will break up and leave bits on the paintwork. If necessary, strain the paint through a piece of muslin or old nylon stocking to remove lumps and other debris.)

When you have finished pouring paint from any tin, hammer the lid back on to provide an airtight seal. A block of wood big enough to cover the whole lid makes the best hammer; a carpenter's hammer will sometimes distort the lid and prevent it from closing properly.

Always mix paint thoroughly, with a circle-and-up movement, so that all constituents are evenly distributed. If using a thinners, do so sparingly; too much can spoil both the depth of colour and the gloss. A newly opened tin of paint normally needs no thinners at all.

Before you begin work, check the light. Daylight is by far the best, but if you must work at night try to pick the brightest place – the kitchen, probably – in the house. Under poor artificial light it is easy, particularly when using a white gloss finish to leave unnoticed 'thin' patches and spoil the job.

Next, protect the floor with newspaper or dustsheets. Never wear woollen clothes, as loose fibres will settle on the paint. Remove fittings, such as knobs or handles, from the unit. Remove the drawers and stand these on end; it is easier to paint a horizontal than a vertical surface, since there is less risk of 'runs' or 'curtaining'.

Now fix wooden blocks under the base of the unit to lift it clear of the floor. This will prevent your brush from picking up dirt from your newspaper, or fluff from your dustsheets. Vacuum clean the unit to get rid of any dust.

Priming

Always work in a set order. If you live in a house where wood-boring insects are particularly troublesome, start by painting the underside of the unit. It is nearest the floor, and therefore most vulnerable. If not, forget the underside and start on the back – where, while you get into your stride, any faults will show up least – and then do the sides. Next, paint the larger top and front areas and, finally, the narrow dividing strips. Never paint the slides on which drawers run – or they won't.

TOP *Clean the unit with a suction head attachment on an ordinary household vacuum cleaner to make sure the surface is completely free from fluff and dust.*

SECOND FROM TOP *Raise the unit clear of the floor by tacking wooden blocks to the base of the unit.*

THIRD FROM TOP *Masking tape can be used to prevent paint from seeping into the dovetail joints which could make the drawers hard to open.*

BOTTOM *Strain off bits of paint flakes and pieces of paint skin by carefully pouring the paint from the tin into a paint kettle through muslin, cheesecloth or an old nylon stocking.*

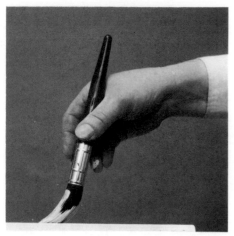

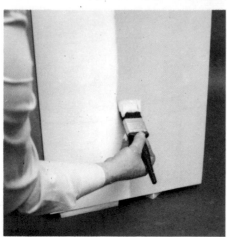

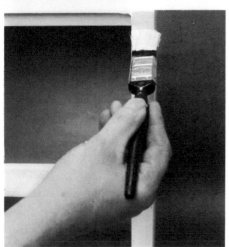

The primer comes first. Its function is to bind loose particles and form a tough, non-porous surface for the undercoat. Pour into the paint kettle just enough primer to cover HALF the depth of bristle in your brush. There should never be more paint than this in the kettle. By using a paint kettle you avoid the inevitable consequence of painting from the original tin – a build-up of thick, sticky paint around the rim which prevents you from getting an air-tight seal when you close the lid. And, by filling the kettle to the right depth, you avoid over-loaded, clogged-up brushes which are hard to clean.

Dip the brush into the primer. Wipe off any surplus paint on the inside of the kettle – not the rim – and lay on the primer with firm strokes along the grain of the wood. Do not be too timid; a firm, wristy action will spread the primer into a thin, but even, coat.

Allow 24 hours for the primer to dry. Then rub it down with grade 0 glasspaper, working along the grain of the wood, until you have a smooth finish. Wipe off the dust with a rag dampened with thinners. Clean the paint kettle and brush with thinners – the back of the paint tin will tell you which kind.

Undercoating

A good undercoat is, more than anything else, the basis of a good paint job. Any 'pimples', rough patches or unevenness of colour in the undercoat will show through the gloss paint, particularly if this is in one of the lighter shades. So the objective in undercoating is a velvet-smooth surface and evenness of colour.

White and the reds, particularly, are likely to show up all imperfections. For white, two coats of undercoat are best. For red, the evenness of colour

TOP *Hold the paint brush in the correct way, by gripping it firmly. To prevent 'curtaining', do not dip the bristles too deeply into the paint.*
SECOND FROM TOP *Apply the topcoat with smooth strokes along the grain of the wood. Breaking the strokes, or dabbing too lightly, will cause curtaining.*
THIRD FROM TOP *Each successive band of paint should slightly overlap the one before. It should be laid on firmly, cross brushed, then finished with the lightest possible strokes to ensure a smooth and even final finish.*
BOTTOM *A small, 2.5cm (1in) brush is best for the tricky edges.*

will be improved if a tube of tint colour the same shade as that of the topcoat is mixed in well with the undercoat.

With the paint in your paint kettle at the right depth, dip in the brush and wipe off any surplus on the inside of the kettle. Beginners often make the mistake of dabbing on too much paint too lightly; this causes the ugly, sagging effect known as 'curtaining'. The correct way is to make the paint spread as far as you possibly can while still looking even in colour.

Paint first *with* the grain of the wood, holding the brush quite firmly and without lifting it except where it naturally rises from the surface at the end of a stroke. Without reloading the brush, and pressing much more lightly, work backwards and forwards *across* the grain. This avoids a striped effect by eliminating the first brush marks. Finally, 'lay back'. Holding the brush almost flat with the work, brush so lightly that you can hardly feel the bristles touching the painted area, and in one direction only – with the grain, and working from the newest edge of the paint (the 'wet edge') back towards the previously painted area.

When you load your brush for the second time, start applying the paint, not on top of the existing wet edge, but one brushload away from it, and work back towards the already-painted bit. This avoids a build-up of paint in one place – the prime cause of curtaining. The strokes, on a wide flat surface, should be about 30cm (12in) long.

Edges are tricky; they catch the tip of the brush and release a globule of paint around the corner. Avoid this by stroking towards edges, where possible, rather than away from them. If you do cause a run in this way, wipe the paint off your brush and 'spear' off the run by pushing (instead of drawing) the brush. The same trick is used to pick up any stray bristles that appear.

Allow 24 hours for the undercoat to dry. Sand off any pimples, brush marks or other irregularities with grade 1 glasspaper, and remove the dust with a thinners-dampened rag. If the undercoat is uneven in colour – remember, the gloss coat will probably not correct this – repeat the whole procedure. It is well worth the trouble to get a first-class job. Once the undercoating has been completed, clean brushes and kettle thoroughly once more.

Topcoating

Gloss paint is stiffer than undercoat, so needs to be applied more firmly –

although the final laying-off strokes should be, if anything, even more delicate than before. It is important, too, that each new brushload should reach the previous one while the wet edge is still wet, and not sticky – with gloss paint, runs and curtaining can happen very easily. Otherwise, the technique is the same as for the undercoat.

One point is worth watching, however; because of its shiny surface, gloss paint can play tricks in poor light, and for this stage of the job only daylight is really good enough.

Gloss paint is touch-dry from three to six hours after application, but takes 16 to 24 hours to dry thoroughly. Edges subject to wear or knocks are best left alone for two or three days while the paint really hardens.

Care of brushes
Poor maintenance, tests have proved, wears out paint brushes much faster than painting does – and there is nothing like a dirty brush for ensuring that the next paint job will be a shoddy one.

If you have to leave a particularly long job unfinished in the middle of a coat, brushes full of paint can be left for a day or two suspended in water. Never let a brush stand on its bristles, since this may 'cripple' (distort) the ends. Suspend the brush by slotting a piece of wire or wood dowel through a hole drilled through the handle. For longer periods, of three or four days, thinning agents should be used instead of water. When resuming painting, rough-dry the brush on a piece of clean board to remove excess water or thinning agent. It is important to remove thinners, since they dilute the paint and produce a patchy surface. However, it is always best to finish a coat of paint completely, as resuming the work half-way through will produce an uneven result.

Brushes should be cleaned thoroughly after each change of paint. Working from the stock towards the tip, scrape off excess paint with the back of a knife and sluice the brush in thinners or a proprietary brush cleaner, finishing off with warm water and soap or detergent, and then clean water. Once dry, the bristles should be wrapped in clean newspaper, fixed with a rubber band, and the brush stored flat. Exposed bristles are subject to attack by moths.

The final result – a perfectly painted Welsh dresser, fit to grace any room of the house.

Learning to paper

For your first attempt at paperhanging, choose walls which are free of awkward obstructions like doors and windows which might make too many difficulties for a beginner. Move as much furniture as possible from the room, put the rest in the middle and cover it. Give yourself plenty of time – paperhanging can't be rushed – and try to work in daylight.

Materials required

For preparing the walls you will need: 1. Bucket. 2. Sponge. 3. Glasspaper wrapped around a cork block. 4. Plaster filler. (Use a cellulose-based proprietary brand.) 5. Lining paper. If your walls were previously papered you will also need: 6. An old distemper brush. 7. A broad stripping knife. 8. Chemical stripper (optional).

For putting up the paper you will need: 1. Plumb bob, chalked line and chalk. 2. Scissors with 28–30cm (11–12in) blades. 3. 1m (3ft) rule. 4. Soft pencil. 5. A table or board supported on trestles. (The board should be at least 55cm (22in) wide and 1.80m (6ft) long to provide an adequate surface for pasting. An old flush door suspended across two chairs could also be used. 6. Adhesive. (Most manufacturers give advice about which adhesive to use for the type of paper.) 7. Buckets in which to mix adhesives. (Plastic ones are better than metal.) 8. Pasting brush. 9. Paperhanger's brush. Have two brushes, if possible, to save delay if one has to be washed (after picking up paste). 10. A hop-up or stepladder, plank and strongly built box (to make a platform from which to reach the top of the walls safely). 11. Seam roller.

Quantities of paper

A roll of standard British wallpaper is about 10m (11yd) long and 52.5cm (21in) wide. Most papers are ready-trimmed but if they are not, this can be done by the retailer. To estimate how many rolls of paper you need, measure the total length right round all the walls you want to paper, and the height of the room from skirting board to ceiling (or to cornice or picture rail). Rolls of paper are produced in batches, so check that they come from the same one (each has a serial number), as rolls from different batches may vary slightly in colouring. If you buy a 'job lot' of paper in a sale, always buy more than you need to cover wastage by matching patterns or through damage.

Preparing the walls

Walls must be carefully and thoroughly prepared in order to make paperhanging a complete success. New wallpaper slapped on is likely to bubble and blister. The walls should be as even as possible, and completely clean and free of grease.

Newly plastered walls containing lime can be papered if they are perfectly dry. Coat the area with an alkali-resisting primer which will neutralize any active lime in the plaster. Alternatively, use one of the papers which has been specially treated for use on new plaster; a lining paper would be useful here.

Distempered walls should be washed down with soapy water to remove all grime.

Painted walls should also be washed down with soapy water to remove all grime. When dry, gloss-painted walls should be keyed by thorough scouring with coarse glasspaper (this slight roughening of the surface will help the paper adhere securely).

Previously papered walls should first be stripped by soaking the paper well with warm water and then using an old distemper brush. A chemical stripper may be added to the water – but if the chemical splashes the paintwork, wipe it off straight away. While the paper is still wet, use the stripping knife to ease it off a little at a time. Properly soaked paper will come away from the wall easily and cleanly.

Once all the paper is off, wash the walls with soapy water, rinse with clean water and, when dry, sand them lightly to remove surface blemishes, such as small pieces of paper and old paint drips.

Making good

Fill any holes and cracks with a proprietary cellulose filler and when it is completely dry, smooth the holes with glasspaper.

TOP *Lining paper is easier to handle if you fold it concertina fashion.*

SECOND FROM TOP *Hold the folded lining paper with your left hand and leave the right hand free to smooth it to the wall (reverse if you're left-handed).*

THIRD FROM TOP *Match the lefthand side of the paper to the righthand side of the cut piece to ensure that a drop repeat matches when the pieces are on the wall.*

BOTTOM *Use a plumb bob to establish a true vertical line.*

Roll Chart	Distance around room in metres (including doors, windows, etc)												
Height from skirting in cms	10	11	12	13	14	15	16	17	18	19	20	21	22
	Number of rolls required												
200 – 220	5	5	5	6	6	7	7	7	8	8	9	9	10
220 – 240	5	5	6	6	7	7	8	8	9	9	10	10	10
240 – 260	5	6	6	7	7	8	8	9	9	10	10	11	11
260 – 280	6	6	7	7	8	8	9	9	10	11	11	12	12
280 – 300	6	7	7	8	8	9	9	10	11	11	12	12	13
300 – 320	6	7	8	8	9	10	10	11	11	12	13	13	14
320 – 340	7	7	8	9	9	10	11	11	12	13	13	14	15

Height Conversion	
6′ 6″ =	198 cms
7′ 0″ =	213 cms
7′ 6″ =	229 cms
8′ 0″ =	244 cms
8′ 6″ =	259 cms
9′ 0″ =	274 cms
9′ 6″ =	290 cms
10′ 0″ =	305 cms
10′ 6″ =	320 cms
11′ 0″ =	335 cms

Distance Conversion	
32 feet =	9.7 metres
36 feet =	11.0 metres
40 feet =	12.2 metres
44 feet =	13.4 metres
48 feet =	14.6 metres
52 feet =	15.8 metres
56 feet =	17.1 metres
60 feet =	18.3 metres
64 feet =	19.5 metres
68 feet =	20.7 metres
72 feet =	22.0 metres

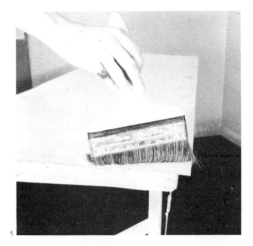

The next step is to 'size' the walls. This prevents them from absorbing the paste too quickly, allowing time to position the paper on the walls correctly. To make size, dilute the adhesive you intend to use according to the manufacturers' instructions (the packets usually give instructions for making it up for both size and adhesive). Coat the walls with it, using a pasting brush.

Adhesive

Make up the adhesive according to the directions given on the packet at least 20 minutes before you want it. This gives it time to absorb the water properly and become completely smooth. Always make up a complete packet at a time to ensure a correct consistency – any paste left over can be kept in a completely airtight jar and be used for touching up, if necessary. Don't mix batches of paste.

When the wallpaper is cut, it is a good idea to test for colour-fastness on a waste piece. If the colours do run, take extra care not to get paste on the surface of your cut pieces.

Lining the walls

For a really first-class wallpapering job, always use a lining paper under the wallpaper. It provides an ideal surface of even porosity, to which the wallpaper and its adhesive will marry, particularly if the wallpaper is heavy

(the principle being that paper sticks to paper more firmly than to plaster). Heavy papers, especially embossed ones, have a tendency to stretch as their fibres first absorb the paste then shrink on drying. This can mean that the joints (joins between pieces) open because the paper loses its grip on the plaster surface. Lining paper prevents this happening. Another advantage of lining papers is that they can disguise a 'bad' surface, as well as having some insulating value.

The method of pasting and hanging lining paper is similar to that for wallpaper (see below – make sure you paste the rougher side so the smooth side is outermost). It is best hung horizontally as the finished effect is smoother. This makes the paper rather difficult to handle on a long wall, so you should fold the paper, without creasing, concertina-fashion (always with pasted side to pasted side). Start

TOP *Paste from the centre to the far edge of the paper.*

SECOND FROM TOP *The paper is pulled back so that it overlaps the near edge of the board. The paste is then brushed out to this edge.*

THIRD FROM TOP *When the paper on the board is pasted, the righthand edges are brought over to make a large fold.*

BOTTOM *When the whole length is pasted, the lefthand edges are brought over to meet the first fold.*

9

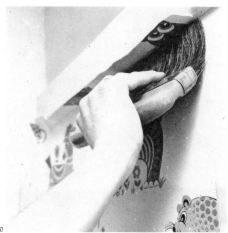

10

11

12

in the right-hand corner of the wall and, holding the paper with your left hand, brush it out with your right hand (reverse this if you are left-handed). If you prefer to hang the paper vertically, stagger the joints with those of the wallpaper to avoid the possibility of ridges. Like wallpaper, lining paper should be butt-jointed (ie, the pieces are positioned edge-to-edge, with no overlap).

Using the plumb bob

As few corners, cornices, ceilings or picture rails are really straight, either vertically or horizontally, it is wise to use a plumb bob to check them and, if necessary, to establish a true vertical line for the position of the first piece of wallpaper.

The easiest way to do this is to chalk the string to which the plumb bob is attached and then suspend it from the top of the wall, about 50cm (20in) from the corner of the wall nearest the light. (As you hang wallpaper, always work progressively away from the light, so that any imperfections or slight over-laps will not cast a shadow.)

When the weighted end of the plumb bob is still, hold it against the wall and pluck the string from the wall and let it snap back to mark the line (this is much easier to do if someone helps you).

To find a true horizontal line for hanging lining paper, use a 1m or 3ft ruler to draw chalk lines at right angles to the vertical. Check the line with a spirit level if you have one.

Cutting the paper

Unroll the wallpaper face ('right' side) upwards. Measure the length required and cut off 5–10cm (2–4in) below this (the additional amount is for easing the paper at the top and bottom). If the paper is patterned, find the first complete motif and cut off 2.5–5cm (1–2in) below. These extra amounts allow you to position the paper accurately, and to ease it in at the top and bottom.

Cut the next length, checking that the pattern matches exactly at the top and sides, again allowing the additional

TOP *Place the first length of wallpaper in position, keeping the side edge exactly level with the chalked plumb line while the paper is eased upwards.*
SECOND FROM TOP *When the paper overlaps at the top, a paperhanger's brush is used to hold it in position.*
THIRD FROM TOP *and* BOTTOM *Smooth down the centre of the paper and then out to the sides in arrowhead movements.*

centimetres at top and bottom. Lay the cut lengths on top of each other. Cut two or three lengths before pasting. Turn the pile over, so that the 'wrong' side now faces upwards, with the first cut length on top.

Pasting the paper

Arrange the pile of paper centrally on the width of the pasting board, so that a little board shows on either side of the paper and the top edge of the paper is on your right. If the paper is longer than the board, have the overhang on your left. Push the top length only so that its far edge slightly overlaps the edge of the board (Fig 5). This is to avoid getting paste on to the board, and then on to the face of one of the other sheets.

Apply a liberal brushful of paste along the centre of the length of the

As each length is pasted, place it on another table to 'rest'. This lets the paste soak in—the time depends on manufacturers' instructions—and the paper becomes supple.

Hanging the paper

Lift the first length of paper over your arm and carry it to the wall. Unfold the top half and, holding the length carefully, place the top edge exactly level with the plumb line. If the corner is vertical, ease the paper into it exactly. Otherwise let it overlap into the corner.

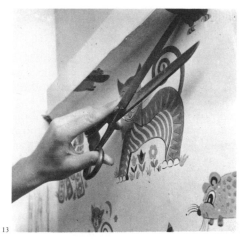

Smooth along the top of the piece with the paperhanger's brush to hold it in place. Now smooth down the centre and out to the sides in a series of arrowhead motions (Fig. 11). This movement eliminates air bubbles, and spreads the paste evenly on the wall. Don't brush from side to side, as this could move the paper out of position. Try not to overhandle or stretch the paper. If any paste seeps out from the sides of the paper, wipe it off with a rag. Keep the paperhanger's brush completely clean, and don't let any paste get on to the 'right' side of the paper.

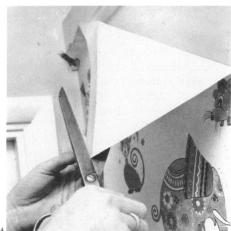

Check again for correct placing, then unfold the bottom section and smooth it out, brushing it as before, until the whole length is completely flat without creases or blisters. The bottom edge will overlap the skirting board.

Run the back edge of the scissors along the paper into the angle between the wall and the cornice or picture rail. Ease the top of the paper from the wall gently, and trim off the excess paper along the crease. Now repeat the procedure at the bottom, where the wall meets the skirting board. If you overlapped the paper into the corner, trim off the excess in a similar way. Smooth the paper back into position.

Hang the next pieces of paper in the same way, butting the edges together (do not overlap them) and carefully matching the pattern. Run the seam roller down the joint to give a completely flat butt edge when the paste is nearly dry.

TOP *Use the back edge of scissors to run along the paper in the angle made by the wall and picture rail.*
SECOND FROM TOP *The top of the paper is eased away from the wall and the excess trimmed off along the crease line.*
THIRD FROM TOP *Match the pattern before smoothing the second length into position.*
BOTTOM *Use a seam roller to give a firm butt edge when the paste is nearly dry.*

Brightly coloured wallpaper, with animal motifs, is perfect for the nursery.

paper, and brush out to the far edge. Always brush outwards, as there is a danger of paste getting on to the face of the paper if you brush inwards. Slide the paper towards you, so that the unpasted side now slightly overlaps the near side of the board. Brush the paste from the centre to this edge.

When the length on the table has been pasted, lift both the corners on the right edge and bring them over to make a large fold (Fig. 7), without creasing (the pasted sides will be facing). Gently draw the paper along the table until the unpasted portion is flush with the left-hand edge of the board. Paste this length as before and then bring this section over and down to meet the first fold (Fig. 8).

17

Using colour

A good sense of colour is essential if your interior decor is to be a success. Apart from the technical skills involved in painting and paper hanging, you need to be able to combine colours and patterns for maximum appeal. With a little care you can choose a colour scheme that will add greatly to the beauty and comfort of your home.

Before starting to decorate your home, you should spend some time considering various colour schemes. When choosing colours that go well together there are no real hard and fast rules to bear in mind, and there is no such thing as a 'good' or 'bad' colour. People's reactions to colour vary tremendously, and your feelings about a particular combination of colours might be quite different from someone else's.

The kind of colour scheme you choose will depend very much on the use to which a particular room is to be put. For instance, a good colour scheme for a study might be mainly brown—dark leather chairs with mahogany furniture and woodwork. The walls could be a cream or light chocolate colour, and the carpet a plum colour. Silverware could be placed around on shelves, or in a glass-fronted cupboard. With this sort of colour scheme the effect will be of solid and subdued comfort. In rooms where you relax for lengthy periods of time the emphasis should probably be on cheerful yet unobtrusive colour schemes.

Try not to be too influenced by the latest fashion in colours. Many people have followed the latest trends slavishly—often with disastrous results. Your own tastes, combined with careful judgement, are far more important. When discussing colour schemes, the main concern is how to combine different colours successfully. It is here that you will benefit on how to get the most out of your personal preferences.

Colour properties

A very great deal has been written about the theory of colour. Before choosing a colour scheme for a particular room you should know about the basic properties of colour. These are hue, tonal value and chromatic intensity.

Hue is the quality which distinguishes one colour from another—red and blue for example. Black, neutral greys, and white have no hue.

There are three basic groups of colour—primary, secondary and tertiary. The colours in the primary group are red, yellow and blue. By mixing any two of these together you can get orange, green and purple. These are the secondary colours. Tertiary colours—adjacent to each other on the colour wheel—are yellow green, blue green, blue violet, red violet, red orange and yellow orange. Altogether, twelve colours go to make the colour wheel. This will be of considerable help to you when you begin to work out possible colour combinations.

Tonal value refers to the lightness, or darkness, of a colour. For example, yellow is lighter than all but the palest of violets.

Light tones are more reflective than darker colours. This is why dark rooms are made brighter by the use of light coloured paints. On the other hand, rooms with large windows, with plenty of access to sunshine, will remain light and cheerful even with a very dark colour scheme.

A colour scheme made up of subtle tone changes will make a room seem larger and play down the appearance of awkward shaped furniture. Such a scheme will give a quiet overall effect. You should pick out something in an opposite shade to the general colour scheme. This will provide a point of interest and prevent the room from becoming boring.

Strong tonal contrasts catch the eye. Your furniture will stand out where such a colour scheme is used. A contrast between the walls and curtains will make a room look much smaller. The reason for this is that the different surfaces will be 'cut up', or separated. You'll find that the effect can be pleasantly lively and stimulating.

An understanding of tone is one way of making sure that you use colour attractively. Two colours which do not seem to combine satisfactorily may well do so when one of them is lightened or darkened.

Chromatic intensity refers to the chromatic brilliance of a colour. Adding grey to any colour will lower its intensity. Of the primary colours,

Most rooms, like the room on the left, will benefit from an all white basic decor. Areas of colour can be used to enliven it and, since the 'base' is muted, strong colours such as orange and purple (as here) can be used to good effect.

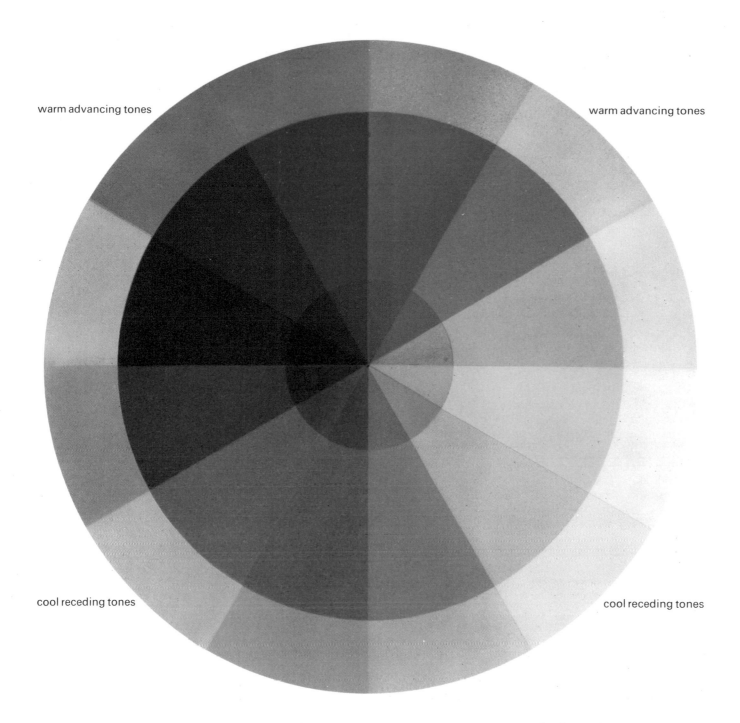

warm advancing tones

warm advancing tones

cool receding tones

cool receding tones

red has the highest intensity, followed by yellow, then blue.

The intensity of the colours you choose will affect your colour scheme in a number of ways. A room decorated in very intense colours will be highly stimulating—reminiscent of the colours at a funfair. However, you'll find such strong colours quite unsuitable for a living room and other leisure areas of your house, where you spend a lot of time. Only use intense colours in small doses. Flowers, cushions and ornaments present excellent opportunities for highly colourful temporary displays. Remember that a room decorated totally in low intensity colours can be very dull. The stimulus of stronger colours in small areas of the room is essential. Try to create a balance between the two extremes.

For living areas, it's a good idea to concentrate on gradual colour changes for the walls. For instance, you could start off with a brilliant red and, by adding more and more green, merge gradually into a rich brown. In the same way, you can merge yellow into cream, or blue into steel grey. By adding white or black you can change a colour totally. For example, red can be turned into a restful pink by adding white.

The intensity of the colour you choose should be related to the size and shape of the surface to be covered. Warm colours like red, orange and

A good colour wheel is indispensable in the planning of colour schemes.

yellow are very dominant—particularly in a small room. This can be extremely tiring on the eye. Such colours are best used for highlighting the colour of objects like lampshades and ornaments.

Blues and greens are cool, retiring colours. They are good when used as background shades. Objects painted in these colours tend to lose definition. This can be useful in painting ugly—but essential—furniture.

You would be well advised to avoid the use of contrasting full intensity colours—such as red and green or orange and violet. They can provide

19

initial excitement, but the long term effect will be tiring and dazzling.

Choosing the colour scheme

Before choosing your colour scheme there are several considerations to be taken into account. If you are fortunate enough to be decorating a large, well-lit room, with a southerly aspect, you will be free to experiment with almost any colour scheme you may have in mind. On the other hand, if the room is on the small side the use of warm colours will make it look smaller still. The effect can be quite cosy—but also claustrophobic. Aim at increasing the sense of space as much as possible. This involves using dull, cool colours on most of the larger surfaces like walls, ceilings and floors. The sense of space can be further increased if you incorporate the colours used in the small room into a larger, neighbouring room. This will prevent the small room from seeming to be cut off from the rest of your home. The pattern of the curtains in the small room might well be used for the wallpaper in the next room.

If you paint one wall in a darker colour than the others, it will have the effect of opening up the room. Don't choose a colour that contrasts too strongly with the others. The effect may be to diminish the size of the room.

A room may be dark either because the window is small or because it faces north. The use of dark colours over large areas of such a room will tend to accentuate the darkness. If the room is used mostly in the evening, find out what the colours you choose will look like by artificial light. Some colours will look very different in the shop compared to your home. Shop lighting is deliberately chosen for display purposes, and is usually much brighter than domestic illumination. It is best to concentate on light colours, as these will brighten the room considerably.

If your room is quite high, paint the ceiling in a dark shade. This will have the effect of lowering the ceiling. Don't use this method if your room is of an average height, as the result will be to 'lower' the room to an uncomfortable extent.

The right scheme for your home

When choosing a colour scheme it is often hard to know where to begin. Colours work best when they are related to their surroundings. For instance, the view from the window may suggest the dominant colour for a particular room. A picture, or the pattern in a set of curtains, may lead to a starting-off point. Select a subordinate colour in the picture, or pattern, as the dominant colour in your scheme for the room.

Remember, there is no such thing as the 'right way' of choosing colours. If you intend to keep existing carpets or curtains it is quite pointless selecting colours which clash with them. Always start with what you have, and build from there.

As far as possible, consider the walls and curtains first. These cover the major area in any room. Next, choose the colour or pattern of the

A skilful use of colours can radically change the character of any room, as both of these pictures illustrate.

On the LEFT, *a clever use of different shades of one basic colour – in this particular case blue – provides a dominant yet very restful colour scheme for an ultra-modern bedroom.*

BOTTOM, *two 'warming' colours provide the basic colour scheme here – brown and pink – and gradations of these colours combine to produce a more traditional bedroom which is elegant yet comfortable, cosy yet with a feeling of space.*

carpet, and the colour of the ceiling. Having selected the colour scheme for the major areas of the room, you should consider the shade and patterns for any upholstery. Now you can think about the smaller objects in the room—like ornaments and small cushions. If your basic colour scheme is in light and restful shades, splashes of stronger colours will add interest to the room. Remember, any colours you consider must be seen in relation to the room you are decorating before a definite choice is made. Mistakes are difficult to avoid completely—but they can be kept to a minimum.

The final result of a successful colour scheme should be one of harmony, and there should also be some sort of theme. Try to establish a definite connection between living areas. This can be done by using the same dominant colour, or pattern, on walls or in curtaining. A living room, where you wish to relax and spend a lot of time, will benefit from subdued

rather than pretty patterns. Also, there should be no strong contrasts in colour or tone. Pretty patterns and strong contrasting colours are best used in rooms which are only used for brief periods—like bathrooms.

A sense of balance and proportion is all important. Colours and patterns should help to highlight the focal point in a room—be it a balance between patterned and plain surfaces. If you do this the eye will be neither over-stimulated nor bored. Every room needs some light areas, no matter how dark the overall effect of the colour scheme is. Some surfaces, or objects, should be accentuated—even in the most subdued of rooms. A room decorated in warm colours needs a cold colour somewhere for visual relief.

Visual emphasis
Every room needs some sort of emphasis in the colour scheme to give point to the whole design. For

Colours or shades of colour carried through from one room to another can give your home an integrated look; in this case the same carpet is used throughout while contrast and progression are provided by changes on walls and furniture.

instance, the table in a dining area could be emphasized with flowers. They will be shown off to better effect if the pattern of the wallpaper is not too strong. The visual emphasis in a room should relate to its function. In a dining area the main function is eating—which centres around the table. If too strong a colour or pattern is used here, the table will be subdued —where it needs to be highlighted.

Once you have learnt the basic rules of planning colour schemes you will be able to experiment more ambitiously. A well planned colour scheme will make your home much more attractive to the visitor—as well as an infinitely more comfortable place in which to live.

Facelifts for the living room/dining room

OVERLEAF *The use of flexible units (with a dining table that can be folded up when not being used) serves to effectively 'divide' this room yet keep its feeling of spaciousness.*

LEFT *When any room has to house a general living area plus a dining section as well, it helps, as here when the room is large enough, to subdivide it according to its functions. In this case, the floor at the end of the room which serves as the dining area has been raised to 'draw away' the table and chairs from the main living area. Yet continuity is provided by connecting the area to the main seating 'pit' by a short flight of steps, and by carpeting both areas in the same material. The seating 'pit' also provides a focal highlight for the room, which otherwise could be somewhat fragmented. The overall effect is streamlined, uncluttered, comfortable – and ultra-modern.*

BOTTOM *A more conventional approach to the problem of creating both living and dining space in one room characterizes this wide, airy flat. The focal point of the room is a wall of windows, which guarantees a light, bright touch. This feeling is emphasized by the sunny yellow and white colour scheme, furniture in cool, modern shapes, and by using shimmering net curtains, gathered and hemmed deeply to give a luxurious 'hang'. The strategic placement of pot plants and flowers heightens the almost alfresco atmosphere.*

Literally thousands of people set up home in small flats, maisonettes, and small houses, and therefore come up against the problem of how to make the most of the actual room space available. For example, one room which does not get the attention it deserves is the dining room. This need not be the case. Modern design for compact living is so advanced that an integrated living/dining room can easily be achieved.

Space saving ideas
If you are lucky enough to start off with a large living room you will probably want to make a permanent feature of the dining area. This means that your table and chairs would be so arranged as to complement your sitting room furniture. It's a relatively simple matter to devise some form of screening arrangement—for instance a partition which could be fitted with shelves on the living room side, displaying books, ornaments and generally comprising a decorative piece of furniture. On the reverse side this partition could be invaluable if you incorporate a combination of drawers and cupboards to house crockery and cutlery. This will minimize the endless to-and-fro of laying the table—as happens when everything has to be brought from the kitchen.

If the room in question cannot afford to be so dramatically cut in half there is a large selection of open dividers available—or you can make one yourself. A very effective version of this idea can be made out of glass, so while your eating arrangements are separate the overall effect is one of space and harmony.

Lighting
Lighting is perhaps the key factor in a successful living/dining room. For example, if the dining area is normally disguised for everyday living but has over it a ceiling light, the fitting of some sort of pulley arrangement, or even a spool fitting, could transform the table when it is lowered, highlighting an attractive setting for instance. Hanging oil lamps are ideal for this type of treatment and are very fashionable nowadays.

With the accent on more modern forms of lighting the subtle use of spotlights can be most effective and very adaptable. The modern spotlight can be angled in many different ways so that where you normally might be emphasizing an attractive picture or ornament, a quick twist will make your table the main point in focus. Most of these spotlight units can be installed by the amateur, and plug-in lamps can be added when more lighting effects are required. The days when spotlights were used only for window displays and the like are long past. They now come in many colours and can produce soft, easy to live with, artificial lighting. Also, conventional wall brackets, strategically placed, can complement your dining facilities.

Tables, chairs and breakfast bars
If you would like a dining recess or specially planned eating area there are a number of ideas for tables that can be incorporated into the main living room which, apart from everyday use, can be quickly converted into a dining table or perhaps breakfast bar. In the case of a breakfast bar this could be used as a writing top, with magazines and ornaments spread around, but when meal time comes it is placed in such a way that a few moments readjustment enables you to eat in comfort. The stools can be stored beneath and being double sided four people can sit around it in comfort.

An idea that has possibilities is where you already have a large coffee table in the centre of the room. This could be adapted to have two sets of legs, low ones for daily use but a higher set screwed or snapped in at meal times to make a serviceable dining table. This is quite a feasible idea especially as many of you must have made your own tables using screw-in legs. It would be a simple matter to alter these. Another good space saving idea, and one that won't cost you anything, is that old gate-leg table Granny gave you.

When choosing chairs for your living/dining room you could be faced with a problem if the room is of such a small size that the chairs must double as both living and dining room furniture. If you look around carefully you could find that a good dining chair will often be more comfortable than large amply upholstered models. A small chair can be with or without arms so that when a number of them are placed around the room they become comfortable resting places without giving any suspicion of their dual purpose. It is always better if you can use the more conventional upright dining chairs when eating as the upright sitting position helps the digestion and in the case of children encourages them to eat properly.

Modern stacking chairs are another alternative; made out of light plastics, they are easily tucked away into the odd cupboard or corner. One attractive design is made out of smoked transparent plastic giving a very airy effect. Like so many things your final overall scheme will depend very much on personal likes and dislikes and the permanent structural features of your home.

Dining tables and crockery storage
An ordinary nest of four tables can be adapted into an original and functional dining arrangement. If you replace existing legs with telescopic ones, all four tables can then be adjusted to any height you like. This means that when the tables are raised to a uniform height a highly unusual yet practical dining arrangement is achieved. Do not try this idea if your tables are valuable antiques!

An attractive wall panel with sliding hinges fitted behind could be lifted up and out giving you a well proportioned table with room for seating on three sides. One of the problems you will encounter in your living/dining room is finding an accessible place to put plates, serving dishes and the like. If you have wall shelves fitted into an alcove you could fit doors across them to make a cupboard to keep your crockery out of view. If your crockery is a matching set with an attractive design you could make a feature of it by storing it on the shelves of a Welsh dresser. Fluorescent tubes, or even ordinary tungsten bulbs, concealed under each of the shelves will highlight the display.

Planning your living/dining room
When starting to plan your room, use only the minimum of furniture as the more cluttered a room gets the smaller it looks. Another advantage in not overdoing the amount of furniture used in your room is that you can live with your layout before you have become committed to a lot of expense. Sometimes what appears to be efficient and decorative is far from a practical proposition for everyday living. Gimmicks wear off and you will wish that you had considered a little longer before going the whole way.

Mirrors have many uses and a large mirror, strategically placed, can dramatically enlarge a slightly dark and difficult room. Another alternative is to build a screen out of panels made from a one way see through

mirror. The sitting area has the benefit of an attractive mirror whereas when eating you can look through into the sitting area. It's best to divide up the mirror side of the screen with well placed shelves and a few ornaments as constantly coming face to face with your full length reflection can be a disconcerting experience.

One of the most pleasant areas of a room for eating is at a table near a window. If your room has a bay window the problem of siting the table will be solved. You can build bench seating into the bay and by choosing a suitable table and a few free-standing dining chairs a comfortable dining area with a view to the outside will be

created. A gate-leg table is a good choice since, when not in use, it can be folded down to take on the role of an occasional table.

If you have a large enough kitchen you may find it simpler to build a dinette for everyday meals and occasional snacks. There is little point in carrying all manner of dishes, cutlery and condiments from the kitchen to the dining area just for a quick meal.

Unless your kitchen is next door to the living/dining room, in which case you can cut a hatchway in the dividing wall, a trolley will prove invaluable. When choosing a suitable trolley do not ignore the aspects of practicality and sturdiness of construction purely

Creating adequate living and dining space from a small room is difficult, but it can be done. In the room above, a cool uncluttered effect is created by using modern plain wood built-in furnishings and cool 'receding' colours.

for the sake of appearance—it is more important that it be well designed and spacious than eye-catching. With the aid of a trolley and using free-standing hot plates you can bring your food to the table still piping hot. A whole course can be brought into the room in one go—saving a lot of fetching and carrying. If you have a step up or down into your living/dining room you can make a small wooden ramp

quite easily. This can be stored away when not in use.

Space will be limited in your living/dining room so you should concentrate on fitted wall units and room dividers rather than free-standing furniture. All the things that clutter up valuable floor space most can be housed in fitted units. The television and the stereo set will be out of the way yet easily accessible. Pot plants which stood, in great danger of damage, on the floor will find a safe home on the shelves.

You needn't confine your fitted units to shelves and cupboards and the like. Why not build in a long couch along one wall—possibly incorporating a corner unit as well? Small table

tops could be included in the structure of the couch. This idea offers a great deal more versatility than conventional free-standing units in the living area and the amount of floor space saved will surprise you.

Ventilation

You should give some thought to the problem of ventilation in your living/dining room as the lingering smell of food can be quite unpleasant when you are trying to relax. Probably the best and cheapest solution is to fit an extractor fan into the window. This will be especially effective if the dining table is near the window.

Today's materials and home furni-

Light, built-in wall units to house the accoutrements of both living and dining areas maximize the space available in this room – and the illusion of space is further emphasized by the use of 'light' furniture such as cane and glass. A richly patterned oriental rug effectively divides the seating area from the dining and work areas.

ture are able to solve almost any space problem in your home. It is up to you to convert your home into the home that you want. Money is no substitute for good ideas, and a little ingenuity can turn your ideas into a reality—in this case the reality of a comfortable and well planned living/dining room.

Facelifts for the kitchen

There are many ways to make a kitchen look smarter without spending a fortune, and while you are giving it a face-lift you can often reorganize it so that it is more practical, too. Whether you are trying to improve an existing, depressing kitchen, or starting from scratch on a new one, the ideas given here should help you.

The kitchen often turns out to be the most expensive room in the house, particularly if you are setting up home for the first time. Once you have bought the large items of equipment such as a stove, refrigerator and washing machine, you may not have much money left to spend on expensive fitted units, let alone smart flooring and ceramic tiles.

If you can't stand your kitchen in its present state, most of the improvements you make will have to be immediate, and on a scale to suit your current finances. If you are working to a budget and don't mind waiting for your dream kitchen, however, you may find a long term plan is preferable.

Long term planning

It can take several years to create a kitchen equipped with all the extras you want, but this waiting is well worth it in a family house that is being improved gradually over the years. With clever planning, your kitchen will look good from the day you put in the first new unit to the day the last one is fitted.

Many large stores and builders' merchants run easy-pay schemes so you can build up your kitchen over the years. If you decide on a long term plan, check with the manufacturer of your kitchen units that the particular line you have chosen will still be available for additions or replacements in three or four years' time when you complete your scheme.

Once you have decided on a rough layout, draw up a plan to scale. It is best to start with the sink and stove, as plumbing and gas pipes are the most expensive things to have altered. Add base units and worktops, which you

You don't have to spend a lot of money or even make major alterations to get results in this kitchen. Bright and cheerful matching wallpaper and blinds, teamed with yellow paint, combine to give the room a completely fresh look.

will buy when you can afford them, leaving space for equipment like a washing machine which may be bought later on. If you are making do with an old stove and refrigerator, remember to leave enough space for the model you plan to buy at a later date.

Finally add the wall cupboards and the flooring. You can easily make do with cheap flooring until you are able to afford the right one. Paint or paper the walls until you are able to give them a more impressive treatment in the form of tiles or wood cladding.

Immediate improvements

Very often the easiest improvement in a kitchen is a simple reorganization of the room itself. The stove may be by itself, with no work surface nearby for putting down hot pots and pans, or the table may be obstructing the path from the door to the stove, or between the sink and the china cupboard.

Altering plumbing or moving a stove is expensive so where possible try to leave the sink and stove where they are and move other units around instead to improve the layout. Free-standing cupboards, the table and even the refrigerator (if it is electric) can easily be re-arranged to create a more streamlined kitchen.

A kitchen always looks better if the working surfaces are all the same height, and this is another improvement that is fairly simple to make. If you have several units the same height, arrange them together to form a continuous worktop, or to link the stove with the sink. An old cupboard which is too low can be raised up on blocks to conform with the height of the other units. A length of blockboard fixed at the right height and covered with sticky-backed plastic makes a perfectly adequate worktop, under which a washing machine can be tucked when not in use. Some old cupboards which are too tall can be brought into line

A small, long kitchen can create problems but, by decorating in bright, light colours and streamlining the arrangement of fittings and worktops, an illusion of space can be created.

with the standard worktops by making their legs shorter, or by removing their base. Try not to affect the balance or looks of a cupboard by chopping off too much.

Colour co-ordination is another simple and quick improvement. You may have a motley collection of old cupboards and units, with the walls one colour, curtains another, and flooring yet another. You can put this right, and cover a multitude of sins at the same time, by painting practically everything in the same colour, right

This large L-shaped kitchen has been modernized to give it the best of both worlds: the built-in cupboards and worktops are modern and efficiently arranged to provide maximum space, while the walls, ceiling and other surfaces are 'wooded' to give a solid, traditional effect, which is further enhanced by the open shelves and crockery rack.

down to the lids of the storage jars. Add a blind or some café curtains to tone, and you will find you have unified a room that looked a jumble before.

Flooring is fairly expensive, especially in large breakfast room-style kitchens. If the flooring is ugly, but you cannot afford to change it, draw attention away from it by having bright things in the rest of the room—posters, storage tins and even pretty tea cloths pinned to the wall can catch the eye effectively. Another way of cheering up a dull floor is with cheap rush matting or a more practical Scandinavian one in thick woven fabric that looks like cotton, but is a wipe-clean plastic fibre. Later on, when you can afford it,

you will be able to lash out on a better flooring of cork tiles or good quality vinyl.

If the floor is covered in ancient linoleum or worn-out sheet flooring, the best way of dealing with it cheaply is to remove it, then sand and seal or paint the floorboards underneath with a polyurethane varnish. This gives a practical finish in a kitchen because it can be easily wiped clean .

As re-plumbing is such an expensive improvement, your best plan is to make the best of what there is, for instance by making pipes merge in with the background by painting them in the same colour as the walls. Alternatively, you may be able to box them in; this is simple for vertical pipes, but more tricky round the edge of a ceiling which is crooked. Make a skeleton shape from 2.5cm (1in) wooden battens, tack on a hardboard casing, then paint it or cover it with wallpaper to match the walls. You can cheer up an old water heater by painting it a bright colour, but be sure to use either a flame-retardant paint or one with a suitable enamel finish. It is not safe to disguise something like this with sticky-backed plastic or anything that is not flame-resistant.

TOP When space is at a premium, bright light colours can help to 'open out' the room considerably. And if provision for eating, or even emergency work space, is necessary, then one useful answer is a flap-top table which can be folded against the wall when not in use, teamed with equally efficient fold-away chairs, which can be stored out of sight until they are needed.

BOTTOM Kitchens which aren't really separate rooms at all but subdivisions of other, larger rooms, are usually small and cramped and therefore need all the help they can get to become both roomy and efficient. Partitions kept below head height help considerably, as here and, with peg-board attached, can do double duty on the kitchen side.

Sinks

It is possible to tidy up old porcelain sinks if they are not badly cracked or chipped. Fit new draining boards for a start, and hang a curtain under the sink to hide any unsightly plumbing. If you cannot afford ceramic tiles, you can make a smart, wipe-clean splashback behind the sink with a length of sticky-backed plastic or vinyl wallpaper. Be sure the wall behind is smooth and free from grease before sticking it on.

Even a new plug and taps will help an old sink take on a new look, also accessories like a plastic washing-up bowl and draining rack in bright colours. If your draining board is too small for a plate rack, hang one on the wall above the sink.

You can replace a really impossible sink fairly cheaply—there are good second-hand stainless steel or enamel ones to be found in some builders' merchants, and even in junk shops. The best ones are those with holes for the taps, otherwise you have to construct a complicated splashback to fit round the pipes behind the sink.

Worktops and tables

All working surfaces must have a practical finish, and plastic laminate combines smart durability with ease of

cleaning. However, a tough polyurethane paint gives almost as good a wipe-clean surface as many plastic laminate sheetings, and has the added advantage of heat resistance. Prepare the surface particularly carefully before painting by smoothing it down with sandpaper, then apply at least two or three coats of paint for a hard finish. One drawback of paint is that it may chip if it is banged hard, but if treated with respect it should provide a bright, hard-wearing surface until you can afford something better.

Another way of giving old wooden worktops and tables a face-lift is to strip off the old paint, rub them down with sandpaper and finish them with a clear polyurethane seal. This gives a tough finish which has the advantage of being non-chip. Sticky-backed plastic is not quite so practical on a worktop because it will not withstand hot pans; however, it does make a pretty surface when used on the top of an old dresser or to cover shelves.

A cheap worktop can be made by using an old door from a house that is being demolished, and is just as solid but less expensive than a new piece of wood the same size. If the door is panelled, nail a piece of hardboard to one side, then cover it with plastic laminate sheeting. For a really smart job, stick a matching strip on the edge which will be the front of the worktop when it is in position.

Some surfaces which are now thought of as being very old fashioned still have their uses. Wooden dressers or table tops make perfect chopping boards, but they do need scrubbing to get them completely clean. Marble is an excellent surface for making pastry on, and you can still pick up old marble-topped dressers or washstands quite cheaply.

You can brighten up an ugly but useful kitchen table with a cloth in a material which matches the blinds or curtains. If you have an old wooden table with a surface you feel you can't improve, cover it with oilcloth or a pvc-coated cotton that can be fixed to the underside with drawing pins. This will brighten up the whole kitchen, especially if you paint the table legs, but remember to use a heatproof mat for hot pots and pans.

An expensive but more durable covering for a kitchen table is a sheet of plastic laminate cut to size and stuck with a strong contact adhesive.

Revamping old units

There are all sorts of ways of making outwardly unpromising old cupboards and dressers into useful pieces of kitchen furniture. Remove the upper doors from an old cupboard, fill in nail holes with plastic wood, paint the whole thing in a bright colour and put sticky-backed plastic on the shelves. If you add new knobs as well, you will

Two marvellously successful budget face-lifts. On the LEFT *gay curtaining cheers up this otherwise dull room, while on the* RIGHT, *every inch has been utilized to the full in this kitchen.*

have transformed an old cupboard into an attractive piece of furniture.

Old glass-fronted cupboards are effective for holding china, and if you cover the shelves and the back with a dark-coloured felt, it will set off the china and prevent it from chipping.

Storage space

Lack of storage space can be a great problem in a kitchen, but there are several ways of providing more. Even orange boxes and tea chests can be used for temporary storage until you can afford something smarter. Build them together to make a 'cube store', then paint them or cover them with sticky-backed plastic.

There may be wasted space under a dresser with high legs, so fix one or two shelves underneath to hold pots and pans or heavy casseroles. A row of crates from a greengrocer's shop can be used as a vegetable store under a dresser, hidden behind a pretty curtain. If your pots and pans and other kitchen equipment are a mass of different colours, shapes and sizes, it's better to hide them in cupboards rather than display them on open shelves.

Tins with polythene tops make

excellent storage jars; just give the tins a coat of spray paint and stick a label on each to unify the look of your larder. Large coffee jars with screw tops are another cheap way of providing storage for dry goods, and have the advantage of showing what is inside; you just have to paint the lids. If you are short of space, keep tall storage jars upright in a deep drawer, then write the name of the contents of each jar on its lid so that you can see at a glance what each one holds.

Walls and ceilings

Tiles are a smart and practical surface for kitchen walls, but if you can't afford the real thing, look for tile-effect wallpapers with a washable finish. If the walls are in a bad condition and re-plastering is not possible, disguise the surface either with tongued and grooved pine panelling, or with much cheaper sheets of hardboard which can be painted or papered to match the rest of the room.

Use a practical washable paint for the walls and ceiling. If the ventilation is bad, choose a paint with a finish that discourages condensation (anything but a gloss finish).

Doors and windows

A good way of smartening up an ugly kitchen door is to nail a sheet of hardboard to it, covering it completely to make a flat surface, then tack or stick green baize or colourful paper-backed felt over it.

You can cheer up windows with new curtains or blinds to make the whole kitchen look brighter. You could buy remnants of suitable fabric and make your own blinds, which are more economical of fabric than curtains. Most laminated fabrics make excellent blinds because they can be wiped clean.

The window sill behind a sink can be given a bright and practical surface by fixing a row of bargain tiles to it.

Camouflage

Blinds and curtains can be great helpers, and if you are experienced in the art of camouflage you will be able to hide a multitude of sins very cheaply in this way. Tall ugly units can be hidden behind a floor-to-ceiling rattan blind, which rolls neatly out of the way when you want to get at the shelves.

Curtains are useful if you want to cover up unattractive shelves under a worktop, but they should not be used near a stove.

Lighting and accessories

New lighting can be a great help for a tired-looking kitchen. Look for inexpensive spotlights that take an ordinary light bulb, which is cheaper to replace than a proper spotlight. Fix them over the working surfaces, stove and sink for direct light to supplement the central pendant fitting. A strip light fixed behind a false pelmet above the working surface will give good all-over illumination to work by. Use bright washable shades on hanging lights, as the greasy atmosphere will tend to make them dirty quickly.

If you are short of storage space, a large section of one wall covered with pegboard can be fitted with hooks to hold everything from pots and pans to wooden spoons. This can look smart if you paint the pegboard in a bright colour. If you hate it when well-meaning friends helping you wash up replace all your kitchen utensils in the wrong places, paint their shapes on the pegboard as a guide to where they belong.

You can make a kitchen notice board from six or eight cork tiles stuck to the wall, then stick cheerful

RIGHT *A well organized broom cupboard – something that's consistently overlooked in most kitchens.*
BOTTOM LEFT *Two hidden assets in one cupboard: an extra worktop to take the mixer and a plastic tray to hold the attachments.*
BOTTOM RIGHT *An excellent way to store pots and pans. This pull-out unit has easy-to-clean plastic-coated shelves.*

posters on it, together with a shopping pad and pencil. Encourage pot plants on the window sill, and paint all the pots in one colour. Even a string of onions or a bowl of oranges will brighten up ordinary kitchens.

The main thing to do when you are trying to refurbish your kitchen on a budget is to look for good junk shop bargains that can be turned into useful kitchen furniture. With some clever ideas and a good eye for colour, you can transform the dullest kitchen into a room that is a positive pleasure to work in.

Facelifts for the bathroom

A bathroom in need of a face-lift can be a very dreary place, but you don't need to spend a fortune to give it a new look. In fact, it is surprising what can be achieved after a relatively simple renovation project.

If your bathroom is in a really bad state, you may need to buy a new suite, which is an expensive proposition. However, if you are working on the cheap, there are several good ways of improving what you have without spending a lot of money.

The bath

One of the best ways of dealing with an ugly old bath is to box it in, as this immediately improves the whole look of the bathroom. It is a fairly easy job to do—you simply have to make a frame that fits round the bath under the lip, on to which you tack sheets of hardboard.

Remember that it may be necessary to get at the drain or the overflow pipe, so make sure there is an easy way for a plumber to reach these. You can do this by making an access door in the boxing, or by making one of the large panels easily removable.

You could also extend the bath panelling beyond the end of the bath, if possible right up to the next wall.

Grooved wood panelling covers the walls and hides all the pipes in this cheerful room. Sealed against moisture, it makes a warm wall covering.

It can then be made into a fitted seat or a neat ledge for plants or towels. If you put a flap-up lid on it, you can use it for storing dirty clothes, or clean towels.

There are many different ways of finishing a newly panelled bath. The simplest one is to paint or wallpaper the panels to blend with the colour scheme in the rest of the room. You can emphasize the rectangular shape by sticking on a striking paper border over a contrasting wallpaper or paint.

If you have a high old bath with cast-iron legs and even ball and claw feet, you may prefer to make a feature of it rather than conceal its elaborate features. Try painting the outside in an outrageous pattern, or even cover it in a mural.

A simpler, though equally effective, idea is to paint the bath in one strong colour and pick out the legs in a contrasting one. If you are painting the outside of a bath, be sure to prepare the surface carefully first. Remove any old paint that is chipping off and start with a smooth, fresh surface.

Ceramic tiles are often thought of as an expensive luxury, but a few courses round a bath will provide an efficient and practical splashback. Tiles last a lifetime, always look smart, and have an easy-to-clean surface, whereas any cheaper alternative will not be as practical and have a shorter life.

If you want to give your bathroom a different look, try one of these ideas for covering the sides and surrounding walls of a bath. Stainless steel tiles give a bright, ultra-modern effect; mirror tiles are much cheaper than a mirror, and create an impression of more space; black or smoked glass gives a less harsh reflection. Mosaic tiles and imitation ceramic tiles made from plastic are effective and much cheaper than the real thing; they can also be moulded over slightly irregular surfaces. Laminated sheeting provides an easy-to-clean surface, so does its cheaper alternative, sticky-backed plastic. However, this should be thought of more as a short-term treatment, and it needs careful bonding so that there is no danger of its coming unstuck in the steamy atmosphere.

If your bathroom is small, carpet for the floor need not be prohibitively expensive, yet creates a luxurious impression. There are foam-backed varieties on the market which are surprisingly cheap, and quite suitable for bathrooms. For an extra touch, continue the carpet up the sides of the bath and tuck it under the lip.

You can steal an idea from sauna baths and use tongued and grooved or plain pine panelling for boxing in the sides of the bath, using it either horizontally or vertically. This can also be used as a splashback or even to cover all the walls of the bathroom for a total effect. However, the wood must be carefully finished with several coats of a tough polyurethane varnish.

If the inside surface of your bath is in bad condition, there are one or two ways of renovating it. Some hardware shops sell extra strong cleansing agents specially made for rejuvenating the bath's surface. Alternatively, try re-enamelling the bath itself with special enamel bath paint.

The wash basin
An old basin can often be something of an eyesore, but it is not difficult to give it a new look. One of the cheapest ways of smartening up a basin with ugly plumbing below it, is to fix skirts round it made in a fabric to match the curtains or roller blind in the bathroom.

It is quite easy to construct a neat cupboard underneath some basins, but a neater idea is to turn it into a fitted unit. This could be a wipe-clean surface of mosaic tiles or laminated plastic sheeting, with cupboards or a skirt below.

If your bathroom is fairly large, you could make a fitted cupboard for the basin with floor-to-ceiling screens on each side, with the basin let into a vanity unit. Complete the unit by fixing up shelves, a mirror and a spotlight, and your bathroom will take on a much more modern look.

The lavatory
The best thing to do with an old high lavatory cistern is to replace it with a modern low flush one. The newest models are slim and take up very little space, which is important in a small bathroom.

If your old cistern is very unsightly but can't be replaced, build a cupboard round it and continue it right along the wall. This will both hide the eyesore and give vital extra high-level storage space. Drill a hole in the base of the cupboard so that the chain can run through easily. While you are doing this, you can make it look smarter by installing a new chain and handle.

A new lavatory seat is another good idea, and there are lots of colourful plastic ones available. If the existing seat is a comfortable old wooden one, smarten it up by removing any chipped varnish. Sandpaper smoothly and finish it with either two or three coats of clear polyurethane lacquer or a good gloss paint.

Many of the newest bathrooms have lavatory cisterns built into the wall. It would not be expensive to give your bathroom this kind of treatment by making a false wall, but be sure

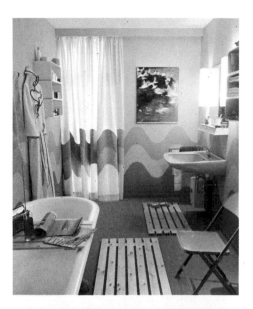

TOP *This spacious room has a fresh and distinctively 'nautical' look.*
MIDDLE *Mirrors 'enlarge' this room and create a look of sunny sophistication.*
BOTTOM *A cool, serene look is achieved by this pretty patterned wallpaper, which covers both walls and ceiling.*

to make an access flap or door in case emergency plumbing is needed.

Building in a low cistern can be a fiddly job, because of having to shape the panel immediately behind the lavatory to fit round the waste pipe. It's easier if you first make a template out of stiff brown paper to be sure of a good fit, then use a jig saw to cut out the difficult shaped sections.

The cistern handle can be installed in the front of the built-in section; make a connection hole for it in the panel, then connect it after the panel is in place. The false wall or panel can then be decorated to match the rest of the bathroom.

In a large old bathroom, you can deal with an ugly lavatory by screening it off from the rest of the room. Either build a floor-to-ceiling fitted cupboard round it with smart double louvred doors, or build one fairly deep full-height screen of hardboard or blockboard, painted or papered to match the rest of the room.

A shower
Another good way of modernizing a bathroom is to install a shower unit. If it is a small room, the shower can be fitted in the bath itself. This is really worthwhile, and it saves on hot water bills since it uses about one-third of the amount of water needed for a small bath.

There are many special mixer taps with shower extensions on the market which can be fitted to a bath. You can buy or make shower curtains to hang from the ceiling to prevent water from splashing over the floor. When the shower is in use, these curtains are pulled to screen the shower end of the bath and hang inside it.

The alternative is to fix splash panels made of glass, acrylic or stiff plastic sheets. These can be fitted on hinges or fixed permanently so that they cover one-third of the side of the bath up to the shower head to keep splashes in.

If you have more space in your bathroom, add a modern touch by fitting a separate shower cabinet. These can be bought complete, or you can make your own quite cheaply by fixing a shower tray with a drain and shower tap unit in one corner of the room. The shower can be enclosed with pvc or plastic curtains, or with corrugated acrylic panels, with a pvc curtain or blind for access.

A more solid idea for a shower tray in a corner is to construct a third wall to make it look like a small cupboard.

Make this of hardboard, fixed to a wooden frame, and cover the inside of the cubicle with tiles. Finish the outside to match the rest of the room, and fix a pretty shower curtain across the open side. You can give it a neater, enclosed look by fixing double louvred or panelled doors so that it looks like a cupboard when it is not being used.

It is important that a shower cubicle must be watertight, and ceramic tiling gives one of the best finishes for this.

Decorations
In many modern houses, the bathrooms are small, so you haven't got much wall area to cover. For this reason, you may feel you can afford matching wallpapers and fabrics which would be too extravagant in a larger room.

Complementary wallpapers and fabrics are well worth using, because they give a room a more spacious appearance. A small window may need only one or two yards of fabric for a smart home-made roller blind, but this simple touch will create a far more effective scheme.

So long as you have a good outlet for steam, in the form of an air brick or ventilator, there is no reason why

A cheerful, gay approach to decorating what can often be the most boring room in the house. And the transformation was effected by one painter with imagination – plus some talent!

you shouldn't use wallpaper in a bathroom, if you use a good strong paste. Modern vinyl wall coverings have a practical washable surface, but if the wallpaper you choose is not spongeable or washable, you can always give it a coat of clear wallpaper lacquer.

For a total effect, you can use the same wallpaper on the sides of the bath, as well as on all the walls and ceiling, plus matching fabric for blinds or curtains.

The best paint choice for a bathroom is one with a washable gloss, egg shell or vinyl finish. If you have problems with condensation and don't want to spend a lot of money on an electric steam extractor, use special paint with a finish that discourages the formation of condensation. Be brave and use a strong colour, then add a bright curtain or blind, and your bathroom will take on a new look at almost rock-bottom cost.

Bathroom walls with a glossy finish look smart, but if the colour you

TOP LEFT *Two shades of turquoise create a bathroom of warmth and elegance.*
TOP RIGHT *Junk shop finds – tiles and a marble-topped basin stand – form the basis of an inexpensive renovation.*
BOTTOM LEFT *The most ordinary bathroom is transformed by a pretty stand containing lots of pot plants.*

choose doesn't come with a gloss finish, you can give it a shine by treating it with a coat of clear polyurethane lacquer. This will make the paint a little darker in colour, but will give it an extremely durable finish that is cheap for the amount of wear it will give you.

If you like the look of ceramic tiles, but can't afford to have them all over the walls, try just a strip around the bath and beside the basin. A cheap alternative is sticky-backed plastic, which comes in tile-effect patterns as well as gay designs.

The floor

There is no need to cover up floorboards if they are in good condition, and well sanded and sealed boards will give you the cheapest flooring of all. If you use a large bathmat, the bathroom will be quite comfortable, so long as there are no wide gaps between the boards.

Vinyl or linoleum sheeting are available in a wide range of grades and prices, and all of them are suitable. Cork, an ideal flooring for a bathroom, is a little more expensive. Keep an eye open for bargain lengths of carpet if you want a luxurious touch in a tiny bathroom.

The window

Whatever treatment you give the window in a bathroom, try not to keep out the light. You may find that frosted glass is not necessary, or only in the lower half of a window, so avoid it wherever possible. A roller blind lets in more light when it is open than full curtains, and is more practical on a window behind a basin, as it doesn't get splashed and tatty.

If you need privacy in your bathroom, but don't want to go to the expense of installing new frosted glass, use one of these ideas. Natural pine louvred shutters let in fresh air when the window is open, allow in a certain amount of light, and look good.

Any blind is a sensible window covering, and paler colours or slightly open-weave blinds will let in quite a lot of light if you need to keep the blind pulled down all the time.

Cover the lower part of the window with a bright café curtain and have a blind on the top half. The café curtain can be a plain strip of stiffened fabric, with a castellated top, and hung on a brass rod. This sort of treatment saves money on fabric, and they are not difficult to make at home.

You can give a window a smart look by making café curtains from an inexpensive fabric like gingham. The lower curtain can be gathered on to a stretchy wire across the middle and foot of the window to prevent it from blowing around, and keep it out of the way if the wash basin is immediately below the window. The top café curtain can be gathered and made up like an ordinary curtain to give a pleasant two-tiered effect.

Accessories

Every bathroom needs at least one mirror, so try to make a feature of it. Mirrors brighten up a dull bathroom, and a large one will make it look bigger and add a new dimension, so hunt around for cheap old mirrors whose frames can be painted brightly. There are also good inexpensive modern mirrors on the market with acrylic or plastic frames.

If you can't afford a modern bathroom cabinet, you can build your own cheaply by adding doors to the front of a small bookshelf unit.

Even something as simple as a row of cheap plastic mugs with toothbrush holders can make a dull bathroom more exciting. Try to keep accessories the same colour for smartness; for instance a white towel rail with matching white soap dish, lavatory brush and paper holder etc. These sorts of accessories can be bought very cheaply, so it is worth getting a completely matching set.

Lighting is all important, even in a bathroom, and you can choose anything from a fluorescent strip to a more dramatic spotlight or a period-style bracket light. You can make a cold bathroom warmer by fitting infra-red spotlights instead of tungsten.

Whatever lighting you choose should give you a good view in the bathroom mirror, so it may be necessary to fit an extra light above it. Some bathroom mirrors have built-in lights, but it is easy to fit a neat strip above a cabinet.

Remember that light switches in a bathroom should be in the form of a string pull for electrical safety, and that they should be well out of the reach of small children.

Extra ideas

If you are short of storage space in the bathroom, you can fix a shelf unit to the back of the door. In a high, dark bathroom, install a false ceiling to make the room seem more cosy and provide masses of dead storage space above. Where a bathroom leads off a narrow landing and space is tight, use double doors instead of one wide door.

With some of these ideas in mind, and a watchful eye for trends and gadgets, you should be able to renovate your bathroom easily and cheaply.

Soft furnishings

Basic cushions

Cushions add greatly to the comfort and decoration of any room. For maximum effect, make several in different shapes and sizes.

The fabric
All kinds of fabric, including dress weights, can be used for cushion covers, although very fine or slippery lingerie fabrics are not ideal because they often need backing and can be difficult to work on. Loosely woven fabrics are not good if you are having a piped edge because the cord will show through, and heavy fabrics may not go through your machine.

As a guide to the amount of fabric you need for square or oblong covers, measure the sides of the cushion pad and allow a minimum of twice this, plus 1.3cm (½in) each way for turnings. If you are having a piped edge, buy about 45cm (½yd) extra for making the casing strips (see below).

For a round cover, measure the diameter, and allow two squares of this length, plus 1.3cm (½in). A round cushion should not have a piped edge because it does not keep its shape well when the pad is inserted.

In all cases, if the fabric you are using has a main motif, allow extra so that you can place it centrally when you cut each side of the cover.

If you are making your own cushion pads the filling should be put into an inner cover so that the main cover can be removed easily for cleaning. This can be made from an inexpensive fabric such as calico, sheeting, cambric, or even remnants of other fabrics if the colours will not show through the outer cover. Allow the same amount of fabric as for the main cover.

The filling
Cushion fillings fall into two types, squashy and firm, but for scatter cushions the squashy sort are more comfortable.

Down is the traditional and most luxurious filling of this type, but it is also the most expensive and difficult to obtain. Feathers are a cheaper and good alternative, and ready-made pads in different sizes and shapes can often be bought from department stores. Sometimes you can buy feathers by weight, but making your own pads with them can be tricky because they tend to fly around, and you need a featherproof fabric for the cover.

If you do want to make your own pads, Terylene or Dacron wadding, a

white man-made fibre, is ideal. It looks like cotton wool, is non-absorbent, washable, and especially suitable for people who suffer from hay-fever. It is sold in bags by weight, and 450g (1 lb) is normally enough to make two average-size cushions.

Kapok, a buff-coloured vegetable fibre, is one of the cheapest fillings obtainable but it has a tendency to go lumpy after a while.

Latex or plastic foam chips are also cheap, but they can be lumpy if the case of the pad is not made in a heavy fabric.

Making your own pads

Cushions can be any shape and size you like and a mixture can be very attractive. To keep the finished cushion a good shape and ensure that it looks well filled, the cover for the pad should be cut 1.3cm (½in) larger each way than the size of the outer cover. When cutting the cover for a 40cm (16in) square or round cushion, for example, the pieces should be 48.5cm (19½in) across. This allows the extra 1.3cm (½in) plus 1.3cm (½in) on each side for turnings.

Square or oblong pads

1. Cut two pieces of fabric, on the straight grain, to your calculated size. Place them together with right sides facing, and machine stitch round on three sides taking 1.3cm (½in) turnings. Leave the fourth side open for the time being, but fold over the turnings on to the wrong side and press down.

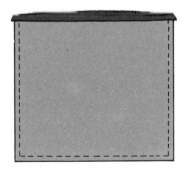

2. Turn the cover right side out and press. Stuff it with the filling, making sure that the corners are well padded but without cramming it too full which would make the cushion hard.
3. Pin the folds of the opening together, tack and machine stitch along the edge.

Round pads

1. To make sure you achieve a good shape, it is essential to make a paper pattern first. This can then be trimmed and used for the outer cover later.

On a large sheet of paper, draw a straight line slightly longer than the diameter of the cushion. Mark the centre point.
2. If you have a pair of compasses, set them to the required radius (half the length of the diameter), put the point of the compasses on the centre point of the straight line, and draw a half circle beginning and ending on the straight line.

If you have no compasses, tie one end of a piece of string round a pencil and measure the radius from the pencil along the length of string. Mark the measurement by pushing a drawing pin through the string and then on to the centre point of the straight line. Holding the pin firmly with one hand and the pencil upright with the other with the string taut, draw the half circle. Cut round the lines.

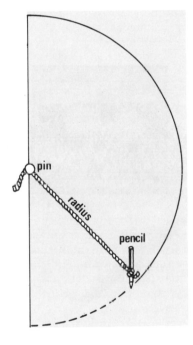

3. Fold the fabric in half along the grain, place the pattern on to it so that the straight edge comes to the fold, and pin in position. Cut round the curved line, but not along the fold. Cut a second piece in the same way, unfold both and place them together with the right sides facing. Tack and machine stitch taking 1.3cm (½in) turnings and leaving an opening of at least 15cm (6in). Finish off as for square cushions.

The main cover

This can be made in the same way as for the cover of the pad (but 1.3cm—½in—smaller each way), and have the sides of the opening slip-stitched together by hand.

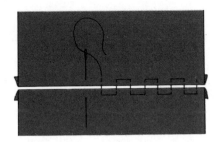

When you cut the cover, place any motif centrally and match a dominant pattern, such as stripes or checks, at the seams.

On square or oblong cushions, if you are likely to have to remove the cover frequently for washing or cleaning, it is a good idea to include a permanent and easy form of opening, such as a zip fastener. And, as a decorative and professional touch, you can also incorporate piping all round the edge of the case. Neither piping nor zip fasteners can be included with round covers because their shape will become distorted.

Piping

Piping both strengthens and decorates seams, and is a common feature of loose covers. It consists of a thin white cotton cord which is encased in fabric to match or contrast with the cover and is inserted in the seam when it is being stitched.

Cord specially made for piping is sold in different thicknesses, and a fine-to-medium one is best for cushions. Buy enough to fit round the perimeter of the cushion, plus about 23cm (9in) to allow for shrinkage. Before making it up into the cover, wash and dry it a couple of times to make sure it is fully shrunk.

To insert piping correctly, you need a special foot for your sewing machine. This is not expensive and can also be used for inserting zip fasteners. The metal foot is in one piece, instead of split as with the standard sewing foot, and can be moved to either side of the needle, enabling the stitching to come close to the piping.

Generally, the needle should be set to the left of the foot, level with the edge. The cushion cover is inserted into the machine with its bulk on the left and the turnings of the seam under the foot, which should be pressed up hard against the side of the piping.

Keep it in this position throughout the sewing. At corners, leave the needle down, lift the foot and turn the fabric round to the new position. Press the foot down again and continue sewing.

Making the piping

To ensure that the fabric moulds easily over the cord and goes round the corners of the cover smoothly, the casing strips for piping should be cut on the bias grain (diagonally) across the fabric because this has more stretch than if it is cut level with the grain.

1. To cut bias strips, check that the edges of the fabric are level with the straight grain, then fold it diagonally so that the selvedge is level with the crosswise threads. Crease this fold without stretching it, and cut along the crease.

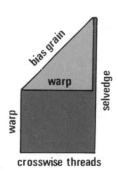

2. Use tailor's chalk to mark off strips of 4cm (1½in) wide from this edge. This allows enough to go round the cord with 1.3cm (½in) for turnings on each side. Cut the short ends of each strip so that they slant the same way and are level with the straight grain, thus making the pieces like a parallelogram.

3. To maintain the stretchiness, seams joining the strips should lie on the straight grain, so place the strips at right angles to each other, with right sides facing and the short edges level. Stitch, taking 0.6cm (¼in) turnings. Press open the seam and trim off the protruding corners.

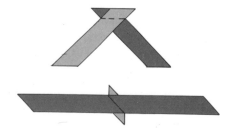

4. Join enough strips in this way to fit the perimeter of the cover, plus 2.5cm (1in) for joining. Leave the final join until you have fitted the casing to the cover.

5. Lay the piping cord centrally along the wrong side of the casing and fold the edges of the casing together, keeping the cord in the middle. Tack the casing round the cord firmly (this can be done by machine), to within 2.5cm (1in) of each end, keeping the stitching as close to the piping as possible.

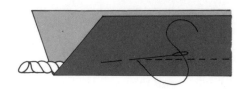

6. Pin the casing all round the edge on the right side of one of the cover pieces, so that the piped side faces in and the raw edges of the casing are level with those of the cover. Clip 1.3cm (½in) into the seam allowance of the casing at the corners to ease the piping round and make it lie flat.

7. To make the final join, unfold the untacked portions of casing, overlap them for 1.3cm (½in), and trim off the excess fabric along the straight grain. Join the strips on the grain as before, making sure that the casing fits the cover exactly.

8. Overlap the cord for 2.5cm (1in) and cut off the excess. Unravel 2.5cm (1in) of both ends of the cord and cut two strands from one end and one strand from the other. Overlap and twist together the remaining ends and oversew them firmly. Fold over the casing and tack in position.

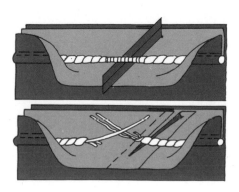

9. To finish the cushion cover, place the sides of the cover together with right sides facing. Tack and machine stitch on three sides and 2.5cm (1in) at each end of the fourth side, keeping the stitching as close to the edge of the piping as possible. Overcast the turnings together if the fabric is likely to fray.

10. Turn the cover right side out and press. Press the turnings of the opening on the fourth side to the wrong side. Either insert a zip fastener, or insert the cushion pad, pin the fold of the unpiped edge to the inside edge of the piping, and slip stitch firmly.

Inserting a zip fastener

One of the neatest methods of inserting a zip fastener is to sew it in by hand after the sides of the cushion cover have been joined.

1. Press under the turning along the piped edge of the opening, and put the edge of the piping on to the right side of the closed zip so that it is level with the centre of the teeth. Tack along the gully between the piping and cover.

2. Fold under the unpiped edge of the opening and put it on to the zip so that it meets the piped edge. Tack in position along the edge of the zip's teeth, curving the stitching into the fold at the top and bottom.

3. Using double sewing thread, prick-stitch the zip to the cover on each side, following the line of tacking. Prick-stitch is like back-stitch, but on the right side of the fabric the stitch should be minute. Be careful not to pull the stitches too tightly, or the fabric will pucker.

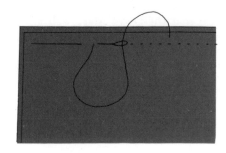

4. Press the cover, insert the pad and close the zip fastener.

Floor cushions

The conventional living-room suite consisting of a sofa and two armchairs is declining in popularity, partly because of its high price, and partly because it takes up so much valuable floor space. It is being replaced in all kinds of homes by large floor cushions. These are very easy to make yourself; by doing this you can get exactly what you want and save money.

Floor cushions can set the mood of the decorative scheme in your living-room. Square shapes covered in plain, smart fabrics can create a formal appearance, while unusual shapes with brightly patterned covers will give a totally different feel to the room. Floor cushions are the perfect answer for bedsitting rooms, where practically every piece of furniture has to have more than one function.

These cushions can vary enormously in shape, size and feel, according to their function. Modular foam units which can be fitted together in different ways, alone or in wooden frames, to form beds, chairs, sofas and seating platforms, are perhaps the most popular, as they are extremely versatile.

A subtler appearance can be created by using large rounded cushions filled with a softer substance such as Terylene wadding, foam chippings, feathers or down. These are not suitable for sleeping on, but provide comfortable sitting accommodation at a low level.

Foam

Foam has become a very popular filling for cushions and mattresses, because it comes in many forms, and its uses are limitless. Latex (natural rubber) and polyether foam are used in solid blocks as the basis for chairs and beds. These blocks can be bought in different densities and thicknesses to suit their function; polyether foam is much cheaper than latex, and is therefore used more often. Crumbed polyether and latex foam chippings are a popular filling for cushions, because they are light and non-allergenic. Other fillings suitable for stuffing cushions are mixed feathers or down, kapok or Terylene fibre.

The chief physical difference between latex and polyether foams is the way in which they react to pressure. When a load is applied to a piece of latex foam, it compresses immediately at an even rate. Most polyether foams

A room that has to be equally at home as a living and sleeping place has to be versatile – and easily and quickly converted from one function to the other. The bed-sitting area above is just that: the foam mattress covered with hard-wearing fabric and a pretty-shaped bolster filled with foam chippings, serve as an attractive seating platform by day, and as a comfortable bed and pillow at night.

currently in use for load-bearing applications are stiffer at first, and then, as the load increases, they tend to 'give' at the same rate as latex. In practice this gives latex a softer, more 'enveloping' feel and polyether foam a firmer support.

The reason for the difference in behaviour between latex and polyether foams is that the hardness or softness of latex depends entirely on its density (ie its weight per cubic foot), but polyether foam, a synthetic product, can be made from scratch with any required stiffness, quite irrespective of its density. Thus a firm latex foam has a lot of latex in proportion to the air it contains, and a soft one less latex and more air. With polyether foam, on the other hand, a firm foam can have either a high or low density.

TOP *Floor cushions provide exotic yet comfortable seating accommodation.*
BOTTOM *Floor cushions are particularly appropriate for a modern decor.*

It is important to remember, however, that high density foams resist wear better than low density foams, and a low density foam used in the wrong application will quickly lose hardness and sag. The choice of foam density and hardness must be related to its use.

Polyether foam

Polyether foam is used as a cushioning material in furniture and bedding, and can be made either in block form or moulded to a required shape. Block foam is produced in a continuous length by the factory and cut into manageable pieces to make it possible to store. These large pieces are then re-cut to the size you order to meet your own needs. When foam is moulded, a metered quantity of liquid polyether is fed into a mould, and foams up to fill it.

The key to the correct use of polyether foam is its density, and this is the first factor to be considered when designing furniture. Densities generally range from 1 lb to 3 lb per cubic foot, corresponding roughly to a range of 16kg to 48kg per cubic metre. The lighter grades from 1 lb to 1.5 lb per cubic foot can be used for back cushions, headrests and arms, but should not be used for seating purposes. Manufacturers of cheap furniture use grades from 1.5 lb to 1.8 lb for seating cushions, but it is better to use a density of 1.8 lb and over; the higher the better.

Once the required density has been decided on, the hardness can be selected in order to give the type of 'feel' required. Polyether foam of a certain density is generally made in two or three hardnesses. The choice depends not only on the 'feel', but also on the thickness of the foam, so this is the next point to consider.

In choosing the thickness, the type of base on which the foam is to be used must be taken into account. With the simplest form of base—a rigid board—the foam will have to provide all the comfort and resilience required, and this is where the thickest cushions are needed. Firm grades need to be at least 9cm (3½in) thick; softer grades usually need a minimum of 11.5cm (4½in) when used for seating.

These thicknesses can be reduced if

the foam is to rest on a sprung or elastic webbing support. Firm grades can be reduced to 7.5cm (3in) and softer grades to 10cm (4in) providing that frame rails are not in direct contact with the cushion. If this cannot be avoided, however, the rail should be padded or the shape of the frame modified to prevent direct contact. Non-elastic hessian webbing and slatter wood bases should be treated as solid bases.

Where the thickness of a cushion has to be reduced below these minimum levels to suit a particular design, this can be done by laminating together different hardnesses of foam. A cushion that would normally be 12.5cm (5in) thick, for example, can be reduced to 10cm (4in) by laminating 7.5cm (3in) of the soft grade to 2.5cm (1in) of a firmer grade. This type of combination is particularly useful for convertible furniture that is used for both sleeping and sitting; the soft grade provides surface comfort in the cushion's lightly-loaded use as a mattress, and the firmer grade prevents undue compression during its heavier daytime use as a seat.

As well as being supplied in solid blocks, polyether foam can also be obtained in profile-cut foam, where one surface is shaped to give an 'egg-box' effect. A typical use for profile-cut foam is in domed cushions or pillows; the shape is achieved by fitting a small flat section between two profile sheets of a larger size. It is also used in conjunction with solid bed bases to give a better air circulation between the mattress and the base.

You can work out all kinds of combinations to produce different grades needed for your various upholstery problems. Cushions can be domed to prevent the effect of cover stretch; cushion sides can be stiffened to give them crisp lines that maintain their shape; and headrests can be made very soft with firmer edges to prevent your head from slumping to one side.

Foam can also be used with other materials; for example a foam core wrapped round with a layer of polyester fibre (such as Dacron or Terylene) produces plump, soft, bulky cushions.

Cutting and sticking foam

Thick slabs of foam are not easy to cut neatly; you should be able to get a satisfactory finish with a fine-toothed hacksaw blade or a really sharp and very long cook's knife. An electric carving knife, if you have one, is an excellent tool for the job, as it makes a

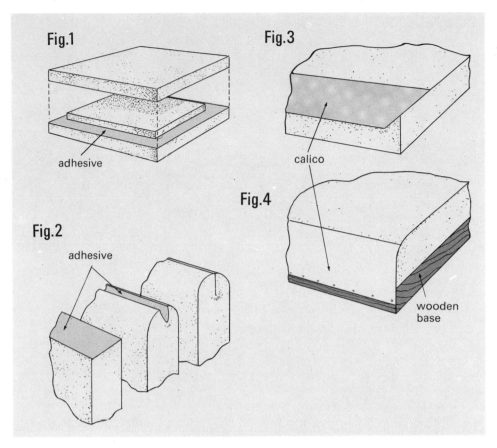

Fig. 1. A domed cushion can be made by sandwiching pieces of foam and sticking them together. **Fig. 2.** Foam slabs can be given rounded edges by pinching and sticking. **Figs. 3 and 4.** Cushions can be fixed to a base by sticking calico to the edge of the foam and tacking it to the base.

clean cut. Always cut foam slightly oversize, but make your fabric covers to the exact finished dimension required. This will put the foam permanently under slight compression, which will ensure clean lines and minimize wrinkles. A mattress should be cut about 2cm ($\frac{3}{4}$in) oversize, most cushions about 0.6cm ($\frac{1}{4}$in).

A contact adhesive such as Dunlop Thixofix should be used for bonding foam either to itself or to other surfaces. To stick two large sheets of foam together, spread a band of adhesive about 4cm (1$\frac{1}{2}$in) wide round the edge of both surfaces, and apply criss-cross bands of adhesive at random over the rest of the area. After the adhesive has been applied the two surfaces should be left for about 10 minutes until they are tacky, then brought together. A strong bond will form immediately on contact. Alternatively, the two surfaces can be pressed together as soon as the adhesive has been applied, and this will allow you to slide them about to a certain extent. You should press

the surfaces together again after about half an hour to ensure a strong bond. The diagrams on this page give ideas for cutting foam and arranging it in laminated layers to suit different purposes.

Fabrics for covers

Large foam cushions are useful both inside the house and in the garden and the fabric chosen for their covers should be suitable for the use to which they are going to be put. Foam slabs for use as cushions on a swing garden seat, for example, can be left outside if they are covered in pvc-coated cotton, which is hard-wearing, waterproof, and comes in a wide range of colours and patterns.

A large floor cushion that will be used as a pouffe must have a strong cover if it is not going to wear out where it rubs against the floor. Foam seating slabs which are also used for sleeping on should not have such a stiff cover that you can feel it through the sheets, but at the same time it should be tough enough to stand up to the hardest daytime use. There are many modern synthetic fabrics on the market—nylon ones are particularly tough—that will fulfil both requirements easily.

Full instructions on how to make up covers for cushions are given in pages 45-46.

Cushion covers

Ready-made covers for boxed cushions—whether for scatter cushions or the larger cushions on armchairs and settees—are expensive and not often available in a wide selection of fabrics, shapes and sizes. Make your own—it is not at all difficult and you will spend a fraction of the amount you would pay to have them made to measure.

The foundation for all these cushion shapes (shown left) may be a soft pad (filled with down and feathers), or a foam biscuit (see pages 38-43 for further information on suitable filling materials).

Plain square box cushions
For the top and bottom cover pieces, measure the width and length of the pad, and add on 2cm (¾in) seam allowance. For the box strip, measure the depth of the pad and add 2.5cm (1in).

If your fabric is wider than twice the total width of the pad, you can cut both sides of the cover from it, so buy an amount equal to the length, plus three times the total depth of the strips. If you can cut only one side from the width, buy double the length of the pad and allow extra if you are not able to cut the box strips from the waste.

If you are having piped edges, for the amount of piping cord and bias-cut casing fabric, measure the perimeter of the pad and double it, allowing an extra 10cm (4in) for joining. As a guide to the amount of fabric needed for the casing, 0.91m (1yd) of 122cm (48in) wide fabric will make about 25.50m (28yd) of bias strip 4cm (1½in) wide.
Making up: Cut out the fabric, on the straight grain and including the seam allowance, for the top and bottom cover pieces. If the fabric has a large motif pattern, position it centrally on both pieces. Next, cut two box strips equal in length to the pad's width, and in width to the pad's depth, including seam allowances. Cut two more box strips of the same width and equal to the length of the pad. For piped edges, cut and join enough bias fabric to make two casings, each 4cm (1½in) wide and equal to the length of the pad's perimeter, plus 5cm (2in) for joining. (See page 39 for details about piping.)

Make one continuous strip by joining all the box strips along their short edges with 1.3cm (½in) plain seams; taper the stitches into the

corners 1.3cm (½in) from both ends on each seam (Fig. 1).

Attach the piping to the 'right' side of the box strip along both edges, so that the stitching line is 1.3cm (½in) from the edges (Fig. 2). With the 'right' sides together, pin one edge of the box strip round the edge of the cover top, positioning the seams of the strip at the corners of the cover (Fig. 3). Clip the casing at the corners; the tapered seams will give enough ease to go round smoothly, so these need not be clipped. Stitch the pieces together and neaten the raw edges if the fabric is likely to fray.

Attach the bottom cover to the other edge of the box strip in a similar way, but leave a large opening in the side which will fall at the bottom of the cushion when it is in position. Turn the cover right side out and press it. Insert the cushion pad and finish the opening either by inserting a zip fastener or by slip stitching the edges together. (These stitches can be unpicked easily for removing the cover for cleaning.)

Round box cushions
For the main cover pieces, measure the diameter of the pad and add on 2.5cm (1in) seam allowance. For the box strip, measure the circumference and depth of the pad and add on 2.5cm (1in) seam allowance to both.

If your fabric is wider than twice the diameter, allow a piece the same length, plus the depth of the box strip including seamage (allow twice the depth if you will have to join pieces to make a strip equal in length to the circumference). For piped edges, allow enough fabric to make two 4cm (1½in) wide bias-cut casings equal to the circumference, plus 5cm (2in) for joining. If you can cut only one side of the cover from the width of the fabric, allow double the amount and cut the piping casing from the waste.
Making up: Using half the total diameter as the radius, make a paper pattern following the method below. Use this to cut out two circular pieces for the main pieces of the cover. Then cut out (join pieces if necessary) the box strip, making its length equal to the circumference of the pad and its width equal to the total depth.

Make both lengths of piping and, taking 1.3cm (½in) turnings, stitch one to the edge of each of the cover pieces.

With 'right' sides together, pin one edge of the box strip over the piping around the edge of the cover top, taking 1.3cm (½in) turnings. Clip the

seam allowance to ease it round smoothly. When the strip fits the circle exactly, join its ends together (Fig. 4). Stitch all the seams, then press them. Join the other edge of the strip to the cover bottom, leaving an opening large enough to insert the pad. Press the seams and neaten all raw edges if you intend to wash the cover. Turn the cover right side out and insert the pad. Finish the opening by inserting a zip fastener or by slip stitching.

Bolster cushions
For the main piece of the cover, measure the length and circumference of the pad and allow a piece of fabric 2.5cm (1in) longer and 2.5cm (1in) wider. For plain ends, measure the diameter of the pad, add 2.5cm (1in) and allow a piece of fabric the same length and twice as wide. For gathered ends, cut two rectangular strips, both equal to the circumference plus 2.5cm (1in) in length, and to half the diameter plus 2.5cm (1in) in width. For piping, you need two lengths of bias-cut casing, both equal to the circumference plus 2.5cm (1in) for joining.

Making up: Cut out the fabric for the main section of the cover and make it into a tube by joining it along its long sides (Fig. 5); leave a large opening in the middle of the seam and insert a zip fastener.

Plain ends: Using half the diameter plus 1.3cm (½in) as the radius, make a paper pattern (see below) and cut out two circular pieces of fabric. Attach the piping around the edges of the circles on the 'right' side. With the 'wrong' side of the tube facing out

Boxed cushions arranged on divans have the two-fold function of adding height and comfort.

(and with the zip undone), join the circles to each end, allowing 1.3cm (½in) turning and clipping the edges of the tube to ease them round. Neaten and press the seams and then turn the cover 'right' side out. Insert the cushion pad.

Gathered ends: Cut out the two strips of fabric to the size given above and make each one into a tube by joining it along its short ends with 1.3cm (½in) turnings. Turn over one raw edge for 1.3cm (½in) on each tube and make a line of gathering stitches 1.3cm (½in) from the fold. Attach the piping to the other edge of the tubes (Fig. 6) and with 'right' sides together, join these edges to each end of the main tube, taking 1.3cm (½in) seams (Fig. 7). Insert the pad and draw up the gathering threads to fit the ends tightly. Secure the ends and then cover the edges with a large covered button.

Sun 'button' cushions
Measure the cushion pad as for plain round covers. Calculate the measurements of the box strip in the same way. For the centre section of main cover pieces, double the width of the strip (less seam allowance) and subtract this from the diameter of the pad. Add on 2.5cm (1in) seam allowance to the remaining figure and then, using half this amount as the radius, make a paper pattern and cut two circular pieces.

Cut out the box strip as for the plain round cover and then cut two

more strips of the same size. Make two lengths of piping, both equal in length to the circumference of the cushion, and stitch it to the 'right' side of the box strip along both edges (Fig. 8). With the 'right' sides together, join the other strips to each side of the box strip, over the piping (Fig. 9), and then make the whole piece into a tube by joining the short ends together (Fig. 10).

Trim off 1.3cm (½in) from the outer edge of the paper pattern and use it to cut two more circular pieces from stiffening (use canvas or the dressmakers' bonded kind). Place the stiffening centrally on the wrong side of the fabric circles and turn in the seam allowance on to the stiffening. Clip the edges of the fabric to keep the circles a good shape, and tack the fabric down (Fig. 11).

Run a gathering thread 1.3cm (½in) from the edge round both ends of the tube and then insert the cushion pad, positioning it so that its edges are level with the edges of the box strip. Draw up the gathering threads to fit the pad and secure them (Fig. 12).

Pin the prepared circles, 'right' side out, centrally over the raw edges of the gathering and oversew them neatly into position. Then, with a long needle and doubled sewing thread, draw the circles together by working through the cushion, from side to side, and drawing up the thread tightly (Fig. 13).

Cutting a fabric circle: Cut a large piece of paper into a square, each side of which is a little longer than the radius (half the diameter) required. Use a pair of compasses set to the radius or tie one end of a piece of string around a pencil and measure the radius from the pencil along the length of string. Mark the measurement by pushing a drawing pin through the string. Lay the paper on a flat surface and push the drawing pin into the top left-hand corner. Hold the pin firmly with the left hand and, with the pencil held upright with the other hand, draw an arc from the top right-hand corner to the bottom left-hand corner. Cut along the pencilled line.

Cut out a square of fabric, each side of which is equal to the diameter. Fold the fabric in half and then in half again, making a square with each side equal to the radius. Pin the paper pattern to the fabric so that its square point is in the corner of the fabric where the folds meet. Cut through the layers of fabric along the curved edge of the pattern only. Do not cut along the folds.

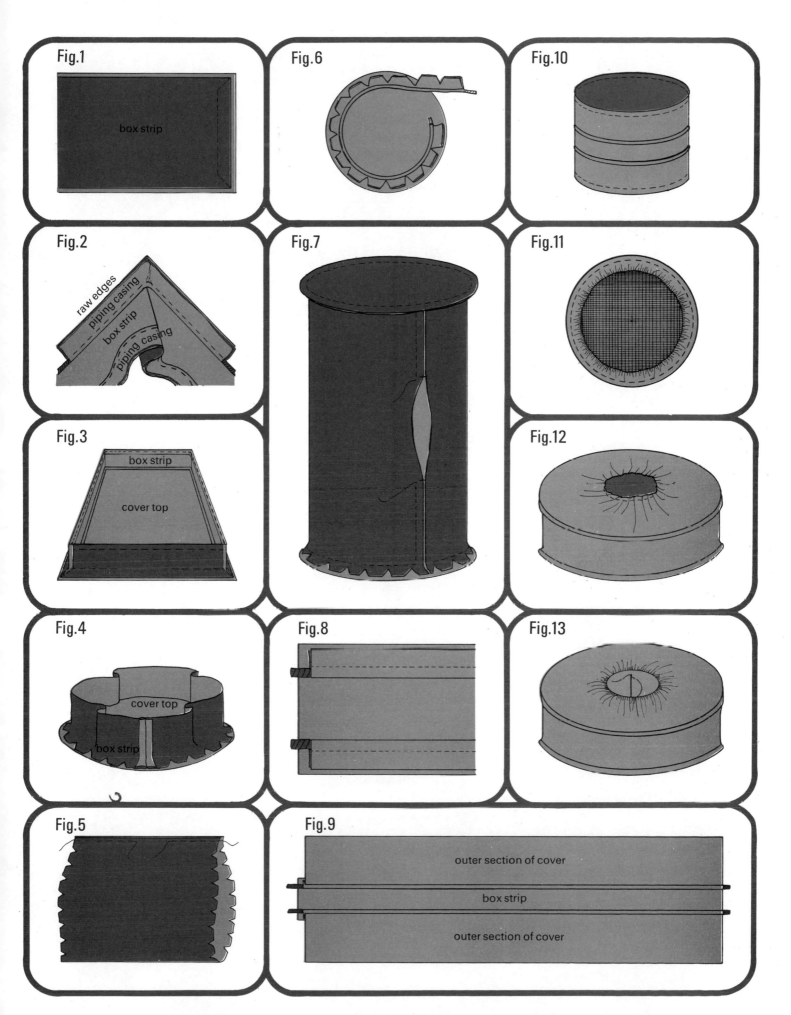

Fig.1

box strip

Fig.2

raw edges
piping casing
box strip
piping casing

Fig.3

box strip

cover top

Fig.4

cover top

box strip

Fig.5

Fig.6

Fig.7

Fig.8

Fig.9

outer section of cover

box strip

outer section of cover

Fig.10

Fig.11

Fig.12

Fig.13

47

The term 'loose cover' is a slight misnomer because the cover should fit the chair like a glove, and be 'loose' only in that it can be removed for cleaning. They do not 'sit' successfully on chairs with leather or plastic covers, and should not be used with velvet because the pile sets up a resistance to the cover fabric which makes it wear badly.

For your first attempt at making covers, choose a simple fireside chair the type which has wooden arms. The cover should be fitted actually on the chair, and never made to match old covers which may have stretched.

Calculating the amount of fabric

Choose fabric which is tough and hardwearing, firm in weave, colourfast and non-shrink. Avoid very thick fabrics—medium-weight furnishing cottons and linens treated for crease resistance are ideal. 75cm (30in) wide fabric is the most economical to use for chairs, but if you do have to buy 122cm (48in) wide, the offcuts can be used for making the piping casing.

Like any other kind of soft furnishing, it is worth making a simple cutting chart showing the measurements of each section. The warp threads of the fabric—those running down the length parallel with the selvedge—should run vertically on all the upright sections of the cover, and on the seat they should run from the back to the front.

Start taking your measurements by putting pins in the padding of the chair on the seam line of the existing upholstery at the top of the back in the centre, and in the seam behind the arms at the widest part of the back, so that the inside and outside measurements are taken from the same point.

Inside back: Measure from the pin at the top (Fig. 1, point A) down to where the back and seat meet (point B). Add on 2.5cm (1in) for the turning at the top and 12.5cm (5in) for the turning and tuck-in at the bottom. For the width, measure between the pins at the sides (points C to D), and add 2.5cm (1in) on each side for turnings.

Outside back: Measure from the pin at the top (point A) to the bottom of the seat (point E) and add 2.5cm (1in) for the turnings at the top and 12.5cm (5in) at the bottom for the turning and tie-under. For the width, measure from C to D (but on the outside of the chair), and add 2.5cm (1in) on each side for turnings.

Seat: In order to cover the section below the seat if it is upholstered, or the seat if it is a fixed one, measure from the back of the seat at point B, to the front (point F). Add 12.5cm (5in) for the turning and tuck-in at the back and 2.5cm (1in) for the turning at the front.

Seat border: For the depth of the seat border, measure from point F to the bottom of the seat (point G). Add 2.5cm (1in) at the top for turnings and 12.5cm (5in) at the bottom for turnings and tie under. For the width of the front border, measure from one arm, round the front of the seat to the other arm, and add 4cm (1½in) on each side. For the width of the side borders, measure from the arm to the back of the chair and add 4cm (1½in) to the front edge and 2.5cm (1in) to the other edge (allow double the amount of fabric, since two side bands are needed).

To calculate the amount of piping cord and bias-cut casing fabric needed for the piping, measure the perimeter of the seat and the chair back (from the back leg, up the side, across the top and down the other side to the leg).

If your chair is different in design from that shown in the diagrams, cut the loose cover sections to correspond with the original upholstery, placing the seams in the same places.

In the chair shown in Fig. 2, for example, there is an extra piece between the inside and outside back sections, and this is in two sections because of the arm.

Fitting the cover

Cut out all the pieces, including allowances, taking care to position any pattern on the fabric the right way up and centrally on each piece.

Find the centre of each section of the chair and mark a line with pins on the padding up the outside back, down the inside back, along the seat and border.

Fold all the pieces of fabric in half lengthwise, with wrong sides together. Place the piece for the inside back on the left-hand side of the chair, with the fold level with the centre pin line. Arrange the fabric so that 2.5cm (1in) projects at the top and then pin the fold to the chair all the way down. Smooth the fabric out to the side of the chair and pin along the top, following the seam line of the original upholstery.

If you have not inserted a strip between the front and back pieces, to fit the fabric round the arms, fold back the edges of the fabric level with the inner edge of the arm. Mark another line with pins on the fabric from the centre of the arm out to the raw edges (Fig. 3). Cut along this pin line from the raw edges to within 2.5cm (1in) of the arm and then snip into the corners of the arm (Fig. 4). Fold under, level

with the arm, remove the pins which hold the fold down and smooth out the fabric to the side of the chair.

Bring the lower piece under the arm to the outside back and pin along the seam line of the original upholstery. Bring the upper piece over the arm and pin. Check that this section fits smoothly and exactly follows the contours of the chair. Make darts to take in any fullness which cannot be disposed of without distorting the fabric.

Place the fabric for the seat section on the left-hand side of the seat, with the fold level with the centre pin line and 2.5cm (1in) projecting over the front of the seat. Pin the fold to the seat padding, smooth the fabric out to the side and pin it at the front and side of the seat. Pin the lower edge of the inside back section to the back edge of the seat section and push in the tuck-in at the back of the seat.

Pin the outside back section to the same half on the outside of the chair, with the fold of the fabric level with the centre pin line and 2.5cm (1in) projecting at the top. Pin it to the inside back fabric along the top of the chair, removing the pins which hold the inside section to the padding as you progress. Smooth the outside back fabric to the side and, working down from the top, pin it to the inside back fabric. Pin it to the padding at the bottom of the chair.

Pin the border sections to the seat fabric in the same way, but do not attempt to fit them round the legs yet. Pin the back edge of the side border to the outside back fabric. Check that all the sections fit the chair exactly, but without the weave of the fabric being stretched or distorted. Then mark with pins the outline of the legs on the border sections (Fig. 5).

Carefully remove the cover from the seat and, with it still pinned together, trim the seam allowance to 2.5cm (1in) where necessary. Cut away the sections for the legs to within 1.3cm (½in) of the outlining pins. Mark the centres of each section with tacking stitches, and cut notches in the seams (use groups of one, two or three) so that all the sections can be fitted together easily. Also mark the points where the seam joining the inside and outside back section divides, and where the seat and border pieces are joined on. Remove all the pins and open out all the pieces.

Facing the arms and legs

Start by finishing off the openings for the arms. Place the inside back section flat on your work surface, with the

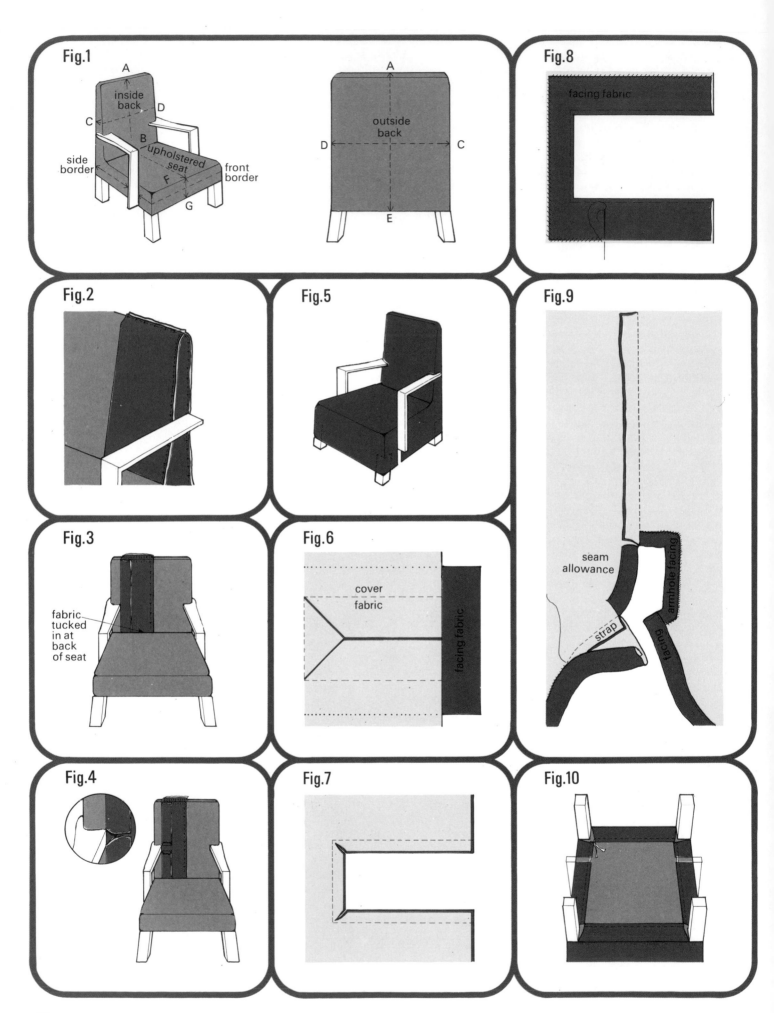

Fig.1

A

inside back

C

D

B

upholstered seat

side border

F

front border

G

A

outside back

D

C

E

Fig.8

facing fabric

Fig.2

Fig.5

Fig.3

fabric tucked in at back of seat

Fig.6

cover fabric

facing fabric

Fig.9

seam allowance

armhole facing

strap

facing

Fig.4

Fig.7

Fig.10

'wrong' side facing upwards.

For the facings, cut two squares of fabric 7.5cm (3in) larger than the total size of the openings and place these, 'right' side facing up, under the openings. Pin and machine stitch the pieces together, following the line where the fabric was folded under level with the arm (Fig. 6). Cut the facings away to within 1.3cm (½in) of the stitching, and snip into the corners (Fig. 7). Turn the facings over on to the wrong side of the cover, tack round the seam line through all thicknesses so that none of the facing shows on the right side, and press. Turn under the outer raw edge of the facing for 0.6cm (¼in) and hem it firmly to the cover (Fig. 8).

Face the openings for the legs in the same way.

Making up the cover
Make all the piping (see page 39) and pin it to the seam line round the sides and top of the outside back section, and around the seat section.

Pin and stitch together the outside back and inside back sections, leaving open the seam below the armhole opening on each side (this will be finished by a placket later). Pin and stitch together the lower edge of the inside back and the edge of the seat.

Turn under 4cm (1½in) on both short ends of the front border and make hems. Turn under 4cm (1½in) on the front short ends of the side borders only, and make hems. Stitch the borders to the seat section, matching all notches carefully, so that all the leg and arm openings are still in the right places, and the tuck-in is left free.

Finishing the opening
Because the opening at the back is made up on one side of the inside back and side border, with the seat tuck-in left free in between, it should be finished with a 'strap and facing' placket.

On the straight grain of the fabric, cut a strip for the strap 9cm (3½in) wide × the length of the opening on the outside back side (excluding the arm opening), plus 2.5cm (1in) for turnings. Turn under 1.3cm (½in) at each short end of the strap and trim the seam allowance on both sides of the opening to 1.3cm (½in). With the 'right' side of the strap facing the 'right' side of the cover seam allowance, and with raw edges level, pin one long edge of the strap to the opening, along the piping line. Tack and machine stitch.

Snip the seam allowance of the cover at the top of the strap. Turn under 1.3cm (½in) along the free side

of the strap, fold over to the wrong side and pin the edge to the other stitching line, enclosing the raw edges (Fig. 9). Tack and stitch in position.

Mark the beginning of the tuck-in section, and measure the length of the opening on the inside back above the mark. Cut a strip for the facing 2.5cm (1in) longer than this measurement × 5.5cm (2¼in) wide. Turn under 1.3cm (½in) at both short ends of the facing, then pin it to the 'right' side of the seam allowance on the inside back, taking 1.3cm (½in) turnings. Tack and machine stitch. Turn the facing completely on to the 'wrong' side of the cover and fold flat. Tack along the seam line so that no facing shows on the 'right' side of the cover. Turn under

the raw edge of the facing for 1.3cm (½in) and slip stitch to the cover.

Make another facing for the border section of the opening in the same way. Press the strap over the facing.

Sew hooks and eyes at 4cm (1½in) intervals along the placket to close it. Turn under the raw edges of the tuck-in section and armhole opening and stitch these down.

Finishing the cover
Turn under a hem to make a 1.3cm (½in) wide casing all round the lower edge of the cover, and machine stitch it.

Place the cover on the chair, insert tape through the hem casing and tie it under the chair (Fig. 10).

Armchair covers

Many people, who would think nothing of making a dress in a weekend, balk at the prospect of making a loose cover for an armchair. But once you know how—and if you take your time—the method is easier and you need fewer techniques.

Use a fabric tape measure and take all the measurements in centimetres or inches. To estimate the length of fabric required, add together the lengths of the sections, including allowances.

If you are using patterned fabric with a one-way design or a large repeat, or if you are making several covers from plain fabric, it is always worth drawing up an accurate cutting chart. The way to do this is described below.

Measuring the chair

The professional way of making loose covers is to cut a block of fabric for each section as in Figs. 1 and 2, and then fit it exactly. Measuring the chair gives the sizes of the blocks.

When fitting the cover for the back and seat, the fabric is folded in half

lengthways and fitted on half the chair, so that the two sides will be identical. For the arms and scrolls, the pieces for opposite sides of the chair are placed together and fitted to one side at the same time.

Because of this, it is simpler to take the initial width measurements across half the chair too, in order to save confusion later on. If you are right-handed, you will find it easier to do the fitting on the right-hand side of the chair (the side which is on your right when you are sitting in the chair). If you are left-handed, fit the cover on the left-hand side. Take the measurements on the same side that you will be fitting on.

Remove the seat cushion if there is one, then mark a line up the centre of the outside back, down the inside back, along the seat from the back to the front edge and down the front border. If you are going to fit the cover straight away, mark this line with pins, pushing them into the existing cover. Or mark the line with tailor's chalk and tack it. All length measurements should be taken along this marked line.

Outside back

For the length, measure from the seam

line at the top (point A) to the bottom of the chair. Add 2.5cm (1in) at the top and 15cm (6in) at the bottom for the turning and tie under. If you are having a skirt instead of a tie under, measure the length to the floor, add 2.5cm (1in) at the top for the turning and subtract 15cm (6in) from the bottom. (The standard length for a skirt is 18cm (7in) finished, regardless of the height of the chair's legs.)

For the width, if there is no extra piece of fabric inserted at the side of the chair between the outside and inside pieces (a side scroll), measure from point C across the back to the centre pin line. If there is a side scroll, measure from the seam joining it to the outside back piece, to the pin line.

Inside back

For the length, measure from the seam at the top of the back (Fig. 1, point A) down to where the back and the seat meet (point B). Add on 2.5cm (1in) at the top for the turning and 15cm (6in) at the bottom for the turning and tuck-in.

For the width, measure across the widest part from the seam line (point C) to the centre pin line. Add 2.5cm (1in) at the side for the turning. Measure again at the bottom of the seat and add 15cm (6in) at the side for the turning and tuck-in. Use the greater of these two measurements for the calculation and cutting-out size.

Seat

If the chair has a removable seat cushion, the cover for this should be made following the method given in pages 49-51. To cover the section below this, or the seat itself if it is a fixed one, for the length, measure from the back (point B) to the seam at the front (point D). Add 15cm (6in) at the back for the turning and tuck-in and 2.5cm (1in) at the front for the turning.

For the width, measure across the widest part from the side of the seat to the centre pin line. Add 15cm (6in) at the side for the turning and tuck-in.

Seat Border

For the length, measure from the edge of the seat (point E) to the bottom of the chair. Add 2.5cm (1in) at the top for the turning and 15cm (6in) at the bottom for the turning and tie under. If you are having a skirt instead of a tie under, measure the length from point E to the floor, add 2.5cm (1in) at the top and subtract 15cm (6in) at the bottom.

For the width, measure from the inner edge of the arm to the pin line. Add 2.5cm (1in) to the edge for the turning.

Arms

The arms should be covered in two pieces. The inside piece should start at the bottom of the seat and finish on top of the arm at its outer edge (the 'sight line'). Decide on the position of this line and mark with pins.

The outside piece extends from this line to the bottom of the chair. This is the only piece of the cover which need not follow the lines of the chair exactly, because if you make it too tight it will be impossible to take the cover off the chair.

Inside arms

For the length, measure from the seat to the pinned sight line and add 15cm (6in) at the bottom for the turning and tuck-in and 2.5cm (1in) at the top for the turning. Double the length when calculating the amount of fabric necessary to allow for the other arm.

For the width, measure along the top of the arm on the pinned sight line and add 2.5cm (1in) to the front edge and 15cm (6in) at the back for turning and tuck-in. On some chairs, the top of this piece will be shaped round to the back of the chair and joined on to the outside back, so it must be made wide enough.

Outside arms

For the length, measure from the highest point on the pinned sight line to the bottom of the chair. Add 2.5cm (1in) at the top for the turning and 15cm (6in) at the bottom for the turning and tie under. If you are having a skirt instead of a tie under, measure the length to the floor and add 2.5cm (1in) at the top for the turning and subtract 15cm (6in) from the bottom. Double the length to allow for the other arm.

For the width, measure across the widest part and add 2.5cm (1in) to each side for the turnings.

Side scrolls

For the length, measure from the top of the back of the chair on its side face, to the top of the arm. Add 2.5cm (1in) at the top and 2.5cm (1in) at the bottom for the turnings. Double the total when calculating the fabric necessary to allow for a scroll on the other side.

For the width, measure across the widest part and add 2.5cm (1in) to

each side for the turnings.

Front scrolls

For the length, measure from the top of the arm on its front face to the bottom of the chair. Add 2.5cm (1in) at the top and 15cm (6in) at the bottom for the turnings and tie under. If you are having a skirt instead, measure from the top to the floor, add 2.5cm (1in) at the top and subtract 15cm (6in) from the bottom. Double the total to allow for the scroll on the other side.

For the width, measure across the widest part and add 2.5cm (1in) to each side for the turnings.

Skirt

For a plain skirt with corner inverted pleats, measure the perimeter of the chair round the bottom and add 122cm (48in). If you will not be able to cut a piece of fabric long enough without joining (and you won't with a patterned fabric) measure each side of the chair and add 30cm (12in) to each. By making the skirt in four sections you will be able to hide the seams inside the corner pleats.

For a skirt with spaced pleats, double the perimeter of the chair. For close pleats, treble the perimeter.

For a gathered frill, allow $1\frac{1}{2}$ times the perimeter.

To calculate the total amount required, divide the length of the strips by the width of the fabric, and multiply this amount by the depth of the skirt.

On professionally made loose covers, the skirt is always made 18cm (7in) deep when finished. To do this, cut strips 23cm (9in) wide, which allows for 1.3cm ($\frac{1}{2}$in) turning at the top and 4cm ($1\frac{1}{2}$in) at the bottom for a 2cm ($\frac{3}{4}$in) double hem.

Making a cutting chart

The simplest way to do this is with a ruler which gives very small measurements, such as a wooden school ruler. Using a scale of 2.5cm to 30cm (1in to 1ft), draw on a long sheet of paper a rectangular strip equal to half the width of the fabric x the estimated length of the amount required. Mark on this the position of the pattern repeats.

Using the same scale, cut out from another sheet of paper small pieces to represent the sections of the cover. Mark the tops of the sections and which pieces should be placed against the fold (the inside and outside back, the seat and the front border). All the

other pieces will be cut through the doubled fabric.

Place the chair section pieces on to the main strip of paper, adjusting them so that the repeats are central both vertically and horizontally. You will then see what fabric there is left over for the smaller pieces and for cutting bias strips for piping.

If you are finishing the cover with a tie under, you may be able to save fabric by stitching on separate pieces for this and reducing the length of the outside back, outside arm, front scroll and front border pieces by 12.5cm (5in) each. The seam joining the fabric should come exactly at the bottom of the chair, and may be piped (Fig. 6).

Cutting out the fabric

Cut out the fabric for each section, following the plan worked out on your chart. Professional cutters always cut the pieces in a set order and mark the top of each piece with a pin for quick identification. You might find it easier and safer to number the pieces in tailor's chalk, or put a tailor's tack in the top of each piece, using a different coloured thread for each.

Fitting the cover

Starting with the outside back piece, place the folded fabric 'right' side out, on to the chair. Keep the fold level with the centre pin line, and position the fabric so that turnings allowed project at the top, bottom and side. Smooth the fabric out to the side of the chair and pin, keeping the grain of the fabric horizontal.

Pin on the seat piece in the same way, so that the allowance for the tuck-ins is at the back and side. When the fabric is completely pinned, fold over these allowances on to the seat for the time being.

Next, pin on the inside back piece. Pin it to the outside back piece at the top of the chair, following the shape of the chair exactly. With some fabrics you may be able to ease out any fullness by stretching it slightly; with others you may have to make small darts at the corners.

If you have side scrolls, fit these (with 'wrong' sides together) between the outside and inside back pieces. This is one of the more difficult pieces to fit neatly, so it is worth taking some time over it, and re-pinning as necessary. Always keep the grain of the fabric vertical and horizontal. In some places you may have as much as 5cm (2in) turning allowances, but this can all be trimmed off later.

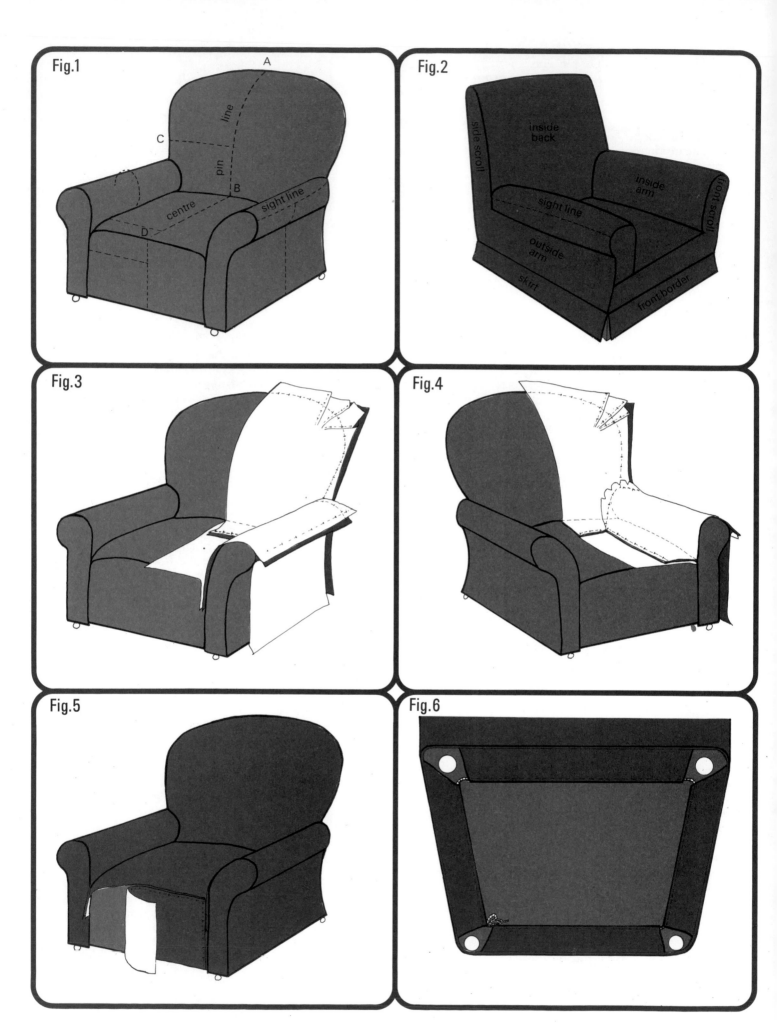

Fig.1

A

line

C

pin

B

centre

sight line

D

Fig.2

inside
back

side scroll

sight line

inside
arm

(front scroll)

outside
arm

skirt

front border.

Fig.3

Fig.4

Fig.5

Fig.6

If there are no side scrolls, pin the inside back piece to the outside back piece at the sides. Work from the top down, keeping the fabric quite smooth. At the arm, you will have to cut into the fabric from the side so that it can be wrapped round to the back smoothly. The fabric below this should be cut so that the allowance for the tuck-in is reduced to 2.5cm (1in) at the top, increasing to the full 15cm (6in) at the seat (Fig. 4).

Fitting the arms
Place the pieces (with 'wrong' sides together) for the inside arm in position. Pin the front edge first so that the 2.5cm (1in) turning allowance overhangs the edge of the arm. Smooth it across to the back of the arm, keeping the grain of the fabric as straight as possible. Pin the bottom edge to the side tuck-in of the seat piece and cut the back edge to correspond with the shape of the inside back tuck-in. Clip into the seam allowance over the top of the arm where necessary to get a smooth fit. If it has to join the back piece, cut away fabric to form the correct shape.

Keeping the crosswise thread parallel to the ground, pin on the outside arm pieces. You will probably have to increase the amount allowed for the turning at the back of the arm, and the edge of the fabric may not stay level with the edge of the inside arm fabric. Pin the back edge of the outside arm piece to the outside back piece, but leave the front edge open (Fig. 3).

Fitting the front scrolls
Place these centrally on the widest part of the scroll and pin carefully to the outside arm piece, following the shape of the chair as closely as possible. Continue pinning to the inside arm as far as the beginning of the tuck-in. Mark with pins the fitting line from this point to the bottom.

Trimming the seam allowance
You will probably find it easier to fit the front border when all the other pieces have been stitched and the tuck-in can be tucked in properly. So, if you are completely satisfied with the fit of the cover so far, trim all the seam allowances to within 1.3cm (½in) of the pins. Try to keep exactly to the 1.3cm (½in) since this will make the fitting together much easier. Cut notches in the corresponding seams in groups of one, two and three, so that you will be able to fit the pieces

together again. Remove all the pins and open out the pieces.

Making the piping
To make quite sure that the piping cord will not shrink when the cover is cleaned, which would have the effect of tightening all the seams so much that the cover would be too small, boil and dry it a couple of times before making up the lengths of piping.

Cut out and join several long lengths of 4cm (1½in) wide bias strips and make the piping following the method given in page 39.

Pin and stitch the piping on the seam line round the vertical and top edges of the side scrolls and front scrolls, along the top edge of the inside front piece, and along the top and back edge of the outside arm.

Stitching the cover
Start by joining the tuck-in seam at the back of the seat and bottom of the inside back pieces. Join the outside arm pieces to the inside arm pieces, then fit these to the seat and inside back pieces.

Join on the outside back piece to the inside back piece along the top edge, and one side edge if there are no side scrolls. If you have side scrolls, fit these between the back pieces.

Leave one of the back seams open for about two-thirds of the way down so that the cover can be pulled on and

off the chair—try to choose the side which will be least noticeable when the cover is on the chair.

Join on the pieces for the front scrolls, continuing the seam down into the tuck-in section on the inside arm piece—it must not be stitched to the tuck-in section which is on the seat piece.

Fitting the front border
Put the cover on to the chair with the 'right' side facing out. Tuck down the tuck-ins neatly, leaving the seam allowance protruding at the front edge. Open out the fabric for the border and place it centrally on to the chair. Pin it to the seat piece and to the seat tuck-in along the top edge, and then to the lower part of the front scroll. Trim the seam allowance to 1.3cm (½in) where necessary, cut notches, then remove the cover from the chair. Unpin the border and re-pin and stitch it with 'right' sides together (Fig. 5).

Finishing off
The opening at the back can be finished with a zip fastener or with a strap and placket as shown on page 51. If you are having a tie under, finish also as shown on page 51. If you are having a skirt, stitch this on round the bottom edge, making a 2cm (¾in) double hem at the lower edge.

Settee covers

A well-made loose cover for a settee looks as good as a fixed cover, and it has several advantages. It can be easily removed for cleaning and repair and, very important, it is simpler, quicker and cheaper to make.

The average life of a settee is likely to be anything from 15 to 30 years. In that time you may find that you tire of the original covering, wish to change the decorative scheme it originally matched, or need to have the settee re-covered because it has become worn and shabby.

Unless the innards of the upholstery actually need attention, it is usually not worth removing the old cover and completely replacing it, particularly if all you need is a different colour or pattern. Even if you are having it done professionally, and almost certainly if you are doing it yourself, the new cover will be simply tacked over the old. But with much less effort, and for rather less cost, you could make a loose cover for the settee—with the

advantage that when you eventually want to change this cover, it will be easy to replace.

The method for making a loose cover for a standard settee is almost the same as for armchairs, the main difference being that the width of a three-seater settee is usually greater than the fabric being used. With a plain fabric, which has no nap or pile, it may be possible to use it so that its length runs across the width of the settee, but with fabrics where the pattern or pile must run vertically you will have to join pieces to make up the full width for the seat, inside and outside back pieces and front border.

As with other soft furnishings, a centre seam should always be avoided because it looks ugly. Instead, you should cut a main panel from the full width of fabric and join narrower strips to each side. If you cut the width of these strips from the selvedge in towards the middle of the cloth, taking care that any pattern is level on all the pieces, it will be possible to match the pattern horizontally and it will run in a line down the back and

Even pale-coloured covers become practicable if you use a drip-dry fabric.

seat pieces. The only difficulty in matching the pattern might occur where the seat has three cushions and the fabric you are using has a main motif.

Cushion covers should always be cut with the motif placed centrally, but this may not correspond with the pattern on the panels on the inside back. Here, you may find it would look better to make each of the inside back panels the same width as the cushions, so that you can centre the motif on each strip. In this case, the panels for the outside back and front border should be cut in the same way.

Calculating the width of the strips
Work out the total width required for the section, including the allowance for the turning and tuck-in. Subtract the width of the fabric, less 2.5cm (1in) seam allowance, from the total width. Add 2.5cm (1in) to the remaining measurement, and divide the total by two.

For example, if the total width required is 165cm (66in) and the fabric 122cm (48in) wide, the width of the strips to be cut out would be 25cm (10in). When joined to the main panel with 1.3cm (½in) plain seams, the centre panel would be 119.5cm (47in) wide and the two smaller panels 24.3cm (9½in).

The strips should be joined on to the main panel before the fabric is fitted on to the settee.

Making up piping

Where you have a large amount of piping to make up, it is much quicker to join up a very wide bias strip and cut this into narrow lengths, rather than to cut several narrow bias strips and then join them in the normal way.

Start by cutting a rectangle of fabric, at least 23-30cm (9-12in) wide, on the straight grain of the fabric. Fold up the bottom right-hand corner (Fig. 1, point D), so that the right-hand edge of the rectangle is level with the top edge (points A-B). Crease the fold well and then cut along it. This line is the true bias of the fabric.

With right sides together, stitch the triangle A-B-X to the left-hand edge of the rectangle so that B and A are together and C and D are together. The fabric will now be shaped like a parallelogram.

On the wrong side of the fabric, mark the width of the strips required down the fabric parallel to the slanting edges (if you are using No. 3 or No. 4 piping cord, the strips should be 4.5-5cm – 1¾in-2in—wide). With 'right' sides together, join the top and bottom sides of the fabric with a 0.6cm (¼in) seam, so that the width of one strip protrudes beyond the opposite edge (Fig. 2), and the marked lines match.

Press the seam carefully, and then start cutting along the marked lines. Make up the whole length of piping by placing the cord (which must previously be boiled and dried twice to prevent subsequent shrinkage) centrally along the wrong side of the bias strip. Fold the strip over the cord so that its edges are level and pin them together.

Fit your sewing machine with a piping foot and machine tack the sides together (using a medium to long stitch), keeping the stitching as close to the cord as possible. As well as holding the piping in place, this stitching helps to prevent the fabric from fraying when it is slashed at corners.

By making up the piping by the 'sleeve' method as above, you will notice that all the joins are running in the same direction, so when you cut off a length, try to cut it in the same direction too. When you have to join edges of piping, pin the ends of the fabric together as shown in Fig. 3.

To join the cord, overlap the ends by 2.5cm (1in) and cut off the excess. Unravel 2.5cm (1in) from both ends and cut off two strands from one end and one strand from the other. Overlap the remaining ends and bind them firmly together (Fig. 3). Fold over the casing and tack it back in position.

Always try to avoid placing a join on the front edge of any of the cover sections, because even if correctly done, the extra thickness of fabric may produce an unsightly ridge.

Once you have reached this stage, you can proceed in exactly the same way as with an armchair. The only difference in method will arise if you have a drop-end settee. It is a good idea, however, to add extra ties under the cover to keep it anchored in position.

Drop-end settee

This type of settee needs a slight alteration to the ordinary method, because it has one folding arm. When the arm is upright, this settee looks very similar to a normal one, but when the arm (normally the right one as seen from the front) is lowered, the settee turns into a sort of day bed.

The general method for making a loose cover for this is very similar to making one for a normal settee, but it needs some modification on the right-hand side so the arm can be lowered

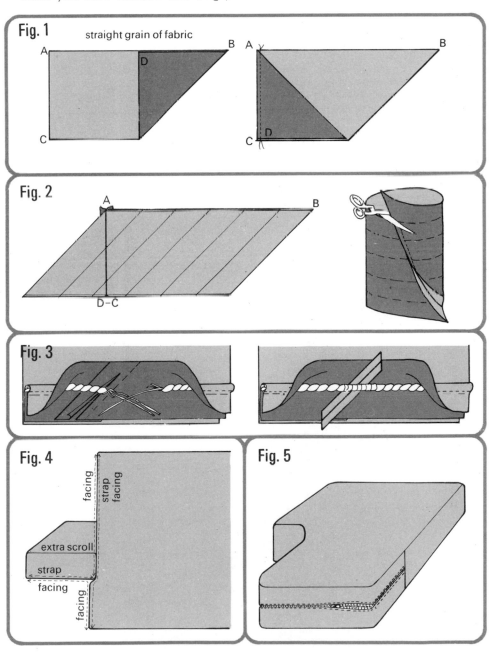

and raised without the cover having to be removed.

Because the cover should be smooth when the arm is lowered, the usual tuck-ins at the back and bottom of the arm are not made. The scroll or border between the outside and inside back sections is made long enough to reach the bottom of the seat (instead of the top of the arm), and an extra scroll is inserted at the back of the arm (Fig. 4).

Measuring the sections

There are various methods of measuring the sections, depending on the type of fabric being used. If you are using a patterned fabric which needs careful placing, you will need to take extra care because the measurements for each side of the cover will not be the same. To make sure of this, the safest way of measuring is as follows.

With the arm upright, measure and mark the centre line down the sections and the sight line on both arms in the usual way. Then lower the arm and measure each side of the sections separately. Mark two columns on your list for the left and right sides, remembering that the right-hand side is always the side which is on your right when you are looking at the settee from the front.

If the arm which drops is on the right-hand side, as it usually is, measure up the left-hand side in the usual way, with all the normal allowances for the tuck-ins and turnings. Then measure the right-hand side as follows.

Inside Back: For the width, measure from the centre line to the side seam line and add 2.5cm (1in) for the turning. For the length, measure from the seam line at the top to the junction of the back and seat. Add 2.5cm (1in) at the top for the turning and 15cm (6in) at the bottom for the turning and tuck-in.

Outside back: As for the other side.
Seat: For the width, measure from the centre line to the junction of the seat and arm, and add 2.5cm (1in) for the turning. For the length, measure from the junction of the back and seat to the front edge. Add 15cm (6in) at the back for the tuck-in and turning and 2.5cm (1in) at the front for the turning.
Inside arm: For the width, measure from the seam at the back of the arm to the seam at the front of the arm. Add 2.5cm (1in) to each side for the turning. For the length, measure from the sight line at the top of the arm to the junction of the arm and seat. Add 2.5cm (1in) to the top and bottom for the turning.
Outside arm: As for the other side.
Front border: As for the other side.
Front scroll: As for the other side.
Side scroll: For the width, measure across the widest part and add 2.5cm (1in) to each side for the turning. For the length, measure from the seam at the top to the bottom and add 2.5cm (1in) to each side for turning.

Back arm scroll: For the width, measure across the widest part and add 2.5cm (1in) to each side for the turning. For the length, measure from the top of the arm to the bottom of the scroll and add 2.5cm (1in) to each side for the turnings.

Cutting out

Although you have measured the sides of the settee separately, the fabric for each section should be cut out in one complete piece wherever possible. The sections which are identical for both sides of the settee can be cut through the doubled fabric in the normal way, but all the other pieces must be cut through single fabric. Cut out all the pieces that can be cut through the doubled fabric first, then lay out the fabric completely flat with the 'right' side facing up and mark a line with pins down the centre.

If the sections for the inside back and seat can be cut from the full width of the fabric without pieces having to

It's not difficult to cover even a comfortable old sofa with separate seats and back covers. And the result is a new, elegant piece of furniture.

be joined on, start from the marked centre line and measure out the widths of the left and right-hand sides, being careful that the pattern is the correct way up. Then cut out the remaining pieces, checking that the pattern is centred if necessary.

If you do have to join pieces for the inside back and seat, you will have to calculate the width of each side panel separately. Subtract half the width of the main panel, excluding seam allowance, from the width of the side being calculated. Add on 1.3cm ($\frac{1}{2}$in) turning allowance to each side to be joined.

For example, when you are using 122cm (48in) fabric full width for the centre panel, this will actually be 119.5cm (47in) wide, because you lose 1.3cm ($\frac{1}{2}$in) on each side for turning. If the right-hand side of the settee measures 91cm (36in), 59.3cm (23$\frac{1}{2}$in) of that will come from the main panel, and the side panel should be 31.7cm (12$\frac{1}{2}$in). Therefore, when cutting out, the side panel should be 33cm (13in), the extra 1.3cm ($\frac{1}{2}$in) being added to the left-hand side for the turning. When you cut out the panel for the right-hand side of the settee, stand so that you are looking at the fabric with the pattern the correct way up. Cut in from the left-hand selvedge for the required width, so when the seam joining the panels is formed by the selvedges of both pieces, the pattern will match. Reverse this for the left-hand panel.

Fitting the cover
Because some pieces are symmetrical and others asymmetrical, the cover must be fitted over the whole settee, rather than with doubled fabric over half as in the normal method.

Keep the fabric the 'right' side out, and match the centre marks on the fabric to the centre line marked on the settee. Pin the pieces together in the normal way, taking care that the grain of the fabric is square to the floor. Trim the seam allowances to 1.3cm ($\frac{1}{2}$in), remove the cover from the settee and re-pin and stitch the seams.

When inserting the piping, be careful to match up both sides. For example, the piping on the left-hand side scroll would come down only as far as the top of the arm, so make the other side to match, even though the scroll actually goes down as far as the seat. This is because the settee will probably be used much more with the arm upright, rather than down, so the sides of the settee should look the same in this position.

To finish the ends of the piping when it finishes 'in mid air' like this, simply cut the piping cord to the right length, cut the bias strip 1.3cm ($\frac{1}{2}$in) longer and turn this under level with the end of the cord. Slip stitch the end of the casing neatly.

Finishing the cover
The strap-and-facing opening on the drop end of the settee should be made in two sections. On the outside back fit a strap. Fit another strap to the outside edge of the back arm scroll. Fit facings to the inside back and outside arm (Fig. 4).

The drop arm is normally worked by a knob in the middle of the outside arm, so an opening should be made for this in the fabric.

Measure the diameter of the knob and mark its position on the fabric with a circular tacked line. Cut a piece of fabric for the facing 5cm (2in) larger than the circle, with 'right' sides together.

Machine stitch the pieces together on the tacked line, then cut away the double layer of fabric inside the circle, leaving a border of 0.6cm ($\frac{1}{4}$in) inside for turning. Clip into the turning at right angles to the stitching at about 1.3cm ($\frac{1}{2}$in) intervals. Turn the facing fabric through to the wrong side of the cover and press and tack it down so that none of the facing shows on the 'right' side. Turn under the outer edge of the facing for 0.6cm ($\frac{1}{4}$in) and hem neatly to the cover.

Covering shaped cushions
Many settees have rectangular seat and back cushions, and these are quite straightforward to cover, following the method given on pages 45-46. If you have cushions which are shaped to fit round the arms, the best way of cutting the fabric for the two mian sections for the top and bottom is from a paper pattern.

Place the cushion on to the paper and draw round it carefully with a pencil, keeping the point as close as possible to the edge of the cushion. Remove the cushion and draw another line 1.3cm ($\frac{1}{2}$in) outside the first one. Cut round this.

If possible, cut the top and bottom pieces at the same time through doubled fabric (folded with 'right' sides facing, so you can check on the placement of the pattern). If you would prefer to cut the pieces singly, lay out the fabric the 'right' side up and cut the first piece. Keep the fabric the same way, but turn the pattern over

for the second piece, so that the shaping is reversed.

For the box strips which are inserted between the main sections, measure the depth of the cushion and cut three strips 2.5cm (1in) wider and long enough to fit the front and each side, plus 2.5cm (1in) for the turning. Join the side strips to each side of the main strip along the short edges, taking 1.3cm ($\frac{1}{2}$in) turnings. Taper the stitching into the corners 1.3cm ($\frac{1}{2}$in) from the beginning and end of each seam.

Cut another strip 2.5cm (1in) wider than the others, and long enough to fit the back of the cushion, plus 2.5cm (1in) for turnings. Cut this strip in half lengthways, and rejoin it for 2cm ($\frac{3}{4}$in) at each end, taking 1.3cm ($\frac{1}{2}$in) turnings. Insert a zip fastener into the remaining opening. Stitch the short ends of the strip to the short ends of the other one, taking 1.3cm ($\frac{1}{2}$in) turnings and tapering the stitching as before.

Attach the piping around both edges of the now circular strip, taking 1.3cm ($\frac{1}{2}$in) turnings. Then, with the 'wrong' side of the strip facing out and the top of the pattern towards the top edge, fit the piece for the top of the cushion to the edge of the strip, matching the corners to the seams. Pin and tack in position, taking 1.3cm ($\frac{1}{2}$in) turnings, and clipping the seam allowance where necessary to turn the curves smoothly. The tapered seams of the strip will open out as you do this, so there is no need to clip into the corners. Stitch the seams and overcast the edges if the fabric is likely to fray. Press carefully.

Still with the wrong side facing out, turn the strip so that the open end is uppermost. Fit the fabric for the bottom of the cushion to this side, matching the corners to the seams as before. Press and turn 'right' side out.

With some very deep cushions, you will find it easier to insert the pad into the cover if the opening is made extra large by extending it round to the sides. To do this, cut the strips for the sides of the cushion about 7.5cm (3in) shorter, and cut the strip for the back 15cm (6in) longer. Join them all as before, and insert the zip fastener. Fit on the main sections so that the zip fastener extends an equal amount into each side. Here you will have to clip into the turnings at the corners, so it is a good idea to strengthen them with an extra line of machine stitching 0.3cm ($\frac{1}{8}$in) outside the main stitching, for about 5cm (2in) at either side of each corner (Fig 5).

Basic bedspread

The focal point of a bedroom should be the bed — and the bedspread is the finishing touch. A throwover bedspread is one of the quickest and easiest pieces of soft furnishing to make and, if you team the fabric with your wallcovering and curtains, it will give the room an immediate co-ordinated effect.

Calculating the amount of fabric

Measure the bed with its bed clothes and pillows as shown in Fig. 1. For the width, measure from the floor on one side, up and across the bed to the floor on the other side. For the length, measure from the top of the pillow to the floor at the foot of the bed. If you wish to tuck the bedspread around the pillows, add an extra 30cm (12in) to the length.

As furnishing fabrics are usually 122cm (48in) or 137cm (54in) wide (plus selvedges), you will need to join two fabric widths for a single or a small double bed, so double the length measurement to calculate how many metres or yards you should buy. Five and a half metres, or about six yards, is usually ample for an average single or double bed. As there will be some wastage when making a single bedspread, a 91.5cm (36in) wide dress fabric might be more suitable here.

If your fabric has a large design or motif, add on extra to the overall length in order to match it at the seams or to position it to best advantage on the bed — the additional amount could vary from an extra half pattern to as much as two patterns (known as repeats). Ask your retailer for advice if in doubt, because so

LEFT *Round corners at the foot of a divan spread are attractive and practical too.*
TOP RIGHT *A feature has been made of the seams on this plain bedspread by stitching on braid. More braid across the foot accentuates the centre panel.*
BOTTOM LEFT **Fig. 1.** *How to measure the bed.* **Fig. 2.** *For square corners, machine stitching is taken to the edges of the hems.* **Fig. 3.** *For round corners, the hem line is marked and the excess fabric trimmed off.* **Fig. 4.** *For cut-away corners, the side panel is folded up and a guide line marked from A to the floor.* **Fig. 5.** *The corner is pinned together on the guide lines.*

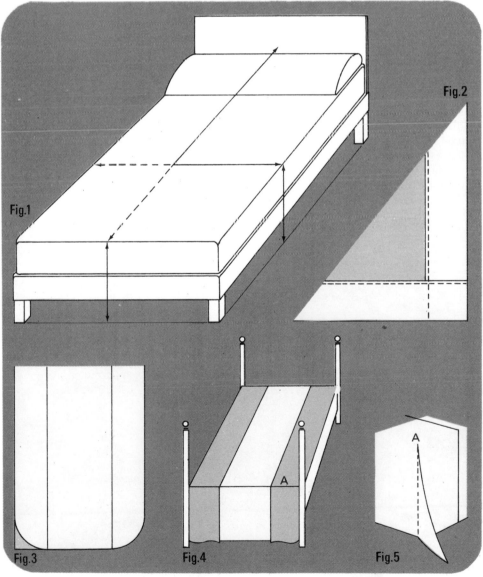

Fig.1 Fig.2 Fig.3 Fig.4 Fig.5

much will depend on where the first measurement is taken on the fabric roll. Choose a time for buying the fabric when the store is quiet and take a note of the bed measurements with you. Ask to have the fabric unrolled so you can examine the design fully and decide how you would like it positioned on the bed.

If you want the first repeat to come on the pillows, for example, allow about 15cm (6in) above this (towards the cut end), and start measuring the length of the bedspread from this point. For the second length, move down the roll to the next complete repeat, start 15cm (6in) above it, as for the first length, and measure as before. This ensures a matching design when you seam the lengths together. With a particularly large pattern, there will be some wastage (at the beginning and between the lengths), but this is unavoidable.

Making the bedspread

To avoid having an ugly seam down the centre of the bedspread, cut the fabric across into two equal lengths and then cut one of these pieces in half lengthways, thus making one full width of fabric for the centre panel and two half widths for the sides. Allowing a total of 10cm (4in) for seams and side hems, with 122cm (48in) wide fabric, the bedspread will have a minimum finished width of 237cm (7ft8in). With 137cm (54in) wide fabric, the finished width will be 268cm (8ft8in).

If your double bedspread is to be narrower, cut off the excess equally from each half width (take it from the raw edges rather than the selvedges if this does not affect the matching of the pattern at the seams). For a 63cm (3ft) bed, however, this would mean that the seams run along the side of the bed, rather than the top, and the panelled effect is lost. To avoid this, cut off the excess from the full width, rather than the halves (the leftover piece could be used for cushion covers). If the fabric is plain, the excess can be taken from one side of the centre panel, but if the pattern runs centrally down the fabric, divide the excess and take off an equal amount from each side.

Joining the panels

To join the side pieces to each side of the centre panel, place the 'right' sides of the fabric together, selvedge to selvedge. Make sure the pattern is matched and the fabric runs the same way on each panel. Pin and tack about 1.3cm (½in) from the edge (more if the selvedges are wide). If you allowed extra on the length to match the pattern, cut off the excess fabric now (remember to allow 2.5cm (1in) at the top and bottom for hems).

Machine stitch the seams, using a medium length stitch, following the tacking line. Remove the tacking. Clip (cut into) the selvedges at intervals if they are tight (this helps the seam to lie flat), and press the seams open. Neaten the raw edges by oversewing by hand or overcasting by machine if any fabric was cut off the centre panel.

Square corners

Make 2cm (¾in) hems down the long sides of the bedspread as follows: fold over the raw edge 0.6cm (¼in) on to the wrong side of the fabric. Make a second fold 2cm (¾in) deep, so the raw edge is now enclosed. Tack and machine stitch through the three thicknesses, along the first fold. Remove the tacking and press the hems. Turn under 2cm (¾in) hems at the top and bottom, making the corners square. Tack and machine stitch them, taking the line of machining over the machined line of the side hems (Fig. 2). Remove the tacking and press the hems and then the finished bedspread all over.

Rounded corners for divans

Join the panels as above. Position the bedspread carefully on the bed and pin a curved line where the fabric touches the floor at the corners of the foot of the bed. Take off the bedspread and use a large plate or something similar as a guide to neaten the curve. Cut away the excess fabric 2.5cm (1in) outside the line of pins — enough for a 2cm (¾in) hem (Fig. 3).

Turn under the hem at the foot and along the sides of the bedspread, easing in the fabric at the corners. Tack and machine stitch the hem, remove the tacking and press the hem. Make a hem the same depth at the top of the bedspread, leaving the corners square. Press the bedspread all over.

Fitting around bedposts

Join the panels as above. Place the bedspread on the bed and fold back the side panels from the edge of the bed, with the fold lying just inside the posts (Fig. 4). Pin a line along the fold from the corner of the bed (point A) down to the floor. Unfold the sides and fold up the foot of the bedspread in a similar way. Pin along this fold from point A to the floor (the pin lines should meet at point A).

Remove the bedspread and, using the pin lines as a guide, pin the corners as shown in Fig. 5. Cut off the corner 1.3cm (½in) from the line of pins. Using this as guide, cut out a similar corner from the other side of the bedspread.

Clip into the angle and make a narrow hem, rounding the angle. Press the hems. Make 2.5cm (1in) hems all round the bedspread, leaving the corners square. Press all over.

For beds with footboards, the corners of the spread can be cut away.

Traditional quilt

If you haven't been converted to using a continental quilt and still prefer traditional sheets and blankets, a good old-fashioned quilt is probably an essential addition in cold weather. You can make one much more cheaply than they cost to buy — and you can choose the fabric, size and weight of filling.

Making a quilt is much easier than it used to be because of the development of Terylene wadding. This looks like cotton wool and is sold in sheet form in different sizes and weights. In the old method of making a quilt, the cover was made up and divided into pockets which were stuffed with down. This was a difficult job, because down is very light and flies away.

Terylene wadding, however, is simply sandwiched between the two sides of the cover. For a traditional looking quilt, the three layers can be held together by quilting stitching or tying.

Or you can leave it unstitched for a bulky, 'puffy' quilt. The composition of the Terylene is such that as long as it is held by the outer seams, it does not actually need quilting to hold it in place.

A quilt made with Terylene weighs about the same as one filled with pure down, or it may be lighter than one filled with a mixture of down and feathers. Other advantages of Terylene are that it does not need a special inner cover to prevent the filling from leaking, as do feathers; it can be washed in a machine and it should not affect hay fever sufferers. It is also more readily obtainable than down in most places.

Calculating the amount of fabric
Make the quilt the same width, or slightly narrower, than your bed and long enough to reach from the foot to within 5-7.5cm (2-3in) of the pillows. Choose cover fabric which is lightweight and preferably crease resisting and drip dry, but not slippery if you also want to use it on the underside of the quilt. Alternatively, the underside could be covered in a fabric like brushed nylon.

For each side of the quilt, allow enough fabric to cut a panel the same size as the Terylene sheet. Allow extra if you want a piped edging. Dress fabric which is 91.5cm (36in) wide is ideal for both single and double quilts. It can be used full width for the single quilt because, although you will lose 2.5cm (1in) from the width in turnings, this can be made up by the edging. On a double quilt it is the right width for the centre panel (to make up the full width strips are joined to each side to form a border).

Although 122cm (48in) wide furnishing fabric can be used, it is more wasteful because fabric would have to be trimmed off for both sizes of quilt. This can be used for the edging, particularly a frilled one because with piping made from bias strips it would need several joins.

Choosing the quilting design
Designing a quilt used to be a craft practised on a scale similar to patchwork and, like patchwork, it originated from a necessity to be thrifty. Old,

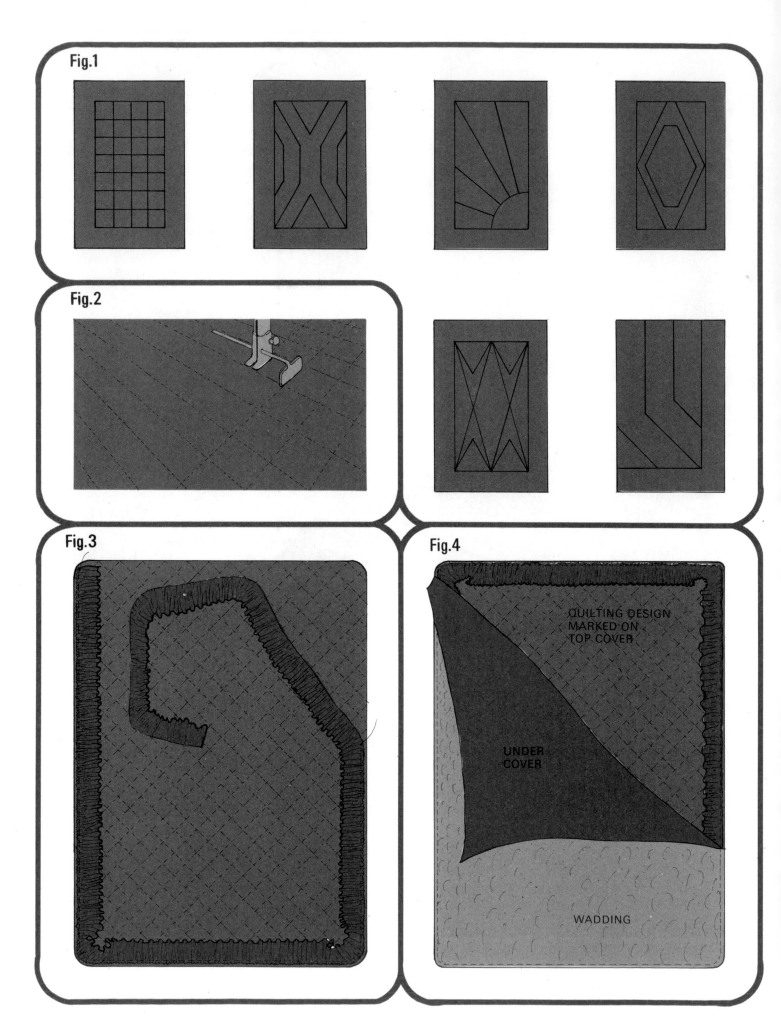

Fig.1

Fig.2

Fig.3

Fig.4

QUILTING DESIGN
MARKED ON
TOP COVER

UNDER
COVER

WADDING

worn blankets, knitted clothes, even raw wool which could not be spun, would be saved and stitched between two pieces of fabric and held in place by all-over hand stitching.

Gradually the craft became an art, and beautiful quilting designs — often made up with traditional emblems and symbols — were incorporated. For convenience of working, the fabric was stretched over a frame and the whole family would take turns at stitching. The finished quilting was used for warm clothing and bedding.

Nowadays, a lot of quilting is done by sewing machine and, although most modern machines can be adjusted to move freely enough to stitch curves and other shapes, the patterns tend to be limited in their design. The most common machine stitching is like a grid, made up from squares, diamonds or ogees (linked lozenges). Once the lines of the quilting have been marked, the actual stitching is easy and quick. Fig. 1 shows some variations on straight stitching.

One way of giving a lift to this basic quilting is to use a fabric printed with a geometric or regular repeat design. The stitching of the quilting can be done following the lines of the design to extremely good effect.

Marking out the design
Some sewing machines have a special attachment which can be used for quilting regularly spaced straight lines, and all you have to do is mark the first line. When the quilt is made up, you stitch the first line, decide how far apart the next lines should be and place the work in the machine as if to start stitching the second line. The attachment is then set at the side of the machine foot so that it runs level with the first line. By keeping it level as you stitch, the second and subsequent lines will be straight and evenly spaced (Fig. 2).

If you have no such attachment, the lines can be marked by using a straight edge or template and tailor's chalk or a dressmaker's tracing wheel and special transfer paper sold with it. The marks made usually brush out easily. Or for a more intricate design you could use an embroidery transfer which is ironed on to the fabric.

Making the quilt
Cut out the fabric to the same size as the Terylene, joining on the borders for a double quilt. Mark the quilting design on the right side of the top cover, leaving a border 1.3cm ($\frac{1}{2}$in) wide all round the edge. Make up the piping or frilled edging (see below), and attach it to the top cover so that the stitching is 1.3cm ($\frac{1}{2}$in) from the edge (Fig. 3).

Next, pin the Terylene to the wrong side of the under cover so that all the edges are level and tack all round. With the right sides of the fabric together, stitch the top cover to the under cover and Terylene on three sides only, taking a 1.3cm ($\frac{1}{2}$in) turning. Turn the quilt right side out, poke out the corners with a pencil and press round the edges carefully. Turn in 1.3cm ($\frac{1}{2}$in) on the fourth side and stitch firmly together to close the opening (Fig. 4).

Doing the quilting
To prevent the fabric from puckering and slipping during the stitching, tack the layers together using long stitches and placing the rows about 15cm (6in) apart across the work in both directions. Start each row from the same side as an extra precaution against puckering.

For the quilting, use regular sewing thread but with your sewing machine set with a fairly long stitch and fitted with a hinged foot. Place the quilt in the machine with the right side uppermost, and start and finish each line of stitching as close to the edging as possible. Stitch slowly, smoothing out the fabric as you progress. Secure the ends with a few reverse stitches or by taking the threads to the underside and knotting them together.

Tying the layers together
As an alternative to quilting, the layers can be tied or knotted together. This is quicker than stitching rows, and is much easier if the wadding is so thick that machine stitching is not practical.

Tack the layers together in the same way as for quilting. Mark out the

position for the knots, spacing them in rows 10-15cm (4-6in) across the quilt in both directions.

To make the knots, spread the work out on your work surface so that it is completely flat and with the underside facing up. Using strong thread and a long needle, make a small stitch through the three layers. Pull the thread through, leaving an end about 5cm (2in) long. Make a back stitch, inserting and withdrawing the needle in the same places as the first stitch, and draw up the thread firmly but not so tightly that the fabric puckers. Knot the ends of the threads together in a reef knot, pull them tightly and cut off 0.6cm ($\frac{1}{4}$in) from the knot.

Making a frilled edging
Cut out and join enough 7.5cm (3in) wide strips of fabric to make one circular piece equal in length to twice the perimeter of the quilt. Fold the strip in half lengthways and press it.

Put marks in the raw edges of the frill to indicate where the corners of the quilt will fall (each section is twice the length of the quilt's sides) and mark the centre of each section. Mark the centre of each side of the top cover.

Insert a gathering thread 1.3cm ($\frac{1}{2}$in) in from the raw edges of the frill (do this in sections to avoid breaking the thread when it is pulled up). Place the frill on to the top cover with raw edges level and with section and centre points matching. Pin the frills at these points, placing the pins at right angles to the edge.

Pull up the gathering threads to make the frill fit the cover, and distribute the gathers evenly. Secure the gathering threads by winding them round the divisional pins. Place the other pins at right angles, so any slight adjustments to the gathers can be made easily. Tack and machine stitch the frill to the cover, then remove the gathering threads.

Continental quilt

A continental quilt is really an extra large eiderdown which takes the place of the traditional bedclothes of upper sheet, blankets and standard quilt. The weight difference is considerable — bedding with wool blankets can weigh as much as 9kg (20 lb) whereas most continental quilts weigh about 2kg (4 lb).

Instead of forming a tent round the body as do normal bedclothes, the quilt drapes round it and it is not tucked in at the sides. Because of the filling which insulates the body, it is just as warm in winter, yet cool enough in all but very hot or humid weather. You will use a bottom sheet and pillows but, instead of a top sheet, the quilt should have a removable cover which can be washed. You can make the bed very quickly — you simply smooth the bottom sheet, plump the quilt and smooth it down before putting on a bedspread. Because of its bulk, a throwover bedspread usually looks better than a fitted one.

Down — the undercoat of water fowl — is the traditional filling for continental quilts but, because of the difficulty of separating it from feathers, it is very expensive. It is more usual for a proportion of feathers to be left with the down, and fillings described as 'down and feathers' should contain 51 percent or more of down, and those described as 'feathers and down' may be mostly feathers but must contain at least 15 percent of down. Down is much lighter than feather and only 850g (30oz) of pure down is needed for a single-sized quilt, as compared with 1.14kg (2½ lb) for a down and feather mixture, or 1.35kg (3 lb) for feathers and down.

The snag about using down and feathers for making your quilt is that they are not readily available and they are not easy to handle. The filling from an old eiderdown may be used, but often this is inadvisable because they become less efficient at a rate of about one percent a year (usually because of dust percolating through the cover). If you do use an old eiderdown, it is worth buying some extra filling to mix with the old, and bulk it up to the required amount. Quilts made with this filling cannot be washed.

Another snag about using down and feathers is that the primary cover must be made from downproof cambric to prevent the filling from escaping and dust filtering through (featherproof ticking is not good enough). Because this is usually available in a 122cm (48in) width only, the cover has to be pieced to make up the total size.

The primary cover may be made like a simple bag and divided into channels down its length by stitching the sides of the bag together or alternatively — and this is the method used professionally because more filling can be inserted — the bag is divided by fabric partitions which are inserted in seams down its length. This is tricky and tedious to do at home, and it is worth buying the bag ready made if possible.

Terylene fibre filling, of the type known as P3, makes an excellent filling for home-made continental quilts because it is light, washable, readily obtainable and not difficult to work with. It is cheaper than down and feathers and also better for hay-fever sufferers. It is sold in large sheets, sandwiched between muslin, and looks like thick cotton wool. The measurements of the wadding sheet should be slightly larger than the finished quilt. The fabric used for the primary cover may be a closely woven sheeting in cotton, cotton/Terylene or a cotton/polyester mixture. These are sold in 175cm (70in) and 225cm (90in) widths.

Calculating the amount of fabric

The finished quilt should be at least the same length as your bed, and at least 46cm (18in) wider. Because these quilts rest simply on top of the bed and are not tucked in at the sides, two

single ones are often more comfortable than one large one for a double bed. You should make two types of cover: a primary cover to enclose the filling, and a couple of secondary covers which are the same size and can be taken off for washing.

Making the primary cover

Feather fillings: If you are making your own simple cover from 122cm (48in) wide cambric, you may find that it is worth drawing a cutting chart to work out the best way of piecing the fabric to calculate the total amount most economically. Basically, the cover fabric should be twice the length of the quilt, plus 5cm (2in) seam allowance x the width of the quilt plus 2.5cm (1in) seam allowance.

For a double quilt, it would be simplest to allow four times the length because, although there will be some wastage, to cut it more economically would be so complicated as to make it not worthwhile. Too many seams would create weak spots, from which the filling could eventually leak. Alternatively, you could reduce the width of the quilt to just under 1.82m (6ft) and allow only three times the length.

Leaving one end open, join all the pieces to make a case the size of the quilt. Take 1.3cm (½in) plain seams, allowing at least 12 stitches per 2.5cm (1in) and make a second line of stitching 0.3cm (⅛in) outside the first for extra strength. Press all the seams and turn the case 'right' side out. Turn under and press down the seam allowance along the opening (Figs. 2 and 3).

Mark evenly spaced—between 23-30cm (9-12in) apart—parallel lines down the length of the case. Pin and then machine stitch the sides of the case together down these lines to divide it into channels (Fig. 3).

When you fill the case, allow at least an hour without interruption. Work in a place which is small, uncluttered and draught-free, such as the bathroom. Close the windows and remove anything to which the filling might cling. Have handy your needles, thread, scissors and some clothes pegs or bulldog clips. It is also advisable to cover your hair and, if you suffer from hay fever, your nose and mouth.

Duvet, or continental quilt, covers, are best made from cotton or man-made fibre sheeting, which is crease-resistant. If you buy extra material, you can make matching pillow cases to complete the effect.

Place the bag of filling in a larger, stout polythene bag to catch any spills, and slit the top of the bag. Place a handful of filling in the first channel of the case and close the opening with a clothes peg or clip. Shake the case vigorously to move the filling to the other end of the bag. Repeat this procedure for the other channels. When all the channels have had one handful of filling, start again in the same way, until the filling has been distributed evenly. Machine stitch the opening together, with two rows of stitching as before.

If you are transferring the filling from an old eiderdown, slit open one quilted division at a time and transfer the filling to the new case, putting one handful in each channel. Clear each section of the old quilt before you slit open the next. If you are mixing it with new fillings, alternate the handfuls of old and new filling and shake the case thoroughly to mix them.

Terylene filling: Use the 225cm (90in) wide sheeting for both sizes of case because, although you can use the 175cm (70in) width for the single size, there is more wastage than if you use the 225cm (90in) 'sideways' on for the length of the quilt.

Cut out two pieces of fabric, both equal in width and length to the finished quilt, plus 2.5cm (1in) seam allowance. Place newspaper on the floor if it is carpeted, lay out one of the cover pieces 'wrong' side up and completely flat, and place the Terylene wadding on top of it. Bulk up the wadding slightly so that its edges, and those of the muslin 'sandwiching' it, are flush with those of the fabric, and pin the wadding to the fabric. Tack it loosely and then machine stitch, allowing at least 12 stitches per 2.5cm (1in) (Fig. 4).

Pin the 'right' side of the other cover piece to the sheet side of the wadded piece and stitch them together round the edge, leaving an opening on one side. Turn the case 'right' side out and close it with machine stitching (Fig. 5).

Measuring in from one long side, use pencil or tailor's chalk to mark the stitching line down the length of the case in panels of 23-30cm (9-12in) wide. Using 5 stitches per 2.5cm (1in), machine or backstitch the panels through all the thicknesses.

Secondary cover
These may be made from sheeting (old 'redundant' sheets are ideal), or any easily washable, and preferably drip dry, fabric. The basic dimensions of the case are the same as the primary cover but, to allow enough fabric to make the pocket to enclose the quilt at the opening end (as for a pillow case), add 25-46cm (10-18in) to the length of one of the sides of the case. (The exact amount for the pocket can be determined by the width or length of the fabric being used—if using 225cm (90in) fabric 'sideways' on, the pocket would be about 25cm—10in—deep.) If you also want to add a flap to the cover which may be tucked in at the foot of the bed to anchor the quilt in position and prevent it from riding up, add the same amount to the length of the other side of the case.

Cut out the sides for the cover, including a seam allowance of 0.6cm (¼in) all round on one piece and of 2cm (¾in) all round on the other. Make narrow hems along the bottom edge of both pieces if the edges are raw and then turn down the remaining amount allowed for the pocket on the narrower piece. Press down 0.6cm (¼in) turnings on to the right side of the other three sides of the wider piece. With right sides together, place the narrower piece on this one, so there is a 1.3cm (½in) margin showing on the side and top edge (Fig. 7). Fold the margin over the narrow piece and stitch through all thicknesses. Repeat this along the sides, and continue this mock French seam in the form of a hem along the sides of the flap (Fig. 8). Press the seams and turn the case right side out.

You can also make a small 'flap' at the top of the quilt to anchor it firmly.

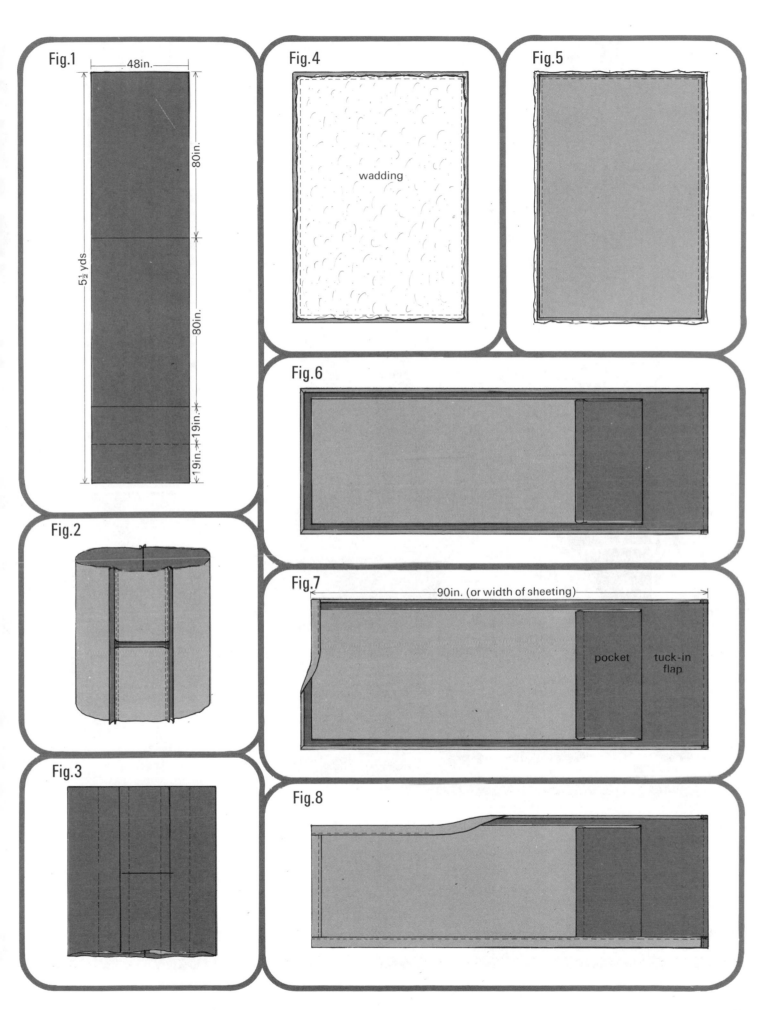

Fig.1

48in.

80in.

80in.

19in. 19in.

5½ yds.

Fig.2

Fig.3

Fig.4

wadding

Fig.5

Fig.6

Fig.7

90in. (or width of sheeting)

pocket   tuck-in flap

Fig.8

Unlined curtains

Unlined curtains are simple and quick to make and are ideal in a room like the kitchen where they may need frequent washing. Make them in a gaily patterned cotton, towelling or any kind of light-weight man-made fibre.

The amount of fabric
This is calculated by measuring the width and height of the window area. If the curtains hang outside the window recess, take the measurements from the track from which they will hang as this probably extends some way on each side of the recess and is fixed a little above it.

Measuring the width
Ideally each curtain should be cut double the width of the area it is to cover, so that when it is gathered it will have a pleasing fullness. Usually however it is simpler to base the width on full and half widths of fabric so there is no wastage. The small difference this makes can be adjusted in gathering.
1. Measure the length of the curtain track with a wood or steel rule. Add 10cm (4in) and divide the width of the fabric into the total, rounding it up or down to the nearest half width.
2. This gives the number of widths required in each curtain, so double it to give the number of widths for a pair of curtains.

Measuring the length
Curtains hung inside the window recess should finish at the sill, or if they are hung outside the recess, 7.5cm–10cm (3–4in) below the sill.
1. Measure from the top of the track to the required length and add 15.5cm (6in) for a double hem at the foot and 4cm (1½in) for the heading.
2. Multiply this figure by the total number of widths to give the minimum amount of fabric required for the curtains.
3. If the fabric is patterned you will have to buy extra so that it can be matched on all the widths. Check on the size of the pattern repeat and as a guide allow one extra on each width. For example, if each curtain is made from two widths, you should allow four extra pattern repeats for a pair of curtains.

4. If the fabric is not guaranteed non-shrink, allow an extra 2.5cm per 90cm (1in per yard), and wash the fabric before cutting out.

Gathering tape
The easiest way of gathering the curtains is to stitch on tape which has cords along each edge which can be drawn up, and pockets for the curtain hooks to be inserted.

For unlined curtains, use tape which is 2.5cm (1in) wide. This is available in a variety of colours, in cotton for natural fibres and nylon for man-made fibres. Buy a piece equal to the width of each curtain, plus 5cm (2in) for turnings.

Cutting out
1. Iron the fabric to remove all the creases and lay it out, right side up, on a large flat surface. You must be able to see a complete curtain length at once, so use the floor if your table is not large enough.

2. Make the top edge square with the selvedges by pulling out a thread across the width. Cut along this line. Measure the total length of the curtain from this point, withdraw another thread and cut along it.
3. Place the top edge of the cut length alongside the next length so you can see how the pattern matches, adjust it if necessary and trim off any wastage from the top edge. Cut the next length in the same way. For a half width, fold the length in half and cut down the fold.

Joining the widths
1. For plain fabrics, pin the pieces together with right sides facing and selvedges matching. Place half widths on the outside edge of each curtain.
2. Tack and machine stitch, taking

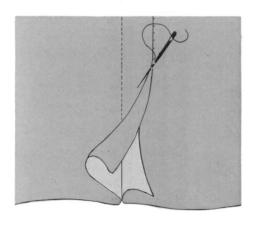

1.3cm (½in) turnings. Trim one side of the turnings to 0.6cm (¼in) and press both turnings to one side so that the untrimmed one is on top. Fold under the edge of this one 0.6cm (¼in) and slip-stitch to complete a fell seam.

3. To join patterned fabrics, press under the turnings for 1.3cm (½in), or width of the selvedge if this is more, on one of the pieces. Place the fold over the edge of the other piece so that the pattern matches.

4. Pin the pieces together from the front and slip-tack in place. To do this, insert the needle into the fold on the first width and withdraw it 0.6cm (¼in) further on. Take it directly across to the second width and insert it. Pass it under the fabric and withdraw 0.6cm (¼in) further on. Continue like this for the length of the curtains. You will then find you can stitch the pieces together on the wrong side in the normal way.

Complete the join with a fell seam as for plain fabrics.

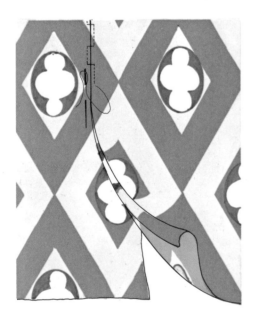

The side hems
1. Make 2.5cm (1in) double hems along the sides of the curtain as these

are heavier than normal hems and prevent the sides from curling back. To make the hems, fold over the edges for 2.5cm (1in) on to the wrong side of the fabric. Press.
2. Fold over the edges for a further 2.5cm (1in), tack and slip-stitch or machine stitch in position. Press.

Attaching the tape
1. Fold over the raw edge at the top of each curtain for 4cm (1½in) on to the wrong side and press down.
2. Cut a length of tape the width of the curtain, plus 5cm (2in). Pull out about 2.5cm (1in) of the cords from their slots at each end of the tape. Knot the cords together at one end but leave the other ends free for gathering.
3. Place the tape on to the wrong side of the curtain so that it covers the raw edge of the turning centrally, and the top edge of the tape is 2.5cm (1in) from the top of the curtain.

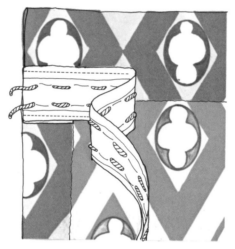

4. Turn under the short ends of the tape, enclosing the knotted cords at one end but leaving them free at the other end. Tack it to the curtain all round the edge.
5. Machine stitch outside the cords on each side, stitching in the same direction on the top and bottom to prevent dragging.

Gathering the curtains
1. Pull the curtain along the cords until it is gathered tightly at the knotted end. Pull out to the correct width, distributing the gathers evenly.
2. Knot the cords to secure the width but do not cut off the surplus ends. These can be wound up and caught to the tape with a few stitches and can be unpicked to release the cords when you wash the curtains.
3. Insert curtain hooks at ends of each curtain and at 7.5cm (3in) intervals

between. Hang the curtains for a few days before taking up the bottom hems as the fabric may drop a little.

Making the hems
1. Mark the required length of the curtain with pins across the width while they are still hanging. Take them down, check that the line is level and that the sides are the same length, and correct if necessary.
2. Turn up the hem along the marked line and tack loosely along it. Turn under the raw edge for half the total depth of the hem allowance and tack. Slip-stitch along this fold and down the sides of the hems.
3. Press the hem, remove all tacking and re-hang the finished curtains.

Lined curtains

Lining improves the look of all curtains, making them seem fuller and better draped, especially important in living rooms and bedrooms. It protects them from fading and soiling on the window side — particularly if the curtains are a pale colour (as above, where the dark border on the edges most handled also helps). In addition, lining intensifies the curtains' colour when seen against daylight, makes them shadowproof and keeps out draughts, especially if they are also interlined.

Buy a neutral-coloured sateen, specially made for curtain lining, in the same width as the curtain fabric and in a comparable quality — if your fabric is an expensive one, don't buy the cheapest quality lining, since it will wear out long before the curtains and you will have the bore and expense of remaking them with a new lining. A good alternative to plain sateen is the type which is metal insulated (the wrong side is silver-grey) as this is completely draught-proof.

For the interlining, use a fabric known as 'bump' which is made in a 122cm (48in) width. It is woven like chenille, with a heavy weft thread and a fine cotton warp, and looks like a thick, fleecy flanelette sheeting.

There are two methods of making lined curtains. One is known as the 'bag' or 'sack' method and should be used only for short curtains made from single widths of fabric. The other method involves more work — and a great deal of hand stitching — as the lining is 'locked' to the curtains at intervals across the width, but it is worth doing as it prevents it from dropping or flapping in the wind when the windows are open.

Making the curtains

Measure the window and calculate the amount of fabric for both curtains and lining as for unlined curtains (see page 71), but allow only 10cm (4in) for the hem. Cut out the fabric for the curtains and join it if necessary. Cut and join the lining, making it 7.5cm (3in) shorter and 10cm (4in) narrower than the curtains. Mark the centre points down the length of the curtain and lining with tacking stitches.

Lined curtains can add a touch of elegance to bathrooms and hallways.

Making the lining

'Bag' method: With the 'wrong' side of the lining fabric uppermost, turn up the bottom edge 1.3cm (½in), then turn up 2.5cm (1in) and make a machine-stitched hem. Lay out the curtain fabric 'right' side up and make a tuck of about 10cm (4in) down the middle (to make the curtain the same width as the lining). Place the lining 'right' side down on the curtain so that the lining top is 4cm (1½in) below the curtain top. Pin the sides together, tack and machine stitch 1.3cm (½in) from the edges and 5cm (2in) from the foot of the lining. Clip the turnings and then press the seams on to the lining.

Turn the curtain 'right' side out and match the centre points together. Lay the curtain out flat and position the lining so that it is centred on the curtain and there is a 5cm (2in) border of curtain showing on each side of the lining. Press. Turn down the top edge of the curtain 4cm (1½in) on to the lining and tack through all thicknesses. Attach the gathering tape and draw up the threads.

Hang the curtains for a few days and then mark and turn up the hem (leaving the lining free), and mitre the corners by folding under the excess fabric (rather like folding the ends of a parcel).

'Locked' method: Make 6.3cm (2½in) turnings on to the wrong side at each edge of the curtain, tack and herring-bone-stitch down. Lay the curtain 'right' side down on a large flat surface and smooth completely flat. Make a 2.5cm (1in) hem on the lining and then position it face down, so that its top edge is 4cm (1½in) below the top of the curtain and the centre points are matching at the top and bottom. Pin the lining to the curtain down the centre line, then turn back one half of the lining (Fig. 7) and 'lock' it to the curtain.

Starting 23cm (9in) from the bottom, and working from left to right up the curtain, pick up two threads of the curtain and lining with the needle, place the sewing thread round it as in Fig. 7, pull the needle through and draw up the thread (rather like blanket stitch). Continue working up the curtain in this way, making the stitches 5-7.5cm (2-3in) apart. Do not pick up more threads than this or the stitches will show on

Lining can be decorative as well as functional. The curtains on the left were made by the 'bag' method, but with lining and curtain pieces cut to the same length.

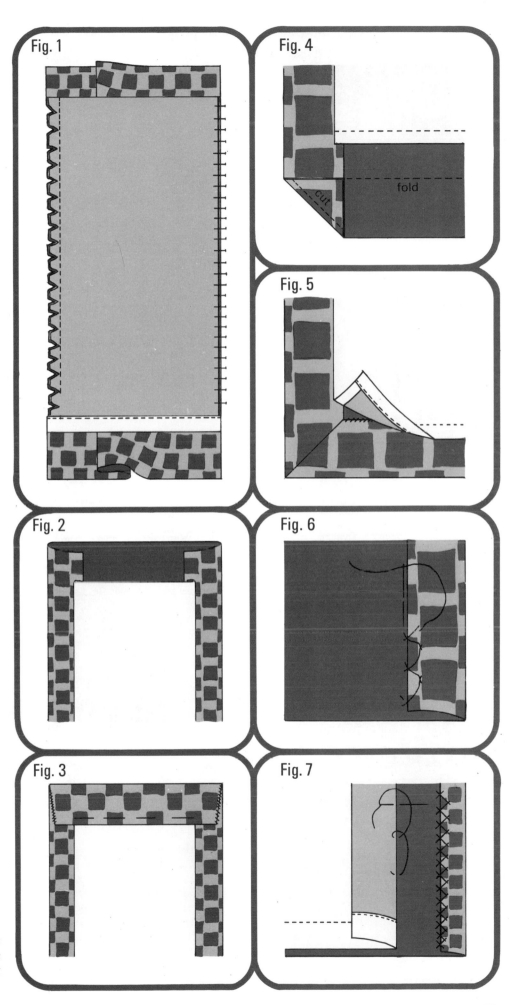

Fig. 1

Fig. 2

Fig. 3

Fig. 4

fold

cut

Fig. 5

Fig. 6

Fig. 7

the right side of the curtain, and do not draw the thread too tight or the stitches will pucker. Repeat this locking process at approximately 46cm (18in) intervals across the width of the curtains and at the seams. Press the lining completely and then tack it to the curtains about 12.5cm (5in) from each edge.

Turn under the sides of the lining for 1.3cm ($\frac{1}{2}$in) and pin them to the curtain, placing the pins at right angles to the fold. Slip stitch the lining

to the curtain and then press. Make the heading and hems as above.

Making the interlining

Cut the interlining to the same size as the curtains, joining it with a lapped seam where necessary because this is much flatter than a plain seam. To make a lapped seam, have both pieces of fabric right side up and lay one edge 1.3cm ($\frac{1}{2}$in) over the other. Backstitch down the centre of the overlap (do not machine stitch this

Dark borders around light-coloured curtains prevent the edges being soiled.

fabric as it tends to stretch).

Lay the curtain face down on a large flat surface and smooth it flat. Place the interlining on it, with the edges meeting. Turn over the edges 6.5cm ($2\frac{1}{2}$in) on both sides, tack and herring-bone stitch down. Place on the lining, lock it to the curtain and interlining, and then finish the curtains as above.

Net curtains

Net curtains — the traditional method of screening windows — are back in fashion. With the modern preference for large windows, they are an ideal way of giving privacy and disguising an unpleasing outlook where necessary.

They are inexpensive and simple to make, modern fabrics make them easy to wash, and they soften the light entering the room rather than reducing it. Whether your other furnishings are modern or traditional, the new fabrics and designs being produced by the manufacturers make it possible to find one which will blend with them.

The main alternative to net curtains is a slatted blind, but these are expensive, tedious to clean and cut out a lot of light. And unless they are in a neutral colour, they do not allow for a radical change in colour schemes.

There are three main types of net curtains.

Sheer fabrics: The most popular type of net curtain is made from a sheer fabric. This is hung right against the window and, although it does not detract from the amount of daylight entering the room, it gives privacy from outside while allowing those inside to see out. It is usually used with main curtains in ordinary fabric which are drawn at night.

Sheer net curtain fabric is mostly white, although some pale colours are available, and has a plain, close weave with a variety of textures, decorative borders and hems. The fabric used to be cotton, but these days it is usually man-made fibre such as Terylene because this can be made in a really fine weave which is strong and resistant to sunlight. This attracts the dirt more quickly than cotton, but it is easily washed and drip dries quickly.

Sheer net fabric is not a difficult fabric to sew provided fine pins and machine needles are used to prevent snagging, and the machine is set with a slightly loose tension to prevent puckering. If you are using a man-made fabric, use a polyester thread, such as Trylko or Drima, because this will 'behave' in the same way as the fabric. Even if you normally don't bother to tack, it is always advisable to tack all folds and seams because the fabric tends to slip while it is being machine stitched.

Patterned net fabric looks best on windows where there are no other curtains.

If you have difficulty with feeding the fabric through the machine, or if it still slips in spite of being tacked, it is often worth putting strips of tissue paper under the fabric as it is being fed into the machine. This can be torn away afterwards.

Another important point about making sheer curtains is that all the hems — side, bottom and top — must be made double (with equal first and second turnings), so that you will not get an ugly raw edge showing through on to the right side of the curtain.

Semi-sheer fabrics: The other main type of net curtaining is made from a semi-sheer open-weave fabric. This cuts off more light than sheer nets, but is more suitable for screening an unattractive outlook. It is made in a variety of weaves and colours, mostly from acrylic fibres which have a warmer 'feel' than Terylene net. Cotton, linen and blends of fibres are also used.

Like sheer nets, semi-sheers are usually left drawn across the window during the day, and main curtains are drawn across at night. Alternatively, because they are heavy enough to hang outside the window reveal, it is possible to make linings which can be pulled across between them and the window for night-time screening.

Curtains made from very open-weave fabrics can be tricky to sew because it is important to plan the size of all the turnings so that the spaces in the weave fall on top of each other and the stitching can be worked on a solid section of the weave.

Vision nets: These are similar to sheer nets, but have an open weave like semi-sheers, so the special techniques needed in sewing both types of fabric have to be used.

Hanging net curtains

Where net curtains are to cover the

whole window, they can be made with a standard or deep curtain tape, and hung with hooks from a track which has an inner 'lane' specially for nets; but because they usually hang against the window, with the main curtains outside the reveal, it may not be possible to have a combined track. Where you do have to have separate tracks, choose one for the nets which is neat and unobtrusive and can be fixed to the ceiling of the reveal, such as Swish Furniglyde.

With sheer nets which will be kept permanently drawn across the window, you can use a rod or an expanding wire which is fixed to the window frame at either side. Wire should not be used for semi-sheer curtains because the fabric is too heavy and would make it sag in the middle.

A curtain tape can be used with this type of fixing, and the hooks are clipped on to the wire itself. More often, the wire or rod is slotted into a casing at the top of the curtain and the gathers are arranged evenly by pulling the curtain along it. This method is also best if you are covering only the lower part of the window. Always choose a logical place, such as a glazing bar, for fixing the rod.

Headings for net curtains

The most common heading for sheer

Floor-length net curtains add a luxurious touch when side curtains are not advisable, or unnecessary.

nets is a casing (see above), but if you are using curtain tape, buy one of the kinds made specially for net curtains. These have an open weave which blends well with the curtain fabric, and are made in a synthetic fibre — usually nylon or Terylene — and so are easily washable and drip dry. They are available in three main widths — 7cm (2¾in) for tall pencil pleats and 2.5cm (1in) or 1.5cm (⅝in) for ruched gathers.

The deep tape is more expensive than the others, but if the main curtains have been made with a pencil-pleated heading, using it on the nets too gives a co-ordinated effect.

On semi-sheer fabrics, try to use a curtain tape which is the same colour as the fabric so that it will not show through unattractively on to the right side of the curtains. Alternatively, if you are using a deep heading tape which is available in white only, on a very open-weave fabric, you could insert a strip of plain fabric in a matching colour between the curtain and the tape. The strip must be in a similar fibre to the curtains, so that it will react in the same way when the curtains are washed — in most cases

a cotton/polyester dress fabric can be used.

Calculating the amount of fabric

The method for measuring and making semi-sheer curtains is very similar to unlined curtains of regular fabric (see page 71), but for sheer curtains there are some important differences.

With most unlined curtains which are gathered with a conventional narrow curtain tape, between one and a half times or double the required width of fabric is used to give fullness. This can appear skimpy on very fine net curtains, so double or even three times the required width should be used.

Achieving the right amount of fullness leads to another difference between regular and net fabrics. Most furnishing fabrics are 122cm (48in) wide, so for any window where the curtain track is longer than 1.22m (4ft) you would have to join on more fabric to the main width in each curtain. The line of the seam would be hidden by the folds of fabric and the turnings out of sight on the back of the curtain.

With net, however, the turnings would show through unattractively on to the right side and, because it is difficult to neaten the raw edges by the conventional method, you would have to join on the fabric by the selvedges. This can lead to the seam puckering if the selvedges are more tightly woven than the rest of the fabric.

Fortunately, most net curtain fabrics are made in a variety of widths up to 402cm (165in), so on many windows the problem of joining will not be encountered. You should work out the minimum width you need, and buy the required length in the standard width which is next above it. There is no need to trim off the excess width because the extra fullness can easily be incorporated.

If you cannot buy the fabric you want in the right width, it is usually better to make up separate curtains with a full width of fabric in each. When these are hung, the edges will be hidden by the folds and the effect will be of one complete curtain.

Alternatively, with sheer fabrics you can solve the problem by buying what are known as 'short nets', which are sold in a variety of standard lengths. Conventional fabrics are sold in set widths and you buy the length you require (sheer curtains of this type are known as 'long nets'). With short nets there is often a ready-made casing heading and a frilled or decorative hem, and you buy the required width in the standard length which is nearest above your own.

In measuring the length for long nets, if you are making a casing you may have to adapt the amount allowed at the top so that the turnings do not show through. Measure the basic length of the curtains from the suspension point of the rod to the window sill, and add on the 15cm (6in) for a double bottom hem in the normal way. Decide on the depth of the casing, making it large enough for the rod or wire to be inserted easily, and add on twice this depth to the length.

If you also want a heading, which protrudes above the rod in a frill and looks very attractive on half nets, decide on the depth of this — usually between 1.3cm ($\frac{1}{2}$in) and 2cm ($\frac{3}{4}$in) because anything greater will fall back — and add on three times this amount to the length.

When you make the curtains, you add together the depth of the heading and casing and turn over this amount for the first and second turnings. Machine stitch along the lower fold and again at a distance equal to the depth of the heading from the top. The rod is inserted into the casing formed by the two rows of stitching.

Semi-sheer nets give a welcome touch of colour to traditionally dark rooms, such as this bathroom. These particular ones have been made café-curtain style.

If you are using cotton net, allow an extra 30cm (12in) length per curtain in case of shrinkage. It is also a good idea to wash the fabric before you cut it out.

Finishing 'short nets'

If the curtains are the right length, before you make the side hems you should unpick the heading for about 7.5–10cm (3–4in) on each side. This frees the fabric so that hems can be made to the top edge and the heading turned down on top of them. If you do not do this, but simply turn down the side hems, you would not be able to insert the rod because you have stitched over the opening.

Trim the side raw edges exactly level with the grain of the fabric, if necessary, and then turn them on to the wrong side for 1.3cm ($\frac{1}{2}$in). Fold over a second turning of 1.3cm ($\frac{1}{2}$in) to make a double hem, tack and machine stitch. Press the hems lightly and then restitch the heading.

If the curtains are too long, unpick the casing across the entire width and press the fabric carefully. Measure the exact length you want the curtain to be from the bottom of the hem up, add on twice the depth of the casing and trim off the excess. Turn the top edge down on to the wrong side of the curtain for the depth of the casing and tack. Fold over a second turning of the same depth, tack and

machine stitch. Press lightly.

Crossover drapes

These are a more decorative style of net curtain, and are ideal where it is more important to distract attention from the outlook than to provide privacy.

Using a fabric tape, measure from the top left-hand corner of the window in a loose curve to the right-hand side at the point you want to tie the curtains back, and then to the window sill. Decide on the depth of casing you need and add on twice this amount to the top, plus 5cm (2in) for a 2.5cm (1in) double hem at the foot. This is the maximum length, which you should double to calculate the amount of fabric needed for the pair of curtains. For the width, measure the length of the curtain track or rod. Buy the width of fabric which is nearest to double this length.

Cut both curtains to the maximum length. Next, work out the minimum length of each curtain by measuring from the curtain track or rod to the window sill. Add on the same allowances as for the maximum length.

Start by cutting the left-hand curtain first. Lay out the fabric flat and mark on the left-hand edge the minimum length, measuring from the top down. Draw a line from this point to the bottom right-hand corner and cut along it. Cut the right-hand curtain in a similar way, but marking the minimum length on the right-hand edge and cutting from this point to the left-hand corner.

Make 2.5cm (1in) double hems along the lower slanting edge and along the side edges. To finish the top, place one curtain over the other, with the short sides on the outside and their 'right' sides facing downwards. Pin and tack them together and then make a 2.5cm (1in) double hem along the top edge for the casing, treating the two curtains as one piece of fabric.

Insert the rod or wire into the casing and hang the curtains in position. Cut the offcuts of net into long strips and make narrow hems along the edges. Use these to tie back the curtains.

If you would like the crossovers to have a flounce on the inner vertical edge, it is possible to use 'short nets' sideways. Work out the length and width as above, and buy the standard length which is nearest above the required width, in a width equal to the required length. Cut the fabric so that the flounced edge in both curtains is the maximum length and the casing

Excellent examples of the three main types of net curtains TOP LEFT *sheer nets,* TOP RIGHT *semi-sheer nets, and* BOTTOM *vision nets.*

edge is the minimum length.

Festoon curtains

These are ideal for a more formal setting on large staircase windows or frosted glass windows. Basically they are curtains which are about three times as long as the window and gathered to the right size by vertical tapes stitched at intervals across the curtain. One curtain is used at each window, rather than the usual pair.

Use a fine Terylene net in a plain weave and allow about three times the required height and one-and-a-half times the required width. Decide on the number of festoon gathers you want, placing one at each side of the curtain and then at 20-25cm (8–10in) intervals across the width (the tapes will be closer together when on the window). If you have to join the fabric to make the full width, plan the gathers so that one will fall on the join. To calculate the amount of gathering tape required, multiply the length of the ungathered curtain by the number of gathers. Terylene curtain tape in the 1.5cm (⅝in) width is ideal.

Make a 1.3cm (½in) double hem along the bottom edge of the curtain and machine stitch with Terylene

thread. Fold over 2.5cm (1in) at each side of the curtain and tack down along the fold and along the raw edge. Press lightly.

Mark the position of the festoons down the length of the curtain, making sure that you keep the lines true to the grain of the fabric. Cut the tape into pieces the same length as the curtain plus 5cm (2in). Pull out the cords for about 5cm (2in) from one end, and then fold under the tape at each end for 1.3cm (½in). Pin the tape to the 'wrong' side of the curtain with the ends where the cord has been pulled out at the top and so that the side tapes come 0.3cm (⅛in) from the outside folds and just cover the raw edges of the turning. Place the remaining pieces centrally over the marks. Tack and machine stitch in position, including the short ends of the tape.

Pull up the cords evenly to make the curtain the right length, adjusting them if necessary so that the loops of fabric fall in regular sweeps. Stitch at intervals to hold in position. To finish the top of the curtain, anchor the gathering cords by making a couple of back stitches with it, and cut off the excess. Then make a 1.3cm (½in) double hem for the casing.

Basic round tablecloth

A square cloth on a round table is like the proverbial square peg in a round hole—it doesn't look right. A round tablecloth is not difficult to make—the only slightly tricky part, you might think, is cutting it out. But if you make a simple paper pattern first, even that problem is overcome.

Measuring for the cloth

First measure the diameter of the table, then decide on the depth of the cloth's overhang (measure from the edge of the table to where you think the bottom of the hem should come). For a small occasional table, the cloth might look best if it goes down to floor level, in Victorian style. For a dining table, however, a drop of 23-30cm

(9-12in)—just clearing knee height when people are sitting at the table—would be more practical. Double the measurement of the overhang and add it to the diameter of the table. Add on 2.5cm (1in) (1.3cm or ½in on each overlap) for the hem, and the total will give you the diameter of the unfinished cloth.

A circular tablecloth is most easily cut from a square of fabric, each side of the square having the same measurement as the diameter of the cloth. Some specialist needlework shops sell fabric suitable for tablecloths in wider than usual widths (up to 225cm or 90in for pure linen or a Terylene/cotton mixture), which means that the cloth can be made in one piece, without a join. You simply buy a length of fabric equal in length to the diameter. Make the paper pattern and cut out the cloth as for the panelled method (see below).

If you have to join more fabric to the main piece, there are two methods of doing so. In the panelled method, the full width of the square is made up by joining two pieces of fabric to the long sides of the main piece (Fig. 1). This method is more suitable for a patterned fabric, as the seams—which fall in an uneven arc on the overhang when the cloth is in position—are less noticeable than in a plain fabric.

For a plain fabric, it would look better to use the circular method, in which a semi-feature is made of the main joining seam. The fabric is cut to fit the tabletop, two semi-circular pieces are joined to it for the overhang, and the main seam falls around the edge of the table (Fig. 2). This method, however, uses more fabric, and there is some wastage.

Panelled method: to calculate how much fabric to buy, determine the diameter of the unfinished cloth as

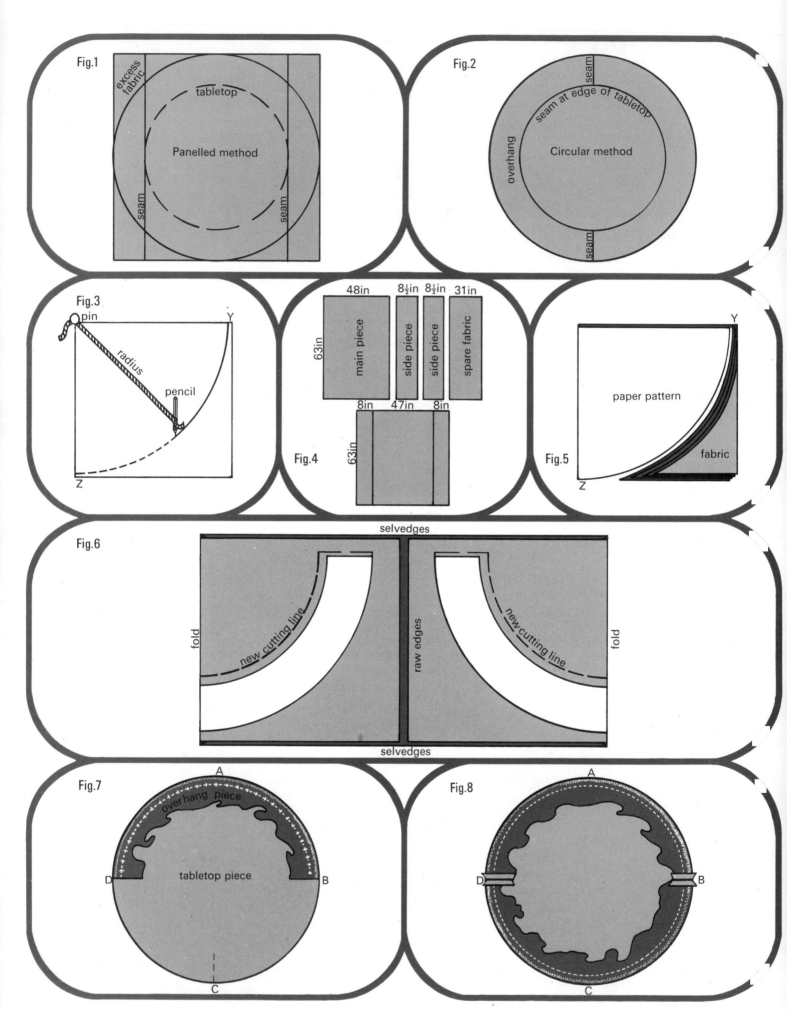

Fig.1

excess fabric

tabletop

Panelled method

seam

seam

Fig.2

seam

seam at edge of tabletop

overhang

Circular method

seam

Fig.3

pin

Y

radius

pencil

Z

Fig.4

48in

8½in

8½in

31in

63in

main piece

side piece

side piece

spare fabric

8in

47in

8in

63in

Fig.5

Y

paper pattern

fabric

Z

selvedges

Fig.6

fold

new cutting line

raw edges

new cutting line

fold

selvedges

Fig.7

A

overhang piece

tabletop piece

D

B

C

Fig.8

A

D

B

C

82

above, and double it (allow extra for matching the pattern).

Circular method: double the diameter of the unfinished cloth, and add it to the diameter of the tabletop, plus 2.5cm (1in) for turnings.

Making a paper pattern

To achieve an accurate shape when cutting out the tablecloth, make a paper pattern first. Cut a large piece of paper into a square, each side of which is a little longer than the radius of the cloth (half the diameter). Tie one end of a piece of string round a pencil, and measure the radius from the pencil along the length of string. Mark the measurement by pushing a drawing pin through the string.

Lay the paper on a flat surface and push the drawing pin into the top lefthand corner of the paper. Hold the pin firmly with the left hand and, holding the pencil upright with the other hand (with the string taut), draw an arc with the pencil from point Y, Fig. 3, in the top righthand corner, to point Z, at the bottom lefthand corner. (Reverse the corners and hands if you are left-handed.) Cut along the pencilled line.

If making the cloth by the circular method, draw a second smaller arc with a radius the length of half the diameter of the tabletop, plus 1.3cm ($\frac{1}{2}$in) for turnings. Cut along this line.

Making the cloth

Panelled method: Cut the fabric across into two equal pieces. Then cut one of these pieces lengthways, as shown in Fig. 4, into panels of the right width to make up the full width of the cloth when these are joined to the centre panel.

To calculate the width of the side panels, subtract the width of the fabric, less 2.5cm (1in) seam allowance, from the diameter of the cloth. Add 2.5cm (1in) to the remaining measurement and divide the total by two.

Match the pattern on the panels carefully, and join the side panels to the centre panel with a 1.3cm ($\frac{1}{2}$in) plain seam. Trim the length down to the same measurement as the width if necessary. You should now have a square of fabric with each side equal to the diameter of the cloth.

Fold the fabric in half and then in half again, to make a square, each side of which is equal to the radius. Pin the paper pattern on to the fabric so that its square point is in the corner of the fabric where the folds meet.

Cut through the layers of fabric

along the pattern edge from point Y to point Z, Fig. 5. Do not cut along the folds. Unpin the pattern and unfold the fabric.

Circular method: Cut off a square of fabric, from the main length, with each side equal to the diameter of the tabletop, plus 2.5cm (1in) for turnings. Fold this square in half and in half again. Pin the triangular pattern piece (for the tabletop) to the fabric as for the panelled method, and cut out. Do not cut along the folds.

Before unfolding the fabric, mark the straight grain four times at opposite points on the cloth by making a few tacking stitches in from the edge along the folds. These stitches will act as guide lines when attaching the overhang, and will ensure that the grain runs straight on the pieces.

Lay the remaining length of fabric flat on the floor. Fold over the raw edges so they meet in the middle. Pin the circular pattern piece (for the overhang) on the fabric so that one straight edge is on one of the folds.

Using tailor's chalk, mark on the fabric the cutting line for the inner edge of the overlap 2.5cm (1in) from the inner edge of the pattern. Mark another line 1.3cm ($\frac{1}{2}$in) from the straight edge of the pattern which is not on the fold of the fabric (see Fig. 6). Cut along these lines and along the outer edge of the pattern. Do not cut along the fold.

Unpin the pattern and pin it to the fabric at the other fold. Mark the cutting line along the inner edges as for the other piece, and cut out. Unpin the pattern. Clip 1cm ($\frac{3}{8}$in) into the inner edge of both overhang pieces at 2.5cm (1in) intervals. With the 'right' sides of the fabric facing, and with the overhang uppermost, match the centre of the inner edge of one overhanging piece to one of the tacking guide marks on the tabletop piece (Fig. 8, point A). Working from this point outwards to the straight edges of the overhang, pin the pieces together 1.3cm ($\frac{1}{2}$in) from the edge (the clips cut in the overhang will open out).

Pin the second overhang piece to the tabletop piece in a similar way, matching its centre to the opposite tacking guide mark on the tabletop (point C). Where the overhang pieces meet at points B and D, pin their raw edges together—the seam line should fall 1.3cm ($\frac{1}{2}$in) in from the edge but adjust this so that the overhang fits the tabletop exactly, and the seam lines correspond with the tacking guide marks at points B and D. Tack and machine stitch these seams. Press them open and neaten the raw edges.

Tack and machine stitch the overhang to the tabletop. Remove the tacking and press the entire seam allowance down on to the overhang. Overcast the raw edges together.

Making the hem

The easiest way to finish a circular hem is with bias binding, as this will give the right amount of ease to go round a curve smoothly. To decide exactly how much bias binding to buy, multiply the diameter of the cloth by 22 and divide the total by seven. This gives the circumference of the cloth (allow about 5cm or 2in extra for overlapping the binding).

Unfold one of the pressed edges of the binding, and place the edge to the edge of the tablecloth, 'right' sides facing. Pin and tack it to the cloth along the crease line of the binding. Neaten the ends by turning them under 0.6cm ($\frac{1}{4}$in) and overlapping them. Machine stitch all round the hem, following the tacking line.

Press the binding over entirely on to the wrong side of the cloth. Tack the binding to the cloth along the outer folded edge of the binding, and machine stitch. Press the hem and then the finished cloth.

This elegantly draped cloth makes a beautiful cover for a bedside table.

Placemats, specially shaped to make the best use of space on the table, can be co-ordinated with napkins and crockery to provide a fresh, attractive setting.

Basic tablecloth and placemats

Ready-made tablecloths tend to come in a few standard sizes which look all wrong if your table is not a standard size too. Try making your own—then you can decide both size and cost.

Measure the length and width of the table top and add 23–30cm (9–12in) for the overhang on each side (23cm or 9in will bring the cloth down to about knee-level). If the cloth is to have a plain hem, add another 5cm (2in) to each side. If you can buy fabric wide enough—usually from a specialist needlework shop—you will only need one length. If you have to join the fabric to make up the width, you may need twice or three times the length, depending on the width of the fabric and the table, and on where the seams are to fall.

Because a centre seam would look ugly, the best method is to join pieces of fabric of equal width to the long sides of the main piece. Ideally the main piece should, when in position on the table, cover the tabletop entirely and overhang the sides, so that any seams are part of the overhang and do not interrupt the smoothness of the top. If, however, the fabric is narrower than the tabletop, rather than having the joining seams so near the edges that they could upset the balance of the place setting, it might be better to make the centre panel narrower still, with the seams 23–30cm (9–12in) from the edges (Fig. 1).

For example, for a table 106cm (3ft 6in) wide, the tablecloth—with a 23cm (9in) overhang and 5cm (2in) hem allowance — would be 162cm (64in) wide unfinished. With 122cm (48in) fabric, you would need an amount twice the length of the table. The full width of the fabric can be used for the centre panel, which is cut from one 'length', and the side panels — each 23cm (9in) wide, including seam allowance — are cut from the second 'length'. The leftover fabric from this would be 75cm (30in) wide.

With 91.5cm (36in) fabric, you might decide to make the centre panel 45cm (18in) wide (47cm or 19in including seam allowance), so that the seams come 30cm (12in) in from the edges. Adapt the formula so that you start by taking the width of the centre panel from the width of the tablecloth. In this case, each side panel, including allowances, would be 34cm (23½in) wide, so you would need fabric three times the length of the table. There would be two leftover lengths, 32cm (12½in) wide.

Making up the panels

Cut out the panels, including 1.3cm (½in) seam allowance on each side of the centre panel and on the inner edge of the side panels. Join with a machine fell seam in which the edges are enclosed, making it flat and easy to press.

Machine fell seam : Make a plain seam, but stitch it with the wrong sides of the fabric together. When the seam is pressed open, trim one side of the seam allowance, press the other side over the trimmed side, turn under 0.3cm (⅛in) and press flat. Tack and machine stitch through all thicknesses, near the fold (Fig. 2).

Making the hem

For plain 4cm (1½in) hems, mitre the corners before stitching, as this will give a flat, neat, effect.

Mitred corners : On adjoining sides of the cloth, fold over the raw edges 1.3cm (½in) on to the wrong side, and press. Make another fold 4cm (1½in) from the first folded edges and press again. Open out the second folds and turn in the corner on a diagonal line going through the point where the fold lines meet, and at an equal distance from the corner on both sides (Fig. 3). Leaving the first folds turned in, trim off the corner 0.6cm (¼in) outside the diagonal crease, cutting firmly through the folded edges (Fig. 4).

Find the centre of the diagonal line, then fold the corner, with right sides facing, at this point so that the sides of the cloth are level. Stitch along the diagonal line, and then turn it right side out, gently easing out the point with a knitting needle (Fig. 5). Press.

Make the other corners in the same way, then stitch the hem using the lines of the folds already made.

Trimmed edge

Turn over the fabric 1.3cm (½in) on to the wrong side, and pin and tack the trimming to cover the raw edge (mitre or lap the corners of the trimming, depending on the type). Stitch along the top and bottom of the trimming.

TOP *Rectangular placemats are ideal for patio dining.*

Napkins

Dinner napkins traditionally tended to be of a good size, not only to cover laps from possible spills but also because they used to be folded into elaborate shapes. Nowadays a practical size — making best use of fabric widths — is 40–45cm (16–18in) square. Cocktail napkins can be 30cm (12in) square, or even smaller.

Finish napkins with plain hems and mitred corners, as for the tablecloth, but turning over the first fold for 0.6cm (¼in) and the second fold 1.3cm (½in). Stitch by machine, or with small, firm slip stitching.

Place mats

These tend to be more informal than a tablecloth and are ideal for tables with a surface which you want to 'show off' but protect from scratches. If you also want to protect it from heat, choose a heavy-weight fabric, in cotton or linen, or use a mat under lightweight ones. If you plan to 'fray' the edges in order to make a self-fringe, use a fairly coarse cotton, as it will keep its appearance better when washed.

A practical size for rectangular place mats is 35cm × 45cm (13½in × 18in) —30cm × 40cm or 12in × 16in finished —but this should be adapted according to the width of the fabric. For plain edges, make hems with mitred corners as for napkins (above). For a frayed edge, remove the threads parallel to the edges to the depth of the fringe required (Fig. 6), then overcast the edges.

Rounded place mats

For round tables, mats which are curved at the outer edge and taper towards the centre of the table can make more economical use of the space (Fig. 7).

In order to make the curve on the mats 'parallel' to the curve of the table, cut a triangular paper pattern to fit the table top, following the method described on page 81. Then measure an equal amount in from the straight sides and draw straight lines parallel to the sides, and to the required depth. Join the lines at the top and then cut off the excess paper, allowing 0.6–1.3cm (¼–½in) hem allowance (Fig. 8).

Cut out the mats so that the grain on the fabric runs parallel to the sides of the mats (otherwise they may stretch and buckle). Finish the edges with bias binding, so that the binding is completely on the wrong side of the fabric.

The corners can be mitred following the method above, or by a simpler method which can be used here because the binding is not bulky and the wrong sides of the mats are not on show.

Unfold one of the creased edges of the binding, and, starting in the middle of one side, pin it to the mat, with edges meeting and right sides together. Clip the binding diagonally at the corners of the mat to ease it round. To join the binding, overlap it at the ends, turning under the raw edges to make a neat join. Tack and machine stitch the binding in position, and then press it over completely on to the wrong side of the mat. Tuck under the excess binding at the four corners, making a diagonal fold. Tack the binding down to the mat along the outer fold, and machine or hem stitch. Stitch the folds and join with small hem stitching.

LEFT *A fresh effect is achieved by this pretty cloth draped over a cane table.*

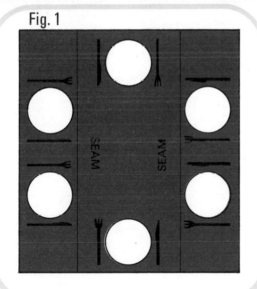

Fig. 1

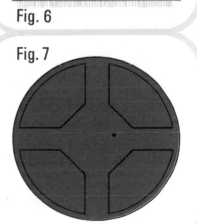

Fig. 3

Fig. 4

Fig. 6

Fig. 7

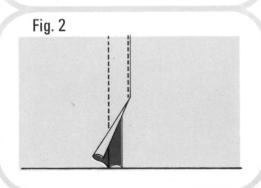

Fig. 2

Fig. 5

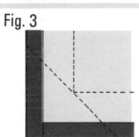

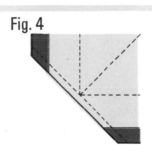

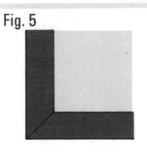

Fig. 8

Fabric lampshades

Artificial lighting is necessary for every home. But just because it's necessary doesn't mean that it can't form an integral part of the decor. Indirect lighting, such as table lamps, etc, can give a room a more 'finished' look, especially when the lamp shades can be co-ordinated with the rest of the fittings

Where you have the choice, large lampshades are better than small ones because they give a greater pool of light and do not restrict the airflow round the bulb. Yet they can be expensive, so it is worth making your own because the materials are simple and cheap.

One of the most simple and quick ways of making a lampshade is to use a fabric which has a stiff backing. There is little or no sewing involved because the cover can be glued to the frame, and there is no need for a lining.

This type of fabric is suitable only for lampshades with straight or sloping sides because it cannot be stretched or moulded to one with curved sides. This is one of the main differences between firm and soft shades: with the latter, the fabric can be stretched to fit, but the backing in a firm shade makes this impossible.

Although standard frames with struts can be used for firm lampshades, all you actually need are the two rings which come at the top and bottom of the shade – the structure in between is formed by the rigidity of the fabric.

Using rings without struts cuts down on the amount of binding needed and, because they are available in a wide range of diameters, you can vary the exact shape and size of the lampshade to suit yourself (Fig. 1). The easiest type to make is where the top and bottom rings are the same size because the cover fabric is cut to a simple rectangle. Where the top ring is smaller than the bottom one, you would need to make a paper pattern to cut out a circular piece of fabric to fit round smoothly. The top ring should also have a fitting suitable for hanging on a table lamp.

Table lamps are a quick and easy way of adding an extra light, and their shades should be chosen to suit both the base of the lamp and the decor of the rest of the room.

Choosing the fabric

Many stores which sell lampshade frames also sell a selection of fabrics already bonded to the stiffening. Alternatively, you can buy the stiffening separately and bond it to the fabric of your choice. There are two main types of stiffening – both white – which are suitable.

One is an adhesive parchment which is ironed on to the fabric. With this, the cover can be either stitched or glued to the frame. The other type is self-adhesive. It is very stiff and so the cover can only be glued to the frame. It is not suitable for open weave fabrics because dust could stick to its uncovered parts.

To calculate the amount of fabric needed where the rings are the same size, decide on the height of shade you want, measure the circumference of the rings and buy enough to cut a rectangle of the same size, plus about 2.5cm (1in) on each side.

Where the rings are different sizes, make a pattern following the method below, place it on another rectangular piece of paper so that one short side of the pattern is level with the edge of the paper, and measure across the pattern at its widest and highest points. Allow a piece of cover fabric of the same size, plus about 2.5cm (1in) each way.

Making a paper pattern

If possible, use a really large sheet of squared graph paper for making the pattern because this makes drawing parallel and perpendicular lines much easier than on blank paper.

Near the bottom left-hand corner of the paper, draw a horizontal line (Fig. 2, A-B), equal in length to the diameter of the bottom ring. Find the centre of the line (C) and draw a perpendicular line upwards from it to the required height of the shade (D).

At D, draw another horizontal line (E-F) equal to the diameter of the upper ring and with D as the centre. Join A-E and B-F and extend these lines upwards until they intersect at G.

Using G-E as the radius, draw a large arc from E, equal to the circumference of the top ring (the length of the arc can be measured with a piece of string). Then, using G-A as the radius, draw another arc from A, equal to the circumference of the lower ring. Add 2cm (¾in) to the length of each arc and then join them (H-I). Cut round A-E-H-I and this gives the paper pattern.

If you prefer, you can omit the graph

stage by assessing the 'slant' height of the shade. To do this, lay the lower ring flat on your work surface and hold the upper ring centrally over the lower one at the required height of the shade. With a long ruler, measure the length of the slant between the rings.

To calculate the radius for the upper edge of the pattern, multiply the radius of the upper ring by the slant height and divide this by the radius of the bottom ring minus the radius of the upper ring.

Radius of upper ring x slant height / *radius of lower ring – radius of upper ring.*

Add the radius of the upper edge of the pattern to the slant height and this gives the radius for the lower edge of the pattern.

If you are using a frame with struts, you can make a less accurate pattern simply by wrapping a piece of paper round the shade, pressing it over the top and bottom rings to make firm creases, and marking where the paper joins following the line of a strut. Cut out the pattern along the crease lines, try it again on the shade and make any necessary adjustments.

Preparing the frame

To prevent the frame from rusting, paint it first with a fast-drying enamel or cellulose paint and allow to dry completely.

If you are going to sew on the cover, bind the rings. If you are sticking on the cover, the binding should also be stuck on.

For this, use 1.3cm (½in) wide adhesive cotton tape. Unwind enough of the tape to fit the circumference of the ring, and press the centre of the adhesive side round the inside of the ring. Overlap the ends by 1.3cm (½in) and cut off. Turn over one edge of the tape smoothly on to the outside of the ring and press down all round. Turn over the other edge in the same way and press down firmly so that it overlaps the first edge smoothly on the outside of the ring. This ensures that the overlap will be secure and hidden when the cover is in position (Fig. 3).

Preparing the fabric

For a lampshade where the rings are the same size, cut out a piece of fabric equal in size to the height of the frame × the circumference of the rings plus 2cm (¾in). For slanting shades, cut out the cover fabric from the paper pattern. In either case, cut out the stiffening to the same height but 0.6cm (¼in) narrower.

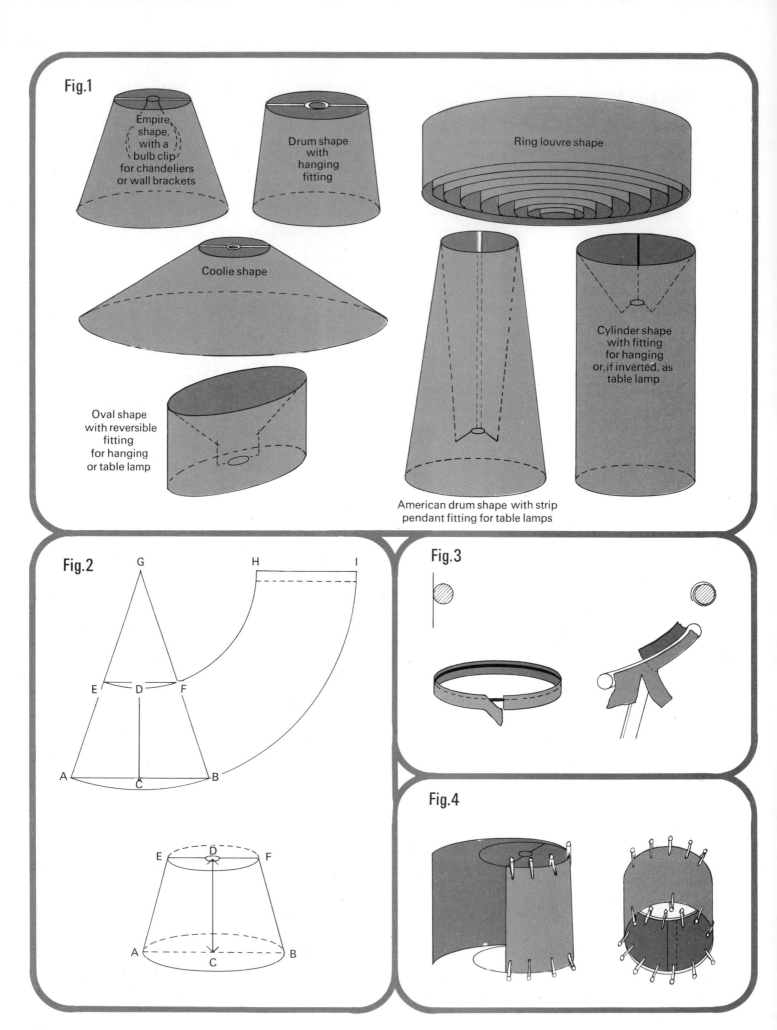

Fig.1

Empire shape, with a bulb clip for chandeliers or wall brackets

Drum shape with hanging fitting

Ring louvre shape

Coolie shape

Oval shape with reversible fitting for hanging or table lamp

American drum shape with strip pendant fitting for table lamps

Cylinder shape with fitting for hanging or, if inverted, as table lamp

Fig.2

G H I

E D F

A C B

E D F

A C B

Fig.3

Fig.4

If you are using iron-on stiffening, first test it for correct iron temperature. Using offcuts of stiffening and cover fabric, place the stiffening on your ironing board with the shiny side up. Place the fabric over it with wrong side down and iron the pieces together. Allow to cool and then check if they have adhered. If you need a high temperature to get a good bond, cover the fabric first with paper to avoid scorching.

Lay out the main piece of stiffening in the same way, and place the cover fabric on it so that one vertical side is level and the other overlaps by 0.6cm (¼in). Iron the pieces together and allow to cool. Check that the edges are correctly bonded and re-iron if necessary

Turn the overlap section of fabric on to the backing and stick down with adhesive (see below). This edge should come on to the outside of the overlap when the cover is placed on the shade, giving it a neat finish.

If you are using self-adhesive stiffening, start unpeeling the protective backing from one vertical edge. Place down the cover fabric carefully and smoothly, with the edges level. It will overlap by 0.6cm (¼in) at the opposite edge. It often helps to roll the fabric, with its right side inside, on to a rod first. The edge of the fabric can then be placed level with the edge of the stiffening, and then unrolled smoothly on to it. Turn the overlap section on to the backing and stick down.

Attaching the cover
Although the cover can be either glued or stitched to the rings, it is usually most satisfactory to glue the overlap

LEFT *If you want to make a shade to match wallpaper, you can stiffen it easily with an iron-on or self-adhesive backing.* RIGHT *One advantage of making a shade with backed fabric is that the only framework needed is two rings for the top and bottom. The fabric forms the structure in between, thus eliminating the need for ugly struts.*

on the vertical seam. Use a clear adhesive, such as Bostik 1 or Uhu, because this will not stain the fabric.

Using sprung clothes pegs (not pins, which would leave holes), peg the cover round the rings as tightly as possible, allowing 1.3cm (½in) overlap and placing the edge where the fabric was turned over on the outside.

If you are sewing the cover on, use strong thread to match the binding tape. Starting about 2.5cm (1in) from the overlap, stab stitch the cover to the tape on the rings, taking the needle out below the ring. Make the stitches small on the inside of the shade, but larger on the outside where they will be hidden by the trimming. Sew round both rings to within 2.5cm (1in) of the overlap, leaving enough thread to finish off.

Check that the seam is straight, then apply a little adhesive to each side of the overlapping section and press firmly together. Finish sewing round both rings.

If you are sticking the cover to the frame, remove about half the clothes pegs and spread some adhesive along the outside of the rings on the portion which is uncovered. Press the cover firmly and carefully back into position. Replace some of the pegs to hold it until the adhesive dries. Repeat this

process on the other half of the shade and stick down the overlap (Fig. 4).

A different way of sticking the cover to the frame may be used where the shade is tapered. Before fitting the rings to the cover, overlap the edges of the seam for the right amount and secure with clothes pegs at the top and bottom. Peg the top ring in position so that it fits tightly—adjust the pegs holding the overlap if necessary. Fit the bottom ring in the same way.

Check that the seam is straight, then mark inside the shade the points where the fabric overlaps. Remove the cover from the rings, apply adhesive along each side of the overlapping section and press together firmly along the marked line (Fig. 4).

Apply adhesive all round the outer edge of the top ring and insert it into the shade, from below, pressing it to the cover firmly. Hold it in place with clothes pegs. When dry, remove the pegs and repeat the process for the bottom ring.

Adding the trimming
Cut pieces of trimming to fit round the top and bottom of the shade, allowing 1.3cm (½in) extra for an overlap. Turn under 0.6cm (¼in) at each end and stick or stitch down. Apply adhesive along the underside of the braid, place one of the folded edges to the seam of the shade and press the braid on to the rim all the way round, so that it covers the stitches and is level with the cut edges of the fabric, finishing with a neat butt join.

Alternatively, you could stick on the braid so half shows on the outside of the shade and the other half on the inside.

Final touches

Hanging pictures

Very often not enough thought is given to the subject of pictures in the home. People spend hours deciding on paint colours, fabric designs and wall coverings, but tend to forget how effective the addition of pictures on the walls can be.

Small rooms
There are several techniques for using pictures to make small rooms look larger, but it is easy to go wrong. Don't put only one or two pictures on each wall, as this breaks up the wall space too much. Instead, hang the whole collection close together on one wall, then the other bare walls will make the room seem larger.

If you have a group of two or three similarly sized paintings, or better still a set, hang them in a row separated by no more then a few centimetres or inches. If they are on the longest wall, hang them towards the corner rather than in the centre, to break up the limited wall space better.

Plain frames or no frames at all are best in small rooms, unless you hang

A collection of old photographs looks effective mounted together in one rich frame.

one special painting as a focal point, say, above a fireplace. Tiny pictures hung one above the other on the side walls of an alcove make it seem deeper.

Large rooms
There is much more scope here, particularly if the room has an interesting shape. One wall, or the back of an alcove, can become a floor-to-ceiling picture gallery, which can have added impact if all the pictures have a common theme. If you want to fill up an empty space, you can often set a picture on a wide mount to make it larger. The proportions of the large frame will suit the room better.

Generally it is more effective to hang pictures in groups rather than dot them singly round a room. A group of four matching prints set on a square or rectangular mount in one large frame can give them added prominence, or a set of four or six hung in an even rectangular arrangement can look just as impressive.

Bedrooms
The bedroom is a good place to display

family photographs – where they are less likely to bore visitors!

Don't put your favourite painting over the bed, because you won't be able to enjoy it there. If you hang it on a side wall or on the wall at the foot of the bed, you will be able to gaze at it while you are in bed.

Bathrooms
If the bathroom is very steamy, it is wisest not to hang any pictures in it at all, or only things that won't spoil. Magazine pictures pinned on a wall of cork tiles can look attractive, and will last longer if varnished with a clear pva wallpaper protector. Unglazed prints treated in this way become washable.

Unimportant pictures in painted wooden frames are usually safe in a bathroom, or even oil paintings on wood, but pictures painted on canvas are likely to suffer damage and metal frames might rust.

Halls
The colours of pictures hung in a hall should be warm and welcoming, because it is here that visitors gain their first impression of what your home is like. If you are hanging prints, mount them on a warm deep red or chestnut card, or a colour to tone with the decorations.

In a hall leading to the stairs, the arrangements of pictures can continue up the staircase wall, co-ordinating the whole circulation area.

Narrow passages
A long passage can be cheered up by hanging two or more pictures together in a group to form a focal point. Light them with a spotlight and this will make the passage seem wider.

Stairs
The wall of a staircase is another good site for a family portrait gallery, but paintings look more impressive here than photographs. Mount and frame them in the same materials to link them, particularly if they vary a lot in shape and size, and then hang them up the wall at eye level.

A group of three or more pictures can be hung diagonally up the wall, or in a close vertical or horizontal line at the top or bottom of the stairs.

When hanging pictures diagonally up a staircase, measure from the step below where the picture is to be, in order to arrange them evenly. Pictures at the top should not be hung too high, because people walking up the stairs won't be able to see them.

Using colour

Pictures can be used to emphasize and enhance the colour scheme of a room and vice versa: a room scheme can be worked out to echo the colours of a much-treasured picture.

Painted frames need to be chosen carefully. White or black are usually safe, but if you are choosing a coloured frame, you should paint it in exactly the same shade as the woodwork – not a different tone or a clashing colour. Grey-white frames in a room where the predominant colours are creamy white would be a mistake. Sage green frames in a room where the main colour is emerald green would also look wrong.

The mounts should also be kept in the same colour range. So a terracotta sketch on cream paper, with a white mount and plain gold frame, would be stunning in a room with cream curtains, white walls and terracotta colours in the furnishings.

Frames

Old frames can easily be renovated and made to look as good as new with a little effort, and badly varnished old wooden frames can be bought cheaply in junk shops. Even a wooden frame taken from, say, an octagonal cane table can become an attractive setting for a piece of needlework or a selection of photographs.

Strip the frames down, then either use them in their natural wood form, or re-polish, paint or gild them. With an ornate metal or wooden frame, the *grooving*, the flat section between the outer and inner moulding, can be *distressed* (picked out in a different colour).

A frame should suit the size and 'weight' of a picture. Carved wooden or ornate metal frames look good on dark old oil paintings, but modern art often looks best unframed, particularly if hung on a wall of plain or unpainted bricks.

Choose a neat, tidy frame for a simple water-colour or sketch. Smoked acrylic and aluminium are suitable frames for a modern picture or print. Try a frame of tiny mirror tiles round soft old prints in a bedroom or bathroom.

Picture glass

Watercolours and drawings should always be protected by glass, but this is not so important for oil paintings. Because of the distraction caused by

reflections it is worth paying extra for non-reflective glass for special pictures.

Always protect pictures with glass if they are hung over a fire, a radiator or a convector heater, because dirt gradually builds up above these and will damage the picture if it is not properly protected.

Modern pictures and prints look smart with no frame at all; just glass fixed at intervals with mirror clips.

TOP *Any colourful picture looks more important if it is framed – whether it's a poster, a child's painting, advertisements or playing cards, as here. Apparently hung at random, this is an eye-catching combination.*

BOTTOM *A mass of pictures (in this case modern prints with simple, aluminium frames) covers one wall, and picks out and enhances the main elements of the colour scheme without actually dominating the whole room.*

Lighting

Lighting is very important when displaying pictures, and the best effect can be achieved by the use of spotlights. These can be either individually fixed to the ceiling or a wall, or in groups on a track. A single spotlight standing on an occasional table is good for low pictures.

If you want to give a particular picture added prominence, use a proper picture light which hangs on a short arm above and in front of the picture, reflecting a bright light on to the picture, but shading the light from the front.

Hanging height

Ideally, pictures should be hung at eye level. They can also look most effective in a living room if they are hung at the eye level of people sitting down, above a low table or in a corner near a sofa.

It is important when hanging a row of different-sized pictures to keep the bottoms in line, not the tops.

It can be almost impossible to

LEFT *Large, modern paintings often need no frame at all, and can make a narrow corridor appear much wider if hung along one wall.*

RIGHT *Pictures need not be large to be impressive. Here, a collection of miniature paintings grouped together on a dark blue bedroom wall are very effective.*

measure accurately when hanging pictures in old houses with uneven walls, floors and ceiling lines, so it is often best to make the final adjustments by eye. Get someone to help you by holding the picture in place, then stand back to see if it looks right.

Never hang pictures in a place where they will catch the sun, because it will fade them.

Formal groupings

A professional effect can be achieved by hanging a collection of pictures of different sizes in a formal arrangement. The best way of working out how to arrange them is to lay them out on the floor first.

Decide on the outside shape of the arrangement – a large square or rectangle – then keep your pictures within this unseen frame. The edges of the pictures on the outside should line up with the unseen frame, and the pictures inside can be arranged as you like.

Start by hanging the four corner pictures, then complete the bottom row. Fix the side and the top rows, then finally fill in the middle.

A formal arrangement of miniatures or cameos can look very attractive if grouped together in an alcove or above a fireplace.

Fixing

It is important to choose a method of fixing to suit the picture.

Use proper picture wire if you can for hanging pictures, particularly heavy paintings, as it lasts longer and does not deteriorate like string or twine. If you use nylon twine, make sure the knots are really tight, because the nylon can easily pull through gradually with the weight of the picture. Steel-cored brass wire is the strongest available for hanging heavy pictures.

Steel screw-eyes which screw into the back of the frame are usually strong enough for light pictures. The wire or twine is then tied through the eye and knotted firmly. Be sure to buy good quality hooks, as a hook can bend slowly, and your precious picture will suddenly crash to the floor.

A safe method of fixing really heavy paintings is to put an ordinary screw on each side of the back of the frame, and wrap the picture wire round each one firmly. A screw is less likely to work its way out than some of the recognized picture hooks.

The wall fixing must also be secure, and correspond to the weight of the picture. Picture hooks such as 'X' hooks or double 'X' hooks, which are sold complete with pins, are the best. It is safer to use two hooks on large or heavy pictures.

If you don't want to mark the wall, or are not sure that the plaster will hold a nail firmly, loop the picture wire over a picture rail hook, one that

is specially designed to hang on a picture rail.

Mounting pictures

Mounting pictures can be a most effective way of building up your own 'art collection'. A simple poster, a magazine photograph, or even a post-card can be transformed into an attractive picture if it is set in a mount, framed and glazed. A small sketch can be made to look much more impressive by the addition of a large mount in a well-chosen colour.

Two main techniques for using mounts are given here; one for posters or all-over drawings, and one for pieces of fabric. The second method is just as effective for adding prominence to pictures or sketches whose design is in the middle of the paper.

Mounting a poster: Cut a sheet of stiff cardboard the size you want the final framed picture to be, that is several centimetres larger than the basic poster. For a large poster, two pieces of cardboard taped together carefully are usually strong enough. This cardboard forms the surface backing on to which the poster is later stuck.

The section between the poster and the frame is called the mount, which is commonly cut out from artists' paper. Cut out from the middle of this sheet a rectangle slightly under the size of the poster. With larger pictures, four strips of artists' paper, mitred and butted at the corners, can be just as effective if they are cut accurately.

Heavy-duty wallpaper paste can be used for sticking the mount and the poster to the cardboard backing, but you should apply the paste to the cardboard in each case. Slop on plenty of paste then, using a plastic or wooden ruler, slide it down the paper to get a thin even coating.

Stick the mount or mounting strips on first, then carefully stick the poster centrally over it, slightly overlapping the rectangular cut-out on each side.

Use a dry paperhanging brush or a paint roller to get rid of the excess paste and any air bubbles, always working in the same direction. A dry cloth is usually adequate on a small picture.

Wallpaper paste remover can be used to clean any excess off the poster or mount.

Pictures hung diagonally up a staircase wall should be measured from the step below to follow the line of the stairs.

Mounting a piece of fabric: Pieces of embroidery or tapestry, samplers, and borders from traycloths or table-cloths can look enchanting if framed. If you want to highlight the central section of the design, but do not want to cut the fabric, a good effect can be achieved by covering the edges with a stiff card mount.

Cut a sheet of stout cardboard the size you want the finished framed picture to be. Using a special fabric adhesive, stick the fabric to the card-board. Apply the adhesive to the cardboard, then carefully lay the fabric on it, taking care not to pull it out of shape.

Using stiff paper, cut out a template the same size as the cardboard surface backing. Cut out from the middle of this template a rectangle roughly the size you want the visible picture to be, and move it around over the fabric. Adjust the template if necessary when you have decided how much of the design you want to be shown.

For the mount, cut a piece of stiff card the size of the finished framed picture, lay the paper template on it, and trace on it the shape of the rectangular cut-out with a soft pencil.

Using a handyman's knife and a straight edge, carefully cut out the traced shape. A professional effect can be obtained by holding the knife at a slight angle, sloping the handle towards the outer edge of the picture.

Artists' paper and stiff card are only two of the materials that can be used for mounting pictures. Wall-paper, and even off-cuts of fabric can create stunning effects, too.

Fillets

A fillet is an additional narrow strip of card or artists' paper inserted between the picture and the mount. Fillets can give various effects. A white one can highlight the picture it frames, and two or more in different shades of the predominant colour can add depth and importance to an otherwise ordinary picture.

Should you want a white or contrasting fillet as well as a mount, cut a sheet of card to the full size as before, in your chosen colour. Cut out from the middle of this sheet a rectangular section slightly smaller than that cut in the mount (for an average picture 0.6 cm – $\frac{1}{4}$ in – is satisfactory), holding the knife at an angle as before. This card is then inserted between the picture and the mount.

Any number of fillets cut to slightly differing sizes can be inserted between the picture or fabric and the main mount. A professional touch that can be applied to a frame with impressive results is brass beading, which can be bought in all shapes and depths from brass founders, who will cut it to your requirements. You simply have to stick it on.

Using dried flowers

When winter comes, and the garden is looking sorry for itself, you automatically want to make the house look a little brighter. If you have planned ahead by drying some decorative summer flowers, you will be able to fill your home with attractive dried flower arrangements, and not just during the winter, but throughout the whole year.

Flowers for drying

Flowers which will dry easily fall into two categories, the 'everlastings', and what are called 'soft flowers' some of which can be dried successfully if the process is quick.

True everlastings, or 'immortelles', are those flowers grown specifically to be dried. They are annuals and grow best in a sunny place. All of the following are good for drying, and are not difficult to preserve.

Acroclinium roseum (*Helipterum roseum*) is a well-known straw daisy with soft petals.

Ammobium alatum grandiflorum (everlasting sandflower) has silvery-white petals and a domed yellow centre.

Gomphrena globosa (globe amaranth or bachelor's buttons) was a favourite in Elizabethan gardens.

Helichrysum bracteatum (straw flower) is probably the best known of all everlastings. It has flowers rather like those of a stiff, shiny-petalled double daisy in an assortment of colours – orange, wine-red, apricot, yellow, gold and white.

Helipterum manglesii, also known as *Rhodanthe manglesii*, has tiny daisy flowers in clusters of florets – white, pink or rose, both double and single blooms.

Statice (*Limonium*) *sinuatum* (sea

lavender) has papery flowers in blue, mauve or white.

Xeranthemum is another everlasting with silvery-pink, mauve or white flowers.

There are many perennials which – although not true everlastings – have flowers, pods or seed heads which can be dried successfully. They can be grown from seed sown in summer for flowering the following year, or bought as plants and planted in spring or autumn. Here are some of the more suitable types.

Acanthus mollis (bear's breeches) has tall spikes of white and purple flowers and large, jagged leaves.

Achillea is a yarrow which is found in many varieties. It has flat white or yellow heads made up of a mass of tiny flowers and feathery grey-green leaves. This dries very well, the yellow keeping its colour.

The silver-grey foliaged *Anaphalis* (pearl everlasting) has clusters of tiny everlasting-type daisy flowers. *Catananche* (blue cupidone or cupid's dart) has large blue daisy-like flowers.

The prickly thistle family includes the superb silver-green and blue *Eryngiums* (sea holly) and the steely, blue metallic balls of *Echinops* (globe thistle). The thistle family as a whole provides a lot of interesting material in various sizes, all of which dry well.

Hydrangeacea (hydrangea) is dried most successfully if it is arranged in fresh water and then just forgotten and left.

Grasses

You can start collecting grasses quite early in the summer, as they should be picked before they are fully mature so that they don't shed seeds. In a whole flower arrangement, grass stems can be used for mounting flower heads and leaves, as their flexible stems fall into soft curves quite naturally. Here is a list of grasses suitable for preserving.

Agrostis nebulosa (cloud grass) has a charming head like a cloud of tiny flowers.

Briza maxima (pearl grass) and *Briza media* (quaking grass) have little hanging pendants or lanterns.

Coix lacryma-jobi (Job's tears) has pea-sized seeds of pearly grey-green and thick leaves like maize.

Eragrostis elegans (love grass) has beautiful panicles (loose irregular arrangements of flower heads) of cloudy florets.

Festuca ovina glauca (sheep's fescue) is a blue tufted grass with pretty, small spikes of flower.

TOP *There are many novel and decorative ways in which you can use dried flowers to decorate your house. For instance, you can bind them into pretty posies, decorate Chinese soup spoons or bowls with a nosegay of flowers, make hanging balls of dried flowers or make a dried flower candle base – if you do this latter arrangement, though, you must be careful not to let the candle burn down too near the base, otherwise it will catch fire.*

LEFT *Dried flowers dyed brilliant colours can make an eye-catching addition to any room – but they are difficult to do yourself and usually have to be purchased ready-dyed.*

97

Another biennal is *Lunaria* (honesty), which is a really good plant for drying. It has purple or white flowers in spring, and through the summer its flat oval pods go from a plummy-green to silvery papery white, thus being useful for flower arrangements throughout the year.

Moluccella laevis (bells of Ireland) is a good and quite distinctive half-hardy annual. It has tiny, shell-like flowers with bell-like sheaths growing around the stems, which turn cream or silvery beige when dried.

Physalis franchetii (Chinese lantern, Cape gooseberry or winter cherry) has orange lanterns which cover its berries. Gather them when the lower lanterns are just beginning to turn orange, and remove all the leaves before drying.

Drying flowers

Wherever possible, cut flowers with long stems and strip off all the leaves. Tie them into small bunches and hang them upside down in a cool shady place with good air circulation. It is important that the place be dry because damp conditions will make the flowers go mouldy, and if there is too much light the colours will fade.

Some flowers lose their heads when the stems are dried out, others look ugly or have very short stems. In these cases, cut the stem 2.5cm (1in) from the head, thread a length of suitable gauge florists' wire up the stem into the flower head and push the wires into sand or dry plastic foam. Leave the flowers to dry in this position, and as they do the wire will rust into place.

Natural-looking false stems for flower heads can be made with preserved grass stems – Timothy grass is particularly useful for supporting flower heads. Pierce the centre of the flower with a matchstick and thread the grass through, stem first, until the grass head touches the flower centre. Trim the grass head off and pull it through a little more until it is almost invisible.

If you are just beginning to experiment with dried flowers, start by drying the brightly coloured varieties – the purples, yellows and golds – as these are less likely to lose all their colour during the drying process.

An alternative method of drying flowers involves the use of borax powder, which is available from chemists. This is a more complicated procedure, but it is worth taking the extra trouble, as it is often more successful with flowers which are not everlastings.

Arrangements of dried flowers look just as pretty in the kitchen as in the living room, and can liven up and give warmth to what is often a cold-looking room.

leaves are popular for this kind of preserving because of the wide range of colours which can be achieved.

The earlier the branches of beech are cut, the deeper the colour will be after drying. Branches gathered later will turn a light tan colour. The early autumn foliage of other deciduous trees such as oak, elm, lime and liquid ambar can all be preserved.

Many evergreens such as holly, spruce, eleagnus, camellia, box and bay preserve well. The evergreens dry green on their own, but have a shorter life than other dried materials.

Seed Heads and berries

You need not limit yourself to drying flowers, grasses and foliage. All sorts of seed heads, cones and fruit can be successfully preserved by the glycerine method if collected while they are still green and unripe. Many are prettier left until they are ripe, and can be preserved by drying, for instance poppies, spiraea, delphiniums and columbines.

Dipsacus silvestris (teasel) and *Dipsacus fullonium* (fuller's teasel) are lovely biennials which can be picked in late summer and dry superbly.

Hordeum jubatum (squirreltail grass) has feathery silver-grey flower heads on spiky wiry stems. Cut it young or the tails will disintegrate.

Lagurus ovatus (hare's tail), with its strong stems and fluffy, silky soft heads, can be used fresh or dry.

Triticum spelta (ornamental wheat) is a very decorative grass.

Leaves and foliage

The leaves on many wooded stemmed trees such as beech, pittosporum, lime and laurel can be preserved on the branch by using a glycerine solution (see below for instructions). Beech

Cover the bottom of a box with borax powder, carefully lay the flowers in it, then pour in more powder until the flowers are completely covered. Take care that the flowers are surrounded by powder but still retain their shape. The borax powder draws all the moisture from the flowers.

Leave the flowers until they are brittle and dry, inspecting them carefully every now and then. The length of time it will take to dry flowers obviously varies, from a few hours to a few days, and you will have to learn from experience.

Drying grasses and leaves

Ornamental grasses are dried in the same way as flowers, tied in tight bunches as they shrink during drying. The darker the place you dry them in the better, as given even a little light they will turn pale and brittle.

Leaves and foliage, and some seed heads and fruits, can be successfully preserved by the glycerine method. After you have cut the branches smash or split their stems and leave 12 hours. Mix a solution of one part glycerine to two parts boiling water, stir and then leave it to cool.

Stand the stems in the mixture and leave them with their branches supported. After a few weeks the leaves should show signs of changing colour as they take up the solution. Remove them from the mixture as soon as they reach this stage, otherwise the leaves may fall.

Evergreens need to be cleaned by washing the leaves in a lukewarm detergent solution. Then rinse them, shaking them gently, and leave them in an airy place. When they are dry lay them between sheets of newspaper in layers each separated by a thick buffer of newspaper. Tie all the layers into a parcel, protecting the top and bottom with a sheet of cardboard, put a light weight on the top and just leave it for a month during which time the leaves will dry.

Arranging dried flowers

Dried flowers can be arranged in exactly the same way as fresh flowers – but without any water, of course. If you are putting the flowers into a lightweight container it is a good idea to put dry sand or gravel in the bottom of the container to give weight and stability to the arrangement.

Don't make the mistake of treating a dried flower arrangement as a fixture. Even though they last for ever, dried flowers soon look sad

when covered with dust after sitting in the same place for months. Rearrange the flowers every few weeks, replace some of them, or move the display to another place.

Hanging ornaments can be made using a ball of Styrofoam or plasticine tied around with ribbon to hang it up by, and filled in with dried flowers. If some of them have fragile stems and prove difficult to insert, pin them in place through the flower head.

Slightly more delicate in appearance are stars with cone centres, in which grasses or flower stalks are glued to the scales of a pine or larch cone. Alternatively, a small cardboard disc can be used as a centre, covered with a combination of sycamore seeds, oat grains and dried flowers and grasses glued to both surfaces.

Ordinary dried flower arrangements gilded with gold spray paint make pretty Christmas decorations; thistles and globe artichokes are particularly suitable for this use.

TOP *An arrangement of grasses and seed heads is given touches of brilliant orange by the inclusion of Cape gooseberries.* BOTTOM *A pretty bowl of grasses, seed heads, everlastings and honesty pods.*

Decorating with flowers

Flowers and plants can make a home come alive, and they give a gardenless town flat a bright, fresh look. Don't just think of flowers as a feature of the summer months; if you choose plants carefully, they can provide a continuous show of colour throughout the year.

Cut flowers

Few things give a house a fresher look than an arrangement of flowers straight out of the garden. If you have a very small garden, you can provide colour outside as well as in by growing plants which are suitable for cutting.

If you are growing your own plants for picking, you must think about what colour flowers to grow. This naturally depends on which colours you want to have around the house. Very dark and very light colours stand out and hold the eye, so use dark flowers to give

depth and emphasis, and light ones to accentuate the shape of the arrangement.

When you are planning a bed for cutting, you should also bear in mind those plants with interesting variegated foliage. These look fresh and attractive at any time, and provide colour in the house when few flowers are out.

Never pick flowers which are in full bloom, as their petals will soon fall. The best ones to choose are those which are half open or just beginning to open. The best times to pick garden flowers are in the early morning and early evening.

Use a good pair of secateurs or sharp flower scissors, as some stems are very tough and you can damage the plants by tearing and pulling at them. Always cut the stems at an angle, so that they present the widest possible area to the water. (Lupin is an exception, as it should be cut straight across.)

Place the flowers in a bucket of water—preferably rain water—in a shady place as soon as they are picked. This water should not be so cold that it gives warm-growing plants an unpleasant shock. Always leave freshly picked or bought flowers standing in deep water in a cool place for a few hours before arranging them.

You can prolong the life of cut flowers by taking a few precautions before arranging them. Plants such as lilac, roses, chrysanthemums and most flowering shrubs with hard woody stems or flowers such as poppies, dahlias and *Euphorbia* (spurge) benefit from being put for half a minute into 5cm (2in) of boiling water.

The flower heads should be protected from the steam by being wrapped in a teacloth. Daffodils, narcissi and similar flowers exude a sticky substance which makes it difficult for them to drink. Hold the stem ends under warm water to remove this. Any leaves growing down stems which will be below water level should be stripped off.

Always arrange flowers in tepid water; it will remain pure if you put a small piece of charcoal in the bottom of the container. Most flowers (except the narcissus family) will last longer if you add sugar to the water in the proportion of two teaspoons to a half litre.

Try to be original when arranging flowers, and use unconventional containers. You don't need a mass of

This graceful pot plant is housed in an unusual swan-shaped plant holder to create a very attractive table decoration.

flowers to make an effective display — in fact, a single bloom or a few broken heads floating in a shallow bowl can be just as pretty.

A large arrangement of flowering shrubs or blossom looks good in a deep jardinière in an open fireplace or an alcove, while a single rose in a slim glass vase will enhance any piece of furniture.

Flowering shrubs

In the spring, when there aren't many flowers in bloom, it is rewarding to cut sprays of flowering shrubs and trees to arrange around the house.

Remember that all shrub and tree stems need to be crushed, split, peeled and given a good drink before being arranged. The lower leaves should be stripped off, as they crowd the container and look out of proportion.

Blossoms should always be cut when the buds are tight, and kept out of a draught when in the house.

Many of the evergreens like bay, laurel, holly and privet are suitable for decorating the house in winter and spring.

There are many flowering shrubs which look most effective if cut for the house. Here is a list of some that are particularly suitable.

Clematis (virgin's bower). Most types are suitable and look very elegant with their pink, white and purple flowers.

Forsythia (golden bells). This shrub, with its yellow starry flowers, can be cut when the buds are only just showing, and it will come into flower in the house.

Jasmin nudiflorum (winter jasmine). This shrub flowers continuously throughout the winter, and looks particularly striking with the dark green leaves of holly and ivy.

Lonicera (honeysuckle). This is a particularly graceful shrub, and its scent fills the air.

Philadelphus (mock orange). This shrub also has a strong scent. You should strip off most of the leaves so that they don't take up all the water that is needed by the flowers.

The branches of some trees look most effective if cut for the house. Alder, hazel and willow will open after being cut. *Aesculus hippocastanum* (horse chestnut) with its 'sticky buds' and *Escallonia*, make very striking displays.

The bright, fresh look in this old house is achieved by a glorious mixture of cut flowers and pot plants.

Pot plants

Pot plants provide a more permanent feature in the home than cut flowers, but most of them need fairly regular attention.

When choosing pot plants, you must bear in mind the conditions under which they will have to live. These include temperature, humidity and light, and you should check on the needs of plants when buying them.

If you are arranging plants on a window sill, be sure to remove them at night if there is any likelihood of frost, as few plants can survive extreme changes of temperature. Equally, if you turn the heating on high, you may deprive them of the humidity they need.

If you feel the atmosphere in your house is too dry for your plants, you can make it more humid quite easily. Either spray them, or put pebbles in the saucers on which you stand the pots. Pour water in the saucers, but don't cover the pebbles, and as it evaporates it will create a humid atmosphere around the plants.

A disused fireplace is an excellent place for a display of colourful pot plants.

All plants need plenty of light, but too much sun can burn them to death. Most plants grow well in the northern hemisphere on south-west facing window sills, except those which grow naturally in the shade. Plants with variegated leaves need good light, otherwise their colours will fade.

Every plant has different needs when it comes to watering, depending on its situation, the time of year, and what kind of plant it is. You must remember, however, that the soil should never be allowed to become completely dry. If it is very dry, plunge the pot into a bucket of water and don't take it out until air bubbles stop coming to the surface.

Always water plants thoroughly by filling the top of the pot with water and leaving it for about half an hour. Then throw away any water which has collected in the saucer, as you must never leave a plant standing with its roots in water.

Naturally all plants need more water in the summer than in the dormant winter season, as they are very thirsty when they are making new growth. Rain water is best, but if this is not available, use tap water which has stood at room temperature for a few hours.

As plants develop, they eventually outgrow their pots, and need repotting. It is wise to replace the soil while you are doing this, but be careful not to remove too much of the old soil from around the roots of the plant. After repotting, give the plant a good drink and leave it in the shade for a few weeks to let it get used to its new pot.

Rather than standing pots around singly on saucers, try making interesting arrangements on trays or planting out a deep trough. If you stand the pots on a bed of gravel or pebbles and pack peat or moss between them, you can water them all together, and the moisture will rise around them.

When arranging different plants together in a trough in this way, be sure that they all like the same conditions. The plants detailed below have been grouped into categories which enjoy the same conditions.

Some plants are happy in almost any conditions. If you are new to the game, try some of the plants in the first list, as they are virtually impossible to kill.

Aspidistra elatior. This plant has dark green leaves, and is happy anywhere except in full sun.

Chlorophytum comosum (spider plant). This has long green and white grass-like leaves which cascade over, with baby plants on the end of runners. These can easily be rooted around the parent plant, or in separate pots, then cut off to provide another plant.

Coleus (ornamental nettle). This large family of plants all have ornamental variegated leaves in reds, yellows, purples and greens. They need good light and frequent watering. It is a good idea to pinch out the growing point and remove the flower buds, to encourage a bushy shape.

Hederas (ivy). This is a large family of climbing or trailing plants with decorative leaves. They are very hardy, and like to be in cool or warm rooms, but the warmer the room the more light and humidity they need.

Tradescantia (wandering sailor). These will grow in practically any soil, temperature and position, although some of the silver and green striped varieties show their colours better in semi-shade.

Plants which do not mind a lack of warm sunlight are ideal for a cool room, so long as they receive sufficient daylight. Here are some suitable plants for cool rooms.

Aechmea rhodocyanea (urn plant or exotic bush). This has silvery grey-green curving leaves and an amazing pink bracted flower which lasts well.

Impatiens (busy lizzie). This is a popular plant with iridescent orange, red or pink flowers and green or crimson tinged leaves, depending on the variety. Give it a lot of water in the summer, but only a little in winter, and keep it in a very light place.

Sansevieria trifasciata (mother-in-law's tongue). This has strong, leathery leaves, but its roots rot easily if it is damp in winter. It needs very little water, and prefers a well-lit situation.

Sparmannia africana (house lime or African hemp). This has large, soft, pale green furry leaves, and produces pretty white flowers in early spring. It can grow up to 1.82m (6ft) high, or it can be made to bush out by picking out the growing point. It needs to be well watered and stood in a light airy position. In winter it prefers a cool place, and in summer a shady situation.

If your room is warm, choose some of the plants listed below. If you have central heating, however, make sure that there is enough humidity for them, as they all need moisture.

Asparagus. This plant needs moisture and a reasonably warm situation, and enjoys good light during the summer.

Bilbergia nutans. This has long narrow, dark green leaves and a striking flower cluster of green, blue and red.

Neoregelia carolinae tricolor. This forms a large flat rosette, has long narrow leaves striped cream and pink, and is happy in shade.

Dieffenbachia (dumb cane). There are many varieties, some of which have ornamental leaves with yellow or cream patterning and green edges. They should all be sheltered from draughts.

Sinningia speciosa (gloxinia). This is a most attractive house plant, and flowers throughout the summer. It has large dark leaves and bell-shaped flowers.

Ferns vary as to the amount of warmth they need, but all require very little light and a moist atmosphere. This makes many of them unsuitable as house plants, but here are two which are reasonably easy to grow in a warm room so long as they do not get too much light.

Adiantum (maidenhair fern). This is rather delicate, but attractive and ornamental. Keep it away from draughts, and make sure it is not in a dry atmosphere. The soil as well as the atmosphere must be kept moist.

Asplenium nidus (bird's nest fern). This has bright green leaves with dark mid-ribs. It enjoys a warm temperature and must be kept moist.

Bulbs
Hyacinths, daffodils and narcissi have always been popular pot plants because they flower in early spring before many garden flowers are available.

Plant bulbs in pots with drainage holes, and make sure they do not touch each other or the sides or bottom of the pot. Use moist potting compost or special bulb fibre, and be careful not to press it down so firmly that it forms a solid, airless mass. The tips of all bulbs (except the really tiny ones) should be just above the top of the soil.

Leave the bulbs in a cool dark place until the green shoots show, and water as necessary to keep the soil moist. Crocus and other small bulbs should be left until the flower buds form but the larger bulbs can be moved to a cool shady place in the house after six to ten weeks, when there is five or six centi-

metres (about two inches) of green shoot visible. After a week you can move the pot to a lighter place, but keep it away from fires, radiators and draughts.

Water the bulbs frequently, especially when they are flowering. As they grow towards the light and tend to become a little lopsided you should turn the pots to make them grow straight.

Plants and flowers around the house
Flowers in the home should look natural, not stiffly formal. A good effect can be achieved by choosing colours in the room. Don't just have a vase of flowers or a pot plant in the living room; other parts of the house benefit equally from the addition of a floral arrangement.

Landings and halls are often neglected, but look very good with a handsome jardinière full of plants. Even if you have small landings, you must be able to find a window sill where you can arrange some pretty pot plants.

If you are having a dinner party, you can improve the look of the dining

A simple planter can be made from a wooden trough overflowing with greenery.

table by having an attractive arrangement of flowers as a centre piece. Don't make it so high that you have to peer round it to talk to your friends. A different idea is to put an individual posy next to each table setting, or just one flower head floating in a shallow bowl.

There is a theory that masses of flowers and plants breathing oxygen during the night can make a bedroom airless. If your guests feel this way, a single rose on the dressing table or a little posy of violets will make a thoughtful touch without upsetting them.

Many plants love the steamy atmosphere of a bathroom, as it reminds them of their humid origins. So don't avoid moisture loving varieties when you are choosing plants.

The important point to remember when dealing with flowers and plants is to look after them properly. If you do, you will be rewarded by a welcoming, friendly home, full of life and colour.

Growing flowers

Window boxes

Window boxes serve two functions; the first is to decorate the outside of a house, thus giving pleasure not only to the owner but also to passers by, and the second is to add to the pleasure of those inside by giving them a tiny foreground landscape of flower and leaf through or across which to look at the world. The view through a window is much improved on a grey morning if it is seen past the nodding heads of daffodils or pot marigolds.

How many boxes: The shape, size and number of window boxes will, obviously, be dictated by the house itself. If you have just one window box it should be colourful and well-tended—it must merit the attention that it will undoubtedly receive. Alternatively, you could have a mixture of troughs, pots and window boxes—each filled with different varieties of flowers. Just think of those pavements, yards and flights of steps in the Mediterranean countries where every kind of pot and pan, even painted petrol tins, contains a glittering cascade of bright flowers which enliven the dullest corner.

Types of window box: Window boxes can be found in many materials. They can either be bought ready-made or made to fit a particular window. The traditional wooden box is still a favourite and will last well provided it is painted with a preservative and one or two coats of paint. Good wood such as teak, elm, oak, pine or red cedar can be treated with preservative against the weather. The less heavy deal boxes need two or three coats of paint. White, off-white, or stone colours are usually good ones to choose. Or a dark blue, green or grey. It is probably best to let the flowers provide all the colour.

How to make a window box: If you want to make your own window box choose wood 2–2.5cm (¾–1in) thick. The usual length for a box is 0.91–1.22m (3–4ft), and the ideal width is 23–25cm (9–10in)—certainly anything less than 18cm (7in) is too narrow for the plants to be happy, and anything wider than 25cm (10in) will hang dangerously far over most sills. The base of the box must have 2.5cm (1in) drainage holes in it, each about 30cm (12in) apart.

Window boxes on a roof and (inset) pots of geraniums add drama to a balcony.

Fixing the box: Place strips of wood under the box to lift the base off the window sill and allow air to circulate and water to drain away. The box must be very firmly attached to both the window sill and wall. And, if there is a gap, drive wedges of wood between the end of the box and the wall.

Soil and planting: Before the box is filled with soil each drainage hole must be covered with a broken crock, and a 2.5–5cm (1–2in) layer of crocks and gravel spread over the bottom of the box. With window boxes, as with any other pot or container, it is vitally important to use a really good soil. Fill the box up to about 2.5cm (1in) from the top.

You can put the plants straight into the soil or, if you prefer, you can put the plants in pots, put the pots in the window box, and pack them around with soil and peat. This second method makes it easier to remove a plant if it dies, and also means that if you have sharp winters your favourite plants can be brought inside in their pots and put into the window box again when all danger of frost is past.

When to plant: Plant window boxes as you would plant a garden. Put in hardy plants in fine weather during winter and spring, sow hardy annuals in early summer or buy them later as plants. Bulbs should be put in in late summer or early autumn.

Which plants to choose: Plants in window boxes tend to have a somewhat hard life, with periods of cold and wind, draughts and little protection. Certain plants are, therefore, almost synonymous with window-box gardening. Choose *Chrysanthemum frutescens* (marguerites), petunias double and single—flowery and floppy in glorious colours—lobelias light and dark, fuchsias, verbenas, *Begonia semperflorens* and, of course, the favourite flowering plants such as geraniums and pelargoniums. Miniature roses, sharing with their fully grown relations a tough disposition, are also good in boxes, as are hydrangeas. Petunias, marigolds, lobelias and verbenas are happy in window boxes which get a lot of sun. Begonias and pansies will prefer a shadier spot.

Ideal for window boxes, and as delightfully edible as they are decorative, are miniature tomatoes with their marble-sized fruits. Team them with green beans; they have beautiful scarlet flowers and you could train them up the sides and around the top of your window, framing it completely. *Ipomoea* (morning glory) can be used for the same purpose as they, too, are good climbing plants.

Flowers all the year round: With some planning and re-planting, a window box can be kept flowering throughout most of the year.

You could start the box with bulbs and sweet-smelling wallflowers and forget-me-nots which will bloom when the bulbs are over. When these are over why not put in *Nicotiana* (tobacco plant) — for their colour — with pansies and, later, nasturtiums with their brilliant flames and oranges.

A window box of herbs: Sweet-smelling rosemary and lavender are good window-box plants and, if you have a convenient sill and are devoted to cooking, have a box for more of your favourite herbs. Many useful ones—chives, chervil, parsley, savory, thyme and marjoram—will thrive in a box if they are kept well watered.

Use of flower colours: A brighter, gayer and generally more daring use of colour is possible in a window box because the flowers are contained in a rigid framework, be it lead, stone, wood, or concrete (or the magic fibreglass which can look like any of these), which effectively cuts them off from nature. What would be unthinkable in the way of colour combinations in a flower bed on a large scale becomes quite acceptable when in a box set off against stone or brick. Shocking, iridescent pink petunias with orange marigolds, for example, or vermilion geraniums with velvety pink and purple pelargoniums.

Although it is often highly successful to have a bright multi-coloured plant pattern in a box, it is also very effective to have shades of one colour, or one colour with white. Try planting yellow and orange marigolds with silver grey foliage plants; pink and white petunias; purple heliotrope with mauve petunias and blue ageratum; or pink and white geraniums with fuchsias.

Care of the plants: As with all flowering plants, but even more so as they are at eye level and more noticeable, take care to remove flower heads as soon as they die, so that you get constant blooms to the end of the season. In the hottest and driest times of the year you must remember to water at least once, and probably twice a day (early in the morning and in the evening) as window boxes tend to dry out quickly. During the summer you could add a plant food once every two weeks or so.

Window boxes in winter: Try not to have a window box which contains only dry dusty soil and a few dead sticks. In winter either clear the box out or remove it entirely to renovate for next year. The soil in window boxes needs to be replaced roughly once a year so this could be a good time to do it. Alternatively, you could fill the window box with winter evergreens like small junipers and cypresses, and tough little heathers and ivies. Either move these into the garden in spring, or put your flowers among them.

Hanging baskets

A basket can look extremely attractive hanging in a porch, on a balcony, or under a verandah. Like window boxes and pot plants, they are a way of compensating for the lack of a garden, so do try to put them where you will enjoy them from indoors—not where they are only visible from outside the house.

You can have hanging baskets indoors, but line them with green plastic or buy special watertight baskets which have their own interior draining devices—otherwise you will have drips all over the floor each time you water.

Size, soil and succour: The basket itself should be at least 23cm (9in) in diameter; if it is smaller than this it will not really hold enough soil to keep many types of plants healthy. Ideally it should be 30–46cm (1–1½ft) in diameter and have a depth of 15–23cm (6–9in).

Hanging baskets are planted at the beginning of summer, to be hung up outside when all danger of frost is past. Make sure you hang them from a strong support; they can get very heavy. Line them with moss—this will help to retain as much water as possible—and then fill them with a mixture of peat and potting soil. They must not be allowed to dry out and in the driest weather must be watered twice a day. If possible, it is better occasionally to take the basket down and immerse it in water rather than water it overhead. If you have very leafy plants, zebrinas for example, clean their leaves occasionally by spraying or wiping them.

Where to hang it: Site the baskets carefully so that they do not cut out any light from the house. They must also be easy to water, but not so low that they thump unwary heads and not where they may drip on the innocent caller.

Which plants to choose: Plants which trail naturally are best; ivies, lobelias, pendant begonias, petunias, zebrinas, *Chlorophytum* (spider plant) and pel-argoniums (particularly the ivy-leaved varieties), with nasturtiums sown among them. Trailing fuchsias can look lovely, too, but they need plenty of space in which to grow, and dislike draughts.

Balconies

For town-dwellers a balcony, if you are lucky enough to have one, offers an opportunity to create a miniature garden. Like window boxes and hanging baskets, a balcony can improve the dreariest outlook. It is so much nicer to look at green growing things and colourful groups of flowers than to be forced to stare at the windows of the house opposite.

Even on the smallest balcony (or flat roof) it is possible to use the space to grow decorative plants, and even useful plants like one or two pots of tomatoes, or a big pot of green beans climbing up canes. If space is very limited, and the position is sheltered enough for them, make use of the wall by having climbing plants.

Some good annual climbers are

Pots of fresh herbs and vegetables framing a kitchen window can add immeasurably to the decor as well as provide ingredients for cooking.

Cobaea scandens (the cup and saucer plant) which has greenish-white flowers changing to violet as the flowers mature, and which can cover a wall in a summer as it grows up to 3m (10ft) high up strings or a lattice; and *Rudbekia hirta* (black-eyed susan) which does best in semi-shade and is covered in vivid yellow flowers from mid-summer until autumn.

The most beautiful of all the annual climbers are, perhaps, the *Ipomoea* (heavenly blue or morning glory) which lives up to its name with its brilliant shining blue trumpets, climbs up canes or string and does best in a sheltered place with a great deal of sun, and *Passiflora caerulea* (passion flower) which is equally delicate and has beautiful flowers. For a narrow little box or sink garden in a less sheltered spot *Sempervivums* (house leeks) are lovely. They spread and propagate themselves and are as tough as you could wish. Other alpine-type plants such as some of the saxifrages could be planted with them.

On a shady balcony you could grow begonias, fuchsias, ferns and trailing vines, in pots and tubs. For a sunnier spot petunias, salvias and geraniums will be happier.

Small conservatories

An attractive and unusual idea is to put shelves across a bay window and have a mixed group of flowering and foliage plants. Outside you could have a window box so that the whole window is a mass of growing things. (Not, of course, if it is a darkish room or a room in which people have to work.) A hall or landing window is ideal for this. On the shelves grow pots of ferns, geraniums, *Tradescantia* (wandering sailor), begonias, hoyas, solanum and trailing ivies.

Alternatively, if your house has a verandah you could have this glassed in and turned into a small conservatory, giving yourself an extension to the house—a garden room.

If this room receives a lot of sun you could grow cacti and other desert plants. If it is warm but shady, receiving little direct sun, create a jungle atmosphere. Grow begonias, philodendrons, monsteras and some of the tropical ferns. Keep the humidity up by hosing down the floor each day and leaving it to steam-dry.

Geraniums and salvias fill a window box while tomatoes, green beans and morning glories decorate a balcony, and petunias cascade from a hanging basket.

TOP Colourful plants grouped in a deep kitchen window can be used to shut out a dismal view.

BOTTOM A hanging basket full of gay flowers adds to the charm of this house.

RIGHT Hanging baskets, creeping plants and plants with sculptural shapes have been used in this small Victorian conservatory and combine to give it an authentic period atmosphere.

Dealing with electrical problems

Electricity is the modern homemaker's all-purpose slave. It powers most of the appliances which have relieved much of the drudgery of cooking, cleaning and washing. But it still has some of the mystery it had over 100 years ago when Edison invented the light bulb, and many people are afraid to make even the simplest repairs around the house.

An understanding, however limited, of what electricity is and how it works could save you hours of frustration when the lights go out.

Currents

An electric current is simply a stream of electrons running at the speed of light along a prepared channel. The channel, or conductor as it is commonly known, most used in today's homes is copper wire though it is important to remember that both earth and water are also good conductors—so be careful in the bathroom! Materials which have the opposite effect to conductors are called insulators. They prevent the conductors from being diverted to other conductors and they also protect the wires from being accidentally touched. The best known insulator is rubber but plastic, Bakelite and wood are also used.

To flow properly, electricity must be able to form a complete circuit. If anything breaks that circuit the current will stop. There are two types of flow—direct current (DC) when the electricity travels along one wire to the appliance and then back along another wire; and alternating current (AC) when the current flows back and forth along the same track. Most mains supplies are AC, while battery supplied electricity is DC. Always check to see if your appliance is AC or DC before using it.

The mains

Electricity enters your home in a cable leading to a sealed box containing the mains fuse.

From here the current passes through the meter which records how much you use (see below) and on to the fuse box and mains switch. This is where you can turn off the entire supply to your house when you need to change a fuse or as a safety precaution when you go away.

Each type of circuit in the house has its own fuse and each has an ampere (amps) rating indicating how much electricity can pass through it at one time. There is usually one for lighting (5 amp wire); one for power such as irons, vacuum cleaners, hair driers (13 or 15 amp wire); and possibly a 30 amp wire for the cooker. Always be sure when changing a fuse that you replace it with a wire of the same amperage.

Reading the meter

Check each of the dials individually, taking the reading from left to right around each clock. If the arrow falls between two digits then take the lower of the two. Check the reading on your last statement, find out how much the charge per unit is in your area and you should be able to calculate the next bill. Don't forget, though, to take into account the fact that not all units are charged at the same rate—the first few are charged at a higher rate than later ones. Also, some of your appliances, such as storage units, work at off-peak hours when charges are lower.

How to wire a plug

The simple 13-amp square-pin plug is always wired up in the same way. The righthand small pin (with the single large pin at the top) is connected to the live wire which has a brown plastic coating. The lefthand small pin is connected to the neutral wire which

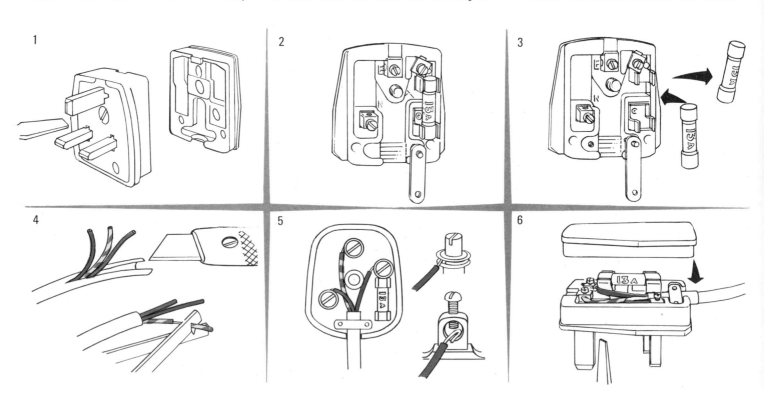

is blue. The large, single pin is connected to the green and yellow earth wire. On some appliances there is no earth wire and the earth pin is left unconnected.

Some older appliances, and those in other countries, have differently coloured wires: red for live, black for neutral and plain green for earth.

The tools needed to wire a plug are: an electrical screwdriver with an insulated plastic handle
a wire stripper or pair of wire cutters
a handyman's knife

Step 1. Remove the lid of the plug by unscrewing the single large screw on the other side. In some plugs the cable must be threaded through a hole in the lid. Remember to do this before attaching the cable to the rest of the plug.

Step 2. Loosen the cable clamp that prevents the cable from tearing out of the plug.

Step 3. Check the fuse cartridge by clipping it into another plug and seeing if it works there. If it has blown replace it.

Step 4. Use the handyman's knife to slit up the outer sheath of the cable for about 4cm (1½in). Pull the wires out of the slit and cut off the empty sheath. Be careful not to cut the wires. Use the wire stripper to pull half the casing off each of the three wires.

Step 5. Put the cable under the clamp so that each wire can reach its pin. Do up the clamp. Then fasten each wire to its pin, making sure that the bare metal wire does not touch another wire or pin. Different plugs have different types of screws. In some plugs the wire is wrapped around a post and held down by a nut. The nut should be removed and the wire looped completely around the post—clockwise so the nut will not unravel it—and twisted around itself. Then the nut should be screwed down on to the loop. In other plugs, where the wire passes through a hole it should be bent double before being inserted to ensure good contact.

Step 6. Clip a working fuse into the fuseholder—it just presses in. Then screw on the top of the plug.

Mending a fuse
There is a limit to the amount of current that can pass through a conductor such as a wire; beyond this limit heat develops which will damage the insulation and cause the appliance to break down. To prevent fire, all domestic circuits are fitted with fuses designed to fail as soon as the circuit becomes overloaded.

When a fuse blows the first thing to do is to remove the cause of the failure. For instance, if switching on a light has made the fuse blow, switch off the light before trying to mend the fuse. If a plugged-in appliance has blown then unplug it.

TURN OFF THE MAIN SWITCH BEFORE YOU BEGIN ANY REPAIRS.

Check at the main fuse box to determine which fuse has blown. It is a good idea when first moving into a new home to label all the different fuses in the main box so that, when anything blows, you can tell at a glance which one is at fault. To do this take each fuse out in turn and then ask your husband or a friend to go around the house to find which appliance is not working. Then mark accordingly.

There are three main types of fuse:
Bridge fuse: In this type of fuse the wire is held in diagonally opposite corners by a screw at each end. Halfway between the screws the wire

crosses a small hump or bridge and, if the fuse has blown, the wire across here will have melted. To mend the fuse loosen both screws and remove the damaged lengths of wire. Cut a new length of wire of the same amperage and wrap it around one of the screws in a clockwise direction so that it does not become loose when you tighten the screw. Then twist the other end clockwise round the second screw and tighten.

Protected fuse: With these it is more difficult to see if the wire is blown because it is threaded through a hole running lengthways through a porcelain cover and you will have to prise the wire out with a screwdriver. This type of fuse is mended in exactly the same way as a bridge fuse.

Cartridge fuse: This, the simplest type of fuse, is completely encased in an insulated cylinder with a metal cap at each end. To mend it you simply unclip the entire cartridge and clip in a replacement of the same rating.

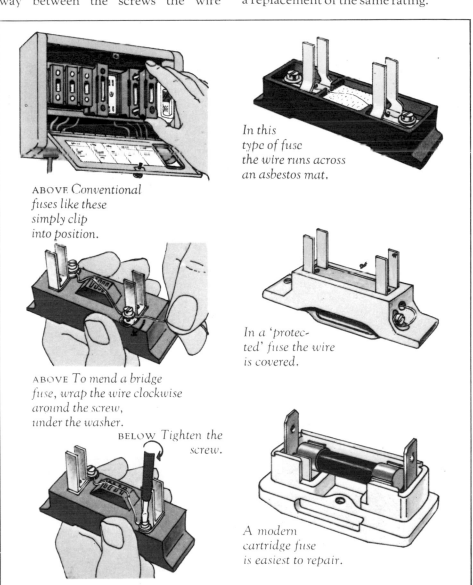

ABOVE *Conventional fuses like these simply clip into position.*

ABOVE *To mend a bridge fuse, wrap the wire clockwise around the screw, under the washer.*

BELOW *Tighten the screw.*

In this type of fuse the wire runs across an asbestos mat.

In a 'protected' fuse the wire is covered.

A modern cartridge fuse is easiest to repair.

Dealing with plumbing problems

Like most other parts of a house, the plumbing system is relatively simple and you should be able to manage day-to-day repairs without having to call in a specialist. A little maintenance goes a long way, too—if you are careful what you put down your sinks, keep gullies and gutters clear, you will be less likely to need professional help to keep things working smoothly.

Blockages
When tea leaves, hair and small bits of vegetables get past the grid over the waste outlet of baths, basins and sinks, they sometimes build up in the elbow joint below and form a blockage. To avoid this, try not to empty any of these things into your sink; but if you must pour hot fat down the drain, always run hot water into it for at least a minute to keep it from solidifying.

To clear a blockage, you will need a rubber plunger. First block the overflow hole at the top of the bath, basin or sink with a wet rag to prevent air in the pipe from escaping. Make sure that the water is deep enough to cover the cup of the plunger. Place the plunger over the water outlet and pump up and down. If the suction and pressure created is enough to loosen whatever is blocking the drain, remove the rag from the overflow hole and run cold water for a minute or two to clear the obstruction completely and fill the trap.

If the plunger brings no results, you will have to drain the U-shaped trap below the sink.

Before you begin, be sure to put a bucket underneath the trap to catch the waste water. Then undo the screw plug at the U's lowest point, or at the base of the newer 'bottle traps'. With a conventional U-trap, be sure to insert a bar between the U to counteract the pressure on the pipework as you unscrew the cap.

After draining away the waste, poke both sides of the pipe with a straightened wire coat-hanger to clear away the blockage. Replace the screw cap and run cold water from the tap above to make sure that the pipes are clear and to refill the trap.

If the drain is still blocked, and there is nothing obstructing the outside waste pipe, call a plumber.

If your toilet becomes blocked, you will need a special type of plunger with a metal disc to prevent the rubber cup from turning itself inside out.

Place the plunger as far down into the pan as it will go, and pump very quickly. If this does not work, call a plumber.

Overflows
Your tank or toilet cistern can overflow if the hollow ball float develops a leak, or the washer (a small rubber or nylon disc with a hole in the centre) in the valve wears out. First, turn off the supply by tracing the pipes back until you find a tap. If the ball float has sprung a leak, you can make a temporary repair by shaking the water out and wrapping it in a plastic bag. Ball floats are easy to replace—you just screw them off the lever and screw a new one on.

If it is the washer that is at fault (check this by holding the ball float up; if the water doesn't stop, the valve is at fault), take out the split pin holding the lever arm, unscrew the cap on the valve case and push the piston out with a screwdriver. Then hold half of the piston with a pair of pliers and turn the other half with a screwdriver held in the slot until you unscrew it. Remove the small rubber washer in the piston and replace it with a new one. After screwing the two parts of the piston back together, washer end first, fix the lever back with the split pin.

A rubber 'diaphragm' operating against a nylon nozzle is used in some

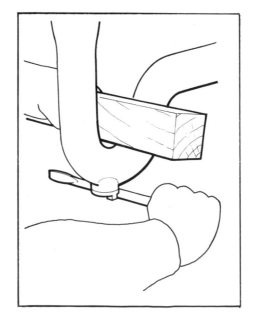

Use a simple bar to avoid undue strain on the pipes when removing a trap plug.

modern cisterns instead of a conventional piston. If you need to replace one of these, just unscrew the cap at the valve end of the lever, pry off the worn diaphragm, replace it with a new one and screw the cap back on.

Dripping taps : changing a washer
That Chinese water torture drip of the kitchen tap late at night when you're trying to sleep is probably due to a worn washer. Despite the fact that there are a number of different types of tap, changing a washer is almost the same for all of them. And it's easy, too, as long as you remember to turn off the water supply first, and use either synthetic rubber or nylon washers.

The most common bathroom and kitchen fixtures are 'bib' or 'pillar' taps. (Bib taps are fixed to the wall behind the sink or basin and pillar taps are fitted directly on to the sink or basin.) The only real difference between them is that pillar taps have a cover which must be removed before you can get at the inside for repairs.

On 'supataps', which have a handle and nozzle in one piece pointing downwards into the sink, new washers can be fitted without turning off the water supply, but it is always best to do so just in case. You can usually find a stopcock underneath the sink or basin. If there isn't one there, trace the pipe back until you find one.

If the hot water tap is the one dripping and you can't find a stopcock somewhere along the line, you'll have to turn off the water at the main stopcock. You'll also have to drain the entire hot water system by opening all the taps. Be sure to turn off the stopcock which supplies the hot water cylinder to avoid draining the cold water system as well.

Once you've turned off all supply of water to the problem tap (and any appliances like hot water heaters and central heating boilers which could burn out without water), open the tap until it runs dry. If it doesn't, check to be sure you've turned off the right stopcock. Don't start fixing the tap until the water is off.

Bib and pillar taps : The handle of the tap will probably have to be removed before you can start. This is a simple operation, requiring only the removal of the screw at its base.

Most taps have a cover or shield which you may be able to unscrew by hand. If not, use an adjustable spanner or wrench. Remember to protect the chromium plating by wrapping a rag around the jaws of the tool. If it won't

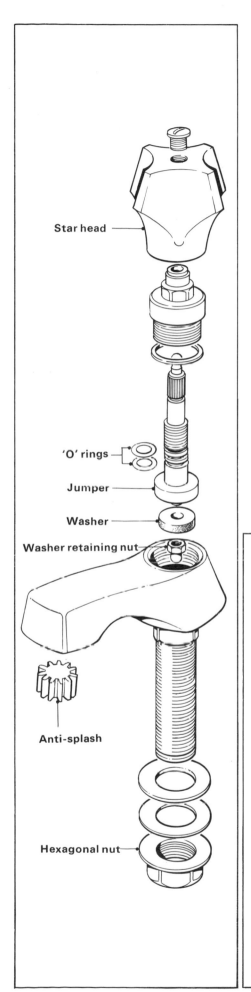

Star head

'O' rings

Jumper

Washer

Washer retaining nut

Anti-splash

Hexagonal nut

move anti-clockwise, try turning it the other way as some older taps have a reverse thread cover.

Once you get the cover clear, you will see the 'gland nut', which holds the headgear to the body of the tap. Use the spanner to undo the nut, holding the tap with one hand to prevent it from twisting.

Now you'll be able to lift the headgear out. The worn washer may be held by a small nut at the bottom of the headgear or will be left in the tap body. If it is fastened on by a nut, use pliers to hold the lower part and undo the nut. Then remove the old washer, put a new one on and replace the nut. If it was the kind left in the tap body, just lift it out and replace it with a new one.

LEFT *A detailed sketch of the conventional pillar tap, with all of the principal components clearly marked.*

If you wish to change a worn washer on this type of tap, first carefully unscrew the cover of the tap. Next, slowly remove the headgear from the cover – you will find the washer at the bottom of the headgear (as on the sketch).

Anchor firmly with a screwdriver while you replace the old washer with a new one – and remember that you should always use a rubber or nylon washer as replacement.

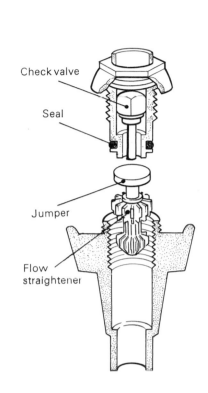

Check valve

Seal

Jumper

Flow straightener

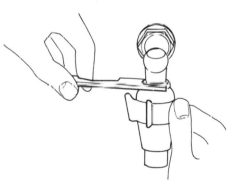

To change a 'Supatap' washer, loosen the nut above the nozzle.

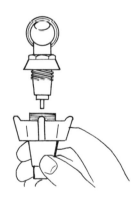

Unscrew the nozzle (you do not need to shut off the supply).

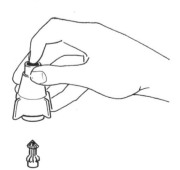

Push out the flow straightener.

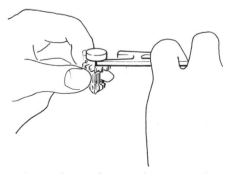

The washer and jumper unit is in the top.

When you re-assemble the tap, grease the threads with a little petroleum jelly so that it will be easier to put back together and take apart the next time.

Supataps: Though you can repair supataps with the water supply still on, some water may escape as you remove the nozzle. This will stop as soon as the nozzle is completely off, but it is still always best to turn off the water at the nearest stopcock.

To remove the nozzle, loosen the locking nut above it by holding the nozzle in one hand and working the nut with a spanner with the other. Then hold the nut still and unscrew the complete nozzle anti-clockwise.

With the nozzle in your hand, push out the anti-splash unit with a pencil or screwdriver. In the top of this unit is the combined washer and 'jumper plate'. Pull it out and replace it with a new unit of the same type, then re-assemble it on the tap.

To get to the gland nut on some modern, more decorative taps, you need to remove their large handles. Just prise up the little button in the centre (which sometimes says 'C' or 'H') with a small screwdriver. Undo the screw underneath the cap, and lift off the handle. The rest is the same as for a normal tap.

Sometimes a small fracture in a supply pipe can cause a steady leak or drip. In an emergency, these fractures can be sealed by rubbing hard soap into them and binding with adhesive tape. This is, however, only a temporary measure.

Drains and gullies

Sometimes blockages can develop in the plumbing outside the house: the drains which carry waste and water from your sinks, basins, lavatories and rainwater drain pipes. This often happens because tea leaves, vegetable scraps, fat, breadcrumbs and so on collect in a bend or trap and block the drain. Sometimes leaves, earth and gravel are to blame when the grating over the trapped gully is blocked. Be careful what you put down your drains and check the gullies regularly to make sure the gratings are free from debris. Be sure not to scrape the debris back into the gully itself as you may block the trap below.

If you've cleaned the grating, but the water is still not draining, the trap is probably to blame. Try poking around with an old spoon tied to a stick. After the water has cleared, empty the trap by pumping with a mop and soaking up the residue with it.

To do a really good job, dig out whatever debris you can see and then rinse with a few bucketsful of very hot water and bicarbonate of soda. Don't replace the grating until after running the cold water taps inside the house to make sure that the drain is completely clear.

If your efforts are still not rewarded by free-flowing water, the next step in the diagnosis and treatment is to open the first manhole cover. The gully leads to two or three of these inspection traps, which get deeper the nearer they are to the sewer, and enable you to locate where the trouble is.

Easy with the manhole cover—it's heavy! It's usually best to lift it from one side only and tip it backwards. If it's stuck, scratch around the edges with a screwdriver and try again.

Once the manhole cover is up, locating the trouble is easy; if the chamber is empty, then the blockage is between the manhole and the house. If it's full, then the problem is further down the line.

Once you've discovered where the blockage is, the best way to clear it is to insert a garden hose into the blocked pipe and turn on the water full pressure. If you adjust the nozzle for the strongest possible jet, you can probably force the blockage through.

Sometimes the build-up will not disperse so easily, and drain rods are needed. Either get a specialist to handle them or, if you don't mind the muck, hire a set yourself. They're not difficult to use, but you must remember to keep turning the rods clockwise as you push them up the drain, or they will disconnect.

Gutters

The most frequent cause of blockages in rainwater gutters and downpipes is fallen leaves, so you must pay special attention to the system in the autumn. If your gutters overflow, you can probably clear the blockage yourself, as long as you can get up to them. If you can't reach them with a ladder (don't forget to secure it firmly at ground level), you might be able to reach them from a bedroom window.

Using a piece of stiff cardboard, cut to the shape of the gutter, scrape the debris into little piles and throw it to the ground or into a bucket. Do not let it enter the downpipe.

If the blockage is in the downpipe, tie a thick rag ball on the end of a cane and ram it down the pipe until it clears and the rainwater can run freely.

Regular cleaning of gutters, especially in the autumn, is the best preventative of blockage. A ball of chicken wire placed at the top of a downpipe (as long as it's big enough not to get stuck inside the pipe) is the easiest way to avoid leaves accumulating in the pipes.

Blockages in downpipes can be dealt with by a thick rag ball on the end of a cane.

Check hopper heads from time to time — they should always be kept clean.

Dealing with general repairs

A man's home is his castle, or so they say, but as we all know, even the best kept castles can still fall into a state of complete disrepair unless carefully maintained...

Locks

It's amazing how careless people are about security. Don't wait until your home is burgled to take out insurance—do it now. If you already have a policy make sure that it is fully paid up and also check that your locks are in good working order. No company will give you cover unless your locks meet their requirements—and they may be reluctant to meet a claim if they discover any locks which are not in perfect order.

Most locks fall into one of two main categories—mortise or rim locks. A mortise lock is inserted into the vertical side member of the door (known as the stile) whereas a rim lock is mounted on to the door stile. These two categories are further broken down into a number of types, including dead locks, tubular locks, cylindrical locks and night latches. Whatever the type, however, the basic maintenance remains the same.

Keep the locks well lubricated—ideally you should clean them once every six months. Powdered graphite (pencil lead) or a light oil are the best materials to use. To lubricate the working parts, just turn the lock to the open position and squeeze in a little oil or graphite. If this doesn't seem to help then you'll probably need to remove the lock and clean the inside with a soft cloth dipped in oil.

If you have trouble getting your key into the lock, rub powdered graphite generously over the key and then slip it in and out of the lock a few times. This should ease the problem.

The time will come, however, when a lock is beyond repair and will need replacement. First, all locks are marked as for 'S' or 'Z' fittings. That is, whether the door *closes* in a clockwise (Z) or anti-clockwise (S) direction. Check which yours is before buying a new lock.

Removing a mortise lock: To remove a mortise lock, unscrew the face plate, the lock front and the door furniture, and then prise the lock out with a screwdriver.

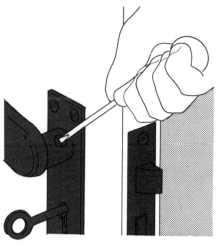

TOP LEFT *Replacing the conventional mortice lock is one of the most basic – and easiest – of home repair jobs. First, using a screwdriver, undo one of the handle screws.*

ABOVE *The next step is to carefully remove the handles and then the handle bar. When they have been removed, you can undo the face plate screws.*

BOTTOM LEFT *Now slowly and carefully lever the lock from its recess. The new lock should be inserted into the door stile in the reverse order to this.*

Fitting a mortise lock: Step 1. Hold the back of the lock face against the edge of the door stile and, with a pencil, mark out the position of the lock case. With a bradawl or long nail also mark the position of the spindle and keyhole.

Step 2. Mark a rectangle the height and width of the lock casing exactly in the centre of the door stile edge.

Step 3. Using a 10mm bit, drill a series of overlapping holes along the centre line of the rectangle.

Step 4. Using the same bit piece, drill out the key and spindle holes.

Step 5. Put the lock in the mortise and mark the place where the face plate is to fall.

Step 6. Remove the lock and chisel out a recess that is the thickness of both the face plate and lock front.

Step 7. Insert the lock and secure the plates with screws. Then slide the spindle into place and mount the door furniture.

Step 8. Close the door and mark the position of the striker plate recesses. Cut out the recess in the frame and fix the plate with screws.

Removing a rim lock: To remove a rim lock, unscrew the lock case and push out the cylinder barrel.

Fitting a rim lock: Step 1. First place the lock at a convenient level and mark the position with a pencil.

Step 2. Bore a hole which will take the cylinder barrel.

Step 3. Mount the cylinder ring and then insert the barrel.

Step 4. Now mount the back plate on the other side of the door and secure it to the cylinder barrel with connecting screws.

Step 5. Using wood screws, fix the back plate to the door stile.

Step 6. Fit the latch case to the back plate.

Step 7. Close the door and mark the position of the keep, relative to the latch.

Step 8. Recess the keep in the frame and secure with wood screws.

Window panes

Having checked and fixed all your locks, don't, whatever you do, let the burglar in through the window. A cracked or missing pane is a real come-on to a prospective thief. It's simpler—and very much cheaper—to

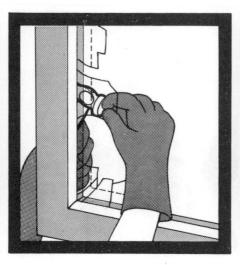

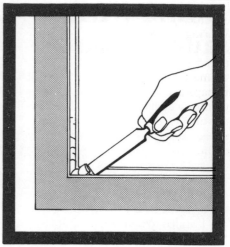

Always wear thick protective gloves when handling broken glass. To remove a broken window pane, score around the edge with a glasscutter.

Starting at the top, carefully tap out the glass, piece by piece, with a hammer. Leave the window open if possible while you're doing this.

Clear away all the old putty from the rebate around the wooden window frame. Some of it may need to be chipped out with a chisel.

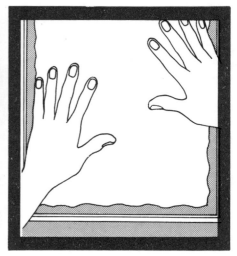

Offer up the new pane of glass to make perfectly sure that it is the right size. Remember that it must be slightly undersize to allow for expansion.

Now mould some putty until it is soft and quite pliable. Then gently press it into the rebate all around the wooden window frame.

Carefully lift the new pane into position and then press it, little by little, into the putty around the edges only – not in the centre.

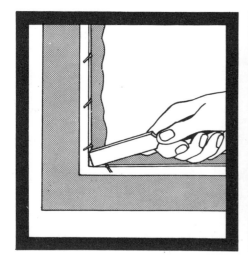

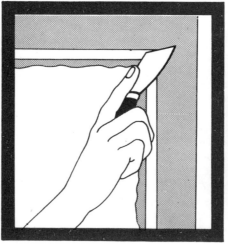

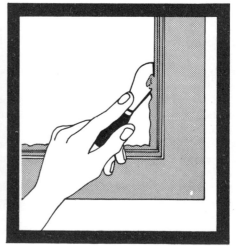

Tap in window sprigs at about 25 centimetre (10 inch) intervals around the window frame to secure the pane of glass in the window.

Press more putty all around the glass on the outside of the window and, using a flat-bladed knife, gently finish it off by smoothing it.

Now trim any surplus putty away with the blunt part of a knife – none of it should be visible above the rebate from the inside of the room.

replace the glass than the contents of your home.

Wearing a pair of thick leather gloves, push away the broken or shattered glass. If there's a lot left in the frame you can knock this out with gentle taps from a hammer. (Do bear in mind, though, where it is going to fall.)

Most glaziers will cut glass to exact requirements for you so measure up your window carefully before ordering. Glass fits into L-shaped rebates on the outside of the window frame so measure the full width and height between the outside edges of this rebate. Deduct about 0.3cm ($\frac{1}{8}$in) from both measurements to allow for expansion once the glass is in place.

Clear away the old putty from around the window frame, using a chisel. Mould some new putty until it is soft and pliable then press it into the rebate all round the frame. Carefully lift up the new pane and press it into the putty. Tap in window sprigs to hold the pane in place. Apply more putty on the other side of the frame, if it is accessible, and smooth it for a neat finish. Trim off any excess so that it is not visible from inside the room. Leave to dry thoroughly.

Furniture

Furniture, unfortunately, is no longer built to last the way it was in our grandparents' time. But minor repairs, requiring only a few simple tools and a basic know-how, can easily be undertaken at home.

Repairing uneven legs: The table or chair with one leg shorter than all the others is funnier on the music hall stage than when it happens at home. So, too, is the idea of sawing down three legs to match the short one. It's also much harder than you think; much more sensible to build up the deficient leg. First, though, check that it is the leg and not the floor which is uneven.

The best way to repair the leg is to use small pieces of wood to build it up until the furniture is standing squarely. If you can find one piece that is exactly the right size all the better, otherwise use a pva adhesive to glue several small pieces until you reach the required height. Use panel pins to hold the pieces together if necessary.

Alternatively, you can buy a nail-on stud such as those used to stop scratches on floors and hammer it into the leg until the height is right.

Repairing wobbly legs: Constant wear and weight, unevenly distributed, can cause furniture to develop wobbly legs. However, legs can be attached in many different ways and before you can remedy the damage you should take a look underneath to determine the type of join. If there are any screws then tighten them as much as possible. If the holes have worn too large then try replacing the screw with a larger one.

If this still does not solve the problem then turn the furniture upside down to check out exactly what bits are loose. Test each leg separately—if it is a chair place it upside down with the seat section on a table so that you can hold it still while you test the legs. When you have located the cause of the wobble you can buy a metal bracket of a suitable size and shape to hold the pieces securely together. Check you have the right size screws for the bracket, then hold the bracket in place and, with a pencil, mark where the screws are to go. Use a bradawl to make holes to start the screws off. Insert the screws into the holes and, with a screwdriver, tightly drive them into the wood.

Problem drawers: Drawers that stick can be infuriating and the temptation to force them open or shut is sometimes overwhelming. However, the problem is usually fairly simply resolved. First find out what sort of drawer it is. There are two main types: those which slide on runners (identified by a groove in the side), and those which slide on their bottom edge (these have plain sides).

It could be that the drawer has swollen due to extra moisture content in the air. This is especially likely if you have just moved house or changed the position of the cupboard with the troublesome door. In either case allow a couple of weeks for the timber to shrink and adjust. If the drawer is completely stuck, try drying out the furniture by directing a fan heater on it from a distance of a metre away—but only do this for an hour or so.

A drawer that is constantly causing trouble sticking can be eased by rubbing down the runners with a medium-grade glasspaper. Do the same, too, for the runners in the cupboard. Brush away any particles of dust and rub over the newly smoothed areas with a bar of soap or a wax candle.

Infected furniture: We all know the tell-tale pin-prick-sized holes left by the woodworm—but not so much about getting rid of this persistent pest.

To treat infected furniture first dust it down then remove any drawers, shelves, or attachments and following the instructions carefully, apply the woodworm fluid, working it well into any cracks. Do the same with any infected drawers or shelves. This should kill any woodworm up to a depth of about 0.3cm ($\frac{1}{8}$in) but to get rid of larvae you will need to follow up with an injection treatment which will force the liquid deeper into the wood. There are several well-known brands on the market. Leave the item for a few days in a well-ventilated room. Wipe off any surplus insecticide with a dry cloth and fill the exit holes with woodfiller—so that you can see at a glance if there are any new attacks.

When one leg is shorter than the others on a chair, it's easier to build up the short leg rather than shorten the others.

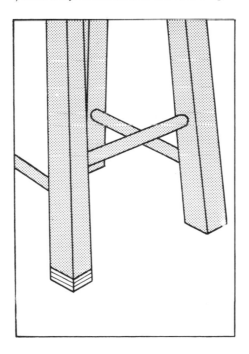

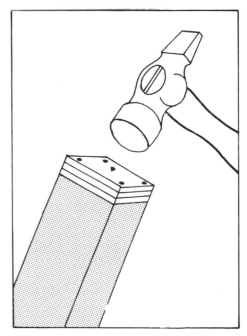

Dealing with stains

Now you see it, now you don't. Stain removal, unfortunately, doesn't work by magic but by knowing what stains are, by knowing what to do—and by doing it quickly—most stains can be easily removed.

There are three principal types of stain:

1. Stains from water-based substances (fruit juices, alcoholic drinks) can, in most cases, be removed by soaking immediately in water.

2. Stains from substances containing oil, waxes or grease (butter, candle grease) require the use of dry solvents such as carbon tetrachloride to effect their removal.

3. Stains from chemical substances (paints, lacquers, glues) are best treated by professional cleaners, although oil based paint can be treated at home.

If a garment or fabric is stained when the proper stain removers are not immediately available (see adjoining table for these), emergency treatment will often prevent a stain from sinking into the fabric. Tea, coffee, fruit juice and alcoholic drink stains must be soaked in cold water immediately, and grease spots should be dusted with talcum powder. Remove the stain with the correct chemical as soon as it is reasonably possible.

Using chemical solvents

Most solvents are highly inflammable, so never use them near a naked flame. Keep all solvents and chemicals out of reach of children, never use in confined spaces and never apply a second, different solvent or chemical until the first one has dried completely and the fabric has been thoroughly rinsed with water.

Cottonwool 'buds' are effective for applying solvents to very small stains. For large stains, pad the end of a small stick with cottonwool, cover with a scrap of cotton fabric and tie with cotton thread.

Place an absorbent pad under the stain, preferably made from white towelling, and, working from the back of the fabric, apply the solvent gently, working in a ring starting from just outside the stain and proceeding towards the centre, using more solvent as you work.

Here is an easy-to-read alphabetical guide to help you when such an emergency occurs.

Furniture and other fabrics		
Stain	Washable	Dry Clean
Alcohol	Blot immediately, rinse in cold water and wash	Blot immediately then sponge with a solution of 1 teaspoon white vinegar to $\frac{1}{2}$ litre water.
Beverages (coffee, tea, milk, soft drinks)	Blot, then wash in a solution of 2 tablespoons borax to $\frac{1}{2}$ litre warm water	Blot, then apply a proprietary stain remover.
Blood, egg	Rinse in cold water straight away	Dab with a mixture of 2 drops ammonia to a cup of cold water. For more stubborn marks mix a paste of cold water and washing starch. Apply to stain, leave to dry, then brush off.
Burns, scorches	Soak in glycerine or sponge with a solution of 2 tablespoons borax to $\frac{1}{2}$ litre warm water	Mix a paste with borax and glycerine and apply to stain. When dry brush off and damp sponge.
Fat	Rub gently with carbon tetrachloride or a brand cleaner.	Same as washable fabric.
Ink (fresh)	Sponge with detergent suds. If fabric is white, also sprinkle with solution of salt and lemon juice. Leave for an hour then wash.	Same as washable except do not give final wash.
Ink (ball-point)	Gently press a cloth dampened with methylated spirits against the stain then wash.	Same as washable except do not give final wash.
Mildew	Apply lemon juice and leave to dry.	Moisten with lemon juice, sprinkle with salt and leave to dry. Sponge gently.
Oil, grease or tar	Sponge with turpentine, rinse and then wash.	Sponge with turpentine, then with clean water.
Paint	Soak emulsion stains in cold water. Dab oil-based stains with turpentine.	Sponge emulsion stains with cold water. Dab turpentine on oil-based stains then sponge with clean water.
Urine and saline solutions	Rinse in clean water. Then immerse in a solution of 1 tablespoon white vinegar to $\frac{1}{2}$ litre water. Rinse then wash.	Sponge with solution of 1 tablespoon white vinegar to $\frac{1}{2}$ litre water.

Carpets

Carpets are a little more difficult to put to rights when they get stained – but they're not impossible to clean, if you know how. There are two basic methods of cleaning carpets (both referred to in the alphabetical guide which follows): dry cleaning and wet cleaning.

Dry cleaning: Apply carbon tetrachloride or trichlorethylene to the stain using a clean towel. Rub in a circular motion starting at the outer edge of the stain and working gradually towards the centre. Keep dampening the towel with the cleaning fluid every 20 seconds or so and blot the stained area thoroughly between each application.

The fumes from these dry cleaning fluids can be very strong, by the way, so do always try to work in a well-ventilated room and, most importantly, keep the solvents well out of the reach of children.

Don't try to clean rubber or latex-backed carpets with these solvents – the fluids will corrode the carpet materials.

Wet cleaning: Apply a good carpet cleaning shampoo to the stain with a sponge or towel. Keep adding more suds until the stain begins to disappear. Blot to remove the lather with clean water. Then leave the area to dry with the pile sloping in the right direction. If possible, do try to remove the carpet from the floor while it's drying so that the air can circulate freely and thus minimize the possibility of mildew occurring.

Carpets	
Stain	**Method of cleaning**
Beer	Wet clean.
Burns, scorches	Clip off the burned fibres. Wet clean wool carpets. Synthetic types will need expert cleaning.
Coffee	Wet clean.
Fruit	Wet clean. If stain persists then rub with methylated spirits.
Grass	Wipe with a clean cloth dipped in methylated spirits before wet cleaning.
Ink	Wet clean fresh ink. Ball-point marks should be wiped with methylated spirits mixed with a teaspoon of white vinegar. Blot quickly to stop stain spreading. Wet clean.
Milk	Wet clean.
Oil, grease	Wipe off as much as possible then dry clean followed by a wet clean.
Paint	Scrape off surplus paint then dry clean followed by a wet clean.
Salt	This attracts moisture and will quickly discolour a carpet unless swept up immediately.
Shoe polish	Scrape off as much as possible then wet clean.
Spirits	Dry clean.
Tea	Wet clean.
Wines	Dry clean.

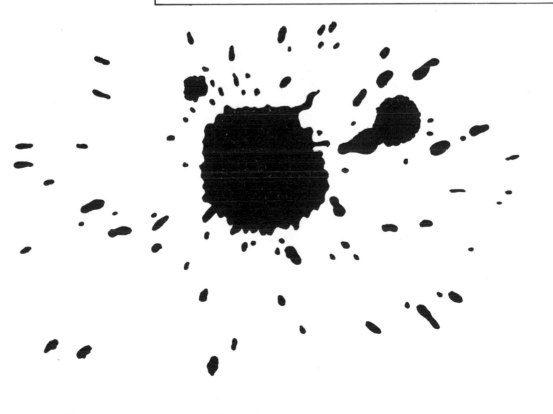

Taking care of your clothes

Clothes need cherishing. Once that meant valets and ladies' maids for the rich—hard work for the rest. Now new fabrics and cleaning aids make it easier to keep clothes looking good.

The secret is good organization, for which there are three golden rules:
1. Take a few minutes each day to put clothes away properly and in good order.
2. Deal with problems quickly—sooner done, easier to put right.

3. Set aside time periodically for a session of catching up and putting right.

Day by day
To get maximum wear out of clothes, especially suits, wear them in rotation. (Never wear a suit more than two days running.) Always hang clothes up immediately after wearing—if left in a warm heap, crumples will set.

For day-to-day care you need a first rate clothes brush, also a sponge or plastic foam 'brush' to deal with surface dirt or dust. Brush outdoor clothes before you hang them up (dust is grit and grit eventually breaks up the

The perfectly planned storage unit, with provision for long and shorter clothes, pull-out drawers and numerous shelves at various levels.

fibres). Close all fastenings as you hang up the garments to help support them. Then give them a while to air before consigning them to the wardrobe.

Aim to put each garment away in the state you would like to meet it next time you go to put it on.

Collars : Clean greasy collars or necklines marked with make-up with a grease solvent. Frequent, light sessions do a much better job than intermittent scrubs.

Defluffing clothes: If your regular clothes brush or sponge won't do the trick, wind a piece of Sellotape around your hand, sticky side out, and rub gently over the surface of the cloth. (Works wonders with velvet.)

Hangers: Good hangers are essential. Heavy coats and suits should hang on shaped wooden hangers. For dresses, pad thin hangers with old laddered tights or stockings, and cover with pretty scraps of material. Longer skirts need an extra, centre skirt carrier; long dresses with waist bands should be hung from the waist.

Wardrobes: Try not to squash too many clothes into too small a cupboard—try to keep out-of-season clothes in bags on a rail in the attic or spare room.

Deal with problems fast

Deal with tears, loose buttons, unstitched hems and stains as soon as possible. Here are a few pointers:

Buttons: Buttons are not always well sewn on ready-made clothes. Sew them on properly before they drop off.

Cigarette burns: Good clothes should always be dealt with by an invisible mender but the following method does a fair patch-up job for unimportant, light-weight clothes. But practise on a scrap first! Snip off all charred threads with scissors, to leave a neat, clean, round hole. Cut out a patch of matching cloth slightly larger than the hole, and another patch of fine polythene sheeting (dry cleaners' bags will do) to the same size. Place the damaged cloth on to a sheet of clean paper, right side down, place the polythene patch over the hole, then the cloth patch, and gently press the lot with a hot iron in order to melt the polythene and 'glue' the two fabrics together invisibly. However, this trick will not work on heavier fabrics.

Hems: If desperate, use Sellotape or double-sided tape to keep up a small length of hem until you can deal with it properly.

Knitwear, piling and matting: It's worth investing in a teazle brush or special knitwear 'defuzzer'. Stroke lightly and in one direction.

Pulls and catches: If the thread is not broken, ease it back as far as possible, then hook the remaining loop through to the wrong side with the head of a pin.

Rips and tears: Again, these should be dealt with by a professional invisible mender or carefully darned. As a last resort, adhesive fabric tape can be

quite successfully stuck to the wrong side of the fabric. It will stand up to washing, but not dry cleaning.

The periodic session

Suits: In between dry cleaning, sponge and press about every six weeks. To do this, you need a stout wooden-backed brush, a pad or wad of fabric for holding under the shoulder seams, a couple of damp cloths—and a firm hand.

First brush the suit vigorously. Lay it flat and rub all over with the dampened cloth to remove loosened surface dust. Lay the area to be pressed carefully on the board, put

over a clean damp pressing cloth and press firmly, lifting the iron carefully each time. Take care! If the suiting is a blend, too hot an iron and too much pressure can ruin the cloth.

Pressing trousers: Press the waist and upper part first. Open the waist band and front fastening and slip the trousers on to the end of the ironing board. Begin by pressing the right fly front, then the right pocket. Move the garment around and press the back

The ultimate in clothes maintenance: an impromptu laundry room, created by screening off a corner of the kitchen which has adequate ventilation.

waist seam, left pocket and left fly front. Use the left hand to flatten pocket linings as you press. Lift the trousers from the ironing board and, holding them by the waist, bring both waist pleats together. With the right hand, grasp the trouser leg bottoms and reverse the trousers so that the waist hangs down, the leg creases in line with the waist pleats. Lay the trousers on the ironing board with the left leg underneath. Turn the right trouser leg back so that the inner seam of the left leg and the crotch is exposed. Press and, holding the leg bottom edges even, stretch the leg to reshape the knee. Press the front and back creases firmly. Bring the right trouser leg back over the pressed leg and turn the trousers over. Turn the pressed left leg back carefully and press the right in the same way as the left.

Pressing jackets: To press a jacket, it's worth making a pressing pad—a 23cm (9in) square bag stuffed firmly with kapok. Start by pressing the collar, opened out and flat. Next, the right hand front, working from the hem to the waist and pressing through a damp cloth. As you work, move the pressed area away from you so that it will not become creased again. Now press the area above the waist (for a woman's jacket, use the pressing pad to press the bust). Press underarm area. Press back. Press left underarm. Press left front. Next, sleeves. Sleeves must never have a crease, and the simplest way to avoid this if you do not have a sleeve board is to lay the edge of the sleeve so that it falls over the edge of the board and therefore does not receive the weight of the iron. Turn the sleeve gradually so that the whole area is pressed. Finish the shoulders by pressing over the pad to keep the curve full. Finish by opening the revers out flat and pressing from the underside. Don't fold the collar or revers back and press — just roll them gently back into position.

Ironing shirts: Set the iron to the correct reading for the shirt fabric — hot for cotton or linen. The shirt should be slightly and evenly damp. Turn the garment inside out and iron the yoke, pleat heading, seams and hems until they are dry. Turn the shirt to the right side and iron the collar, both inside and outside, and then the cuffs, stretching the material taut and ironing until the fabric is quite dry. Next, iron the sleeves, using a sleeve board if available, or fold the sleeve along the underarm seam and

iron to within 0.6cm ($\frac{1}{4}$in) of the outer fold. Then refold and iron the un-ironed strip, taking care not to make a sharp crease along the sleeve. Do both sleeves in the same way, setting the pleat in the cuff edge.

Iron first the back and then the front of the shirt, working the point of the iron around the buttons and taking care with the shoulders. Fasten the buttons and iron the front again and, if there is a pocket, press it flat.

Turn the shirt over and lay it front downwards. Fold the fronts back on the shirt so that the sleeves lie flat on the shirt back. You will probably find that a piece of cardboard cut to measure 35.5cm (14in) long and 18cm (7in) wide will be of help in keeping the two sides equally folded. Slip the cardboard out. Fold the shirt tail up about one-third of the length of the shirt, and then fold again.

Shine: Removing shine is a temporary affair, since shine usually means that the cloth has worn thin. Before attempting any remedial action, brush the suit thoroughly, then sponge the worn area with a solution of vinegar and warm water. Rinse with a clean cloth wrung out in warm water. Pass a hot iron very lightly over a damp cloth on both sides of the shiny area — to 'swell' the fibres, not to flatten them! For light materials use the same system, but add ammonia to water (about 1 tablespoon to half a litre).

Baggy skirts, trousers and elbows: You may be able to shrink the cloth back to its original shape. To do this, lay the affected area on the ironing board and cover with a well damped cloth. Stroke the cloth with the iron without pressing, to force the steam into the fibres. Leave to 'set' and dry before further handling.

Trouser and pleat creases: For a crisp crease, rub the inside of where it should be with hard yellow household soap. Then press in the normal way with a damp cloth, making sure the crease is in exactly the right position.

Perspiration: If the garment is washable, soak in cool enzyme detergent (test for colour fastness first). To try to revive colour, sponge with a weak solution of vinegar or ammonia before washing (again, test first). Sponge clothes (except rayon) which can't be washed with methylated spirits and rub gently in a circular motion with a dry cloth. To remove odour, first soak the garment in warm water with borax (1 teaspoonful to half a litre). Wash in warm soapy water to which a few drops of ammonia have been added.

Rinse well. If the fabric is suitable, try to dry in sunshine — sun always has a sweetening effect.

Linings: A cheap, unlined skirt always looks better for having a lining. Choose a firm, inexpensive rayon.

Knitwear, stretched collars and cuffs: If careful washing and flat drying can't remedy this, darn two or three rows of shirring elastic round on the wrong side of the garment.

Metallic embroidery and lamé: To clean gold work or other metallic embroidery, gently brush in bicarbonate of soda. After a few minutes, brush out with another soft, clean cloth.

Artificial flowers: These revive if

held in the steam from a boiling kettle.

Feathers: Shake several times in soapy lather. Rinse well in warm, then cold, water, and dry slowly in a warm oven with the door open, taking them out from time to time to curl them over the edge of a blunt knife.

Care of clothes brushes: To get fluff out of a bristle clothes brush, rub warm porridge flakes or oatmeal into the bristles and leave for a few hours. Shake, comb out, and rub with a clean cloth. (Too much washing makes bristles soft.) Nylon brushes can of course be washed.

Storage

As mentioned under day-by-day care, it's useless to overhaul a dress and press it beautifully — then plunge it into an overcrowded wardrobe. If you have a corner anywhere in the house to hang out-of-season clothes in plastic bags, do so. (Remember to clean them before putting them away.) Keep heavy clothes at one end of the wardrobe, lighter ones at the other. The greatest treat for all clothes is adequate storage space. Store knitwear in a drawer, not on hangers. Allow air to circulate, rather than keeping jerseys, etc in bags. Always store metallic embroidery and lamé in acid-free tissue paper.

Work basket

A well-stocked work basket is in-valuable. It should include small supplies of the following: elastic (sufficient for a pair of underpants), dressmaker's pins, needles, cotton, assorted safety pins, Sellotape, pearl and trouser buttons, adhesive fabric tape, cash for emergencies, foam pad and spot removal fluid — with ammonia, vinegar and borax near to hand, plus clean cloths and a pressing pad.

Even if your ambitions stop at making adequate repairs to clothes and soft furnishings, a well-organized sewing area, with some space for ironing or laying out materials is a good idea. If possible, choose somewhere with lots of natural light.

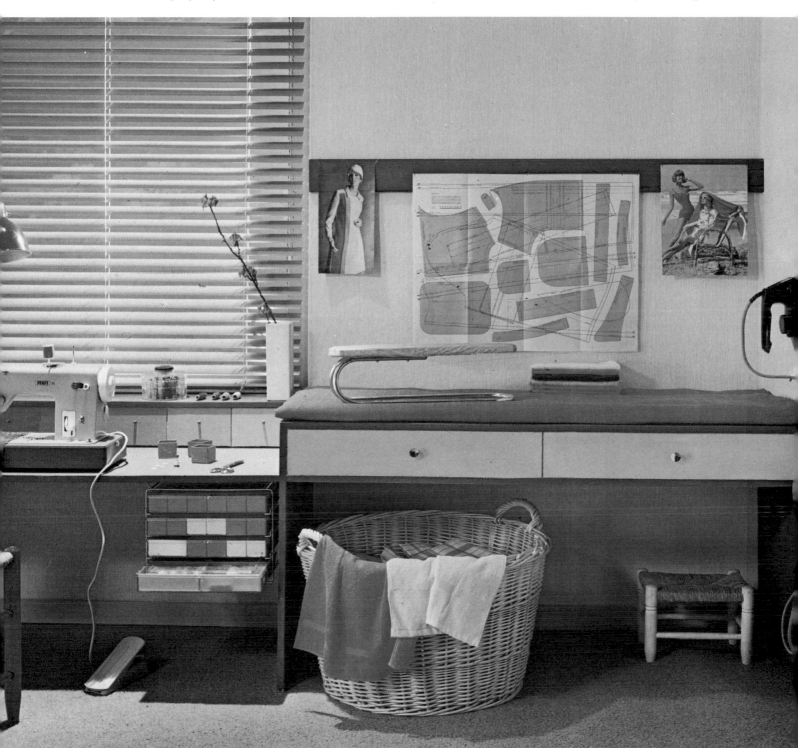

Kitchen crafts

Shopping shrewdly

Running a household for the first time can be a daunting experience; there's a budget (usually limited) to be adhered to, a new husband to be fed, a new flat or house to be kept up to scratch. And nowadays, more often than not, all of this has to be done in addition to a full-time job. So planning your shopping wisely is not just moderately desirable—it's absolutely necessary in order to maintain even basic sanity!

Organizing your shopping trips
If it's at all possible, organize your buying expeditions in advance, perhaps even on a weekly cycle. Sit down (say on Friday evenings or Saturday mornings) and work out your menus for the week and just what you will require to be able to cook them. You don't have to be too exact, of course, but doing this will help to cut down journeys to the supermarket (if you're a working wife, you'll be anxious to do that), and if you happen to be fortunate enough to possess a refrigerator or freezer it will enable you to use them efficiently. Most foods can be stored in the refrigerator for at least two or three days — and many foods can be stored

in the freezer for several months (storing and freezing are dealt with in detail on pages 132 – 141).

Buying sceptically
Armed with your shopping list, you can now put your consumerism to the test. Don't just race through the supermarket, picking up the first jar of coffee that meets your eye. Be selective —and sceptical.

Be suspicious of the 'bargains' that scream at you from prominent shelves. Some are genuine of course (and should therefore be snapped up) but the word is often used 'loosely' and a product offered at a reduced price may be cheaper simply because the quality is poorer than a more expensive brand. A cheap strawberry jam, for instance, may well be made from sweetened fruit pulp rather than genuine fruit and may ferment quickly, so it certainly would not turn out to be the bargain it first appeared to be. In other cases, the price of the reduced product may have been raised before being brought down again. This practice is, in fact, strictly illegal and if you do happen to come across instances of it happening you can take legal action against the offending shopkeeper.

Be sceptical about packaging too. Instead of looking at the pretty illustrations and breathless prose, check the small print. Every prepacked product is required by law to describe accurately the contents of its package, tin or carton. If the small print says 'tuna fish' you can therefore be certain you're getting tuna fish and not some other, cheaper type of fish with tuna flavouring added. That flavour phrase is something else to watch out for, by the way. The words 'rum flavour', 'caramel flavour', or 'strawberry flavour', don't mean that rum, caramel or strawberries are ingredients in a given product but that substances that taste somewhat similar to them have been added.

Take a sharp look at labels. By law, manufacturers are required not only to list all of the ingredients used in, say, their Irish stew or vegetable soup, but also to list them in descending order by weight. So avoid an Irish stew that lists the lamb or mutton halfway down the list of ingredients!

Finally, keep a sharp look out for manufacturers who package their goods wastefully — *you're* ultimately paying for that inner layer of waxed paper enclosed by cardboard which in turn is covered in cellophane.

Buying in bulk

A bit of planning also comes in useful when you decide what you can safely buy in 'family packs' and what would be more convenient in smaller quantities. The important prerequisite for buying in bulk is to ascertain in your own mind that the product in question is something you will use regularly and use up fairly quickly — even dry food deteriorates somewhat in time. A large-size bag of flour may seem a great saving at the time — and so it will prove to be if you're an enthusiastic bread or cake maker, but if you only use flour to thicken the occasional sauce or stew, then you're probably saving money in the end by sticking to smaller bags. Things like pasta, rice and olive/cooking oil do store well, however, and are almost always worth buying in bulk. Herbs and spices are NOT usually worth buying in large quantities; they lose their potency eventually and are used in such minute amounts that even a few grams will last quite a long time.

Remember that fresh produce, such as fruit, vegetables, meat or fish do not, as a rule, lend themselves to bulk buying unless you have a freezer; they are best eaten on the day or a day or two after purchase and unless you can consume prodigious quantities, it's probably safer — and better — to assess only what you need and buy as you go along.

Buying for convenience

The advent of frozen food on the market has probably revolutionized both cooking and eating habits in this country, and there is no doubt that, used sensibly, they can be a real boon to the busy housewife. But *DO* remember before you get over-enthusiastic at the frozen food counter that they are *always* considerably more expensive than their fresh food equivalents. If convenience is not a problem and you have a choice between, say, fresh and frozen vegetables, the interests of economy alone should dictate your choice.

Frozen foods do come into their own as standby foods, however. And it is a good idea to keep a couple of packets of vegetables and perhaps some fish in your refrigerator or freezer for emergency use — or for that evening when you simply can't face the idea of preparing yet another meal from scratch. Remember to follow the storage instructions when you buy packets of frozen food, though. If a manufacturer specifies that a packet of frozen peas will keep for two weeks at a given temperature, he has a reason for it. So check that your refrigerator can be set to that level and *don't* keep the peas for any longer than the manufacturer recommends.

Buying fresh

Buying fresh food the day you intend to eat it is getting the best of all possible worlds. But it is important not to over-buy and that means sitting down and making some brief calculations about just how much you think you can consume within the two or three days most fresh food will be worth eating. Items like lamb or pork chops are easy — just buy one large one each or two small ones; but what about stewing beef or mince, say? All recommendations of amounts of food depend on individual appetites, of course, but a rough guide, a starting-off point, would be to allow about 450 grams (1 pound) of stewing beef or minced beef for two people, then adjust up or down according to consumption. On roasts or meat you buy on the bone, allow between 175 and 250 grams (6 and 10 ounces) per person; on meat off the bone, such as fillet steak, about 125 to 175 grams (4 to 6 ounces) is probably enough — and probably all you can afford anyway!

Fish is best bought by number rather than weight. Allow one medium-sized whole fish per person, and one medium-sized fillet (very small sole fillets may not be filling enough and you may need one and a half for a really hungry man). For fish steaks, let your eyes be your guide; one fairly good-sized one would probably make a very adequate helping for one.

Fruit and vegetables are more difficult to assess but both will keep somewhat longer than meat or fish, so it isn't so critical if you over-buy a little. Potatoes, for instance, will keep reasonably well for a week or so and can be bought safely in money-saving quantities such as a kilo to a kilo and a half or three or four pounds, especially if you serve them at most evening meals. Allow at least one or two large potatoes per person. Vegetables such as carrots, turnips, Brussels sprouts or cabbage all depend on personal taste but assuming they will be served as a second vegetable with meat or fish, then about 450 grams (1 pound) (weighed before peeling) should be adequate for two people.

If you buy fruit mainly as a mid-evening snack, then you should probably buy it in fairly small quantities, but if you buy it, as an increasing number of people do, as a nourishing and easy-to-serve dessert, then obviously quantities can be slightly larger — although one average-sized apple per person is probably enough and, say, two or three plums.

Cutting corners

Buying food can be an expensive business; planning can help somewhat of course but in addition most housewives concoct their own short cuts as they go along. There are some general money-saving devices well worth passing along, to start you off:

Buy fruit and vegetables seasonally whenever possible, that is when they're at their cheapest and best.

If you've acquired some pretty herb and spice jars as a wedding gift, you can save quite a bit of money by purchasing your dried herbs and spices 'loose' from delicatessens rather than in those small — and costly — jars. Or, better still, invest in a window box and grow your own herbs — fresh ones taste better than dried and a small herb box on a kitchen window can add a pretty finishing touch to your decor.

It's worthwhile investing in some large storage jars, some small storage jars and some screw-top jars. There's nothing worse than slightly damp sugar or salt, and all dried foods will keep better — and look prettier — if neatly stored away in airtight containers. Smaller jars come into their own in the case of products in daily use, such as coffee or tea; if you buy in bulk, pour a small amount into a small storage jar and put away the remainder; thus a nasty accident such as spilling the coffee or tea all over the kitchen floor is a bit less fatal — both in terms of money lost and temper expended on cleaning up the mess! Screw-top jars are a particularly good investment. They enable you to make salad dressings in bulk, to store home-made stock and such things as pasta sauces until you next fancy spaghetti. They were obviously invented with the busy housewife specially in mind!

Buy own brand goods whenever possible. Despite what brand manufacturers say, at least a proportion of the difference in price is in advertising and public relations for the brand name product. It's certainly worthwhile experimenting anyway and then you can decide for yourself whether you want to spend the extra and invest in the known brand product.

Nutrients in your food

Nutrients	What they do	Where to find them
Carbohydrates **Sugar**	Sugar is easily digested and can provide energy quickly	Sugar—fine, coarse, brown, white, icing or confectioners' Sweet foods such as cakes, puddings, chocolate, candy, jams and preserves, honey, treacle, molasses, syrup Soft drinks Fresh and dried fruits
Starch	Starch is a major source of heat and energy	Cereals including wheat, maize, corn, oatmeal, rice Potatoes, arrowroot, cassava, yams Peas, beans, lentils Bread, pastry and pasta
Cellulose	Cellulose forms the structural material of plant cell walls. The human body is unable to digest cellulose, but it does provide valuable bulk and fibre	Present in most fruit and green, leafy vegetables
Fats	Provide energy and insulate the body against heat loss	Vegetable oils and fats, including sunflower, corn, palm, olive, coconut, groundnut or peanut, soya and kernel oils Animal fats Fish oils Butter and margarine Milk, cheese and cream Nuts
Proteins	Play a vital role in the growth, repair and maintenance of body tissues and provide energy	Meat, poultry, fish Milk, cheese, eggs Lentils, beans, peas
Vitamins **Vitamin A**	Necessary for growth especially in children, an aid to good eyesight and healthy skin	Deep-yellow foods, such as carrots, sweet potatoes, apricots, peaches, cantaloup. Also butter, margarine, Cheddar cheese, liver, and dark green vegetables, such as spinach and broccoli

Nutrients	What they do	Where to find them
Thiamine (B)	Assists the metabolism of carbohydrates, proteins and fats and chemical processes giving a steady release of energy	Meat, especially pork and ham, poultry Whole grain or enriched breads and cereals Eggs
Riboflavin (B_2)	Helps the body to get energy from food and is found in all body tissues	Milk and cheese Eggs Fish, poultry, liver and kidney Whole-grain breads, yeast and cereals
Niacin (Nicotinic Acid)	Plays an important role in growth, healthy skin and nerves. Helps the body obtain energy from food	Meat, liver, poultry, fish Milk Nut butters Bread, yeast, beans, peas
Biotin	Necessary for the health of the skin and helps liberate energy from food	Intestinal bacteria in healthy people usually manufacture enough Biotin to supply requirements, but good food sources are egg yolks, liver, kidney
Folic Acid (Folacin)	Helps in the formation of red blood cells and the reproductive system	Meat, kidney and liver Whole-grain cereals, yeast Spinach, watercress, cabbage Dried peas, beans and nuts
Pantothenic Acid	Involved in releasing energy from carbohydrates and the metabolism of fatty acids. Aids the health of the skin, growth and the production of antibodies	Widely distributed in animal tissue Whole-grain cereals, yeast Egg yolk Beans and peas
Vitamin B_6 (Pyridoxine)	Concerned with growth, the nervous system, fat, protein and carbohydrate metabolism and the health of the skin	Since B_6 is not a single substance but a collection of substances, it is available from both animal and plant sources. Liver, ham, butter beans, lima beans, yeast and corn are good sources

Nutrients	What they do	Where to find them
Vitamin B$_{12}$	Essential for the normal functioning of all cells, necessary for growth especially of nerve cells	Liver is the richest source, also other meat, milk, eggs and fish. It is mostly found in foods of animal origin and therefore can be a problem for strict vegetarians
Vitamin C (Ascorbic Acid)	The main function is to assist in the formation of connective tissue, bone, skin and cartilage. It has multiple functions to do with blood vessels, red blood pigment, iron deposits, wound healing and resistance to infection	Found predominantly in green peppers, Brussels sprouts, broccoli, cabbage, cauliflower, potatoes, tomatoes, citrus fruits, blackcurrants, strawberries and cantaloup. This is a dangerously lacking vitamin for followers of all-grain diets
Vitamin D	Vital for healthy teeth and bones, especially important in infants, adolescents, during pregnancy and during old age	Simple exposure to sunshine may fill all the required needs. Other sources of vitamin D are fish—liver oils, liver and egg yolk. Because of its scarcity in foods, margarine and butter are fortified with Vitamin D
Vitamin E	Essential for normal metabolism. There are no proven advantages to large intakes of Vitamin E, except in cases of malabsorption of fats	Wheat germ, Brussels sprouts, spinach, cauliflower, cabbage, vegetable oils, margarine, meat, eggs and nuts
Vitamin K	Essential for the normal clotting of the blood	Green leafy vegetables, cauliflower, green peas, liver, egg yolk and soya oil
Minerals Calcium	Necessary for the proper development and maintenance of bones and teeth, the normal clotting of blood and the functioning of muscles. Widespread deficiency in calcium exists where iodine and fluoride supplies are low	Milk, cheese, bread, fortified flour, green vegetables, parsley Fish, such as sardines, where the bones are eaten
Phosphorus	Together with calcium it forms most of the hard structure of bones and teeth. It is involved in reproduction and the transfer of hereditary characteristics	Present in nearly all foods and calcium sources, also in meat, fish, eggs, milk and cereals

Nutrients	What they do	Where to find them
Copper	Involved in the chemistry of the blood and aids in the absorption and utilization of iron. Copper deficiencies in human beings are rare	Ordinary diets provide a sufficient supply. Good sources are liver, kidney, shellfish, nuts, raisins, cereals, peas, beans, spinach, lettuce and cabbage
Fluoride	Incorporated in the structure of bones and teeth and necessary for the resistance of tooth decay	Fish, cheese, milk and seafoods are good sources. Water fluoridation is recommended where the fluoride level is low
Iodine	Important to the healthy functioning of the thyroid gland. Deficiency may cause goitre	Seafoods and iodized salts
Iron	Most iron in the body is present in the red colouring pigment in the blood. It is now considered the most lacking nutrient, especially among women. Deficiencies also exist where iodine and fluoride supplies are low	Red meats, especially organ meats, whole-grains, prunes, raisins, molasses, dried fruits, dark green vegetables, such as spinach, broccoli, cabbage. Also present in water and wine
Magnesium	An important constituent of all soft tissue and bone. Involved in the release of energy during metabolism	Sea salt, olives, nuts, peas, beans, cocoa, chocolate
Sodium, Potassium and Chloride	These minerals are often called electrolytes. They maintain an inner balance of body fluids. Contribute to metabolic processes	All are readily available in common foods, particularly in salt and sea salt. Frequently sodium (table salt) intake can be harmfully high
The trace minerals Chromium, Cobalt, Manganese, Molybdenum, Silenium, Zinc and possibly others	In minute amounts these minerals are necessary for normal metabolism	Spinach, lettuce, cauliflower, cabbage, organ meats and lean meats
Water	Water is not usually considered a nutrient, but it plays a vital role in bodily functions. It is well known that human beings can survive without food much longer than they can without water	Water or other fluids. 80 to 90 per cent of fresh fruits are composed of water and 10 to 15 per cent of such foods as flour

Storing food

Food	Storage	Best preparation	Source of
Apples Keep in a cool room	Peel only when necessary. Rub cut apples with lemon juice so that they will not turn brown. When stewing, use only a tiny bit of water.	Very little vitamin C	
Artichokes, globe 2 to 3 days in a dark, dry place or covered in the refrigerator	Wash under running water. Trim the stems, remove tough outer leaves and cut off the spiky tips of inner leaves. Rub cut places with lemon juice to prevent discolouration. Cook in boiling, salted water for 20 to 30 minutes. Serve hot with melted butter or cold with vinaigrette sauce.	A little of vitamins B and C	
Asparagus 2 days in a plastic bag in the refrigerator	Wash carefully. Cut off a little of thick white base of stalks. Tie in bunches and steam for about 25 minutes. Serve with melted butter.	Vitamin C	
Aubergine 3 days in warmest part of refrigerator or crisper drawer	Wash. Remove any hard stalk. Bake in casserole with butter and a little milk for 30 minutes.	Vitamin B group. Very little vitamin C	
Bananas Keep in a cool place—never in the refrigerator	Eat raw, in salads (particularly good with coconut) or fried as a dessert or accompaniment to pork or chicken.	Very little vitamin C	
Beans, green Buy only on the day they are needed or they will go limp	Wash and string. Cook quickly in a very little boiling water until barely tender. Drain, salt and toss in melted butter.	Vitamin C a little iron	
Beetroot Up to a week, loosely wrapped in a cool, dark place	Wash and boil until tender when pierced with a fork. Peel and serve hot with hollandaise sauce. To serve cold with salads, allow to cool unpeeled until required.	A little iron	
Blackcurrants Buy only on the day they are needed	Eat fresh with a little sugar and cream, or mash and stew with brown sugar until just tender.	Very rich in vitamin C	
Broccoli Buy only on day needed to prevent withering	Wash quickly in cold, running water. Steam until just tender and serve with melted butter or hollandaise sauce.	Vitamin C and iron	

Food	Storage	Best preparation	Source of
Brussels sprouts 2 to 3 days in a plastic bag in the refrigerator		For preparation and cooking instructions, see page 171.	Vitamin C and iron
White Cabbage 3 to 4 days in a plastic bag in the refrigerator		Best of all served raw, finely shredded, in salads. For preparation and cooking instructions see page 171.	Vitamin C and iron
Carrots 2 to 3 days in a cool, dark place		For preparation and cooking instructions, see page 171.	Vitamin A, a little vitamin C
Cauliflower 2 days in refrigerator, or 1 day loosely wrapped in paper in a cool, dark place		For preparation and cooking instructions, see page 171.	A little vitamin C and some iron
Celery 2 to 3 days in refrigerator if possible		Eat raw, after washing, in salads and with cheese. Or braise in a covered dish in a moderate oven.	Very little vitamin C
Cheese About 1 week, covered, in a cool, dark place		Use fresh or in any favourite recipes, but never cook for a long time.	Protein and vitamin A. High in calcium
Chicken Fresh—only keep 1 day in refrigerator. Frozen—cook immediately after defrosting		Use any recipe you choose, but try to use the juices from the bird in a sauce or gravy.	Protein. A little of the B-group vitamins
Courgettes 2 days in refrigerator		Wash, cut off stem end and slice thinly without peeling. Toss in melted butter over a low heat for 5 minutes. Salt lightly, add freshly-ground black pepper and serve with butter sauce from pan.	Very little vitamin C
Eggs 1 week, in cool, dark place, preferably not in the refrigerator			Protein. Vitamins A and D and B-group vitamins. Iron

Food	Storage	Best preparation	Source of
Fish Buy, cook and eat on the same day	Dry with kitchen paper towels before cooking. Use in any favourite recipes, retaining juices for sauces.	Protein, vitamins A and B and a little iron. Fatty fish such as kippers and salmon have vitamin D	
Grapefruit 3 to 5 days in refrigerator or cool place	Eat as a first course or add to salads. Try tossing it with chicory and orange segments or top with honey and grill for 5 minutes.	Vitamin C	
Leeks 3 to 5 days in a refrigerator. 1 day loosely wrapped in paper in a cool, dark place	Cut off roots and tough outer leaves and wash well. Melt butter, add leeks and cook in covered pan for 5 to 10 minutes. Add salt and freshly ground black pepper. Use in soups and stews in place of onions.	Some vitamin C	
Lemons 1 week in refrigerator	Squeeze and drink sweetened with brown sugar or use instead of vinegar in salad dressing.	Vitamin C	
Lettuce Buy on the day required	Wash quickly under running water and dry thoroughly. Toss in vinaigrette dressing just before serving.	A very little of vitamins A and C	
Meat 2 to 3 days covered in a refrigerator or buy on the day it is needed	Wipe with a damp cloth or kitchen paper towels before cooking. Use any recipe you like. Always use any juices that escape from the meat during cooking to make a sauce or gravy.	Protein. Vitamin B group. Liver and kidneys are exceptionally high in vitamin A and iron	
Melon 2 to 3 days when ripe	Eat sliced with no added sugar or dice and add to salads.	A little of vitamins A and C	
Milk Do not leave exposed to light. Keep in refrigerator	Do not boil or keep hot for any length of time.	Vitamins A and some B-group vitamins. Very rich in calcium	
Mushrooms Buy on the day they are needed	Wash thoroughly, but do not peel cultivated mushrooms. Trim stems. Try cooking in the oven for 20 minutes in aluminium foil parcel with pepper and lemon juice.	Very little of the B-group vitamins	

Food	Storage	Best preparation	Source of
Onions	Onions 2 to 3 weeks loosely wrapped in paper in a cool, dark place. Do not refrigerate	Use peeled in soups and stews, roast with meat, steamed with cheese sauce or stuffed and baked. For preparation and cooking instructions, see page 172.	Very little vitamin C
Oranges	Oranges Keep 4 to 6 days	Eat freshly peeled whenever possible. Try adding to salads.	High in vitamin C
Parsley	Parsley Wash and dry. Keep no longer than 3 to 6 days in a plastic container in refrigerator	Use as a garnish for salads, soups, sauces, meat and fish.	Vitamin C and iron
Peaches	Peaches 2 to 3 days in a cool place when ripe	Eat raw.	Vitamin A
Pears	Pears 2 to 4 days when ripe	Eat raw or bake, tightly covered, in the oven for about 30 minutes with a little butter. Then pour on single cream and serve immediately.	Only a very little vitamin B. Calcium and iron
Peas	Peas Buy and cook on day of purchase	For preparation and cooking instructions, see page 172.	Some of the B-group vitamins and vitamin C
Peppers	Peppers Wash and dry. Keep in plastic bag in refrigerator for crispness	Eat raw, sliced in salads. Try baking them. If you add them to casseroles, first blanch for a moment in boiling water and then refresh by pouring cold water over them.	Vitamin C and a little vitamin A
Pineapple	Pineapple Buy and eat when ripe	Eat without sugar. Sprinkle with a little liqueur for a change.	A little of vitamins A and C. Small amount of vitamin B
Potatoes	Potatoes Store in a dark place and never eat when they go green	For preparation and cooking instructions, see page 172.	Vitamin C and a very little vitamin B. Iron

Food	Storage	Best preparation	Source of
Plums 2 to 3 days when ripe	Eat raw or stew gently with brown sugar in a tightly covered pan until just tender.	Vitamin A
Raspberries Buy on day they are needed. Pick out bad or over-ripe fruit. Wash and dry before use	Eat as they are with cream and a little sugar if necessary.	Rich in vitamin C
Spinach Buy on the day required	Wash leaves thoroughly. Place in a pan without water and cook, shaking, over very low heat for about 10 minutes. Drain and salt. Serve with melted butter and freshly ground black pepper.	Vitamins A and C, calcium and iron
Spring Onions Keep 4 to 6 days in a plastic bag in the refrigerator	Use chopped in salads or as a garnish for stews and soups.	Some vitamin C
Strawberries Buy on day they are needed. Pick out any bad or over-ripe fruit. Wash and dry before use	Eat as they are with cream or sprinkled with kirsch.	Rich in vitamin C
Sweetcorn Buy on the day required and keep in plastic bag in refrigerator	Remove husk and 'silk'. Wash and cook in a little rapidly boiling water for 20 minutes. If cooked for too long, sweetcorn becomes tough. Serve with melted butter and salt to taste.	Vitamin A and a little B
Tomatoes Buy when really firm and store in refrigerator	Use raw in salads. When soft can be used in soups and stews.	Vitamins A and C
Turnips 3 to 4 days loosely covered in a cool, dark place	Wash, peel and use in soups and stews or steam and serve mashed with butter.	Little vitamin C
Watercress Buy on day required	Wash thoroughly under running water. Use raw in salads and as a garnish for meat and fish. Also makes a delicious soup.	Some of vitamins A and C and some iron and calcium

Freezing food

Freezing is the most natural way to preserve food if it is to retain the flavour, texture and colour closest to the original. To ensure successful freezing and to obtain the longest high-quality storage life, as well as justifying the preparation time, food selected for freezing *must* be really fresh.

The process of freezing retards the natural decay of food by inhibiting chemical and enzymatic changes which, if allowed to continue, result in food spoilage. It is important that food should be frozen as quickly as possible and this can only be achieved at home in a genuine food or home freezer.

What is a freezer?

A freezer is an appliance designed to extract heat quickly and to reduce the temperature of food down to $0°F$ ($-18°C$) or colder.

It is especially important that food passes quickly through the critical temperature range of $30°F$ ($-1°C$) to $23°F$ ($-5°C$). It is in this temperature range that most of the water in food freezes and small ice crystals are formed. If food is frozen slowly between these temperatures, large ice crystals are formed which puncture the cell walls in the food, causing eventual loss of colour, flavour and texture and a reduction in quality.

Food storage cabinets (conservators) and star-marked frozen food storage compartments in refrigerators should not be used to freeze food. These are only for storage of food already frozen.

Until recently, it has been difficult to distinguish between a conservator for storage and a chest type freezer. They look similar and both have top opening lids. However, an agreed symbol used internationally now marks genuine home freezers.

When using this symbol the appliance manufacturers must also indicate the maximum weight of food which will pass quickly through the critical temperature range and be frozen down to 0°F (—18°C) within 24 hours. In a genuine home freezer, this can be done without affecting the quality or texture of any of the frozen food already in the freezer.

Types of freezers

There are three different types of freezers: chest, upright and refrigerator freezers or combinations. Each type is available in a wide range of sizes — the size is expressed in cubic feet or litres. The choice of freezer is a personal one, depending on where it is to be located and the size required.

Chest freezers occupy proportionately more floor space, there is no work top, and access to particular packages of food is more difficult if the model is a large one.

The upright freezer takes up the minimum of floor space, having a front opening door, and it is easy to pack food on the shelves and find particular packages quickly.

The refrigerator/freezer combines a two-door refrigerator and a freezer, the refrigerator compartment preferably being located above the freezer. The larger two-door models usually have the refrigerator and freezer compartments arranged side by side.

When choosing a freezer it is well worth over-estimating the capacity required, providing, of course, it will fit into the planned space. Once installed, you'll find yourself using it more and more to store bought frozen food, and to freeze and store favourite dishes and basic recipe ingredients.

Wrapping Food for freezing

When food is prepared for freezing, it is very important that it is wrapped correctly, using special freezer packaging materials. If this isn't done, the very low temperature air will eventually dry out the food, making it tasteless and unpleasant to eat.

Freezer packaging materials are moisture and vapour-proof and resistant to breakage at low temperature. There is a wide range of wrapping materials and containers. Some of these are:

Freezer or heavy duty aluminium foil: This is one of the most convenient materials for wrapping as it is pliable, and easy to fold and to make airtight seals.

It can be used for meat, fish, poultry, cakes and breads. It can also be used for stews, soups and sauces. To freeze such liquids, line a dish with aluminium foil, leaving enough to wrap over. Pour the stew, soup or sauce into the lined dish and freeze. Remove the dish after the food is frozen, ensuring that the edges of the foil are properly sealed (if necessary using freezer tape). Return the foil-wrapped food to the freezer for storage.

Polythene bags: These are ideal for meat, poultry, vegetables, breads and scones, etc. The bags should be sealed with freezer tape or 'tite-tie' fasteners.

Special 'boil-in-bags' are useful for freezing vegetables in sauce and for fish, such as kippers or smoked haddock. The food can be reheated in the same bag in a saucepan of boiling water, thus retaining the maximum natural juices and flavour.

Cartons and tubs: These come in a variety of shapes and sizes and are made from waxed board, aluminium foil or polythene. They also have their own lids. Use flat cartons for fish fillets, small cakes or biscuits — these should be interleaved with foil for ease of separation when individual portions are required. Other shapes are suitable for soups, sauces, fruit purées and ice-cream. Liquids packed in cartons should have at least 1.3-centimetre or ½-inch 'head space' left between the level of the liquid and the top of the container to allow for expansion during freezing.

Cooked meat, poultry, fish dishes, pies and puddings packed in aluminium foil containers can be reheated in the same container.

Whichever wrapping is chosen, it is wise to pack food in family-meal-size portions. Keep packages as thin as practicable to ensure fast freezing, and follow the freezer manufacturer's instructions when putting the food into the freezer.

Label or colour-code each package with the name of the food and date it was frozen.

What to freeze and what not to freeze

Most raw and cooked foods freeze well, the exceptions being salad greens (they go soft and mushy when thawed), eggs in shells (they expand and the shells will crack), hard-boiled eggs (go hard and rubbery), mayonnaise (it will curdle), bacon (after 2 to 3 weeks it goes rancid), tomatoes (they go soft when thawed, but can be used in cooking), bananas (they discolour and go soft), milk, sour and single cream with less than 40 percent butterfat (they will separate), royal icing and frosting (they go soft and spongy), and custards (they tend to separate).

Soups and sauces with cream in the ingredients can be cooked and frozen, but it is advisable to add the cream when the food is being reheated. Otherwise, there is a tendency for the mixture to separate.

As seasonings may increase or decrease in strength during storage, add small amounts in the preparation for freezing and adjust to the taste required when thawed or when reheating.

Meat

All kinds of fresh meat can be frozen at home, but pork, lamb and veal joints and small cuts are better for freezing than beef, which usually loses a little tenderness and flavour. All types of meat in cooked dishes, stews and casseroles, for example, can be frozen with complete success.

Any fresh meat to be frozen at home should be purchased from a reliable butcher, preferably one who specializes in the preparation of meat for freezer owners. The skill and experience required in cutting a whole carcass into family-size joints and cuts normally means that carcass meat, while cheaper at the outset, is not in the end a worthwhile purchase. Family-size joints and individually portioned cuts, such as chops and steaks prepared by a skilled butcher, are usually the best buys.

With all meat, trim off the excess fat and remove unnecessary bones, which can be used for stock.

Large joints should be wrapped in

foil or polythene, protecting any sharp projecting bones with a double layer, pressing out as much air as possible.

Small cuts of meat — chops, steaks and cutlets — are packed in the same way, but should be interleaved with polythene or aluminium foil to ensure easier separation before cooking.

When freezing meat dishes, the longest storage life is achieved by removing all the fat from the surface of the cooled dish before packing and freezing.

Beef and lamb
    large joints: 9 months
    small cuts: 6 months

Pork and veal
    large joints: 4 months
    small cuts :   3 months

Offal, minced meat and sausages   :   1 to 2 months

Cooked meat dishes   :   2 to 3 months

Poultry and game

Like meat, fresh whole birds and joints, cooked poultry and game dishes can be frozen. When selecting whole birds, choose best quality young poultry that has been thoroughly cleaned and eviscerated. The liver and giblets should be frozen separately and whole birds should not be stuffed before freezing. (The stuffing, if required, can be prepared and frozen separately.) Truss the bird as for normal cooking and protect any projecting sharp bones with a piece of greaseproof or waxed paper or cheesecloth. Wrap in aluminium foil or in a large gusseted polythene bag, pressing out as much air as possible.

Poultry joints and quarters can be wrapped individually or interleaved with aluminium foil or polythene in one large pack. After jointing whole birds, make stock from the carcass, but skim off all excess fat from the surface if the cooled stock is to be frozen. Ice-cube trays and small containers are ideal for freezing stock.

Game birds are prepared in the same way as poultry except that the hanging period is usually longer before freezing to obtain the taste preferred.

All whole birds must be thawed out completely before cooking, remembering that a large turkey may take two or three days and a large chicken 24 hours in a refrigerator.

Small joints and quarters can be cooked from the frozen state, firstly using a gentle heat and increasing the temperature as cooking proceeds to ensure that each piece is cooked through to the centre.

Chicken	:	9 months
Duck	:	6 months
Goose	:	6 months
Turkey	:	6 months
Game	:	6 months
Hare and rabbit:		6 months

Fish

Once taken from the water, fish deteriorates very quickly, so only really fresh fish should be frozen at home. This restricts the opportunity of home freezing fish to those who can obtain fish at the quayside or riverside. Other home freezer owners should rely on the well-known brands of commercially frozen fish available in most supermarkets and grocery stores, which can also be used in cooked dishes and then refrozen.

Round fish should be washed and gutted, the scales, fins and eyes removed; then drain and dry the fish. Flat fish is prepared in the same way and the dark skin may be removed if preferred. It is usually more convenient to cut the whole fish into fillets or steaks and, after thorough washing and drying, to wrap individually in polythene or aluminium foil. Interleaving of fish steaks and fillets packed in larger quantities will greatly help separation when required. The smaller pieces of fish can be cooked from the frozen state.

Shellfish, including crabs, lobsters, scallops, prawns and shrimps, should be home frozen only if they are kept cool and frozen within a day of being caught. Crab and lobster should be cooked and the meat removed from the shells and claws before freezing. Shells can be washed and then stored

for later serving of the meat. Oysters and scallops are frozen uncooked. Remove them from their shells, reserve the liquid and pack the fish into suitably sized containers. The reserved liquid should be poured on to the fish before closing the container. Prawns and shrimps are best frozen raw as they tend to toughen during storage if precooked. They can be frozen in their shells and then shelled and deveined during thawing.

White fish: cod, haddock, plaice, sole and whiting:	6 months
Oily fish: herring, mackerel, mullet, turbot, salmon, trout:	3 months
Shellfish:	3 months

Vegetables

All vegetables, with the exception of salad greens, can be successfully home frozen, although those which are normally cooked before eating, like peas, beans and Brussels sprouts are usually better than those eaten raw, onions, for example. The latter lose some texture after freezing, but are useful as ingredients for recipes. Home freeze only the really seasonal vegetables — there is little to be gained by freezing vegetables like potatoes, which are always available.

Again, like all other foods, select only really fresh, young vegetables and prepare them as for normal cooking. All vegetables require blanching in boiling water for a few minutes before freezing to inactivate enzymes and retard the development of 'off flavour' during storage. The blanching time depends upon the type and size of the vegetables. At the end of the blanching time, the vegetables should be chilled in iced water before draining and packing for freezing.

All frozen vegetables can be used as ingredients in recipes for soups, casseroles and stews that are to be prepared for freezing. Frozen vegetables should be cooked in the minimum quantity of boiling water until they are just tender, to retain the full flavour, texture and nutritional value.

Most vegetables	:	12 months
Carrots and cauliflower	:	8 months
Beetroot and leeks	:	6 months
Onions	:	3 months
Herbs (unblanched)	:	3 months

Fruit

The best time to freeze fruit is when it is at the peak of its maturity. Over-ripe fruit is too soft and may result in a disappointing product when thawed.

Fruit will have a longer storage time if it is packed with dry sugar or a sugar syrup. Soft fruit which has a lot of juice — strawberries, raspberries and blackberries, for example—is better packed with dry sugar. When thawed, the sugar and juice in the fruit form a syrup.

Other fruit can be packed in a sugar syrup or dry sugar. The amount of sugar to use depends on the sweetness of the fruit and personal taste.

Light coloured fruit — apples, pears and peaches — discolours quickly. This can be stopped by the addition of ascorbic acid available from chemists in tablet or crystalline form. Once the fruit has been peeled and sliced, it should be dipped into a solution made with 5 grams or $\frac{1}{4}$ teaspoon of ascorbic acid to half a litre or one pint of water. If the fruit is to be packed with dry sugar, dip the fruit into the ascorbic acid solution, drain and dry it. If the fruit is packed in a sugar syrup then the ascorbic acid should be dissolved in 1 teaspoon of water and added to the sugar syrup.

Some citrus fruit is worth freezing, particularly that with a limited season or which is difficult to obtain, such as Seville oranges and limes. The fruit can be frozen whole or, like oranges be used for marmalade, it can be prepared up to the point of cooking then packed in polythene bags.

Fruit purées are a useful standby for sauces, cold desserts, baby foods or drinks. Apples and tomatoes should be cooked first and then passed through a nylon strainer.

Fruit in sugar or sugar syrup	:	12 months
Fruit with no sugar	:	6 months
Purées	:	6 months

Cakes, breads and pastries

All cakes, breads, pastries, scones and biscuits freeze well. Generally cakes, breads, scones and biscuits have a better texture if they are baked before freezing, whereas pastry dough is crisper if it is frozen before baking. If the dough is used for pies with a cooked filling — steak and kidney, chicken or game — then this should be cooked first of all — and thoroughly cooled before covering with dough.

Uncooked bread dough can be frozen, but a better rise is ensured if the amount of yeast is increased by half. Pack the unrisen dough in a greased polythene bag, leave 2.5 to 5 centimetres or 1 to 2 inches of space above the dough, and seal the bag with a 'tite-tie' fastener. To prepare the dough for baking, remove the fastener and allow the dough to thaw out and rise in the refrigerator overnight, or for 2 to 3 hours at room temperature. Knead and shape the dough as usual before baking.

For ease of serving, large cakes should be divided into pieces before wrapping and freezing. The required amount can be taken from the freezer and the remainder returned to it for storage.

It is easier to wrap soft and sponge cakes and those with a buttercream filling and decoration after they have hardened in the freezer. Cakes that are to be filled when thawed should be packed with a piece of foil between each layer to prevent them from sticking together.

Fresh white breadcrumbs will keep well in the freezer packed in polythene bags. The required amount can then be removed when needed.

Bought, sliced bread should be over-wrapped in foil or a polythene bag. Slices required for toast can be taken straight from the freezer and toasted while still frozen.

Baked bread, croissants and Danish pastries	:	1 month
Cakes, scones and biscuits	:	6 months
Unbaked bread dough	:	2 months
Baked pastry	:	6 months
Unbaked pastry dough	:	9 months

Dairy foods

As most dairy foods — butter, cream, cheese, eggs and milk, etc — are always available, it seems a waste of space to freeze these in quantity. On the other hand, some butter, cheese and double cream are useful to have as a standby.

Butter and cheese which are commercially prepared and wrapped should be over-wrapped in polythene or aluminium foil before freezing. Grated cheese, packed in a polythene bag, can be taken straight from the freezer for use in sauces and other savoury dishes. Whole milk should not be frozen, but pasteurized and homogenized milk can be frozen and stored for a short time. Freeze it in wax cartons, leaving a head space before covering and sealing.

Eggs should not be frozen in their shells as they expand and crack. The

yolks and whites should be lightly beaten together with salt or sugar added — ½ teaspoon of salt or ½ tablespoon of sugar to every 6 eggs. Label the cartons with the number of eggs and whether with sugar or salt. Approximately 3 tablespoons of the thawed egg mixture is the equivalent of 1 egg.

Like whole milk, single cream does not freeze well. Double cream, with not less than 40 percent butterfat, will freeze well and if it separates when thawing, stirring will correct it.

A home freezer is ideal for ice-cream and this can be packed in wax tubs or cartons. Commercially made ice-cream can be stored in the freezer and to reduce shrinkage, over-wrap the packet with aluminium foil.

Butter	:	3 months
Cheese, soft or blue	:	3 months
hard or grated	:	6 months
Ice-cream, home-made	:	3 months
commercial	:	1 month

Eggs, whole mixed	:	6 months
Milk, homogenized	:	3 months
Double cream	:	3 months

This chest-type freezer, which opens at the top, displays some of the most popular of an ever-increasing variety of packaging materials – aluminium containers (which can be heated in the oven), plastic tubs and cartons, and polythene bags.

Kitchen equipment and utensils

A well equipped kitchen is every cook's dream. To have the right pan, whisk, casserole or pie dish for every recipe — what heaven that would be! But most kitchens grow slowly and cooks collect equipment and utensils as they gain experience.

Because cooks are individuals, a list of kitchen equipment and utensils that would suit one may not suit another. But there are certain essential items that every cook needs and they are so defined because of the frequency with which they are used.

When choosing kitchen utensils it is better to buy a reliable brand and the best quality. Although the initial expense may seem a lot, it is more economical as the utensil will stand up to more 'wear and tear'.

The following list is a guide to the basic essential items that are invaluable to all cooks. The extra items will be useful to more experienced cooks and will also help to make the job easier.

Essential kitchen equipment
large kitchen, vegetable and palette knives
carving knife and sharpener
large kitchen and slotted spoons
wooden spoons — large and small
fish slice
large two-pronged fork
plastic or rubber spatula
rolling pin
set of spoon measures
can opener
whisk (balloon or rotary)
kitchen scissors
chopping board
mixing bowls — large and small
strainer and grater
saucepans — small, medium and large
heavy-based frying-pan
flameproof casserole
kettle
one ovenproof pie dish
ovenproof casseroles
one medium-sized sandwich tin
one medium-sized cake tin
large loaf tin
pastry cutters and pastry brush
two baking sheets
roasting tin
wire cake rack
weighing scales
measuring jug

Extra kitchen equipment
fat and sugar thermometers
pestle and mortar
steamer and double saucepans
deep-frying pan with basket
electric blender and mixer
selection of special cake tins, e.g.
    savarin mould, baba moulds, spring-

form cake tin, charlotte mould, brioche mould, moule à manqué (a shallow cake tin with sloping sides) and tartlet tins
icing equipment, e.g. forcing bags and nozzles, cake turn-table
soufflé dishes
kitchen timer

Glossary of cooking terms

Al dente

Al dente is an Italian cooking term which, literally translated, means 'to the tooth'. It is used to describe the point at which food, particularly pasta, is properly cooked—that is, firm to the bite, but not soft.

Bain marie

A bain marie is a large shallow pan, which may be used on top of the stove or in the oven. It is often used, half-filled with boiling water, to cook delicate sauces, custards or mousses. A deep roasting pan can be used as a substitute.

Bake blind

Bake blind is the term used to describe cooking a pastry shell without its filling (aluminium foil and/or dried beans or uncooked rice are placed over the base of the shell to preserve the shape during the baking).

Baste

To baste means to moisten food by spooning hot fat or liquid over it while it is cooking.

Beurre manié

Beurre manié is a paste made up of equal parts of flour and butter which is used to thicken stews, sauces and gravies.

Blanch

To blanch is to soak items of food in boiling water in order to remove the outer skins (for example, almonds or peaches).

It also means to plunge ingredients into boiling water either to harden them or, in the case of some green vegetables, to cook them partially.

Braise

Braising is a method of cooking meat, fish, game, poultry and some vegetables. It is a combination of steaming and baking, in a little liquid, which requires heat to be applied from above and below, ie on top of the stove then, for the greater part of the cooking time, in the oven.

Cocotte

Cocotte is the name given to an ovenproof pot, usually round or oval, with a tightly fitting lid. It comes from a French children's word for chicken because, technically, a cocotte should be large enough to hold a fowl.

Similar small pots, suitable for individual servings, with or without lids, are also called cocottes.

Court bouillon

Court bouillon is a rich stock, acidulated with vinegar, which is often used for poaching fish.

Dégorge

To dégorge means to remove excess flavour or liquid from food by sprinkling with salt, setting aside for 30 minutes to 1 hour and then draining. Aubergines and courgettes are two vegetables commonly dégorged to get rid of excess water.

Decant

To decant is to pour wine from its bottle, usually through muslin or, in extreme cases, a handkerchief, into another container such as a carafe or decanter. Red wines, particularly claret or Burgundy, which have been laid down for a long period of time, need to be decanted in order to separate the wine from sediment which gathers in the bottle during aging.

Julienne

Julienne is the description applied to vegetables which have been finely shredded into 'matchsticks'.

Knead

To knead is to combine all the ingredients in a mixture, using your hands to pummel it into a smooth dough.

Macerate	To macerate means to soften by soaking. The word is usually applied to fruit, both fresh and crystallized, which is moistened in wine, brandy, rum or liqueur.
Marinade	A marinade is a mixture of liquids, highly seasoned with herbs and spices, in which meat, fish or game is left to soak prior to cooking.
Purée	Purée is a term used to describe meat, fish, vegetables or fruit which have been first cooked and then either pounded or put through a strainer, food mill or electric blender to produce a smooth paste.
Ramekin	The word ramekin was originally used to describe cheese which had been toasted. Now, however, it means a small, circular, individual fireproof dish used both as a baking and serving dish for pâtés and mousses.
Render	To render is the process of cooking pieces of fat or fatty meat until the fat runs clear from the connective tissue. The liquid fat may then be drained off, clarified, solidified and stored for future use, or used immediately for frying.
Roux	A roux is an equal mixture of butter and flour cooked together, then used to thicken liquids such as sauces.
Scald	To scald is to place a liquid, usually milk or cream, in a saucepan and bring it to just under boiling point. Scalding can also mean to rinse something out with boiling water, for example a cheesecloth or muslin bag used in jellymaking.
Sauté	To sauté means to fry small pieces of vegetables or meat very quickly in a little hot fat or oil until lightly or completely browned. To hasten the browning process, the pan is usually shaken gently so that the ingredients are tossed and turned constantly.
Simmer	To simmer means to cook food over low heat in liquid, which is kept just below boiling point. Foods which have a delicate texture, such as fish, are often simmered rather than boiled, to prevent them from breaking up.
Skim	To skim is to remove scum or other substances from the surfaces of liquids—cream from milk, or scum from stock or jam, for instance. It is usually done with a large metal spoon or a flat slotted spoon called a skimmer.
Sift	To sift means to pass dry ingredients through a sieve in order to aerate them. Ingredients such as flour, baking powder, sugar and salt, or a combination of these, are usually sifted before being made into dough or batter.
Whip	To whip means to beat air into a substance such as egg whites or cream so that it becomes light and fluffy and increases in bulk. Whipping may be done with a fork (although this can be a laborious process), a wire whisk, rotary beater or an electric beater.
Zest	The zest is the coloured exterior rind of citrus fruits. It can be removed from the fruit by using a very fine grater or by rubbing a lump of sugar over the skin until it becomes saturated.

Basic cooking

Beef

Beef, the meat of the young ox or bullock, can be more variable in quality than other meats and the price will fluctuate according to availability. Obviously, the prime, tender cuts are always more expensive because there are fewer of them on the carcass.

When buying beef, look for meat with a fresh red colour that has a brownish tinge. If the colour is too bright it means that the meat has not been sufficiently aged and will be tough and lacking in flavour. The meat should be marbled with fat; this will make it moist and tender when it is cooked. The fat should be a creamy colour.

The amount of meat you buy depends on family requirements, but an approximate guide is 125-175g (4-6 oz.) of boned meat or, 175-225g (6-8 oz.) of meat with bone per person.

Roasting
Suitable Cuts: Ribs (Top, Fore and Back), Sirloin, Top Rump, Fillet.
Preparation: Preheat oven to hot 425°F (Gas Mark 7, 220°C). Place a little cooking fat in a roasting pan and heat in the oven. Place meat in the hot fat then turn over to seal all sides. After cooking for 15 minutes reduce temperature to moderate 350°F (Gas Mark 4, 180°C).
Cooking Time: Rare: 16 minutes to the half kilo (15 minutes to the pound) and 16(15) minutes over (Meat thermometer temperature 60°C or 140°F).
Medium: 27 minutes to the half kilo (25 minutes to the pound) and 27 (25) minutes over (Meat thermometer temperature 72°C or 160°F).
Boned and rolled beef: 32 minutes to the half kilo (30 minutes to the pound) and 32 (30) minutes over (Meat thermometer temperature 80°C or 175°F).

Braising or pot roasting
Braising is a mixture of roasting and stewing. The meat is cooked on a bed of vegetables with a little liquid, in an ovenproof casserole with a tight-fitting lid. Pot roasting is similar, the only difference being the meat is cooked in a saucepan on top of the stove.
Suitable Cuts: Brisket, Silverside, Thick Flank, Topside.
Preparation: Preheat oven to moderate 350°F (Gas Mark 4, 180°C). Fry both sides of the meat in hot fat for 2 minutes to seal in the juices. Place on a bed of fried vegetables (or according to recipe). Cover the casserole with a tight-fitting lid.
Cooking Time: 44 minutes to the half kilo (40 minutes to the pound) for thinner cuts. 48 minutes to the half kilo (45 minutes to the pound) for thicker, or stuffed, cuts.

Stewing or casseroling
Suitable Cuts: Chuck (also called Shoulder or Blade Bone), Leg, Neck, Oxtail, Shin, Skirt, Thick Flank, Salted Brisket or Silverside.
Preparation: Preheat oven to cool 300°F (Gas Mark 2, 150°C), or cook on top of the stove over low heat. Cut meat into pieces and continue according to recipe, or leave whole as in the case of salted meat.
Cooking Time: Most stews require at least 2½ hours.

Frying or grilling
These are the best ways of cooking pieces of the prime cuts. The grill should be glowing red or the frying-pan very hot, as the meat should be cooked as quickly as possible.
Suitable Cuts: Fillet, Entrecôte, Minced Beef (made into hamburgers), Rump.
Preparation: Add a little butter and oil to the frying-pan and preheat. Grill or fry for 4 to 8 minutes on both sides depending on thickness and how you like steak cooked.
Rare: about 3–4 minutes each side.
Medium: about 5–6 minutes each side.
Well done: about 7–8 minutes each side.

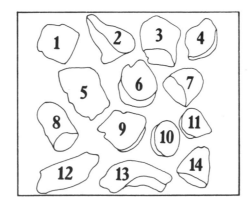

1 *Neck* 2 *Foreribs* 3 *Sirloin* 4 *Rump Steak*
5 *Chuck* 6 *Back ribs* 7 *Topside* 8 *Rolled and boned Brisket* 9 *Top rib* 10 *Top rump*
11 *Silverside* 12 *Shin* 13 *Flank* 14 *Leg*

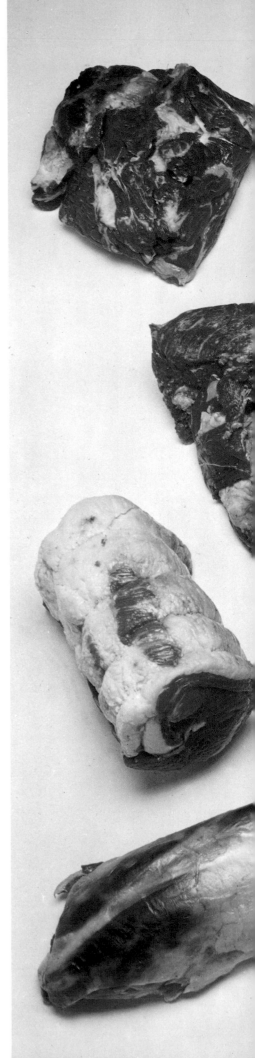

Lamb

Lamb is a young sheep. In culinary terms the word refers to either an unweaned baby lamb or to an animal less than a year old.

When buying lamb, look for meat with a light colour, fine grain and firm texture. The fat should be creamy-white and soft. Imported lamb has a whiter, firmer fat. Yellowish fat indicates an older animal and brittle white fat one that has been frozen too long.

The amount of meat you buy depends on family requirements, but an approximate guide would be 175 to 225 grams (6 to 8 ounces) of boned meat for each serving. For meat on the bone, allow 350 grams (12 ounces) of leg, 350 to 450 grams (12 ounces to 1 pound) of shoulder, saddle and loin and 225 to 350 grams (8 to 12 ounces) of breast or best end for each serving.

The prime cuts of lamb are the saddle, the leg and the shoulder. The saddle is the choicest and biggest cut, from which the best end and the loin are cut. These are always roasted.

The leg, which may be cut into two, the fillet end and the shank or knuckle end, is suitable for roasting, braising and, when boned, for use in casseroles.

Roasting

Most cuts except the scrag end are suitable for roasting. The breast should be boned and rolled and is usually stuffed. The meat may either be placed on a rack, sprinkled with flour or put in a roasting pan with a little dripping or fat. The meat is best roasted in a fairly hot oven 400°F (Gas Mark 6, 200°C) for the first 20 minutes. The heat is then reduced to warm 325°F (Gas Mark 3, 170°C). The meat should be basted every 30

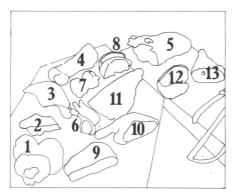

1 Scrag 2 Middle neck 3 Best end 4 Loin 5 Saddle 6 Cutlets 7 Loin chops 8 Chump chops 9 Shoulder – fillet end 10 Shoulder – shank end 11 Breast 12 Leg – fillet end 13 Leg – shank end

minutes with the juices in the pan.

The traditional accompaniments to roast lamb are gravy and mint sauce or redcurrant jelly.

Cooking time: 22 minutes to the half kilo (20 minutes to the pound) and 22 (20) minutes over. If you are using a meat thermometer the temperature must register between 80°C and 82°C (175°F and 180°F).

Braising

The cuts of lamb suitable for this method of cooking are leg, boned and stuffed shoulder and stuffed breast. The meat is first browned and then placed on a bed of sautéed vegetables with herbs and wine or stock. The dish is then covered and braised in a moderate oven 350°F (Gas Mark 4, 180°C).

Cooking Time: For leg and shoulder 27 minutes to the half kilo (25 minutes per pound) and for breast 16 minutes to the half kilo (15 minutes per pound).

Boiling

Boiled leg of lamb is a traditional English dish. The leg is tied in a cloth and boiled in salted water with vegetables and a bouquet garni. It is traditionally served with a caper sauce.

Cooking Time: 16 minutes to the half kilo (15 minutes per pound) plus 16 (15) minutes.

Stewing

The cuts of lamb suitable for slow cooking are breast, scrag and middle neck. As these cuts are usually very fatty, it is advisable to make the stew some time in advance, allow it to cool and skim the fat off the top. The stew is then reheated before serving.

Frying or grilling

Suitable cuts for quick cooking are loin chops, chump chops and cutlets from the best end of neck. Chops and cutlets should be trimmed of excess fat.

The grill must be preheated to very hot. If the meat is very lean brush it over with melted butter or oil. Grill the meat for 2 minutes on each side. Reduce the heat to moderate and continue cooking the chops or cutlets until they are done.

To fry chops and cutlets, use butter or oil or a mixture of the two. Fry the meat over high heat for 2 minutes on each side. Reduce the heat to moderate and continue frying, turning the chops once, until they are done.

Cooking Time: 7 to 10 minutes for cutlets and 10 to 20 minutes for chops.

Pork

Pork is the fresh meat from a pig, as opposed to ham and bacon which are cured before cooking.

When buying good-quality pork the points to look for are fine-textured, firm, pink-coloured, smooth flesh, with no gristle.

All pork should be thoroughly cooked and never served underdone. This is because pork sometimes harbours a parasite dangerous to man; thorough cooking destroys it.

The amount of pork you buy depends on family requirements, but an approximate, if generous guide, is 175 to 225 grams (6 to 8 ounces) of boned meat or 225 to 350 grams (8 to 12 ounces) with bone per person.

The prime cuts of pork are the leg, which is sometimes divided into fillet and knuckle; loin, the best and most expensive joint from which loin chops are cut and which is sometimes divided into hind and fore loin; blade or blade bone, which is a joint cut from the top part of the foreleg.

The medium cuts are the hand and spring; belly; spare ribs from which cutlets and neck chops are cut; and chump chops. Fillet is a fatless cut which is removed from either side of the backbone.

Roasting

The leg, loin, blade, hand and spring, spare ribs, chops and head are all suitable for roasting. The only extra fat needed for roasting pork is 1 tablespoon of oil to grease the tin. To prepare a pork loin for roasting ask the butcher to chine it — this makes carving and serving simple. For a special occasion, two loins may be chined and bent outwards to form a 'crown'.

Preheat the oven to fairly hot 375°F (Gas Mark 5, 190°C). Allow 38 minutes to the half kilo (35 minutes per pound) plus 32 (30) minutes over; for joints without bone, i.e. boned and rolled, allow 44 minutes to the half kilo (40 minutes per pound) plus 44 (40) minutes over; for boned, rolled and stuffed joints allow 48 minutes to the half kilo (45 minutes per pound) plus 48 (45) minutes over.

Accompaniments for roast pork are brown gravy, apple sauce, cranberry sauce, and redcurrant jelly.

Braising

Pork is not usually braised, since it produces a lot of fat during cooking. If you wish to braise pork, use spare ribs or cutlets or neck chops. Allow 27 to 32 minutes to the half kilo (25 to 30 minutes per pound) for spare ribs and 22 to 27 minutes to the half kilo (20 to 25 minutes) for the chops.

Stewing

Although the cuts suggested for braising may be used in casseroles and stews, they give out so much fat that they should be cooked a day in advance, so that the stew may be cooled and the fat removed and discarded. However fillet, which has no fat, is ideal for casseroles and should be cooked for 1 to 1¼ hours.

Boiling

All cuts of pork may be boiled for serving cold, although salt belly of pork is the cut most often boiled. Allow 32 minutes to the half kilo (30 minutes to the pound) and 30 minutes over.

Frying and grilling

To fry pork chops, in a large frying-pan, melt a mixture of butter and oil, (2 tablespoons of butter and 1 tablespoon of oil will be enough for 4 to 6 chops) over moderate heat. Add the chops, fry them for 5 minutes on each side or until they are well browned all over. Cover the pan, reduce the heat to low and cook for 25 to 35 minutes, depending on the thickness of the chops. Test the chops by piercing them with a sharp knife; if the juices run clear, the chops are done. To grill pork chops, preheat the grill to moderate. Place the chops on the grill pan and cook the chops for 15 to 20 minutes on each side — depending on the thickness of the chops.

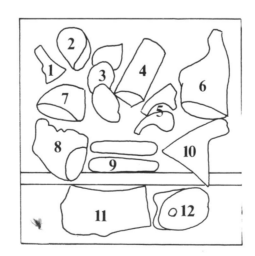

1 *Spare rib chops* 2 *Spare rib* 3 *Chump chops* 4 *Loin* 5 *Loin chops* 6 *Leg* 7 *Blade* 8 *Hand and spring* 9 *Fillet* 10 *Knuckle* 11 *Belly* 12 *Fillet end of leg*

150

Veal

Veal is the flesh of young calves, 10 months old or sometimes younger. The flesh is pale pink in colour and darkens as the animal gets older. It has very little fat on it and, because of this, the leanest cuts should be barded before cooking. Good veal is soft and moist in texture and if the flesh has a blue or brown tinge, it means it is stale and should not be bought. Veal bones contain a large amount of gelatine and because of this, veal stock is ideal for use in moulds and pies.

There are two kinds of veal available: from milk-fed calves and from grass-fed calves. Milk-fed calves are considered to have the more delicate flavour and finer texture and are also more expensive.

Allow 125 to 175 grams (4 to 6 ounces) of boned meat for each person; for meat on the bone, allow 225 grams (8 ounces) of leg; and 350 to 450 grams (12 ounces to 1 pound) of shoulder, neck, hock and knuckle for each person.

The prime cuts of veal are the leg, fillet, loin, shoulder and saddle. Loin chops, chump chops and cutlets are cut from the loin and can be grilled or shallow-fried. Leg, fillet, loin and saddle are usually roasted.

The cheaper cuts are the breast, neck, hock and knuckle and are suitable for roasting, boned, stuffed and rolled, or for braising, boiling and stewing. Neck is also suitable for moulds and pies.

Roasting

The meat can be boned and stuffed or cooked in one piece. Place the meat in a roasting tin with 50 to 125gr (2 to 4oz) of fat, or barded with slices of streaky bacon. The meat is best roasted in an oven preheated to fairly hot 400°F (Gas Mark 6, 200°C) for the first 20 minutes. Reduce the oven temperature to warm 325°F (Gas Mark 3, 170°C) and continue cooking, basting every 20 minutes with pan juices.
Cooking Time: On the bone, 22 minutes to the half kilo (20 minutes to the pound) plus 22 (20) minutes. Boned and rolled 32 minutes to the half kilo (30 minutes to the pound) plus 32 (30) minutes. If you are using a meat thermometer, the temperature should register 85°C (185°F).

Braising

In braising, the meat is first browned and then placed on a bed of sautéed vegetables with herbs and wine or stock. The dish is then covered and braised in an oven preheated to fairly hot 375°F (Gas Mark 5, 190°C).
Cooking Time: 32 minutes to the half kilo (30 minutes to the pound).

Boiling

Some of the cheaper cuts of veal are boiled in salted water with vegetables and herbs.
Cooking Time: 16 minutes to the half kilo (15 minutes per pound) plus 15 minutes.

Stewing

Again, the cheaper cuts of veal are ideal for stewing. These are usually more fatty and it is best to make the stew a few hours before it is required and leave it to cool completely. The fat can then be removed from the top of the stew, and the stew reheated before serving.

Grilling and frying

Suitable cuts for quick cooking are loin chops, chump chops, cutlets and escalopes.

Preheat the grill to very hot. Brush the meat with melted oil or butter and grill the meat for 3 to 5 minutes on each side for chops or cutlets or 3 to 4 minutes on each side for escalopes. Reduce the heat to moderately low and continue cooking until they are done.

To fry chops or cutlets, use butter or oil or a mixture of both. Fry the chops over moderate heat for 3 to 5 minutes on each side. Reduce the heat to low and continue cooking until they are done.
Cooking Time: 15 to 30 minutes for cutlets and chops. (The cooking times will, of course, depend on the thickness of the chops and cutlets.) Escalopes take between 6 and 8 minutes to cook through.

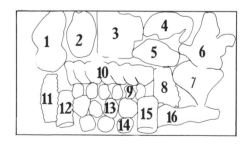

1 *Stuffed breast* 2 *Chump chops* 3 *Middle neck* 4 *Saddle* 5 *Oyster* 6 *Knuckle* 7 *Breast* 8 *Escalopes* 9 *Medaillons* 10 *Chops* 11 *Rolled shoulder* 12 *Rolled best end* 13 *Osso buco* 14 *Paupiettes* 15 *Rolled loin* 16 *Fillet*

Poultry and game, recognizing and trussing them

Poultry is the collective term used to describe domestic birds which are reared for the table. Game, on the other hand, is defined as being wild animals and birds which are hunted for sport and then prepared for eating. Poultry includes chicken, turkey, duck, goose, guinea fowl and pigeon, among others; popular game includes grouse, partridge, pheasant, rabbit, hare and deer (which provides venison), among others.

Poultry must be plucked, hung and drawn before cooking — jobs usually done these days by the butcher before the poultry is sold. Game is usually hung after it has been shot to allow the flesh to 'mature' — the length of time depends upon the game in question and, to some extent, the time of the year. Game is plucked and gutted immediately before it is sold — a service again performed (if you're lucky) by the butcher.

When you are buying fresh poultry, look for chickens with tender, firm flesh and plump breasts. Ducks should have rich, fatty flesh, while good-quality turkeys can be recognized by their firm white flesh and bright red wattles.

When you are buying fresh game, look for hare with dark, strong-flavoured flesh and plump rabbits with pale meat. Venison should have dark red meat with creamy white fat.

If you are using frozen poultry or game, always make sure that the meat is thoroughly thawed out before you truss or stuff it, or otherwise prepare it for cooking.

Both poultry and game are traditionally roasted whole (see the roasting chart on page 158 for specific details on how to roast individual birds and joints), and served with traditional sauces or gravies. Most poultry can now also be purchased jointed (as can the larger game such as rabbit and hare) and in this case can be used in stews and casseroles.

Trussing Poultry

Poultry is trussed so that it keeps its

shape during cooking and is therefore easier to carve.

The simplest way to truss a bird is with a skewer and a piece of string. Push the skewer through the bird just below the thigh bone. Turn the bird on to its breast. Catch in the wing pinions with the string, pass the string under the ends of the skewer and cross it over the back. Turn the bird over, pass the string over the drumsticks and tie under the parson's nose.

To truss poultry in the traditional way it is necessary to have a long trussing needle and strong fine string or trussing thread.

1. Place the flap of skin neatly over the back of the neck and fold the pinions or ends of the wings backwards over the flap to hold it in position.

2. Put the bird on its back with the breast away from you. Press the legs well into the sides, as this raises and plumps the breast. Thread the needle and push it through the lower part of the carcass.

3. Pass the string or thread over one drumstick, through the tip of the breastbone and over the other drumstick. Tie it firmly.

4. Re-thread the needle and thrust it through the carcass where the drumstick and the second joint meet and then out the other side.

5. Turn the bird over and push the needle through the wing, then the neck flap on either side of the back bone, and the other wing. Tie it firmly.

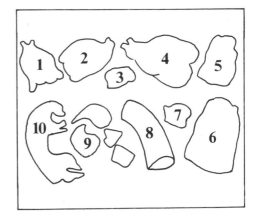

1 *Chicken* 2 *Duck* 3 *Poussin* 4 *Goose* 5 *Capon* 6 *Turkey* 7 *Pigeon* 8 *Boned and rolled joint of Venison* 9 *Hare, cut into individual serving pieces* 10 *Rabbit*

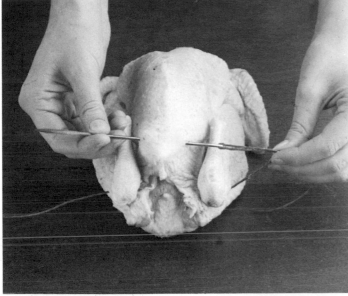

Push the needle through the lower part of the carcass. Pass the string over one drumstick, through the tip of the breastbone and over the other drumstick. Tie firmly.

Then re-thread the needle and thrust it through the top of the carcass, above the wings, where the drumstick and the second joint meet, and then out the other side.

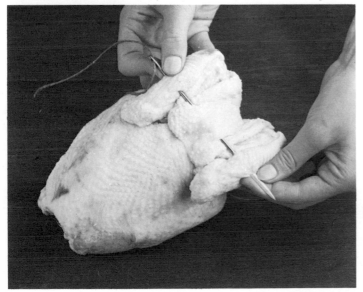

Turn the bird over and push the needle through the wing, the neck flap and then the other wing. Tie firmly.

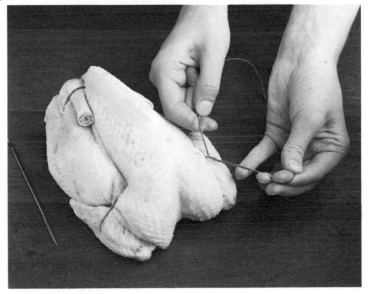

Tie the string ends firmly together. Rub salt and pepper all over the skin of the bird. It is now ready to be cooked.

155

Roasting Chart for Meat, Poultry and Game

	Suitable Cuts	Oven Temperature	Cooking Time	Meat Thermometer
Beef	Ribs (top, fore and back), sirloin, top rump, whole fillet.	Cook in the oven preheated to hot 425°F (Gas Mark 7, 220°C) for 15 minutes. Reduce the temperature to moderate 350°F (Gas Mark 4, 180°C).	Rare: 16 minutes to the half kilo plus 16 minutes. Medium: 27 minutes to the half kilo plus 27 minutes. Boned and rolled: 32 minutes to the half kilo plus 32 minutes.	60°C 72°C 80°C
Lamb	Leg, shoulder, saddle, loin, breast.	Cook in the oven preheated to fairly hot 400°F (Gas Mark 6, 200°C) for 20 minutes. Reduce the temperature to warm 325°F (Gas Mark 3, 170°C).	22 minutes to the half kilo plus 22 minutes.	82°C
Mutton	Leg, shoulder, loin.	As for lamb.	27 minutes to the half kilo plus 27 minutes.	80°C
Pork	Leg, loin, blade, hand and spring, spare ribs, chops and head.	Cook in the oven preheated to fairly hot 375°F (Gas Mark 5, 190°C). Increase the temperature to hot 425°F (Gas Mark 7, 220°C) for the last 20 minutes.	On the bone: 38 minutes to the half kilo plus 38 minutes. Boned and rolled: 44 minutes to the half kilo plus 44 minutes. Boned, rolled and stuffed: 48 minutes to the half kilo plus 48 minutes.	88°C
Veal	Leg, shoulder, saddle, loin, breast.	Cook in the oven preheated to fairly hot 400°F (Gas Mark 6, 200°C) for 20 minutes. Reduce the temperature to warm 325°F (Gas Mark 3, 170°C).	On the bone: 22 minutes to the half kilo plus 22 minutes. Off the bone: 32 minutes to the half kilo plus 32 minutes.	85°C
Chicken	Poussins, young chickens, capons.	Cook in the oven preheated to hot 425°F (Gas Mark 7, 220°C) for 15 minutes. Reduce the temperature to moderate 350°F (Gas Mark 4, 180°C).	A 1 kg oven-ready chicken takes about 1 hour to roast. Add between 10 and 16 minutes for every additional half kilo.	82°C
Duck	Domesticated or wild ducks in prime condition.	Cook in the oven preheated to very hot 450°F (Gas Mark 8, 230°C) for 15 minutes. Reduce the temperature to moderate 350°F (Gas Mark 4, 180°C).	15 minutes to the half kilo.	85°C
Goose	Young geese in prime condition.	Cook in the oven preheated to very hot 450°F (Gas Mark 8, 230°C) for 15 minutes. Reduce the heat to moderate 350°F (Gas Mark 4, 180°C).	22-27 minutes to the half kilo.	85°C
Turkey	Young turkey in prime condition.	Cook in the oven preheated to very hot 450°F (Gas Mark 8, 230°C) for 10 minutes. Reduce the heat to warm 325°F (Gas Mark 3, 170°C).	On the bone stuffed: 22 minutes to the half kilo plus 22 minutes. Unstuffed and on the bone: 16 minutes to the half kilo.	85°C
Grouse	Young birds in prime condition.	Cook in the oven preheated to moderate 350°F (Gas Mark 4, 180°C).	1 hour.	80°C
Partridge	Young birds in prime condition.	Cook in the oven preheated to hot 425°F (Gas Mark 7, 220°C).	20-25 minutes.	85°C
Pheasant	Young birds in prime condition.	Cook in the oven preheated to moderate 350°F (Gas Mark 4, 180°C).	1 hour.	85°C
Venison	Haunch, leg and loin, saddle, neck, fillet.	Cook in the oven preheated to very hot 450°F (Gas Mark 8, 230°C) for 30 minutes. Reduce the heat to moderate 350°F (Gas Mark 4, 180°C).	27 minutes to the half kilo plus 27 minutes.	85°C

Carving meat and poultry

To carve meat and game. Carving, the cutting or slicing of large cuts of meat or whole game, is a very useful skill to acquire. To know how to carve meat correctly is very important — it avoids wastage, improves presenta-tion, saves time (thus avoiding bringing cold meat to the table), and helps make the most of leftovers — the sight of cold, messy remains will defeat even the most economical cook!

If you have any doubts at all about your prowess as a carver, or if you are relatively new to the craft, then it's per-haps a good idea for you to test your expertise (or conduct your experi-ments, depending on how confident you are of your progress!) in the safety and privacy of the kitchen. To have a go at the table, with all the family and or dinner guests looking on expectantly, takes courage, and in such circumstances even the strongest nerve can fail!

The basic tools required for carving are: sharp knives, long and thin for slicing and shorter and thick for jointing (these knives should be used

To carve the back and fore wing of beef, first carefully remove the chine bone from the rest of the joint, using a thick carving knife.

Using a carving fork to anchor the fore wing of beef steady, carefully carve the meat thinly down on to the rib bone with the knife.

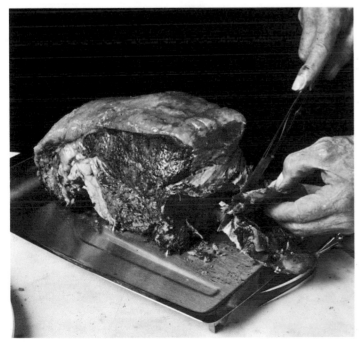

To carve sirloin of beef, on the bone and with the fillet, first grasp the chine bone firmly and, using the carving knife, sever it from the meat.

Now steady the sirloin by anchoring it with the carving fork, then, using the carving knife, carve the meat right down into thin slices.

specifically for carving and nothing else), a long two-pronged fork, preferably with a thumb-guard, and a carving dish. Carving dishes may be made of stainless steel, aluminium or wood, and may have short protruding spikes to hold the meat steady, as well as grooves or depressions to contain the juices or blood that run out of the meat when it is carved.

The most important point to note about carving is that each type of meat has a particular grain which, generally speaking, runs lengthways along the carcass. The meat is usually carved against the grain as this produces more tender slices. One of the few exceptions to this rule is loin of veal, which is carved with the grain.

Before carving the meat, remove and discard any trussing thread or string, or skewers.

Avoid cutting the meat in short or deep cuts — aim for large, thin, even slices.

The pictures and directions below are a guide to how to carve cuts of meat which have been cooked with the bone. Directions for boned or rolled cuts of meat are not given as they are simple to carve — the only point to remember is that they should be carved fairly thinly.

To carve roast leg of lamb, on the bone, using the carving knife, begin carving from the shorter, or knuckle end, and in short, thick slices.

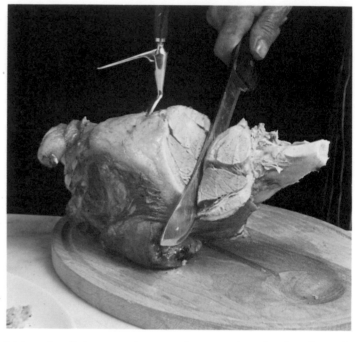

Using the fork as anchor, continue carving the leg from the knuckle, graduating to longer, thinner slices towards the aitch bone.

To carve best end of lamb, first anchor the joint firmly with the carving fork. Then, using the knife, sever the chine bone from the rib bones.

Now carefully turn the lamb over so that the fatty side is uppermost. Carve the meat between the rib bones into cutlets.

Beef

Back and fore wing is a sirloin cut with the fillet removed. This cut can be cooked on the bone, but is also sold boned or rolled.

Top, fore and back rib cuts are all carved in the same way — the only difference in the cuts is that the lengths of the rib bones differ, fore rib having the longest bones. These cuts are also sold boned or rolled.

Sirloin is a large cut which should weigh at least 2¼ kilos (5 pounds) if cooked with the bone. Sirloin is also sold boned or rolled, cut into steaks, or sold on the bone with the fillet removed.

Brisket is the meat covering the breast bone. It may be cooked with the bone, but more commonly is boned and rolled, or salted.

Lamb

Lamb cuts are the same as mutton, and the methods of carving are the same. The only basic difference between lamb and mutton is that mutton is older, usually tougher, and the cuts are generally larger.

Leg of lamb is cooked whole, on the bone, or, if the leg is very large, divided into two pieces—the shank and the fillet which are sold separately. Leg can be boned, but it is more commonly cooked on the bone. It is also sometimes boned and cut into

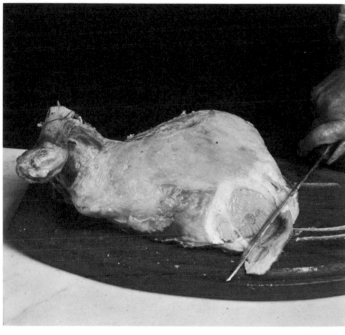

To carve shoulder of lamb, start from the blade end, cutting the slices as thinly as possible and going with the grain.

Then turn the shoulder of lamb over, anchoring it with the fork. Carve the meat into thin slices, across the thicker end of the meat.

Now turn the shoulder over once again so that the fatty side is downwards on to the carving board, and cut the meat, with the grain, into thin slices.

Hand and spring of pork is carved with the crackling when there is any. Carve from the neck end downwards into thick slices.

cubes for kebabs, curries and casseroles.

Loin is usually chined by the butcher, cooked whole on the bone and then carved into chops. Loin may also be sold boned or rolled, or separated into chops.

Shoulder is cooked whole on the bone, or, if it is very large, cut into 2 or 3 pieces which are sold separately. Shoulder is also sold boned or rolled, or sometimes boned and cut into small pieces for kebabs, curries and casseroles.

Saddle, a very large cut, is always sold whole, on the bone, with the kidneys attached.

Pork

Leg of pork can be cooked whole on the bone, or cut into two—the fillet end and knuckle end. Leg can also be sold boned and rolled.

Loin may be chined and cooked whole on the bone, or it can be boned and rolled. Loin is also separated into chops.

Hand and Spring is the front leg and it is generally cooked whole on the bone.

Blade is cut from the shoulder and it may be cooked whole, on the bone or boned, stuffed and rolled.

Gammon and Ham are the hind leg of the pig and are smoked or cured before cooking. Gammon is either sold whole,

To carve loin of veal, first turn the meat on to its side and anchor it on the carving board with the carving fork. Cut off the chine bone.

Now turn the loin over so that the fatty side is uppermost and carve it into medium-thick slices, between the rib bones.

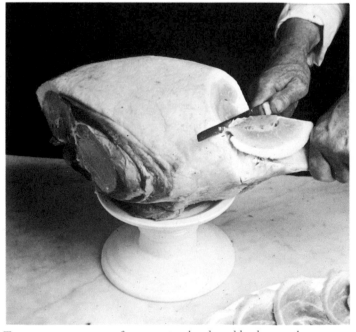

Half-shoulder of veal is also sometimes called the Oyster. To carve it, slice it straight down, with the grain, into thin slices.

To carve gammon, first grasp the knuckle bone, then carve in thin slices towards the knuckle end, down to the leg bone.

162

or cut into three pieces, Corner, Middle Cut and Hock, which are sold separately. Ham is sold whole and is generally cooked on the bone.

Veal

Leg of veal, called chump end of leg, is usually cooked whole, on the bone. Leg of veal is also sometimes sold boned or rolled.

Loin can be chined and cooked whole on the bone. It is also sometimes sold boned and rolled, or it can be separated into chops.

Shoulder can be cooked whole on the bone. It is also sold boned and rolled, or boned and cut into pieces.

Neck is cooked whole on the bone, or sold boned or rolled. It is also separated into chops and known as neck cutlets.

Game

Small game birds such as pheasant, grouse and partridge are served in three different ways, according to the size and toughness of the bird — whole (very small birds only), jointed, before or after cooking, or carved in the same way as poultry, although sometimes only the breast is eaten.

Hare is usually sold in serving pieces, or jointed (with the blood reserved).

Rabbit is also usually sold already cut into serving pieces.

To carve poultry

The basic tools required for carving poultry are the same as those used for carving meat or game.

With the exception of very small birds, the legs are removed first before you carve. To do this, pull the leg away from the body with a two-pronged fork and sever through the thigh joint. Separate the drumstick from the thigh by cutting through the knee joint. To remove the wings, use the fork to hold down the pinion and cut through the shoulder joint. If the fowl is large the breast may be carved in thin slices, parallel to the breast-bone. With a smaller bird, the breast is removed in one piece and then cut in half. If the bird has been stuffed, then this is removed after carving and a small amount is served with the meat.

When you're serving poultry, by the way, especially chicken and turkey, it's traditional to serve a little white meat (meat from the breast area) plus a little dark (from around the thighs, wings and legs) per serving — always allowing for personal preferences, of course.

To carve poultry, using the carving knife and fork, pull the leg away from the body and sever it through the joint.

If the bird is a large one, carve the meat from the breast in thin slices, slicing it parallel to the breastbone.

If the bird is small, the breast should be cut off in one piece with sharp scissors, then halved before serving.

163

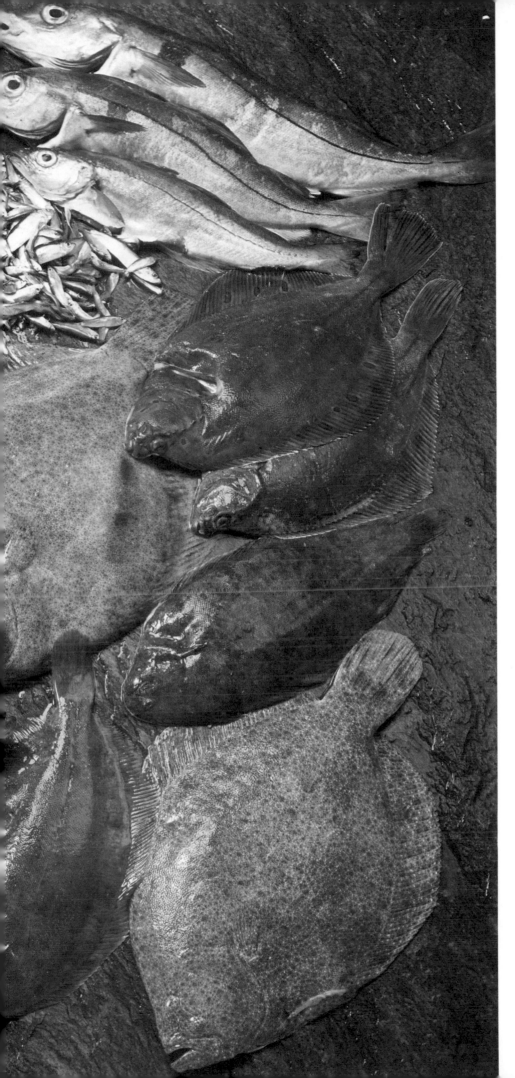

Fish, recognizing and filleting them

Fish is a readily available, relatively cheap source of food which is high in proteins, vitamins and minerals.

Fish is classified by its source, either fresh or salt water, and by type, white, oily or shell fish.

Fish is extremely perishable, so it must be cooked as quickly as possible after being caught, and must be kept cold until it is cooked.

Packets of frozen fish are a convenient and ideal way of buying. Providing the manufacturer is a reputable one, quite often frozen fish is fresher than that bought from the fishmonger, as it is quick-frozen as soon as it is caught. If you have a refrigerator, frozen fish can be kept for the time stated on the packets.

Fish in the fishmonger's can be recognized as fresh by having a clear, shining eye, flesh which is fresh-smelling and firm when pressed, and pink or bright red gills.

Fish can be bought whole, in steaks or in fillets. A fishmonger will usually clean, dress and cut the fish. However, if you catch your own fish, preparation at home is not difficult.

Preparing fish
Scaling: To scale a fish, dip it first in

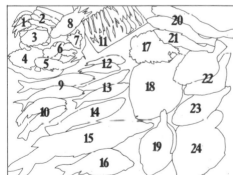

Fresh from the market – a large selection of shellfish, and freshwater and saltwater fish. **1** *Pacific prawns* **2** *Dublin Bay prawns* **3** *Crab* **4** *Prawn* **5** *Lobster* **6** *Oysters* **7** *Shrimp* **8** *Langouste* **9** *Mackerel* **10** *Rainbow Trout* **11** *Sprats* **12** *Red Mullet* **13** *Herring* **14** *Sea Trout* **15** *Pike* **16** *Carp* **17** *Whitebait* **18** *Turbot* **19** *Lemon Sole* **20** *Haddock* **21** *Whiting* **22** *Plaice* **23** *Dover Sole* **24** *Brill*

cold water and lay it on a board. Grasp the fish by the tail and, with a sharp knife, scrape from tail to head against the grain of the scales. Wash the fish thoroughly in cold water.

Cleaning or gutting: To clean the fish, cut off the head (if the recipe does not specify leaving it on) and make one long cut down the underside. Using a spoon, scrape out the intestines, which should come out in one piece. Wash the inside of the fish well, holding it under cold water to get rid of any remaining blood.

Cleaning a fish which is to be kept whole is done by removing the intestines through the gills; part of the gut will come away with the gills and the rest can be removed by inserting your fingers.

Next, cut off the tail and cut away all the fins—the pelvic fins on the underside near the head, the pectoral fins on either side behind the gills, the dorsal fin on the back and the ventral fin on the underside at the back.

The fish is now ready to be cooked, and if it is particularly large it may be cut into steaks or fillets.

Filleting: To fillet a fish is to remove the flesh in lengthways pieces from the backbone. Some fish provide two fillets and some four. First make an incision right down the backbone.

Then with short, sharp cuts, separate the flesh from the bone and carefully work the flesh away. Drop the fillets into a bowl of cold water and dry them with a clean cloth or on kitchen paper towels.

The fillets may now be skinned by inserting a knife between the flesh and the skin and removing the skin in one piece. Cut fish is usually improved if the fillets or steaks are sprinkled with a little salt and left for a few minutes before cooking.

As a general rule, you will require between 175 and 225 grams or 6 and 8 ounces of fish steaks or fish fillets or 450 grams or 1 pound of whole fish per person.

There are numerous ways of cooking fish—frying, grilling and poaching are perhaps best known, but steaming and baking are also suitable. The most popular method of cooking fish is to shallow or deep-fry it.

The length of the cooking time varies according to the method used and the type of fish, but generally the fish is cooked if it flakes easily when tested with a fork.

Cooking Fish

Frying: Fish which is fried is usually coated in seasoned flour, egg and breadcrumbs or batter.

To deep-fry fish, vegetable oils are best as they are lighter and leave the surface of the fish crisp and dry. The thinner the fish, the higher the temperature of the fat may be. Fill a large saucepan one-third full of oil. Heat the oil over moderate heat until it reaches 370°F (183°C) on a deep-fat thermometer, or until a cube of stale bread dropped into the oil browns in 45 seconds.

Successful deep-frying requires a frying basket which fits easily into the pan. This should be heated before the fish is put in so that the fish does not stick to the basket. Depending on the size, the coated pieces of fish will take from 3 to 7 minutes to cook through. The breadcrumbs should turn a light golden brown in colour. Drain the fried fish on kitchen paper towels before serving.

Grilling: To grill fish, preheat the grill to high. Brush the fish with melted butter and place it under the grill. Cook for 10 to 15 minutes, depending on the thickness of the fish.

Fish steaks and fillets only need to be grilled on one side to be cooked right through, whereas whole fish must be turned to brown them evenly on both sides. Whole fish should be

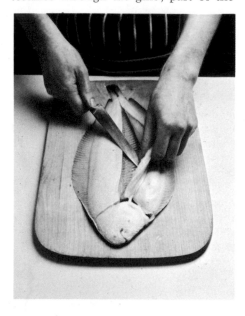

To fillet a fish, make an incision down the backbone and, with a sharp knife, carefully ease the flesh away.

Turn the fish round so that the head is facing you and remove the other fillet in the same way.

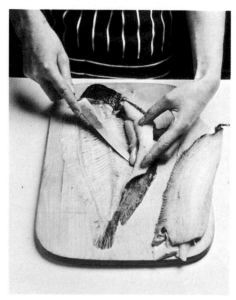

Turn the fish over on to its front and remove the remaining two black-skinned fillets with any roes.

Rub your fingers with salt for easier handling and carefully ease the flesh off the skin in one piece.

scored with three shallow slits on each side to speed up the cooking process and to prevent the fish from curling.

Poaching: Fish may be poached in milk, court bouillon, fish stock, wine or water. Poaching can be done on top of the stove or in the oven. To poach in the oven, preheat it to moderate 350°F (Gas Mark 4, 180°C). Lay the fish in a shallow baking dish. Heat the poaching liquid until it is boiling and pour it over the top. Cover the dish with foil and place it in the oven.

To protect a large white fish from breaking up, and also to make it easy to lift out, wrap it in cheesecloth. When poaching on top of the stove, place the wrapped fish in warm, not boiling, liquid and bring it to the boil. Reduce the heat to low and simmer the fish until it is cooked. Baste occasionally so that the cheesecloth remains wet at all times. When the fish is cooked, lift it out of the poaching liquid with the two ends of the cheesecloth. Unwrap the fish and place it on a serving dish.

Allow 10 to 12 minutes per half kilo (8 to 10 minutes per pound) for large whole fish, 15 to 20 minutes in all for small whole fish like plaice, flounder or sole, 8 to 12 minutes for fillets and 10 to 15 minutes for steaks lying in a single layer in the dish. An onion, lemon slices, chopped carrots and celery may be put in the poaching liquid to add flavour to the fish.

Steaming: Steaming is the best way of retaining flavour in a delicate lean fish. If you do not possess a fish kettle with a steaming shelf, a steamer can be easily improvised by placing a perforated tray over a deep saucepan half-full of water or fish stock. The fish must be kept out of contact with the liquid. Cooking times are the same as for poaching.

Baking: To bake a whole fish, lay the fish on a large piece of aluminium foil. Place a bay leaf, salt, pepper and thin slices of onion and lemon inside the fish. Rub the fish all over with oil, if you are eating it cold, or butter if it is to be served hot. Wrap the fish like a parcel, leaving space inside for the air to circulate, and carefully fold the edges to seal. Place the fish in a roasting tin and bake it in the oven preheated to cool 300°F (Gas Mark 2, 150°C). A 1 to 1½ kg (2 to 3 pound) fish will take about 1 hour.

Carefully remove the fish from the foil and while it is still hot, remove the skin gently with a knife. This is a good way of cooking salmon and salmon trout.

Smoked fish of all kinds are becoming an increasingly popular part of the diet. Kippers, pictured below, are inexpensive and delicious to eat.

Eggs and how to cook them

Eggs have always been symbols of birth, rebirth and fertility. Now, however, it is chiefly valued as a food in itself. The egg is high in protein and fat, as well as calcium, iron and vitamins.

Eggs should be eaten as fresh as possible; if you must store eggs, store them in a cool, airy place. If you store them in the refrigerator, allow them to warm to room temperature before using. To test the freshness of an egg, lay it, horizontally, in a bowl of cold water. If it stays horizontal it is fresh, but if it stands vertical it is stale.

Preparing eggs

Separating eggs: to separate eggs, crack them sharply then open them carefully just enough to let the white slip out. Tip the yolk carefully from one half of the shell to the other to let out all the white.

Beating egg whites: whichever type of bowl you use, it must be without a trace of grease anywhere. To ensure this, the inside of the bowl may be rubbed over gently with a piece of lemon.

Begin by beating slowly. When the whites begin to foam, add a pinch of salt (if you are using a stainless steel bowl add a pinch of cream of tartar instead) and quicken the pace of beating gradually until you are beating vigorously and the whites resemble stiff snow.

Beaten egg whites will not remain firm for long unless sugar has been added, and even then it will be for a short time only.

Cooking eggs

In cooking, eggs may be prepared in so many ways that they need never become boring. The basic methods are: boiling (hard or soft), scrambling, frying, poaching and baking. Eggs can also be made into omelets or soufflés.

Boiled eggs: Boiled eggs should not, in fact, be boiled, but simmered gently to prevent them from cracking. There are two chief ways of soft-boiling an egg.

1. Place the egg in a pan of boiling water. Boil for 1 minute. Turn off the heat, cover the pan and leave for 5 minutes.

2. Place the egg in a pan of boiling water and simmer for 3 to 4 minutes according to the size of the egg. At the end of this time the egg white will be lightly set and the yolk runny.

For a hard-boiled egg, put the egg in a pan of boiling water and bring the water back to the boil. Simmer over moderate heat for 10 minutes.

Scrambled eggs: In a small bowl, beat 2 eggs together with $\frac{1}{2}$ teaspoon of salt, $\frac{1}{4}$ teaspoon of black pepper and, if liked, 2 tablespoons of milk, cream or water, until the mixture is frothy. In a medium-sized saucepan, melt 1 tablespoon of butter over moderate heat. Pour the egg mixture into the pan and cook for 3 to 4 minutes, stirring constantly with a wooden spoon until it thickens. Remove from the heat and stir until the mixture is creamy.

Fried eggs: In a small frying-pan, heat 1 tablespoon of olive oil or butter or bacon fat over moderate heat. When the oil or fat is sizzling, break an egg carefully into the pan. Reduce the heat to low and cook gently, basting frequently with the hot fat, until the white is set and the yolk is firm.

Poached eggs: Poached eggs may either be cooked in boiling water, or steamed in a poaching pan.

For the first method, half-fill a small saucepan with water. Add $\frac{1}{2}$ teaspoon of salt and 1 teaspoon of vinegar. Place the pan over moderate heat and bring the water to the boil. Break an egg into a cup. When the water is boiling, carefully tip the egg into the centre of the bubbling water. Reduce the heat to moderately low and simmer gently for 3 minutes.

To use an egg-poaching pan, half-fill the bottom of the pan with water. Place $\frac{1}{4}$ teaspoon of butter in the centre of each cup, unless you are using a non-stick pan. Place the pan, with the cups in place, over the heat. When the water boils, break the eggs into the cups. Cover and simmer for 3 to 5 minutes or until the eggs are lightly set.

Baked eggs: One of the oldest

methods of cooking eggs, baked eggs are usually prepared in individual cocotte dishes, although several may be baked together in a small oven-proof dish. Place the dishes or dish on a baking sheet. Put ½ teaspoon of butter in each dish and place the baking sheet in the oven preheated to fairly hot 400°F (Gas Mark 6, 200°C) for 2 minutes. Break an egg into each dish, season with a little salt and pepper and return the dishes to the oven. Bake for 4 to 5 minutes or until the eggs are lightly set. Serve at once, in the dishes.

Omelet: To make good omelets, you will require a special omelet pan. The pan should be thick with a good smooth surface and should never be used for cooking anything else.

Never make too large an omelet. The best size is with 4 eggs and the limit should be 6 eggs. A medium-sized pan, one with a base 18 centimetres or 7 inches in diameter, will do for the smaller omelet and a pan with a 23-centimetre or 9-inch base for the larger.

Omelets must never be over-cooked. The perfect omelet has a soft, creamy nearly semi-liquid centre.

To make an omelet for 3 people, break 6 eggs into a bowl. Add ¼ teaspoon of salt and pepper (or more if you like) and 2 tablespoons of cold water. Beat well to mix with either a fork or a wire whisk.

Heat the pan over moderate heat for 10 seconds or until it is quite hot. Add ½ tablespoon of butter and when the foam subsides, pour in the beaten eggs. Stir the eggs, then leave them for a few seconds until the bottom sets. Reduce the heat to low. Using a palette knife or spatula, lift the edge of the omelet and at the same time tilt the pan away from you so that the liquid egg escapes from the top and runs into the pan. Put the pan down flat again over the heat and leave until the omelet begins to set. Tilt the pan away from you again and, with the help of the palette knife, flip one half of the omelet over to make a semi-circle.

Soufflé: To make a cheese soufflé for four, first generously grease a medium-sized soufflé dish with butter. Sprinkle about 4 tablespoons of grated cheese (preferably a hard cheese, such as Cheddar) around the inside of the dish.

In a large saucepan, melt 50 grams

or 2 ounces of butter over moderate heat. With a wooden spoon, stir 4 tablespoons of flour into the butter and cook, stirring constantly, for 1 minute. Remove the pan from the heat and add 300 millilitres or 10 fluid ounces of milk, stirring constantly. Return the pan to the heat and cook the mixture, stirring constantly, for 1 minute or until it is thick and smooth.

Remove the pan from the heat and add salt, pepper and spices (mace, paprika, etc.) to taste. Beat 5 egg yolks, one at a time, into the hot sauce. Set aside to allow the egg yolk mixture to cool slightly.

Meanwhile, in a large mixing bowl, beat 6 egg whites with a wire whisk or rotary beater until they form stiff peaks.

Stir 125 grams or 4 ounces of grated cheese (again preferably a hard cheese, such as Cheddar) into the cooling egg yolk mixture. When the cheese is thoroughly blended, using a metal spoon, spoon the egg whites on to the top of the yolk mixture, then quickly fold them in.

Spoon the mixture into the prepared soufflé dish and cook in a fairly hot oven 400°F (Gas Mark 6, 200°C) for 25 to 30 minutes or until the soufflé is well risen and golden brown on top.

Vegetables and how to cook them

Vegetables may be classified as plants which are cultivated for human consumption. They are usually cooked or eaten raw as part of the main or savoury course.

Vegetables are an essential part of the diet. They supply, in varying quantities, vitamin A in the form of carotene, vitamin C and vitamins of the B group, as well as natural sugars and starch. Leafy vegetables introduce cellulose into the diet, which is essential for natural bodily functions.

Many vegetables may be eaten raw and those that call for cooking should only be cooked long enough to make them tender. Vegetables may be cooked by boiling, steaming, braising, frying and, in some cases, baking and roasting.

On the following pages is some basic information and cooking instructions for the most commonly used vegetables.

Brussels sprouts

Brussels sprouts are a variety of miniature cabbage and were brought to Britain from Belgium during the nineteenth century—hence their name. They are winter plants and are a good source of vitamin C.

Ideally, Brussels sprouts, in appearance, should be small and solid, with the leaves closely curled, green and very fresh.

To prepare sprouts for cooking, cut the base of the stalks and remove the tough outer leaves. Wash them well. With a sharp knife, cut a cross in the base of each sprout. Cook them, uncovered, in boiling salted water over moderate heat for 10 minutes or until they are tender but still crisp. Remove the pan from the heat and drain the sprouts thoroughly.

If you plan to serve the sprouts plain, put them back in the dried pan with a large piece of butter and sprinkle over some pepper and salt. Toss them over low heat until the butter melts and the sprouts are thoroughly coated with the butter. Serve them at once.

A tempting display of garden-fresh vegetables – simple and quick to cook, even easier to eat!

Cabbage

Cabbage is one of the oldest known vegetables and is cultivated in many varieties, such as cauliflower, Brussels sprouts, kale and broccoli, all of them, like true cabbage, being descended from the wild cabbage. The two main types of green cabbage are those with curled leaves and those with smooth leaves.

Cabbage contains vitamin A, iron, calcium and varying amounts of vitamin C. It may be eaten raw, in salads or cooked. Red cabbage, another variety, is chiefly used for pickling although it tastes delicious braised.

To prepare cabbage for cooking, wash it thoroughly and remove the coarse outer leaves and hard core. Cut into quarters, then soak in cold salted water for about 10 minutes. Drain the cabbage thoroughly.

Cook the cabbage, covered, in a small quantity of boiling salted water over moderately low heat for about 10 minutes or until it is tender but still crisp. Remove the pan from the heat and drain the cabbage thoroughly (if necessary press it between two plates to get rid of the excess moisture). Slice the cabbage, return it to the dried pan; add a large lump of butter and sprinkle over some pepper and salt, and some lemon juice. Toss over low heat until the butter melts and the cabbage is thoroughly coated with the butter. Serve at once.

Carrots

The carrot is a herbaceous plant with a large, edible root. The roots range from long and tapering to short and bulbous; although white, yellow and even purple carrots exist, the orange variety is the most popular. Carrots are a good source of vitamin A and contain a good amount of sugar.

Although carrots are available throughout the year, it is best to buy them when they are new—the older ones (sold during the winter months) have coarser skins and, sometimes, woody cores which have to be removed. Carrots should never be peeled, by the way, as the flavour and vitamins lie very close to the skin.

To prepare carrots for cooking, scrape them with a sharp knife or stiff scrubbing brush, and cut off the root end. If they are large cut them into short lengths or rounds. Cook them, uncovered, in a small quantity of boiling salted water for about 15 minutes or until they are tender but still crisp. Remove the pan from the

heat and drain the carrots thoroughly.

If you wish to serve the carrots plain, garnish with butter, pepper and salt as indicated under Brussels sprouts.

Cauliflower

The name cauliflower is derived from the old English word for flowering cabbage—and as that suggests, cauliflower is indeed a variety of cabbage. It is cultivated for its flowerets which form a compact, round, hard white head surrounded by leaves. Cauliflower is a good source of vitamin C (it provides about half a day's requirement per average portion). In appearance, a cauliflower should have a firm white head and bright green leaves.

To prepare cauliflower for cooking, cut off the leaves, leaving only the very tender small leaves closest to the stalk, and trim the stalk. Either leave the head whole or separate into flowerets. Soak the cauliflower in cold salted water for 20 minutes to draw out any insects. Cook, covered, in boiling salted water for about 15 minutes, if you are cooking the cauliflower whole, 7 to 10 if you have broken it into flowerets. Remove the pan from the heat and drain the cauliflower thoroughly.

If you plan to serve the cauliflower plain, garnish it with butter, pepper and salt as indicated under Brussels sprouts.

French beans

French beans, also known as string beans or haricots verts, are South American in origin. There are many varieties, shapes and colours but the most common has a pod that is deep green in colour.

French beans are best picked when very young, before the seeds have had time to form. With older beans, it is necessary to cut away the stringy edges with a sharp knife before cooking. When the beans are allowed to mature on the plant, the pods should be shelled and the peas inside cooked fresh or when they have been dried.

To prepare French beans for cooking, cut away the stringy edges of older beans with a sharp knife. If the beans are large, halve or cut them into lengths. Soak the beans in cold water to clean them thoroughly. Drain. Cook them, uncovered, in a little boiling salted water, for 5 minutes for young beans, about 15 minutes for older beans.

If the beans are not to be eaten immediately, drain them well and pour cold water over them — this ensures that the texture will be preserved. Garnish them as indicated under Brussels sprouts.

Onions

The onion is a hardy, bulbous plant of the lily family. There are many varieties, all of them edible. The onion has numerous culinary uses—it may be eaten raw, boiled, steamed, fried, braised or baked and is used in stews, sauces, curries, pickles, chutneys and salads. It may be cooked whole, sliced, sliced and pushed out into rings, chopped or grated.

The onion is rarely cooked well; high heat and prolonged cooking can burn it, giving it a bitter flavour; undercooking can leave it too raw, thereby spoiling the flavour of the finished dish. As a general rule, when the full flavour of the onion is required, it should be fried until it is golden brown; when a milder flavour is required it should be fried more gently until it is translucent but not brown. For a dish such as French onion soup, the onion should be cooked until it is deep brown.

To prepare onions for cooking, cut away about ½-inch of the sprouting end since this is mostly outer skin. Remove the brown outer casing and the skin immediately underneath it if it is brown or green. Do not cut off the root until just before cooking because this is where the irritant oils are—the ones that make you cry!

To boil 450 grams (1 pound) of whole onions, pour enough water into a large saucepan to make a 2.5 centimetre or 1-inch layer. Bring the water to the boil and add salt. Add the onions, cover, reduce the heat to low and simmer the onions for 15 to 30 minutes or until they are tender when pierced with the point of a sharp knife. Remove the pan from the heat and drain the onions thoroughly.

If you wish to serve the onions plain, garnish as indicated under Brussels sprouts. Serve at once.

To steam 450 grams (1 pound) of whole onions, half-fill the lower half of a steamer with boiling water. Add the onions to the upper half and place it in position. Place the steamer over moderate heat and steam the onions for 30 to 35 minutes or until they are tender. Remove the steamer from the heat and serve at once.

To fry 450 grams (1 pound) of sliced or chopped onions, in a large frying-pan, melt 1 tablespoon of butter with 1 tablespoon of cooking oil over

moderate heat. When the foam subsides, add the onions and fry, stirring occasionally, for 5 to 7 minutes or until they are soft and translucent but not brown. If you wish to fry the onions until they are golden brown, fry them, stirring occasionally, for 8 to 10 minutes. (The cooking times given are approximate and extra time should be allowed if you are cooking very large quantities.)

Peas

The pea originated in the Near East, although it now grows extensively all over the world. There are two basic types, usually classified as edible-podded or shelling peas, depending on whether the outer casing may be eaten or not.

Garden peas, the most common type of shelling pea, may be bought fresh in season, canned or frozen.

To cook fresh garden peas, place 450 grams (1 pound) (weighed after shelling) in a large saucepan and pour over enough water just to cover. Add a little salt and, if you wish, a sprig of mint. Place the pan over high heat and bring the water to the boil. Reduce the heat to low and simmer the peas for 10 to 12 minutes or until they are tender. Remove the pan from the heat and drain the peas thoroughly. Garnish the peas with butter, pepper and salt as indicated under Brussels sprouts and serve at once.

Petits pois, the smallest and sweetest of the shelling peas, are cooked in the same way.

The mange-tout or snow pea is an edible-podded variety of pea and should be cooked in the same way as French beans.

Potatoes

The Irish or white potato, one of the most important food plants in the world, originated in the Andes region of South America.

There are numerous varieties and each producing country grows 'early' varieties and 'maincrop' varieties, thus ensuring supplies all the year round.

Potatoes have a high water content (about 77 percent) and contain small amounts of minerals, vitamins B and C and about 2 percent protein. However, as they are generally eaten in comparatively large quantities, the sum total of nutrients can be an important contribution to the diet. They should always be eaten cooked, when they make an easily digestible and palatable food.

All potatoes may be cooked and eaten unpeeled, in their jackets, and this is recommended as most of the nutrients lie immediately beneath the skin. If you must peel potatoes, peel only old ones; new potatoes need only be scrubbed.

To boil potatoes, choose potatoes of uniform size, or cut them to size so that they cook in the same amount of time. Cook the potatoes in boiling salted water for 15 to 20 minutes or until they are tender. Remove the pan from the heat and drain the potatoes carefully. Garnish the potatoes with butter, pepper and salt as indicated under Brussels sprouts and serve at once.

To mash boiled potatoes, cook and drain the potatoes as above and mash and stir the potatoes to a rough purée with a potato masher or fork.

To cream boiled potatoes, cook and drain the potatoes as above and beat in 25 grams or 1 ounce of butter and 2 tablespoons of milk or single cream to every kilo or 2 pounds of potatoes. Beat until the mixture is fluffy.

To steam potatoes, half-fill the lower half of a steamer with boiling water. Add the potatoes to the upper half and place it in position. Place the steamer over moderate heat and steam the potatoes for 15 to 20 minutes or until they are tender. Remove the steamer from the heat and serve at once, with melted butter.

To sauté potatoes, prepare the potatoes and cut them into slices, about 1-centimetre or ⅜-inch thick. In a large frying-pan, heat enough butter and oil together to cover the bottom of the pan. Place the pan over moderately high heat. When the foam subsides, add enough potato slices to make a single layer on the bottom of the pan. Fry the slices, turning them frequently, for 10 to 15 minutes or until they are tender and golden brown. Transfer the potatoes to kitchen paper towels to drain. (Cooked or parboiled potatoes may also be sautéed; cut them into slices and fry for 5 to 8 minutes or until they are golden brown. Transfer to kitchen paper towels to drain.)

To cook French-fried potatoes or chips, first cut the potatoes into fingers, 1 to 1.3-centimetres or ⅜ to ½-inch thick and pat them dry with kitchen paper towels. Fill a deep-frying pan one-third full with vegetable oil and heat it over moderate heat until the temperature registers 182°C (360°F) on a deep-fat thermometer or until a small cube of stale bread dropped into the oil turns golden brown in 50 seconds. Place about two handfuls of the potato fingers in a deep-frying basket, which has first been dipped in the hot oil, and lower the basket into the oil. Fry the potatoes for 5 minutes or until they are golden brown. Lift the basket out of the oil and allow the excess oil to run back into the pan. Drain the potatoes on kitchen paper towels and keep them hot while you cook the remaining potato fingers in the same way. French-fried potatoes should be crisp on the outside and floury on the inside.

To bake potatoes in their jackets, preheat the oven to fairly hot 375°F (Gas Mark 5, 190°C). Choose uniform-sized unblemished potatoes. Scrub the skins to remove any soil and prick the skins, in several places, with the prongs of a fork. Distribute the potatoes over the rungs of the oven shelves, being careful to arrange them so that they do not touch. Bake the potatoes for 45 minutes to 1½ hours, depending on the size of the potatoes. The potatoes are cooked if they feel soft when you pinch them. Remove the potatoes from the oven. Cut a cross on one of the flat sides of each potato. Pinch the lower part of each potato with both hands so that the 'cross' opens out. Place a little butter in the 'opening' and sprinkle with a little salt and pepper.

To roast potatoes, either leave them whole if they are small or medium-sized, or cut them into large cubes if they are large. Preheat the oven to fairly hot 400°F (Gas Mark 6, 200°C). Heat an 0.6-centimetre or ¼-inch layer of vegetable oil in a baking tin in the oven for 8 minutes or until the oil is very hot. Remove the tin from the oven and place the potatoes in the oil. Brush them all over with some of the hot oil. Return the tin to the oven and roast the potatoes for 1 hour, brushing occasionally with the oil and turning once, or until the potatoes are deep golden brown. Remove the tin from the oven and transfer the potatoes to kitchen paper towels to drain.

To roast potatoes with meat, par-boil the potatoes, drain and add them to the pan in which the meat is roasting, for the last hour of cooking.

Fresh from the garden – a cool, nutritious selection of vegetables and fruit. They are equally delicious raw or cooked.

Pastry and how to make it

Pastry is an unleavened dough, generally made from shortening (fats), flour and liquid, which is rolled out and used to line flan and tart tins, or to envelope or cover sweet and savoury fillings.

The basic ingredients used to make pastry are:

Flour: in almost every kind of pastry dough, refined plain white wheat flour is used. Self-raising flour is used only when a heavier ingredient such as suet is incorporated.

Salt: in most doughs, salt is added in amounts varying from $\frac{1}{8}$ teaspoon to 1 teaspoon.

Sugar: sugar is added to sweet pastry doughs.

Shortening: all pastry dough includes a shortening (a general term which describes fats used in doughs) in proportions which vary according to the richness of the pastry — the more shortening, the richer the pastry. Generally, butter is used, but margarine, suet, lard, vegetable fat and oil or a combination of shortenings — such as butter and vegetable fat in shortcrust pastry — are also used.

Liquid: liquid is added to the flour and shortening mixture to bind it and make it more pliable. Water is most commonly used, but other liquids such as eggs, milk, cream, sour cream and buttermilk may be used.

Flavourings: Cheese, herbs, spices and essences may be added to the basic pastry dough.

The method by which the shortening is incorporated into the flour determines the texture of the finished pastry. In puff pastry, for example, the shortening, generally butter, is added either in one large or several smaller pieces and rolled and folded into the flour and liquid mixture. The resulting texture is, as the name of the pastry indicates, very light and flaky. For closer-textured pastries, such as shortcrust, the shortening is cut into small pieces and rubbed into the flour with the fingertips until the mixture resembles fine or coarse breadcrumbs. For cooked and even closer-textured pastry doughs, such as choux or hot water crust, the shortening is melted with the liquid and then stirred or beaten into the flour. The eggs in choux pastry open out the texture.

The basic points to remember when making pastry dough are:

1. Unles the dough is made with yeast, or cooked, the ingredients and implements should be kept cool. For some pastry doughs, such as puff pastry, the ingredients should also be chilled.

2. Again with the possible exception of yeast and cooked doughs, a minimum of handling is desirable. When possible, use a table knife or pastry blender to incorporate the shortening into the flour. When rubbing the shortening into the flour, use your fingertips and work quickly and lightly. The more you handle the dough, the stickier and less manageable it becomes.

3. When rolling out dough, place it on a lightly floured working surface and use a floured rolling pin. Make sure that the dough does not stick to the surface as it is rolled out. Roll the dough lightly away from you. Do not turn the dough over or it will absorb too much flour from the working surface. If the dough is sticky or contains a high proportion of shortening, chill it in the refrigerator before rolling it out to make the handling easier.

4. Generally speaking, pastry should be baked, or at least start its baking time, in a hot oven. Long, slow baking produces rather hard, flat-tasting pastry.

5. Closer-textured pastry doughs, such as shortcrust pastry, are more suitable for lining flans and pie dishes and for baking blind. All types of pastry doughs are suitable for covering pies and enveloping sweet or savoury fillings, although puff pastry is the one traditionally used for savoury pies and turnovers.

If you have a freezer, it is well worth your while to make extra dough and store it in the freezer. Wrap it in quantities that are suitable for use, for example 225 grams or eight ounces and 450 grams or one pound. Remember to remove the dough from the freezer at least 30 minutes to one hour before using so that it has time to thaw out thoroughly.

Pastry pies, tarts and flan cases can also be frozen. For the most successful result, it is best to freeze the pastry dough uncooked. If the pie has a cooked filling, such as steak and kidney, this should be cooked and cooled before covering with the pastry dough. Make sure all pastry doughs are wrapped in special freezer packaging.

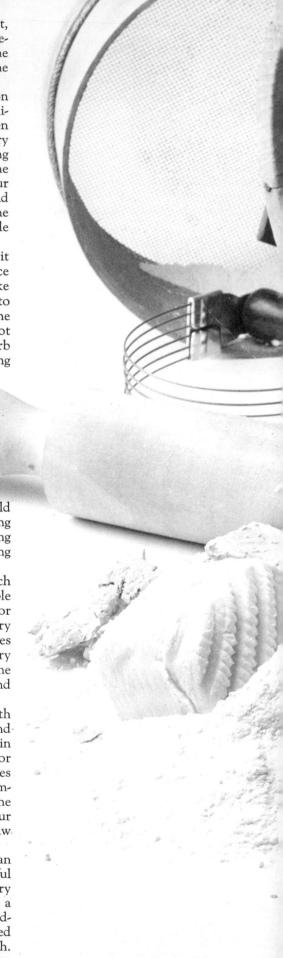

Pastry recipes

Use Shortcrust Pastry as a pie or flan crust for either sweet or savoury fillings; Rich Shortcrust Pastry, should be used for heavier fillings.

Use Puff Pastry when you're making turnovers, or savoury pies.

Use Hot Water Crust Pastry for 'raised' pies such as pork or veal and ham.

Choux Pastry is usually made into puffs, which are baked in the oven and then filled with savoury mixtures such as creamed seafood or sweet ones such as crème pâtissière.

Suetcrust Pastry is usually used in sweet or savoury steamed puddings or roly-poly puddings.

Shortcrust Pastry

225 GRAMS (8 OUNCES)

225g (8oz) flour
½ teaspoon salt
50g (2oz) butter
50g (2oz) vegetable fat
3 to 4 tablespoons iced water

Sift the flour and salt into a medium-sized mixing bowl. Add the butter and vegetable fat and cut them into small pieces with a table knife. With your fingertips, rub the fat into the flour until the mixture resembles coarse breadcrumbs.

Add 3 tablespoons of the iced water and, using the knife, mix it into the flour mixture. With your hands, mix and knead the dough until it is smooth. Add more water if the dough is too dry. Form the dough into a ball and chill it in the refrigerator for 30 minutes.

The dough is now ready to use.

Rich Shortcrust Pastry

225 GRAMS (8 OUNCES)

225g (8oz) flour
¼ teaspoon salt
125g (4oz) butter, chilled
1 teaspoon sugar
1 egg, lightly beaten
2 to 3 tablespoons iced water

Sift the flour and salt into a medium-sized mixing bowl. Add the butter and cut it into small pieces with a table knife. With your fingertips, rub the butter into the flour until the mixture resembles fine breadcrumbs. Stir in the sugar.

Add the beaten egg with a spoonful of iced water and mix it into the flour mixture with a table knife. Add more water if the dough is too dry.

Turn the dough out on to a lightly floured board and knead it for 1 minute. Form the dough into a ball, and chill in the refrigerator for 30 minutes.

The dough is now ready to use.

Choux pastry

300 GRAMS (10 OUNCES)
(OR 8 LARGE CHOUX PUFFS)

300ml (10floz) water
75g (3oz) butter, cut into small pieces
1 teaspoon salt
⅛ teaspoon grated nutmeg
300g (10oz) flour
5 large eggs

In a large heavy saucepan, bring the water to the boil over moderate heat. Add the butter, salt and nutmeg. When the butter has melted, remove the pan from the heat and beat in the flour with a wooden spoon. Continue beating until the mixture pulls away from the sides of the pan.

One by one, beat the eggs into the mixture, beating each one into the dough until it is well blended before adding the next. When the eggs have all been completely absorbed, the mixture should be thick and somewhat glossy.

The dough is now ready to use.

Suetcrust pastry

225 GRAMS (8 OUNCES)

225g (8oz) flour
½ teaspoon salt
125g (4oz) shredded suet
150ml (5floz) cold water

Sift the flour and salt into a medium-sized mixing bowl. Using a table knife, stir the suet and water into the flour mixture to form a firm dough. Form the dough into a ball and wrap it in greaseproof or waxed paper. Place the the dough in the refrigerator to chill for 10 minutes.

Remove the dough from the refrigerator and remove and discard the paper.

The dough is now ready to use.

Puff pastry

450 GRAMS (1 POUND)

450g (1lb) flour
½ teaspoon salt

450g (1lb) butter
200ml (8floz) iced water

Sift the flour and salt into a large mixing bowl. With a table knife, cut 125 grams (4 ounces) of the butter into the flour. Crumble the butter and flour with your fingertips and, with the water, mix to a firm dough. Knead the dough to make it pliable and form it into a ball. Cover with greaseproof or waxed paper and place the dough in the refrigerator to chill for 15 minutes.

Put the remaining butter between two pieces of greaseproof or waxed paper and beat it with the back of a wooden spoon or a wooden mallet into a flat oblong slab about 2 centimetres (¾ inch) thick.

On a floured board, roll out the dough into a rectangular shape 0.6 centimetres (¼ inch) thick. Place the slab of butter in the centre of the dough and fold the dough over it to make a parcel. Place the dough in the refrigerator to chill for a further 10 minutes.

Place the dough, with the folds downwards, on the board and roll out away from you into a rectangle. Fold the rectangle in three. Turn so that the open end is facing you and roll out again. Chill the dough in the refrigerator for 15 minutes. Then repeat this process twice more.

The dough is now ready to use.

Hot water crust pastry

350 GRAMS (12 OUNCES)

350g (12oz) flour
1 teaspoon salt
150ml (5floz) water
125g (4oz) vegetable fat or lard
1 egg yolk, lightly beaten

Sift the flour and salt into a large mixing bowl.

In a small saucepan, bring the water and vegetable fat or lard to the boil over high heat, stirring frequently with a wooden spoon until the fat or lard has melted. Remove the pan from the heat.

Make a well in the centre of the flour and pour in the egg yolk and water and fat mixture. With a wooden spoon, gradually draw the flour mixture into the liquids. Continue until all the flour is incorporated and the dough is smooth.

Turn the dough out on to a floured board and knead it well with your hands until it is shiny.

The dough is now ready to use.

Bread and how to make it

It is easy to buy a commercially made loaf of bread or even freshly baked bread from a bakery, but neither of these will give you the sense of satisfaction you will have when your family and friends tuck into a loaf of bread you have made yourself.

Making bread is an art, but, contrary to some opinion, it can be easily mastered. Bread recipes vary considerably and the general guidelines set out here will not fit all of them exactly, but if you understand what each ingredient is meant to do and what the techniques are, you will be on your way to successful breadmaking.

In addition to the principles and techniques that follow, three 'basic' bread recipes are given, including one for soda bread which traditionally uses bicarbonate of soda rather than yeast for rising.

Ingredients:

Flour: The type, or types, of flour you use for your bread is really a matter of personal taste, but the best flours for both yeast and non-yeast bread doughs are milled from hard wheat. These flours have a high gluten content which produces a more elastic springy dough – soft wheat flours make a rather sticky dough.

Almost all white flour sold commercially is soft household flour. Health food stores, however, usually stock wholewheat flour, stone-ground flour, 100 percent wholemeal flour (the whole grain of the wheat with nothing removed and nothing added) and 85 percent or 90 percent wholemeal flour (the husk and bran removed). And some larger stores and supermarkets sell strong plain white flour which is particularly recommended for breadmaking.

You can mix several different kinds of flour together. For example, you can make a good loaf of pale brown bread if you use a mixture of 125 grams (4 ounces) of 100 percent wholemeal flour and 350 grams (12 ounces) of soft household flour. Even better bread is produced if you use 85 percent or 90 percent wholemeal flour with strong plain white flour in the same proportions.

When making bread, it is best if the temperature of the flour is the same as that of the room and of the liquid used in the recipe. If the flour is too cold, you can warm it in the oven.

Yeast: the most important thing to remember about yeast is that it is a living cell which must be provided with a 'friendly' environment if it is to do its job properly.

Yeast is a very tiny fungus which grows by sending off buds to form new plants, and by forming spores which may also become new plants. As yeast grows it gives off carbon dioxide gas. This gas, when the yeast is mixed into the dough, causes the elastic cell walls of the gluten in the flour to expand – the phenomenon of the dough rising.

The yeast also gives off alcohol which, if growth is allowed to continue too long, develops into acetic acid and causes the dough to become sour. The heat of baking, however, drives off the alcohol.

Controversy still rages over fresh yeast versus dried yeast. Fresh bakers' yeast or compressed yeast (*not brewers' yeast*) is sold by health food shops and by some bakers and supermarkets.

In a large, warmed bowl, make a well in the flour, salt and sugar mixture. Pour in the liquid ingredients.

Using your hands or a spatula, gradually mix the ingredients together until all the flour is incorporated.

On a floured board or marble slab, knead the dough for about 10 minutes or until it feels elastic and smooth.

Because the plants are active and alive it is highly perishable and can be kept for only about four to five days in an airtight container in the refrigerator. Fresh yeast should feel cool and like putty to the touch. It should be grey in colour and practically odourless. When you use it, it should break with a clean edge and crumble very easily. Do not use yeast that is dry or sour-smelling, or has dark streaks.

Dried yeast in granule form (activated dried yeast) will keep for six months in a cool place because the plants are inert and will not become active until they are mixed with a warm liquid.

The quantity of yeast given in the receipes which follow are for fresh yeast – so you should halve the quantities if you are using dried yeast. As a general guide, use 15 grams ($\frac{1}{2}$ ounce) of fresh yeast for 450–675 grams (1–1$\frac{1}{2}$ pounds) of flour and 25 grams (1 ounce) for 1·35 kilograms (3 pounds) of flour.

Yeast is destroyed by extreme heat. If you add hot water to yeast or try to speed up the rising process by leaving the dough in a very hot place, the yeast will be killed.

Sugar: sugar provides food for the yeast which helps it to grow and also adds flavour to the bread. Sugar also plays a part in browning the crust. If there is not very much sugar in the dough, the yeast will use it all in making carbon dioxide and alcohol, and the baked bread will not be golden brown.

Too much sugar, however, retards the yeast's activity and the dough will take longer to rise.

Liquid: the moisture in the dough is supplied by water or milk or a mixture of the two, and may be cold when it is added. The ideal temperature, however, is lukewarm. Test the milk on the inside of your wrist.

Milk should be scalded (that is, brought to just under boiling point) and then cooled to lukewarm before it is added to the flour. This scalding action destroys certain bacteria in the milk which could cause the dough to sour. It also makes the dough easier to handle.

Salt: salt should never be mixed directly with the yeast because it slows down the fermentation process. But a sufficient amount of salt must be added to the dough or the bread will have a very uninteresting flavour.

Eggs and butter or oil: Eggs and butter or oil are variables. When eggs are added to the dough, as in sweet breads or brioches, the finished bread is richer and more yellow. Butter or oil increase the volume of the baked bread because the gluten network of the dough is lubricated so that it expands more smoothly and easily. Butter or oil also improve the flavour and keeping qualities of the bread.

Techniques
Dissolving the yeast: crumble the yeast into a small bowl. Using a fork, cream a small amount of sugar with the yeast and add a little lukewarm water. Mix to a paste and set aside in a warm, draught-free place to ferment. At the end of 15 to 20 minutes the yeast will be puffed up and frothy.

If you are using dried yeast, dissolve a small quantity of sugar in lukewarm water in a small bowl or teacup and sprinkle on the yeast. Leave it for 10 minutes to allow the yeast cells to separate, swell and become active.

The yeast is now ready to begin its work as soon as it is worked into the dough.

Mixing the dough: put the dry ingredients, the flour, salt and sugar, in a large, warmed bowl. Make a well in the centre and pour in the liquid ingredients, the dissolved yeast, milk and/or water, butter melted in the milk or oil. Then, using your fingers or a spatula, gradually draw the dry ingredients into the liquids and continue mixing until all the flour is incorporated and the dough comes away from the sides of the bowl. If the dough is too soft and wet, more flour may be worked in.

Kneading: turn the dough out of the bowl on to a floured board or marble slab to knead. This will thoroughly mix the flour with the liquid. The kneaded dough will hold in the gas bubbles manufactured by the yeast.

Fold the dough over on to itself towards you and then press it down away from yourself with the heels of your hands. Turn the dough slightly and fold and press it again. Continue kneading for about 10 minutes or until the dough feels smooth and elastic. Dough made with hard wheat flours requires a little more kneading than dough made with soft flour.

If the dough feels sticky while you are kneading, you may work in a little more flour, but be careful not to add too much or the dough will become stiff.

Rising: shape the kneaded dough into a ball and place it in a lightly greased bowl. Sprinkle the surface of the dough with a little flour and cover the bowl with a damp cloth. The flour will prevent the dough from sticking to the cloth as it rises and the cloth is dampened to increase the humidity. Do not cover the bowl tightly because to grow the yeast needs air as well as

Leave it in a warm place for 1 to 1½ hours or until the dough has almost doubled in bulk. Remove the cover.

When the dough has risen, punch it to break up the air pockets, and fold the edges to the centre.

Shape the dough into pieces and press them into greased loaf tins. Leave the dough to rise again.

moisture, warmth and food. Place the bowl in a warm, draught-free place until the dough has almost doubled in bulk.

If your kitchen is cold you may want to place the bowl on top of the stove with the oven on at cool 300°F (Gas Mark 2, 150°C).

Rising times vary greatly depending on temperature, the amount of yeast in the dough and the kind of flour used, but, generally speaking, 1 to 1½ hours is adequate. The longer the fermentation, the better-flavoured and better-textured the bread will be. However, the dough should not be left to rise in a warm place for too long or it will become rather tough. You can tell if this is happening because a crust will form on the top of the dough.

If you want to speed up the rising process, place the covered bowl on an oven rack over a pan of boiling water. But be sure that the bottom of the bowl is not too close to the water or the heat will kill the yeast.

To test if the dough has risen sufficiently, press two fingers deep into the dough and withdraw them quickly. If the indentation remains the dough has risen enough.

If you are preparing the dough the day before the bread is to be baked, you can prolong the rising process by putting the covered bowl in a cool place or in the refrigerator for 8 to 10 hours or overnight. When the dough is fully risen it will be lighter and more spongy than dough which has risen in a warm place. It will require more kneading the second time as well as a longer proving.

Second kneading: push your fist into the centre of the dough and fold the edges to the centre. This punching down breaks up the large gas pockets

and makes available a new supply of oxygen for the yeast plants.

Turn the dough out of the bowl on to the floured work surface. Knead it thoroughly and vigorously for 2 to 3 minutes (a larger batch of dough requires a longer kneading). This second kneading is more important than the first because it temporarily checks the action of the yeast.

Use a sharp knife to cut the dough into the number of loaves you are baking. With your hands, shape these pieces into balls.

Proving: what you are proving is that the yeast is still active. To do this the balls of dough are put into the greased tins and pushed out slightly so that they are roughly the shape of the tins. The tins should only be about half full. Sprinkle the surfaces of the loaves with a little flour. Cover the tins with a damp cloth and return them to a warm place for 30 to 45 minutes. During this time the dough will rise to the top of the tins.

The proving may be done on an oven rack over a pan of boiling water, but be careful not to place the bottoms of the tins too close to the water.

If you want your bread to have a shiny crust, instead of sprinkling the dough with flour, just before baking (using a pastry brush) brush the tops of the loaves with a mixture of beaten egg and milk.

A country-style finish can be produced by making a criss-cross gash in the top of the dough with a knife or kitchen scissors.

Baking: the bread must always be started in a hot oven so the oven should be preheated to the correct temperature for at least 5 minutes before the dough is put in to bake. Baking stops the fermentation of the

yeast and evaporates the alcohol.

Place the tins in the centre of the oven and bake for 15 minutes. In this initial stage the loaf rises dramatically. This is caused by the leavening gas expanding rapidly and the gluten cells stretching to accommodate it.

Transfer the tins to a lower shelf and reduce the oven heat. The gluten cells will gradually be set by the heat, and after 25 to 30 minutes the bread should be done, having shrunk slightly in the tins.

To increase the crustiness of the loaves, brush the tops of the loaves with lightly beaten egg white or cold water 10 minutes before the end of the baking time. For a soft crust, brush the tops with melted butter about 10 minutes before the baking time is completed.

Remove the tins from the oven and turn the bread out, upside down, on to a wire rack. Rap the bottoms of the loaves with your knuckles. If they sound hollow, like a drum, the bread is cooked. If they feel soft, return them, upside down, to the oven with the heat reduced and bake for a further 10 to 15 minutes.

A shiny, glazed crust, characteristic of French and Vienna loaves, can be obtained by placing a flat pan of boiling water in the bottom of the oven just before the bread is put in and leaving the tin in the oven throughout the baking. The steam from the water forms a coating of moisture on the surface of the dough which gives it time to expand and develop a crust.

Cooling: bread should be cooled on a wire rack so that the air can circulate around it and prevent moisture from spoiling the crispness of the crust. For the very best results, serve the bread while still slightly warm.

Basic white bread

FOUR 450 GRAM (1 POUND) LOAVES
2 teaspoons butter
25g (1oz) yeast
1 tablespoon plus 1 teaspoon sugar
**900ml (1½pints) plus 4 teaspoons
    lukewarm water**
1.35kg (3lb) flour
1 tablespoon salt

Grease four 450 gram (one pound) loaf tins with the butter.

Crumble the yeast into a small bowl and mash in 1 teaspoon of sugar with a fork. Add 4 teaspoons of water and cream the water and yeast together to form a smooth paste. Set the bowl aside in a warm, draught-free place for 15 to 20 minutes or until the yeast is puffed up and frothy.

Put the flour, the remaining sugar and the salt into a warmed, large mixing bowl. Make a well in the centre and pour in the yeast and the remaining water. Using your hands or a spatula, gradually draw the flour into the liquid. Continue mixing until all the flour is incorporated and the dough comes away from the sides of the bowl.

Turn the dough out on to a floured board or marble slab and knead for about 10 minutes, reflouring the surface if the dough becomes sticky.

This basic white loaf is very easy to make and tastes much better than commercially made bread. If possible, try to use strong plain white flour (available in most larger supermarkets).

The dough should be elastic and smooth.

Rinse, dry and lightly grease the bowl. Shape the dough into a ball and return it to the bowl. Dust the top of the dough with a little flour and cover the bowl with a damp cloth. Set the bowl in a warm, draught-free place and leave it for 1 to 1½ hours or until the dough has risen and has almost doubled in bulk.

Turn the risen dough out of the bowl on to a floured surface and knead for about 8 to 10 minutes. Using a sharp knife, cut the dough into four pieces and roll and shape each piece into a loaf. Place the leaves in the tins, cover with a damp cloth and return to a warm place for 30 to 45 minutes or until the dough has risen to the top of the tins.

Preheat the oven to very hot 475°F (Gas Mark 9, 240°C).

Place the tins in the centre of the oven and bake for 15 minutes. Then lower the temperature to hot 425°F (Gas Mark 7, 220°C), put the bread on a lower shelf in the oven and bake for

another 25 to 30 minutes.

After removing the bread from the oven, tip the loaves out of the tins and rap the undersides with your knuckles. If the bread sounds hollow, like a drum, it is cooked. If it does not sound hollow, lower the oven temperature to fairly hot 375°F (Gas Mark 5, 190°C), return the loaves, upside down, to the oven and bake for a further 5 to 10 minutes.

Cool the loaves on a wire rack.

Basic soda bread

ONE 20CM (8IN) LOAF

1 teaspoon butter
450g (1lb) flour
1 teaspoon bicarbonate of soda
1 teaspoon salt
125-250ml (4-8floz) buttermilk

Preheat the oven to hot 425°F (Gas Mark 7, 220°C).

Grease a large baking sheet with the butter and set it aside.

Sift the flour, soda and salt into a large mixing bowl. With a wooden spoon, gradually beat in 125 millilitres (4 fluid ounces) of buttermilk. The dough should be smooth but firm. If necessary, add more buttermilk.

Transfer the dough to a floured

This basic soda bread is Irish in origin but is now enjoyed throughout the world. It is one of the few genuine breads that is traditionally made without yeast.

board or marble slab and shape it into a flat round loaf, about 20 centimetres (8 inches) in diameter.

Place the loaf on the baking sheet. With a sharp knife, cut a deep cross on top of the loaf.

Place the loaf in the oven and bake for 30 to 35 minutes or until the top is golden brown.

Remove the loaf from the oven and allow it to cool. Serve slightly warm.

Basic wholewheat bread

FOUR 450 GRAM (1 POUND LOAVES)
2 teaspoons butter
25g (1oz) yeast
1 teaspoon soft brown sugar
**900ml (1½ pints) plus 4 teaspoons
  lukewarm water**
**1.35kg (3lb) stone-ground
  wholewheat flour**
**1¼ tablespoons rock salt or 1
  tablespoon table salt**
2 tablespoons clear honey
1 tablespoon vegetable oil

Grease four 450 gram (one pound) loaf

tins (or clay flower pots as above) with the butter.

Crumble the yeast into a small bowl and mash in the brown sugar with a fork. Add 4 teaspoons of water and cream the water and yeast together to form a smooth paste. Set the bowl aside in a warm, draught-free place for 15 to 20 minutes or until the yeast has risen and is puffed up and frothy.

Put the flour and salt into a warmed, large mixing bowl. Make a well in the centre and pour in the yeast, the honey, the remaining water and the oil. Using your fingers or a spatula, gradually draw the flour into the liquid. Continue mixing until all the flour is incorporated and the dough comes away from the sides of the bowl.

Turn the dough out on to a floured surface or marble slab and knead for about 10 minutes, reflouring the surface if the dough becomes sticky. The dough should be elastic and smooth.

Rinse, dry and lightly grease the bowl. Shape the dough into a ball and return it to the bowl. Dust the top of the dough with a little flour and cover the bowl with a damp cloth. Set the bowl in a warm, draught-free place and leave it for 1 to 1½ hours or until the dough has risen and has almost doubled in bulk.

Turn the risen dough out of the

This basic wholewheat loaf makes an extra special treat. You can make it in any shape you like – in conventional loaf tins, in clay flower pots, as above, or shaped into a round and baked on a baking sheet.

bowl on to a floured surface and knead vigorously for about 10 minutes. Using a sharp knife, cut the dough into four pieces. Roll and shape each piece into a loaf. Place the loaves in the tins or pots. Cover the tins or pots with a damp cloth and return to a warm place for 30 to 45 minutes or until the dough has risen to the top of the tins or pots.

Preheat the oven to very hot 475°F (Gas Mark 9, 240°C).

Place the tins or pots in the centre of the oven and bake for 15 minutes. Then lower the temperature to hot 425°F (Gas Mark 7, 220°C), put the bread on a lower shelf in the oven and bake for another 25 to 30 minutes.

After removing the bread from the oven, tip the loaves out of the tins or pots and rap the undersides with your knuckles. If the bread sounds hollow, like a drum, it is cooked. If the bread does not sound hollow, lower the oven temperature to fairly hot 375°F (Gas Mark 5, 190°C), return the loaves, upside down, to the oven and bake for a further 10 minutes.

Cool the loaves on a wire rack.

Preparing for 2

Magazines can provide helpful new ideas for dinner or supper.

Having gone to the trouble of organizing shopping for food and storing it (see pages 126–141), it makes sense to plan your cooking in the same way. In fact, if you're a working wife (and most newly married women are nowadays) you will probably find that having a cooking and eating routine, especially during weekdays, is not so much a desirable luxury as an absolute necessity.

Planning for weekdays
One way to tackle the problem of providing what seems like an endless procession of meals is to pre-cook. Have a giant session on, say, Saturday afternoon (specially recommended for football, cricket or golf widows!) or on Sundays (perhaps during the hiatus between reading the papers and the start of evening television) and cook enough to see you through at least the first couple of days of the working week. This is only really feasible if you have a refrigerator, though; of course, if you're the proud owner of a freezer, then most of your cook-ahead troubles are over — you could, technically at least, limit your cooking to a mammoth binge once a month.

Pre-cooking has other advantages. Stews, casseroles and soups — the type of food most often pre-cooked — often actually improve on the second or even third day after cooking and, since they are not the sort of food that it is practicable to cook during the week for consumption the same evening, by definition they extend and vary the diet. Cold desserts, too, can be concocted and left to set overnight or even for a couple of days in the refrigerator and thus provide an 'instant' addition to any mid-week meal.

You could also rely on quick-cooking foods — lamb chops, a slice of liver or fried fish fillets, for instance. You will still have to do *some* work (breading the chop or fish perhaps) but, on the whole, such foods take little time to prepare yet provide substantial and nutritious meals.

Quick-cooking foods have obvious advantages — if you arrive home late, and hungry, the meal can often be on the table within 30 minutes if you really set your mind to it. They can be fairly economical, too, since you'll probably rely on a plain piece of meat or fish (going up or down the cost scale as you prefer) and serve it with vegetables, which also can be inexpensive when chosen judiciously.

Alternatively, you could concentrate on frozen, pre-cooked foods — fish, for example, which comes in a wide variety of types and is often accompanied by a pre-cooked sauce, or perhaps pre-prepared roast beef or roast turkey.

The advantages of frozen food are self-evident. For those who don't like to cook (and that's all of us sometimes, even the most enthusiastic experimenters), it cuts down the preparation and cooking of meals to an absolute minimum. You can literally plunge some little bags in boiling water and 15 minutes or so later your meal is complete and ready. All of which can be soothing in the extreme after a hard day at the factory or the office! However, frozen foods do have major disadvantages: used on a regular, everyday basis, they can and do work out to be much more expensive than freshly made meals, and the cost really does have to be calculated against the convenience if you're trying to exist within some sort of budget. And despite a great many improvements in quality and taste in recent years, frozen foods, indeed any kind of pre-packed, pre-cooked food, does not — and probably never will — taste quite the same as freshly bought, freshly made food in season.

The most efficient way to plan your working, cooking week is probably to plan some sort of combination of all three of the above suggestions, using frozen food as a 'rest' or when you honestly can't quite face preparing yet another meal from scratch. Say, pre-cook one or two stews on Sunday for early in the week, then have liver or kebabs or fish for the next couple of days; or make some soup on Sunday (or Monday even — particularly possible if you have a roast on Sunday, use up the leftovers on Monday and still have a carcass or bones to boil up for stock) and serve it with a sustaining pudding, perhaps a roly poly with custard. Man *can* live without meat — it's just a matter of proving it to the average Western male! On the days when you have a pre-cooked stew, you might feel more like making a salad or a hot dessert, whereas on the days you plan to have chops or steaks, those pre-prepared cold desserts can come into their own, or you can serve fruit and cheese as a refreshing and nutritious change-of-pace dessert.

Planning for weekends
This is when you'll probably feel most like cooking — and entertaining, too, which is where our special section on pages 207–231 comes in. Even if you're only cooking for the two of you, there's more time to do it in, more time to appreciate it and to relax over it.

At first sight, buying a roast can be a bit expensive for just the two of you, but second thoughts may well change your mind (and if they don't, our suggestions on how to get three meals out of a joint on pages 198-203 ought to do the trick). It does add a touch of luxury to anyone's eating routine, especially if most of the rest of the week is spent eking out cheaper cuts, or trying to disguise them in one way or another, and since at weekends meals assume an even greater significance than during the week, it's well worth investing just that little extra both in terms of money and energy on them.

Preparing ahead

If you're the type who likes to come home and put your feet up for 15 minutes before doing *anything* (weekdays *and* weekends), then maybe you should consider preparing ahead, or changing long-held habits a little.

Preparing ahead (apart from pre-cooking) means peeling/scraping vegetables and making salad dressings in bulk ahead of time, making up the minced meat mixture for the hamburgers — either before you go to work in the morning during the week or before you go out at weekends.

Preparing ahead could also mean the introduction of a little women's lib into the kitchen, with the institution of the golden rule that first in, from work, football game or shopping, peels the spuds (if they haven't already been done, that is) or puts the oven on to heat up the evening's offering.

Changing long-held habits a little means, perhaps, increasing the use of pasta or rice as the main accompaniments to a main course (thus cutting out the fiddly preparations associated with preparing fresh vegetables), serving fruit as a dessert rather than a troublesome trifle or mousse.

It will all cut down on the time consumed in preparing the meal and thereby allow you more time for the really important things in life—like a sherry or Scotch before dinner.

Cutting corners

Preparing tasty meals can be an expensive business; planning can help somewhat of course but it is an essential part of good housekeeping to learn some simple ways of cutting down the cost of good eating — and, contrary to popular opinion, these don't consist solely of finding wonder substitutes for fillet steaks that cost

half the price (although you can be sure that somewhere in the world there's a back-street restaurant proprietor working exclusively on this very problem!). Here are some 'stretchers' that are well worth considering:

Turkey fillets, for instance. They can be bought in most large supermarkets and butcher chains now, look and taste quite similar to veal escalopes and retail at roughly half the price. So if you really want to impress your man, buy some turkey fillets (one fairly large one per person), dip it in flour, then egg, then breadcrumbs, fry it in lots of butter and garnish it with a lemon quarter. And you have a quite delicious dish, indistinguishable from a genuine Wiener Schnitzel!

Whiting fillets don't taste exactly the same as sole fillets (nothing, unfortunately, does) but, poached gently in stock and/or white wine and covered with a delicate white or cheese sauce, they make a much more than passable substitute. And again they cost approximately half the price.

Everyone's talking about the new soya protein meat substitute (TVP to the initiated); unfortunately, it CAN look a bit like dog biscuits or sawdust when dehydrated (depending on whether you're looking at the chunky or mince version), but when cooked it looks and tastes quite delicious (although, manufacturers claims notwithstanding, it doesn't as a rule taste exactly like meat — but does in fact have a pleasant taste of its own). If you don't fancy cooking the protein on its own, it can also be added to meat to stretch out stews, casseroles or any recipe calling for mince or meat chunks; they really do blend into the taste of the meat in such cases and mixed with meat to serve four in the proportion of roughly 50 grams or 2 ounces soya protein to 450 grams or 1 pound of meat, it is indistinguishable from the real thing. And again the cost is a definite plus — a 150-gram (5-ounce) bag of mince soya protein (which used on its own will feed about four people) costs approximately three-quarters the price of 450 grams (1 pound) of minced meat.

At the moment, soya protein products are available mostly in health food stores and some delicatessens, but at least one large food manufacturer now markets a brand of mince protein which is generally available at supermarket chains throughout the country.

A little cream added to almost

anything makes a luxury out of the mundane. Of course cream isn't cheap but there are some things that shouldn't be skimped on too much and cream is one. Besides if your recipe calls for fairly large quantities, there are ways of economizing. If your recipe calls for, say, 400 millilitres (15 fluid ounces) of double cream, then this can be 'stretched' by beating 150 millilitres (5 fluid ounces) of single cream into 300 millilitres (10 fluid ounces) of double cream; if you have to whip the cream stiffly, you'll have to use your elbow a little longer, otherwise the result will be exactly the same as if you'd used all double cream. Beating an egg white into double cream (roughly in the proportion of one egg white to 150 millilitres or 5 fluid ounces of double cream) can also 'stretch' it out considerably.

If you're planning to use your oven to cook a roast, why not use up the extra space by cooking a dessert, or perhaps tomorrow's tart or cake as well? The saving on fuel bills (over a period of time) could be quite substantial. Of course you must check first that all of the things you plan to cook together can be cooked at the same temperature!

And on those occasions when you indulge yourself by buying a roast or a roasting bird, when you've had the roast AND made tasty meals of the leftovers (see pages 198–203 for some fabulous ideas), then you could be super-economical and boil up the bones and carcass to make stock. It really is no trouble at all and homemade stock is not only cheaper than the bought variety, it tastes much better as well.

Menu suggestions

On the pages following (from 184-197) are some suggested menus for dinners for two — normally a much neglected area where cookery books are concerned. Most are of the quick-cooking dish type but most of the stews recommended on pages 224-231 for small dinner parties could also be adapted happily to family eating. And for those evenings when you just don't feel particularly hungry, or for Saturday lunch, there are pages of snacks, ranging from soups (guaranteed as filling snack meals in themselves) through main dishes to desserts.

All are specially chosen to mix and match — the main criterion for their selection for this section being their flexibility; your individual tastes and appetites will dictate the rest.

Suppers for 2

> **Porterhouse Steak with Red Wine Sauce**
> **Baked Potatoes**
> **Tomato and Lettuce Salad**

Porterhouse Steak with Red Wine Sauce

1½ tablespoons black peppercorns
2 porterhouse steaks
1 garlic clove, crushed
½ teaspoon salt
25g (1oz) butter
1 medium-sized onion, thinly sliced
50g (2oz) mushrooms, wiped clean
  and thinly sliced
50ml (2fl oz) red wine
¼ teaspoon dried thyme
1 teaspoon butter blended with
  1 teaspoon flour

Using a mortar and pestle, or a rolling pin, crush the peppercorns coarsely and set them aside on a plate.

Rub the steaks all over with the garlic and salt, then press each steak into the crushed peppercorns, coating both sides. Shake off any excess pepper and set the steaks aside.

In a large frying-pan, melt half of the butter over moderate heat. When the foam subsides, add the onion and cook, stirring occasionally, for 5 to 7 minutes or until it is soft and translucent but not brown. Stir in the mushrooms and cook, stirring occasionally, for 3 minutes. With a slotted spoon, transfer the onion and mushrooms to a plate. Set aside while you cook the steaks.

Add the remaining butter to the pan and melt it over moderate heat. When the foam subsides, add the steaks and cook them for 2 minutes on each side. Reduce the heat to low and cook them for a further 2 minutes on each side. This will produce rare steaks. Double the cooking time for well-done steaks.

Remove the steaks from the pan and transfer them to a warmed serving dish. Keep them hot while you finish making the sauce.

Return the onion and mushroom mixture to the pan and pour over the red wine. Stir in the thyme. Boil the mixture, stirring occasionally, for 2 minutes or until the liquid has reduced slightly. Stir in the butter mixture, a little at a time, and cook, stirring frequently, for a further 2 minutes or until the sauce is hot and has thickened.

Remove the pan from the heat and pour the sauce over the steaks. Serve at once.

Baked Potatoes

(see page 173 for how to bake large potatoes)

Tomato and Lettuce Salad

(to make the dressing, in a small bowl beat 4 tablespoons olive oil, 2 tablespoons wine vinegar, 1 teaspoon lemon juice, ¼ teaspoon French mustard, salt, pepper and herbs to taste together.)

Succulent steak, with mushrooms and red wine, and served with salad and baked potato is an easy-to-make dinner that's downright festive to eat.

Chilli con Carne
Bean Salad

Raspberries with Ice-cream and Maraschino

Chilli con Carne

1 tablespoon olive oil
1 medium-sized onion, thinly
    sliced
1 garlic clove, chopped
450g (1 lb) lean minced beef
125g (4oz) canned tomatoes
50g (2oz) canned tomato purée
1 bay leaf
½ teaspoon ground cumin
½ teaspoon dried oregano
½ teaspoon cayenne pepper
1 tablespoon mild chilli powder
1 teaspoon salt
175ml (6fl oz) beef stock
225g (8oz) canned red kidney beans,
    drained

In a large frying-pan, heat the oil over moderate heat. Add the onion and garlic and fry them for 5 to 6 minutes, stirring constantly. Add the meat and brown it, stirring from time to time to make sure the meat breaks up properly and does not stick to the bottom of the pan.

Put the mixture into a large, heavy saucepan and, mixing well, add the tomatoes, tomato purée, bay leaf, cumin, oregano, cayenne pepper, chilli powder, salt and stock. Cover the pan and bring the liquids to the boil over moderate heat. Reduce the heat to low and simmer the mixture, stirring occasionally, for 1 hour. Add the kidney beans, cover the pan again and continue simmering the chilli for 30 minutes.

Remove the bay leaf and serve.

Bean Salad

125g (4oz) red kidney beans
75g (3oz) white beans, such as
    haricot or butter beans
50g (2oz) chick-peas
½ red pepper, white pith removed,
    seeded and coarsely chopped

Exotic Chilli con Carne makes a perfect mid week supper dish. Make it in large quantities and eat till it's finished – you'll never get tired of it!

½ small onion, finely chopped, or
    2 spring onions, trimmed and finely
    chopped
1 garlic clove, crushed
1 tablespoon finely chopped fresh
    chives
1 tablespoon white wine vinegar
3 tablespoons olive oil
½ tablespoon lemon juice
¼ teaspoon freshly ground black
    pepper
¼ teaspoon salt

Soak the beans and peas in water overnight. Put them in a large saucepan, cover with water and bring to the boil over high heat. Cover the pan, lower the heat and simmer for 40 minutes or until tender. Drain the beans and peas and set them aside to cool.

In a large salad bowl, combine the beans, peas, red pepper, onion, crushed garlic and chives.

In a small bowl, combine the wine vinegar, olive oil, lemon juice, salt and black pepper. Mix, add to the bean mixture and, using two large spoons, toss well.

Refrigerate for about 30 minutes before serving.

Raspberries with Ice-Cream and Maraschino

2 tablespoons Maraschino liqueur
225g (8oz) fresh raspberries, hulled
1 tablespoon flaked almonds
300ml (10fl oz) vanilla ice-cream
SYRUP
50g (2oz) sugar
50ml (2fl oz) water
1 teaspoon finely grated lemon rind

Place 2 sundae glasses in the refrigerator to chill.

First make the syrup. Place the sugar, water and lemon rind in a small saucepan. Set the pan over low heat and cook, stirring constantly, until the sugar has dissolved. Increase the heat to moderately high and boil the syrup, without stirring, for 4 minutes. Remove the pan from the heat and set the syrup aside to cool completely.

Strain the syrup into a medium-sized mixing bowl and stir in the Maraschino, raspberries and flaked almonds. Chill the mixture in the refrigerator for 30 minutes, stirring occasionally.

Remove the sundae glasses from the refrigerator. Remove the raspberry mixture from the refrigerator and divide it equally between the 2 glasses. Using an ice-cream scoop, scoop balls of ice-cream into each glass. Serve immediately.

185

Lamb Kebabs with Noodles

Honey-Baked Pears

Lamb Kebabs with Noodles

450g (1 lb) boned leg of lamb, cubed
1 tablespoon olive oil
1 tablespoon red wine vinegar
$\frac{1}{2}$ tablespoon fresh lemon juice
$\frac{1}{2}$ teaspoon cumin seeds, crushed
$\frac{1}{2}$ teaspoon salt
$\frac{1}{8}$ teaspoon black pepper
1 tablespoon pine nuts, crushed
225g (8oz) noodles
25g (1oz) butter, cut into pieces

Preheat the grill to moderate.

Thread the lamb cubes on to 4 skewers. Set aside.

In a small mixing bowl, combine the oil, vinegar, lemon juice, cumin seeds, $\frac{1}{4}$ teaspoon of the salt, the pepper and half of the nuts. Using a pastry brush, brush the lamb cubes with half of the oil mixture. Place the skewers under the grill and grill, turning and brushing frequently with the remaining oil mixture, for 15 to 20 minutes or until the lamb is cooked through.

Meanwhile, half-fill a large saucepan with cold water. Add the remaining salt and set the pan over high heat. Bring the water to the boil. Reduce the heat to moderate, add the noodles and cook them for 6 to 8 minutes or until they are 'al dente' or just tender.

Remove the pan from the heat and drain the noodles in a colander. Place the noodles on a large warmed serving platter. Add the butter and, using two large spoons, toss the noodles until the butter has melted and they are coated. Set aside and keep warm.

Remove the skewers from the grill. Slide the lamb cubes on to the bed of noodles. Sprinkle over the remaining nuts and serve at once.

Lamb Kebabs with Noodles.

Honey-Baked Pears

15g ($\frac{1}{2}$oz) plus 1 teaspoon butter
2 large firm pears, peeled, halved and cored
2 tablespoons lemon juice
2 tablespoons brandy
50ml (2fl oz) clear honey
$\frac{1}{4}$ teaspoon ground cinnamon
$\frac{1}{8}$ teaspoon grated nutmeg

Preheat the oven to moderate 350°F (Gas Mark 4, 180°C).

Grease a baking dish with the teaspoon of butter. Arrange the pear halves in the dish, cut sides down.

In a small saucepan, warm the lemon juice, brandy and honey together over low heat, stirring the mixture with a wooden spoon until it is hot and smooth.

Stir in the cinnamon and nutmeg and remove the pan from the heat. Pour the mixture over the pears. Cut the remaining butter into pieces and dot them over the mixture. Place the dish in the oven and bake the pears for 30 to 35 minutes or until they are tender but still firm.

Remove the dish from the oven and cool before serving.

Lamb and Apricot Pilaff
Mixed Green Salad

Lamb and Apricot Pilaff

50g (2oz) butter
1 small onion, very thinly sliced
450g (1 lb) boned leg of lamb, cut into cubes
50g (2oz) dried apricots, soaked overnight, drained and halved
2 tablespoons raisins
1 teaspoon salt
$\frac{1}{2}$ teaspoon ground cinnamon
$\frac{1}{4}$ teaspoon black pepper
550ml (18fl oz) water
150g (5oz) long-grain rice, washed, soaked in cold water for 30 minutes and drained

In a large frying-pan, melt the butter over moderate heat. When the foam subsides, add the onion and cook, stirring occasionally for 5 minutes, or until it is soft and translucent but not brown.

Add the lamb and cook, stirring and turning occasionally, for 5 to 8 minutes, or until it is lightly browned all over. Stir in the apricots, raisins, $\frac{1}{2}$ teaspoon of the salt, the cinnamon and pepper.

Pour in 250 millilitres (8 fluid ounces) of the water and bring to the boil, stirring occasionally. Reduce the heat to low, cover the pan and simmer the meat for 1 to $1\frac{1}{4}$ hours, or until the meat is tender when pierced with the point of a sharp knife.

Meanwhile, put the rice in a medium-sized saucepan. Pour over the remaining water and add the remaining salt. Place the saucepan over high heat and bring the water to the boil. Reduce the heat to very low, cover the pan and simmer the rice for 15 minutes. If all the liquid is not absorbed, continue to cook the rice, uncovered, until it is dry. Remove the pan from the heat.

Preheat the oven to moderate 350°F (Gas Mark 4, 180°C). Place one-third of the rice in a medium-sized oven-proof casserole. Cover with a layer of one-half of the meat mixture, then top with another one-third of the rice.

Continue to make layers in this manner until all the ingredients have been used up, finishing with a layer of rice. Cover the casserole and place it in the oven. Bake the pilaff for 20 minutes.

Remove the casserole from the oven and serve at once.

Mixed Green Salad

$\frac{1}{2}$ lettuce, outer leaves removed, washed and shaken dry
$\frac{1}{4}$ cucumber, sliced
$\frac{1}{2}$ green pepper, white pith removed, seeded and cut into strips
3 spring onions, trimmed and chopped
DRESSING
2 tablespoons olive oil
1 tablespoon wine vinegar
1 garlic clove, crushed
salt and pepper to taste

Place all the salad ingredients in a large bowl and set aside.

In a small bowl, combine all the dressing ingredients until they are mixed. Pour the dressing over the salad and toss well to blend. Serve the salad at once.

Lamb and Apricot Pilaff makes a wonderfully sustaining supper, served with a mixed green salad.

Pork Chops with Cranberry Sauce
Courgettes, Provençal-Style
Mashed Potatoes

Orange Pudding

Pork Chops with Cranberry Sauce

15g (½oz) seasoned flour, made with
    15g (½oz) flour, ½ teaspoon salt,
    ⅛ teaspoon cayenne pepper and ¾
    teaspoon dried rosemary
2 large boned pork chops
½ tablespoon butter
½ tablespoon vegetable oil
2 tablespoons canned cranberries,
    drained
75ml (3fl oz) dry white wine
¼ teaspoon salt
¼ teaspoon freshly ground black
    pepper
1 tablespoon double cream

Place the seasoned flour on a plate and
dip each chop into it, coating thoroughly on all sides. Shake off any
excess flour. Set aside.

In a large frying-pan, melt the butter
with the oil over moderate heat.
When the foam subsides, add the
pork chops and fry them for 5 minutes on each side or until they are well
browned all over. Reduce the heat to
moderately low and continue cooking
the chops for 20 to 30 minutes or
until they are thoroughly cooked and
tender when pierced with the point of
a sharp knife. Using tongs, transfer
the pork chops to a warmed serving
dish. Cover the dish and keep the
chops hot while you finish making the
sauce.

Remove the pan from the heat and
pour off all but a tablespoon of the
cooking fat. Return the pan to the
heat and stir in the cranberries, wine,
salt and pepper. Bring the mixture to
the boil.

Stirring constantly with a wooden
spoon, cook the sauce for 5 minutes.
Stir in the cream and cook for 30
seconds more. Remove the pan from
the heat and pour the sauce over the
chops.

Serve immediately.

*Succulent Pork Chops with Cranberry
Sauce, served with lots of Courgettes,
Provençal-Style and Mashed Potatoes – a
welcome home-coming for a hungry man!*

Courgettes, Provençal-Style

4 courgettes, trimmed, cleaned and
    blanched
2 tablespoons olive oil
½ teaspoon salt
½ teaspoon white pepper
2 garlic cloves, crushed
25g (1oz) fine dry breadcrumbs
1 tablespoon finely chopped fresh
    parsley

Cut the courgettes into slices, crosswise, and dry them thoroughly on
kitchen paper towels.

In a large frying-pan, heat the olive
oil over moderate heat. When it is hot,
add the courgettes to the pan and cook
them for 8 to 10 minutes, stirring
occasionally to prevent them from
sticking to the bottom of the pan.

Raise the heat to fairly high and stir

in the salt, pepper, garlic, breadcrumbs
and parsley. Remove the pan from the
heat and, using two serving spoons,
toss gently to coat the courgettes
thoroughly. Transfer the mixture to a
warmed serving dish and serve
immediately.

Mashed Potatoes
(see page 172 for how to cook and
mash potatoes)

Orange Pudding

3 medium-sized thin-skinned oranges,
    peeled and with the white pith
    removed
1 tablespoon soft brown sugar
50g (2oz) currants
1 tablespoon orange-flavoured
    liqueur

With a serrated-edge knife, slice the
oranges very thinly. Arrange the
orange slices in a serving dish and
sprinkle the sugar and the currants over
them. Spoon over the orange-flavoured
liqueur. Place the dish in the refrigerator and chill for 2 hours.

Remove the dish from the
refrigerator and serve at once.

Cream of Tomato Soup

Sautéed Chicken with Basil
Boiled Potatoes

Cream of Tomato Soup

25g (1oz) butter
1 shallot, finely chopped
450g (1 lb) ripe tomatoes, blanched,
   peeled, seeded and chopped
$\frac{1}{4}$ teaspoon sugar
$\frac{1}{4}$ teaspoon dried basil
$\frac{1}{2}$ teaspoon salt
$\frac{1}{2}$ teaspoon black pepper
$\frac{1}{4}$ teaspoon dried sage
600ml (1 pint) hot chicken stock
$\frac{1}{2}$ tablespoon flour
50ml (2fl oz) single cream
$\frac{1}{2}$ tablespoon chopped fresh dill

In a saucepan, melt half the butter over low heat. When the foam subsides, add the shallot and cook for 5 minutes. Add the tomatoes, sugar, basil, salt, pepper and sage and cook for a further 10 to 15 minutes. Stir in the stock. Cover and simmer for 15 minutes. Strain the mixture into a bowl.

In another saucepan, melt the remaining butter over moderate heat. Remove the pan from the heat and stir in the flour, mixing to a smooth paste. Return the pan to the heat and mix in the strained tomato mixture. Bring to the boil.

Remove the pan from the heat and stir in the cream, mixing briskly until all the ingredients are blended. Reduce the heat to low and return the pan to the heat. Heat the soup very gently until it is hot but not boiling.

Pour the soup into a warm tureen, sprinkle it with dill and serve at once.

Sautéed Chicken with Basil

50g (2oz) butter
2 chicken breasts, rubbed with $\frac{1}{2}$

If you're still hungry after the soup, serve Sautéed Chicken with potatoes AND stuffed tomatoes.

teaspoon salt and $\frac{1}{2}$ teaspoon black
   pepper
125ml (4fl oz) dry white wine
125ml (4fl oz) chicken stock
2 teaspoons chopped fresh basil
1 teaspoon butter blended with
   1 teaspoon flour

In a flameproof casserole, melt the butter over moderate heat. When the foam subsides, add the chicken breasts and cook, turning frequently, for 8 to 10 minutes or until they are evenly browned.

Reduce the heat to low, cover the casserole and cook for 20 to 25 minutes or until the breasts are tender. Transfer the chicken to a warmed serving dish. Keep warm.

Skim any fat from the juices in the casserole. Add the wine, stock and basil and bring the liquid to the boil over high heat. Boil for 10 minutes or until the liquid is reduced by half.

Add the butter mixture, a little at a time, stirring constantly until the sauce is smooth and has thickened.

Remove from the heat, pour the sauce over the chicken and serve.

Boiled Potatoes
(see page 172 for how to boil potatoes)

Herrings in Butter Sauce

2 large herrings, filleted
3 tablespoons seasoned flour, made
    with 2½ tablespoons flour,
    1 teaspoon salt and ½ teaspoon
    black pepper
50g (2oz) butter
2 teaspoons lemon juice
1 tablespoon chopped fresh parsley

Wash the herring fillets under cold running water and pat them dry with kitchen paper towels.

Place the seasoned flour on a plate and, one by one, dip the herring fillets into it, shaking off any excess. Set aside.

In a large frying-pan, melt the butter over moderate heat. When the foam subsides, add the herring fillets to the pan and cook them for 3 minutes on each side, or until they are lightly browned and the flesh flakes

easily when tested with a fork.

Remove the pan from the heat and, with a slotted spoon, transfer the herrings from the pan to a warmed serving dish. Spoon over the lemon juice, then the pan juices.

Sprinkle on the parsley and serve.

Boiled Potatoes
(for how to boil potatoes, see page 172)

Glazed Carrots

450g (1 lb) carrots, scraped and cut
    into slices
250ml (8fl oz) water
1 tablespoon sugar
1 tablespoon butter
1 teaspoon salt
1 tablespoon chopped fresh parsley

Put the carrots in a medium-sized

saucepan with the water, sugar, butter and salt. Cover the pan and cook over low heat for about 30 minutes, or until the carrots are tender and a small amount of thick rich syrup remains.

Turn into a hot serving dish. Sprinkle with the parsley and serve at once.

Banana and Raspberry Cream

3 bananas
225g (8oz) fresh or frozen and
    thawed raspberries
150ml (5fl oz) double cream
2 tablespoons castor sugar

Peel the bananas and cut them into rounds. Arrange the slices in a dish.

Mix the raspberries with the cream and, using the back of a wooden spoon, carefully push the mixture through a strainer. Mix in half the sugar. Taste to check the sweetness and add the rest of the sugar if necessary. Pour the cream mixture over the bananas.

Chill well in the refrigerator before serving.

Herrings in Butter Sauce, served with lots of freshly cooked vegetables and a smooth cream and fruit dessert, makes an ideal, inexpensive and nutritious supper for two — and it's easy to cook too!

Italian Rice with Shrimps
Tomato and French Bean Salad

Peach Dessert

Italian Rice with Shrimps

25g (1oz) butter
1 tablespoon olive oil
1 small onion, finely chopped
1 garlic clove, finely chopped
1 small red pepper, white pith
  removed, seeded and chopped
50g (2oz) button mushrooms, wiped
  clean and chopped
1 teaspoon chopped fresh basil or
  ½ teaspoon dried basil
1 teaspoon salt
½ teaspoon freshly ground black
  pepper
175g (6oz) Italian rice, such as
  Avorio
175g (6oz) frozen shrimps, thawed
  and shelled
400ml (15fl oz) boiling fish stock or
  water
50g (2oz) Parmesan cheese, finely
  grated

In a large, heavy frying-pan, melt half of the butter with the oil over moderately high heat. When the foam subsides, reduce the heat to moderate. Add the onion, garlic and red pepper and fry them, stirring occasionally, for 5 to 7 minutes, or until the onion is soft and translucent but not brown. Stir in the mushrooms, basil, salt and black pepper. Cook, stirring occasionally, for 5 minutes or until the mushrooms are cooked through and tender.

Add the rice, reduce the heat to low, and cook, stirring frequently, for 5 minutes. Stir in the shrimps and cook for 1 minute. Add approximately one-third of the boiling stock or water. Regulate the heat so that the rice is bubbling all the time. Stir the rice occasionally with a fork. When the rice swells and the liquid is absorbed, add another one-third of the stock or water. Continue cooking the rice in this way until the rice is tender and moist but still firm.

Remove the pan from the heat and stir in the remaining butter and the cheese. Turn the mixture into a

Italian Rice with Shrimps, served with a colourful salad and dessert, is economical enough for a midweek supper for two, elegant enough for a special dinner.

warmed serving dish.
Serve at once.

Tomato and French Bean Salad

225g (8oz) tomatoes, very thinly
  sliced and seeded
225g (8oz) French beans, trimmed,
  cooked and drained
DRESSING
2 tablespoons wine vinegar
4 tablespoons olive oil
¼ teaspoon salt
¼ teaspoon black pepper
¼ teaspoon prepared mustard
¼ teaspoon sugar
1 garlic clove, crushed

Place all the dressing ingredients in a screw-top jar and shake vigorously until they are mixed. Set aside.

Place the tomatoes and beans in a large serving dish and pour over the dressing. Using two large spoons, toss the salad until the vegetables are thoroughly coated with the dressing.

Chill the salad in the refrigerator before serving.

Peach Dessert

400g (14oz) canned peach halves,
  drained
1 tablespoon soft brown sugar
150ml (5fl oz) yogurt
1 tablespoon butter
4 tablespoons medium oatmeal
1 tablespoon clear honey

Put the peach halves into a medium-sized serving bowl and, using a fork, mash them to a smooth purée. Beat in the brown sugar, then the yogurt, beating until the mixture is well blended. Place the bowl in the refrigerator to chill for 15 minutes.

Meanwhile, in a small saucepan, melt the butter over moderate heat. When the foam subsides, add the oatmeal and fry, stirring constantly, for 3 minutes or until it is lightly toasted. Stir in the honey and remove the pan from the heat. Set the mixture aside to cool completely.

Remove the bowl from the refrigerator and spoon the oatmeal mixture on top. Serve at once.

Soups for 2

Cabbage and Sausage Soup

25g (1oz) butter
½ white cabbage, coarse outer leaves removed, washed and shredded
900ml (1½ pints) beef stock
1 bay leaf
    salt and pepper to taste
125g (4oz) pork sausages, sliced
1 tart apple, cored and chopped

In a saucepan, melt the butter over moderate heat. When the foam subsides, add the cabbage and cook, stirring occasionally with a wooden spoon or a spatula, for 15 to 20 minutes or until the shredded cabbage is soft and translucent but not brown, and still retains its shape.

Add the stock, bay leaf, salt and pepper. Reduce the heat to low and simmer the soup for 30 minutes.

Add the sausages and apple, and simmer for a further 20 minutes or until the sausages are cooked. Remove the bay leaf and serve at once.

Chicken Corn Soup

2 tablespoons vegetable oil
1 medium-sized onion, thinly sliced
2 celery stalks, trimmed and sliced
900ml (1½ pints) chicken stock
5 black peppercorns, crushed
450g (1 lb) cooked chicken, shredded
50g (2oz) large thick egg noodles
200g (7oz) canned sweetcorn, drained
¼ teaspoon dried sage
¼ teaspoon dried savory
½ teaspoon salt
½ teaspoon ground saffron threads

In a large saucepan, heat the oil over moderate heat. When the oil is hot, add the onion and cook, stirring occasionally, for 5 to 7 minutes or until it is soft and translucent but not brown. Add the celery and cook, stirring, for 5 minutes.

Pour in the chicken stock and add

Warming, filling Chicken Corn Soup is a dish with man appeal! Served with lots of crusty bread, it's practically a meal on its own.

the peppercorns. Bring the liquid to the boil over moderately high heat. Reduce the heat to low and simmer for 20 minutes.

Add the chicken, noodles, sweetcorn, sage, savory, salt and saffron and stir well to mix. Increase the heat to moderately high and bring the mixture to the boil. Reduce the heat to low and simmer the soup for 15 to 20 minutes or until the noodles are just tender.

Remove from the heat and serve.

Clam Chowder

50g (2oz) salt pork, diced
1 onion, finely chopped
75ml (3fl oz) water
125ml (4fl oz) milk
2 medium-sized potatoes, peeled and chopped
450g (1 lb) canned clams with their juice reserved, chopped
¼ teaspoon salt
¼ teaspoon black pepper
½ teaspoon paprika
125ml (4fl oz) double cream
1 tablespoon butter

In a large saucepan, fry the salt pork over moderate heat for 4 to 5 minutes, or until there is a thin film of fat covering the bottom of the pan. Add the onion and cook it with the salt pork for 5 minutes, stirring occasionally. The salt pork dice should resemble small croutons by the end of this cooking period.

Pour the water and milk into the pan and add the diced potatoes. Increase the heat to high and bring the liquid to the boil. Reduce the heat to low and simmer for about 10 minutes or until the potatoes are tender but still firm.

Add the chopped clams with their broth or juice, the salt, pepper and paprika. Increase the heat to moderately high and bring to the boil. Remove the pan from the heat and gradually stir in the cream. Return the pan to low heat and heat the chowder gently until the cream is warmed, taking care not to let the mixture come to the boil again. Add the butter, stirring until it melts.

Remove the pan from the heat and transfer the chowder to a warmed tureen or individual bowls. Serve.

Vegetable Soup

25g (1oz) vegetable fat
1 large carrot, scraped and diced
½ small swede, peeled and diced
1 large leek, trimmed and coarsely chopped
1 large potato, peeled and diced
1 celery stalk, trimmed and coarsely chopped
3 tomatoes, blanched, peeled and coarsely chopped
50g (2oz) dried butter beans, soaked overnight and drained
½ teaspoon salt
½ teaspoon black pepper
900ml (1½ pints) beef stock
1 bay leaf
50g (2oz) frozen peas, thawed
1 tablespoon chopped fresh parsley

In a large saucepan, melt the vegetable fat over moderate heat. When the foam subsides, add the carrot, swede, leek, potato and celery and cook, stirring occasionally, for 10 minutes.

Stir in the tomatoes, beans, salt and pepper and pour over the stock. Add the bay leaf, increase the heat to high and bring the mixture to the boil,

Colourful, nourishing Vegetable Soup is easy to make, even easier to eat.

stirring constantly.

Reduce the heat to moderately low, cover the pan and simmer, stirring occasionally, for 20 minutes or until the vegetables are soft.

Remove the pan from the heat and strain the soup through a large, fine wire strainer into a large mixing bowl. Remove and discard the bay leaf.

Remove about half the vegetables remaining in the strainer and add them to the strained stock in the bowl. With the back of a wooden spoon, rub the remaining vegetables through the strainer into a small mixing bowl.

Transfer the purée to the saucepan and stir in the reserved stock and vegetable mixture. Place the saucepan over high heat, add the peas and bring the liquid back to the boil, stirring frequently. Reduce the heat to moderately low and simmer for a further 5 minutes or until the peas are tender.

Remove the pan from the heat and pour the soup into a warmed tureen or individual bowls. Sprinkle over the parsley and serve immediately.

Main courses for 2

Bobotie

1½ tablespoons butter
½ tablespoon vegetable oil
1 medium-sized onion, chopped
1 garlic clove, finely chopped
1 tablespoon curry powder
50g (2oz) shredded almonds
50g (2oz) sultanas
½ teaspoon mixed herbs
    juice of ½ lemon
½ teaspoon salt
½ tablespoon sugar
½ tablespoon wine vinegar
⅛ teaspoon black pepper
450g (1 lb) lean minced beef
2 slices white bread, crusts removed
175ml (6fl oz) milk
2 small eggs, lightly beaten

Preheat the oven to moderate 350°F
(Gas Mark 4, 180°C). Grease a deep
pie dish with ½ tablespoon of the
butter.

In a small frying-pan, melt the remaining butter and oil over moderate
heat. When the foam subsides, add
the onion and garlic to the pan and
fry for 8 to 10 minutes or until the
onion is golden brown.

Remove the onion and garlic from
the pan and place them in a large mixing bowl. Sprinkle the curry powder
over the onion and add the almonds,
sultanas, mixed herbs, lemon juice,
salt, sugar, vinegar, pepper and meat.
Mix well.

Soak the bread in the milk. Squeeze
the milk from the bread and mash
the bread into the meat mixture with
1 beaten egg. Turn the mixture into
the buttered pie dish.

If necessary add a little extra milk
to the milk squeezed from the bread
to make up 125 millilitres (4 fluid
ounces).

Beat the remaining egg into the milk
with a whisk. Pour the milk-and-egg
mixture over the meat in the pie dish.
Stand the pie dish in a pan of water
and bake for about 1 hour, or until
the top is brown and firm to the touch.

Hamburgers

450g (1 lb) lean minced beef
2 tablespoons fresh breadcrumbs
½ teaspoon salt
½ teaspoon black pepper

*Light, spicy Bobotie makes a delicious
snack supper dish.*

½ teaspoon dried thyme
1 small egg, lightly beaten
ACCOMPANIMENTS
1 tomato, thinly sliced
1 small onion, thinly sliced and
    pushed out into rings
2 large lettuce leaves
2 hamburger or large soft buns
25g (1oz) butter

Preheat the grill to high.

Preheat the oven to cool 275°F (Gas
Mark 1, 140°C).

In a medium-sized mixing bowl,
combine the beef, breadcrumbs, salt,
pepper, thyme and egg, using your
hands to mix the ingredients together
thoroughly.

Form the beef mixture into two
balls and flatten them into patty
shapes.

Arrange the tomato slices, onion
rings and lettuce leaves on a large
serving plate.

Split the hamburger buns in half
and butter each half. Re-assemble the
buns and put them on a baking sheet.
Place the sheet in the oven while you
cook the hamburgers.

Place the beef patties on the grill
rack and put them under the grill.
Grill for 2 to 3 minutes on each side,
or until the hamburgers are well
browned. Then reduce the temperature
to moderate and grill for a further
5 to 7 minutes on each side, or until
the hamburgers are well cooked.

When the hamburgers are cooked,
place one on each bun, transfer them
to individual serving plates and serve.

Spaghetti alla Carbonara

25g (1oz) butter
125g (4oz) lean bacon, rinds
    removed and chopped
2 tablespoons double cream
2 eggs
50g (2oz) Parmesan cheese, grated
½ teaspoon salt
¼ teaspoon black pepper
225g (8oz) spaghetti, cooked
    according to packet instructions,
    drained and kept hot

In a small frying-pan, melt 1 tablespoon of the butter over moderate
heat. When the foam subsides, add the
bacon and cook, stirring occasionally,
for 5 minutes or until it is crisp.
Remove the pan from the heat and
stir in the cream. Set aside.

In a medium-sized mixing bowl,
beat the eggs and 25 grams (1 ounce)
of the Parmesan cheese together with a

Serve Spanish Rice as a very 'different' vegetarian supper dish.

fork until the mixture is smooth and the ingredients are well blended. Stir in the salt and pepper. Set aside.

Place the spaghetti in a large, deep serving bowl and add the remaining butter. Using two large spoons, toss the spaghetti until the butter has melted. Stir in the bacon mixture, tossing well. Finally, mix in the egg mixture, tossing until the spaghetti is well coated.

Serve at once, with the remaining grated cheese.

Spanish Rice

3 tablespoons olive oil
2 onions, thinly sliced
1 garlic clove, crushed
1 green pepper, white pith removed, seeded and thinly sliced
2 red peppers, white pith removed, seeded and thinly sliced
350g (12oz) mushrooms, sliced
400g (14oz) canned tomatoes, chopped
40g (1½oz) stoned green olives
1 teaspoon dried oregano
½ teaspoon dried basil
½ teaspoon salt
¼ teaspoon black pepper
150g (5oz) cooked rice

In a large frying-pan heat the oil over moderate heat. Add the onions and garlic to the pan and cook, stirring occasionally, for 5 to 7 minutes or until the onions are soft and translucent but not brown.

Add the green and red peppers and cook for 4 minutes, stirring frequently. Add the mushrooms, tomatoes with the can juice, olives, oregano, basil, salt and pepper to the pan and cook, stirring occasionally, for 3 minutes. Add the rice and cook for 3 to 4 minutes, stirring constantly, or until the rice is heated through.

Transfer the mixture to a warmed serving dish. Serve immediately.

Welsh Rarebit

½ tablespoon butter
½ tablespoon flour
1 tablespoon milk
2 tablespoons brown ale
1 teaspoon Worcestershire sauce
½ teaspoon dry mustard
¼ teaspoon salt
¼ teaspoon black pepper
125g (4oz) Cheddar cheese, grated
2 slices toast, buttered and kept hot

Preheat the grill to high.

In a saucepan, melt the butter over moderate heat. Remove the pan from the heat and, with a wooden spoon, stir in the flour to make a smooth paste. Gradually add the milk, ale, Worcestershire sauce, mustard, salt and pepper, stirring constantly. Return the pan to low heat and cook, stirring constantly, for 2 to 3 minutes or until the mixture is thick. Add the cheese to the mixture and cook, stirring constantly, for a further 1 minute or until the cheese has melted.

Remove the pan from the heat and divide the mixture between the slices of toast. Place the toast in the grill pan and place the pan under the heat. Grill for 2 to 3 minutes or until the mixture is golden. Remove the pan from the heat.

Transfer the toast slices to individual warmed plates and serve immediately.

Desserts for 2

Apricot Cinnamon Crumble

175g (6oz) canned apricots, drained
   and with a little of the can juice
   reserved
2 teaspoons soft brown sugar
2 teaspoons ground cinnamon
½ teaspoon ground ginger
¼ teaspoon mixed spice
TOPPING
40g (1½oz) butter, at room
   temperature
75g (3oz) wholemeal flour
1 tablespoon rolled oats
2 tablespoons soft brown sugar
1 teaspoon ground cinnamon

Preheat the oven to moderate 350°F
(Gas Mark 4, 180°C).

Arrange the apricots in a small
greased baking dish. Sprinkle over
1 tablespoon of the can liquid, the soft
brown sugar, cinnamon, ground
ginger and mixed spice.

To make the topping, rub the butter
into the flour until it resembles coarse
breadcrumbs. Mix in the oats and soft
brown sugar. Arrange the crumble
mixture lightly over the apricots,
sprinkle the teaspoon of cinnamon on
top and place the dish in the oven.
Bake for 45 minutes or until the top is
golden and crispy.

Remove the dish from the oven and
serve the crumble warm, with lots of
whipped cream.

Baked Apples

2 cooking apples
light brown sugar
butter
water

Preheat the oven to moderate 350°F
(Gas Mark 4, 180°C).

Wash the apples and, with an apple
corer, remove the cores. Peel off
about 2.5cm (1in) of skin from the
tops of the apples.

Arrange the apples in a baking dish
and fill the centres with sugar. Top
each apple with a little butter and pour
enough water into the baking dish to a
depth of 1.3cm (½in).

Bake the apples for about 30
minutes or until they are soft, basting
frequently with the syrup in the baking
dish.

Remove the baking dish from the
oven and carefully transfer the apples
to individual serving plates.

Serve hot or cold.

Fruit Salad with Kirsch

225g (8oz) fresh strawberries,
   washed, hulled and halved
6 fresh apricots, peeled, stoned and
   sliced
2 large green or yellow apples, cored
   and sliced
1 large banana, peeled, sliced
   crosswise
225g (8oz) large black grapes,
   halved and seeded
3 tablespoons sugar
50ml (2fl oz) kirsch
1 tablespoon slivered almonds

Place all of the fruit in a large serving
dish and mix carefully to avoid bruis-
ing. Sprinkle on the sugar and chill in
the refrigerator for 10 minutes.

Remove the dish from the refrigerator and pour over the kirsch, stirring
carefully to coat the fruit. Sprinkle
over the almonds and serve the salad
at once.

Honey and Walnut Pudding

1 teaspoon butter
3 eggs, separated
½ tablespoon sugar
125 ml (4fl oz) clear honey,
   warmed
50g (2oz) flour, sifted with
   ½ teaspoon baking powder
50g (2oz) walnuts, very finely
   chopped
75ml (3fl oz) double cream

Preheat the oven to warm 325°F (Gas
Mark 3, 170°C). Using the teaspoon
of butter, lightly grease a medium-
sized soufflé dish. Set aside.

In a medium-sized mixing bowl, beat
the egg yolks and sugar together with a
wire whisk or rotary beater. Gradually
beat in the warmed honey and continue beating until the mixture is well
blended.

With a metal spoon, fold in the
flour mixture and then the walnuts and
double cream.

In another mixing bowl, beat the
egg whites with a wire whisk or rotary

*This sustaining traditional pudding is a
perfect dessert for cold winter days.
Apricot Cinnamon Crumble may be
served hot or cold, with lots of thick home-
made custard or freshly whipped cream.*

beater until they form stiff peaks.

With a metal spoon, carefully fold the egg whites into the honey mixture.

Turn the mixture into the buttered soufflé dish and place it in the oven.

Bake the pudding for 40 minutes, or until it has risen and is firm to the touch.

Remove the dish from the oven and set it aside to cool. When the pudding is cold, run a knife around the edge of the pudding. Hold a serving dish, inverted, over the soufflé dish and reverse the two. The pudding should slide out easily. Serve at once.

Lemon Bread Pudding

1 teaspoon butter
6 large slices white bread, with the
  crusts removed and generously
  buttered
2 tablespoons blanched flaked
  almonds
50g (2oz) finely chopped mixed
  candied peel
$\frac{1}{4}$ teaspoon ground mixed spice or allspice
  finely grated rind of 2 large
  lemons
2 tablespoons soft brown sugar
CUSTARD
2 eggs
$\frac{1}{4}$ teaspoon vanilla essence
$\frac{1}{8}$ teaspoon almond essence
400ml (15fl oz) milk
1 tablespoon sugar

Preheat the oven to fairly hot 375°F (Gas Mark 5, 190°C).

Using the teaspoon of butter, lightly grease a medium-sized shallow baking dish.

Cut the bread slices into quarters. Place a third of the bread quarters, buttered sides up, in the bottom of the baking dish. Sprinkle over half the flaked almonds, candied peel, mixed spice or allspice, lemon rind and sugar.

Cover with a second layer of bread quarters. Sprinkle over the remaining almonds, candied peel, mixed spice or allspice, lemon rind and sugar. Cover with the remaining bread quarters, buttered sides up. Set aside.

To make the custard, beat the eggs, vanilla and almond essences together in a medium-sized mixing bowl. Set aside.

In a medium-sized saucepan, heat the milk and sugar over moderate heat. When the sugar has dissolved and the milk is hot, remove the pan from the heat. Beating constantly,

gradually pour the hot milk into the beaten egg mixture.

Pour the custard through a fine wire strainer on to the bread layers in the dish. Set aside for 15 minutes, or until the bread has absorbed most of the liquid.

Place the dish in the centre of the oven and bake the pudding for 35 to 40 minutes, or until the top is golden and crisp.

Remove the pudding from the oven and serve immediately, straight from the dish.

Rich Rice Pudding

1 tablespoon butter
75g (3oz) round-grain rice
250ml (8fl oz) milk
75ml (3fl oz) single cream
2 tablespoons sugar
1 egg, separated
125ml (4fl oz) apple sauce
1 tablespoon redcurrant jelly
50g (2oz) blanched almonds,
  chopped
2 tablespoons hazelnuts, finely
  chopped

Using the tablespoon of butter, grease a medium-sized soufflé dish or straight-sided baking dish and set aside.

Place the rice and milk in a medium-sized heavy-based saucepan and bring them to the boil over moderate heat,

There can't be anything that's easier to make or more refreshing to eat than Fruit Salad with Kirsch – and you need never get tired of it since you can change the combinations of fruit according to the seasons of the year.

stirring constantly. Reduce the heat to low and cook the rice for 15 to 20 minutes or until the milk has been absorbed and the rice is tender. Remove the pan from the heat.

Preheat the oven to warm 325°F (Gas Mark 3, 170°C).

Stir the cream, 1 tablespoon of the sugar and the egg yolk into the rice mixture.

Place one-third of the rice mixture in the prepared dish and cover with half the apple sauce and $\frac{1}{2}$ tablespoon of the redcurrant jelly. Sprinkle over half the almonds. Continue making layers until the ingredients are used up, finishing with a layer of rice.

In a medium-sized bowl, using a wire whisk or rotary beater, beat the egg white until it forms stiff peaks. Using a metal spoon, fold the remaining sugar and hazelnuts into the egg white. Carefully spoon the egg white mixture on to the rice mixture.

Place the dish in the oven and bake the pudding for 25 to 30 minutes or until the top is pale golden brown. Remove the pudding from the oven and either serve immediately or allow to cool before serving.

Economy roasts

Three ways with beef

1. Roast Beef with Roast Potatoes

Always allow meat plenty of time to come up to room temperature again if it has been stored in your refrigerator or the butcher's. It is a good idea to rub seasonings into the meat as soon as it comes out of the refrigerator, then leave it at room temperature for one to two hours so that it can lose its chill and absorb the flavours at the same time.

1 × 2kg (4¼ lb) topside of beef
   salt
   freshly ground black pepper
50g (2oz) butter
450-675g (1-1½ lb) potatoes, peeled

Preheat the oven to hot 425°F (Gas Mark 7, 220°C).

Wipe the joint with kitchen paper towels and season to taste with salt and pepper.

In a roasting pan, melt the butter over moderate heat. When the foam subsides, add the joint and brown well, turning occasionally, for 5 to 8 minutes. Remove the pan from the heat.

Place the roasting pan in the centre of the oven and roast the joint, basting it with the hot melted butter occasionally, for 15 minutes. Then reduce the oven temperature to moderate 350°F (Gas Mark 4, 180°C) and continue to roast the meat until it is cooked to your liking. Allow 16 minutes to the half kilo plus 16 minutes for rare beef, 27 minutes to the half kilo plus 27 minutes if you prefer your meat medium and 38 minutes to the half kilo plus 38 minutes for well-done beef. Continue to baste the meat with the pan liquid from time to time throughout the cooking period. You can test the beef for doneness by inserting a skewer or the point of a sharp knife into the centre of the joint. For rare meat, the juices will run out bloody, for medium they should be pale pink and for well-done the juices should run out clear.

If you are using a meat thermometer, by the way, the temperature should read 60°C for rare beef, 72°C for medium and 80°C for well-done.

Meanwhile, cut the potatoes into even-sized pieces. About an hour before the end of the beef cooking time, add the potatoes to the roasting pan, and arrange them in the hot fat around the beef. Turn them over and round from time to time during the cooking period to ensure that they are cooked and evenly browned.

When the meat is cooked to your liking, remove the roasting pan from the oven and, using two large forks or spoons, carefully transfer the joint to a warmed serving platter or a carving board. Set aside and keep warm.

Raise the oven temperature to hot 425°F (Gas Mark 7, 220°C) and return the potatoes (still in the roasting pan) to the centre of the oven. 'Crisp' them for 5 to 10 minutes or until they are a deep golden brown on the outside but soft on the inside.

When the potatoes are 'crisped' to your liking, remove the pan from the oven and transfer the potatoes to a serving platter or individual serving plates.

Carve the beef, as illustrated on page 159 and serve the beef, in thin slices, with the roast potatoes.

2. Minced Beef Curry

25g (1oz) butter
1 medium-sized onion, finely chopped
1 apple, peeled, cored and roughly chopped
2 tablespoons curry powder
1 tablespoon flour
450g (1 lb) cooked beef, coarsely minced
300ml (10fl oz) beef stock (or thin gravy)
1 tablespoon mango chutney
2 tablespoons sultanas or seedless raisins
1 tablespoon lemon juice
125g (4oz) long-grain rice, washed, soaked in cold water for 30 minutes and drained
1 teaspoon salt
125g (4oz) frozen peas, thawed
2 tablespoons sour cream (optional)

In a medium-sized saucepan, melt half the butter over moderate heat. When the foam subsides, add the onion and apple and fry, stirring occasionally, for 5 to 7 minutes or until the onion is soft and translucent but not brown. Stir in the curry powder and cook, stirring occasionally, for a further 2 minutes.

Add the flour, cooked minced beef, stock, mango chutney, sultanas or raisins and lemon juice. Bring the mixture to the boil, reduce the heat to low and simmer, uncovered, for 30 minutes, stirring occasionally to prevent the mixture from sticking to the bottom of the pan.

About 20 minutes before the end of the cooking time, boil the rice in salted water until it is cooked and tender and all the water has been absorbed, stirring in the peas when the rice is half cooked. Add the remaining butter to the rice mixture and stir well to blend thoroughly.

Remove the rice from the heat and arrange it, in a ring, on a heated serving dish.

Stir the sour cream, if you are using it, into the curry, then pour it into the centre of the rice ring. Serve at once.

3. Cottage Pie

2 tablespoons olive oil
1 Spanish onion, finely chopped
450g (1 lb) cooked roast beef, coarsely minced
300ml (10fl oz) beef stock
2 teaspoons Worcestershire sauce
2 tablespoons finely chopped fresh parsley
½ teaspoon dried mixed herbs
½ teaspoon salt
½ teaspoon black pepper
1 packet instant mashed potato (2-3 servings)

Preheat the oven to fairly hot 400°F (Gas Mark 6, 200°C).

In a medium-sized frying-pan, heat the oil over moderate heat. When the oil is hot, add the onion and fry, stirring occasionally, for 5 to 7 minutes or until it is soft and translucent but not brown. Stir in the beef, stock, Worcestershire sauce, chopped parsley, mixed herbs, salt and pepper. Remove the pan from the heat and spoon the mixture into a deep ovenproof dish.

Make up the instant mashed potato according to the instructions on the packet. Spread the mixture over the beef in the dish.

Place the dish in the oven and bake for 20 to 25 minutes or until the top is browned.

Remove the dish from the oven and serve at once.

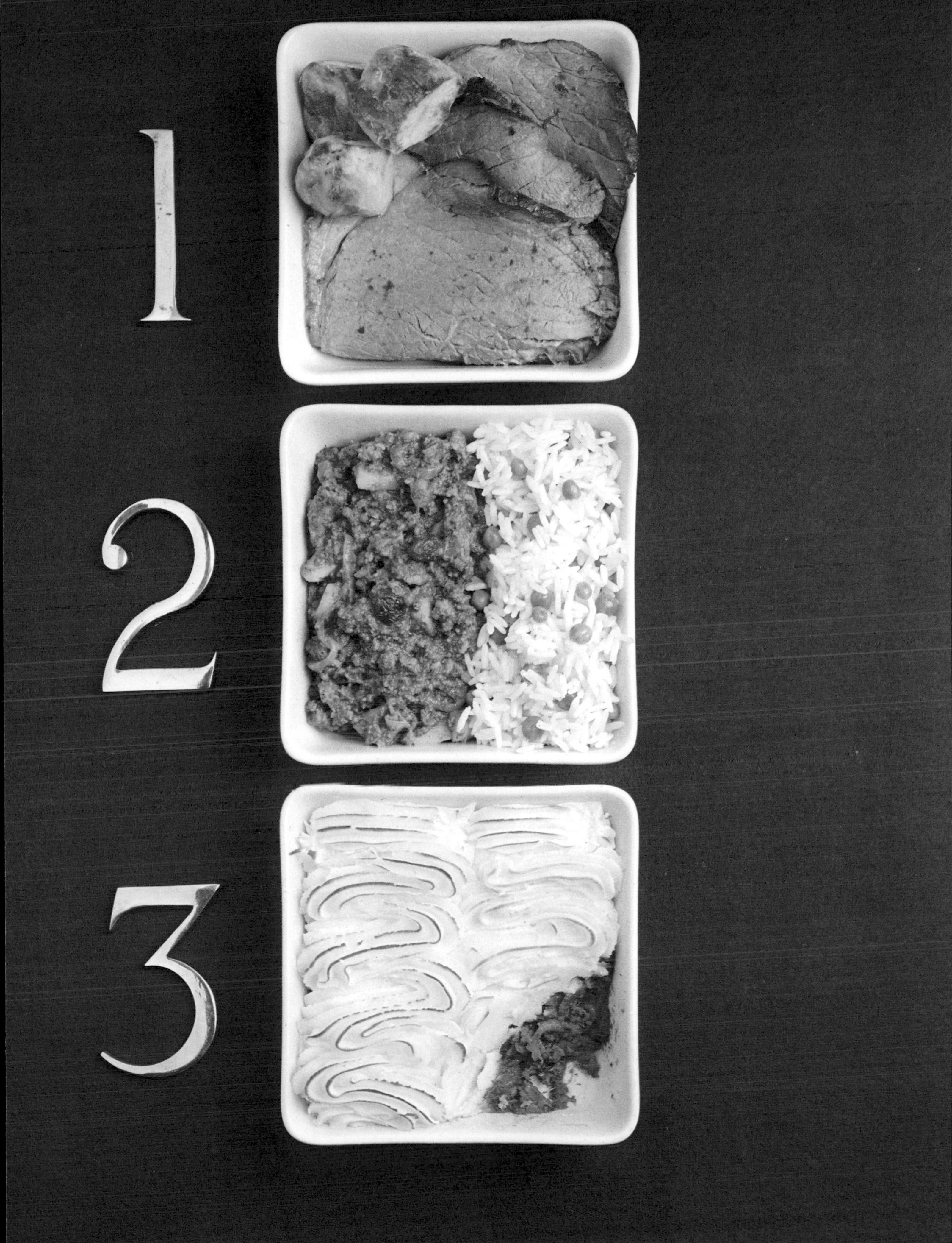
1
2
3

Three ways with lamb

1. Roast Lamb with Rosemary

1 × 2kg (4¼ lb) leg of lamb
2 garlic cloves
65g (2½oz) butter
2 teaspoons chopped fresh rosemary
   or 1 teaspoon dried rosemary
   juice of 1 lemon
   salt
   freshly ground black pepper
300ml (10fl oz) beef stock
1 tablespoon flour

Preheat the oven to fairly hot 400°F (Gas Mark 6, 200°C).

Wipe the joint with kitchen paper towels. Cut the garlic cloves into about 20 slivers. Using a sharp knife, make enough slits all over the meat to insert them.

In a small bowl, beat 50 grams (2 ounces) of the butter, rosemary, lemon juice, salt and pepper together. With a flat-bladed knife, spread the mixture over the lamb.

Place the meat in a roasting pan and place the roasting pan in the centre part of the oven. Roast the lamb for 20 minutes, then reduce the oven temperature to warm 325°F (Gas Mark 3, 170°C) and continue to roast the meat until it is cooked to your liking. Allow 22 minutes to the half kilo plus 22 minutes over for medium to well-done lamb. Baste the lamb with the pan juices from time to time during the cooking period. You can test the meat for doneness by inserting a skewer or the point of a sharp knife into the centre of the joint. For medium lamb, the juices that run out should be pale pink; if you wish the meat to be well-done, however, continue to roast until the juices that run out are clear.

(If you are using a meat thermometer, by the way, the temperature should read 82°C.)

When the meat is cooked to your liking, remove the roasting pan from the oven and, using two large forks or spoons, carefully transfer the joint to a warmed serving platter or to a carving board. Set the joint aside and keep it warm while you make a sauce from the pan juices to serve with the lamb.

Pour the stock into the roasting pan and bring to the boil, stirring constantly and scraping the pan. Make a paste of the remaining butter and the flour and add, little by little, to the hot stock, stirring constantly. Cook the sauce for 2 to 3 minutes, stirring constantly, or until it is smooth and has thickened. Pour the sauce into a sauceboat.

Carve the lamb, as illustrated on page 160 and serve the lamb, in thin slices, with the sauce.

2. Lamb Croquettes

25g (1oz) butter
1 small onion, finely chopped
2 tablespoons flour
300ml (10fl oz) beef stock
350g (12oz) cooked lamb, coarsely minced
2 tablespoons finely chopped fresh parsley
1 teaspoon Worcestershire sauce
   salt
   freshly ground black pepper
1 egg
1 tablespoon milk
75g (3oz) fresh white breadcrumbs
   sufficient vegetable oil for deep frying

In a saucepan, melt the butter over moderate heat. When the foam subsides, add the onion and fry, stirring occasionally, for 5 to 7 minutes or until it is soft and translucent but not brown. Stir in the flour and cook, stirring constantly, for 2 minutes. Add the stock and bring to the boil, stirring. Cook the mixture for 2 minutes. Stir in the meat, parsley, Worcestershire sauce, salt and black pepper.

Remove the pan from the heat and spoon the mixture on to a large plate. Place the plate in the refrigerator and chill the mixture for at least 8 hours or until it has cooled completely and is 'set'. (If you haven't a refrigerator, put the plate in a cool place such as a larder, and chill the mixture overnight.)

When the mixture is cold and 'set', divide it into eight portions. Using the palms of your hands, roll each portion into a sausage shape.

In a shallow dish, beat the egg and milk together. Place the breadcrumbs in a second plate. Coat each shape first in the egg mixture, then in the breadcrumbs, gently shaking off any excess crumbs.

Fill a deep-frying pan one-third full with vegetable oil. Set the pan over moderate heat and heat the oil until it registers 375°F (190°C) on a deep-fat thermometer or until a small piece of stale bread dropped into the oil turns golden in 40 seconds. Carefully lower the croquettes into the oil, a few at a time, and deep-fry them for 2 to 3 minutes or until they are golden. Remove the croquettes from the oil and drain on kitchen paper towels. Set the croquettes aside, cover them and keep them warm while you cook and drain the remaining croquettes in the same way.

When all the croquettes have been cooked, transfer them to a warmed serving dish or individual serving plates and serve at once.

3. Turkish Lamb Pilaff

4 tablespoons cooking oil
175g (6oz) long-grain rice, washed, soaked in cold water for 30 minutes and drained
1.2 l (2 pints) stock
25g (1oz) butter
2 tablespoons blanched almonds
1 medium-sized onion, finely chopped
350g (12oz) cooked lamb, cut into strips
2 tablespoons seedless raisins or sultanas
1½ teaspoons ground cinnamon
   salt
   freshly ground black pepper

In a medium-sized saucepan, heat half the oil over moderate heat. When the oil is hot, add the rice and cook for 3 minutes or until it becomes transparent. Pour in the stock and bring to the boil over high heat. Cook for 12 minutes; do not allow the rice to overcook.

Meanwhile, in another saucepan, heat the remaining oil with the butter over moderate heat. Add the almonds and cook them for 3 minutes or until they are golden. Remove them from the pan and set aside.

Add the onion to the pan and fry, stirring occasionally, for 5 to 7 minutes or until it is soft and translucent but not brown. Add the meat and cook for 5 minutes or until it is lightly browned and heated through.

Remove the rice from the heat and pour it through a strainer. Add the rice to the onion and meat, stir in the almonds and raisins or sultanas. Stir in the ground cinnamon, and sprinkle over salt and black pepper to your taste.

Heat the pilaff gently for 2 to 3 minutes, remove it from the heat and serve it immediately.

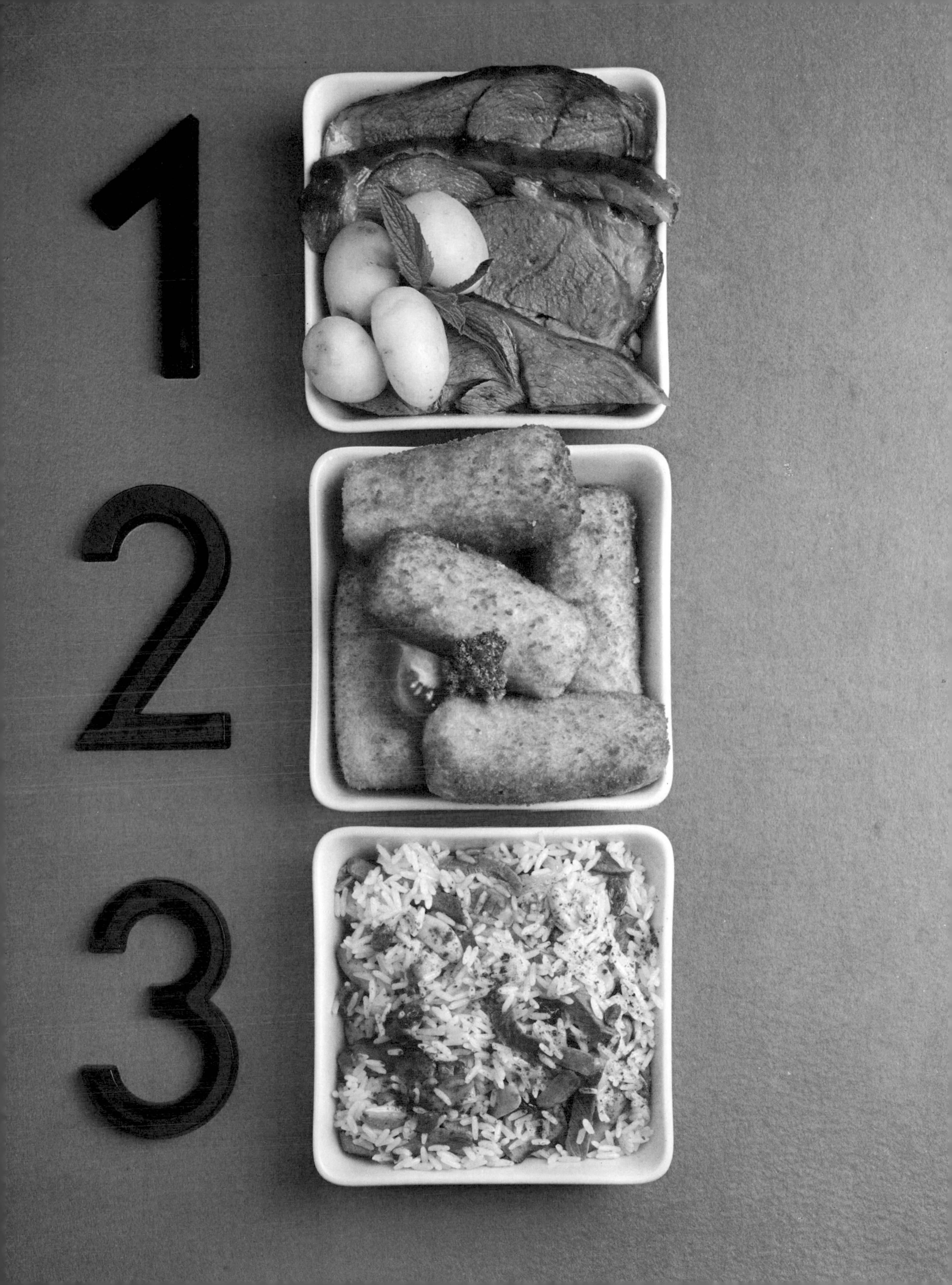
1
2
3

Three ways with turkey

1. Roast Stuffed Turkey with Cranberry Sauce

1 × 3kg (6½lb) oven-ready turkey
25g (1oz) butter, softened
    salt
    freshly ground black pepper
APRICOT STUFFING
50g (2oz) dried apricots, soaked
    overnight
50g (2oz) fresh white breadcrumbs
½ teaspoon mixed spice
½ teaspoon salt
½ teaspoon black pepper
2 teaspoons lemon juice
1 tablespoon melted butter
1 small egg, beaten
CHESTNUT STUFFING
675g (1½lb) chestnuts
    turkey or chicken stock
25g (1oz) butter
CRANBERRY SAUCE
225g (8oz) cranberries
150ml (5fl oz) water
75g (3oz) sugar
    a little dry sherry or vermouth

Wipe the bird, inside and out, with kitchen paper towels.

To prepare the apricot stuffing, drain the apricots, then chop them. Stir in the breadcrumbs, mixed spice, salt, pepper, lemon juice and melted butter. Bind with the egg. Free the skin from the turkey breast and gently push the apricot mixture under the loosened skin, pushing down and over the sides of the breast so that it will keep the meat moist during cooking. Secure the neck skin with skewers or with a trussing needle and thread.

Now prepare the chestnut stuffing. First, you must peel the chestnuts by removing the hard, outer shells. To do this, make a small slit in the hard skin at the pointed end of each chestnut with the point of a sharp knife. Put the chestnuts into a medium-sized saucepan and pour over just enough cold water to cover. Place the pan over high heat and bring the water to the boil. Boil the chestnuts for 2 minutes, then remove the pan from the heat. With a slotted spoon, remove the chestnuts from the water and, as soon as you can handle them, peel them and remove the inner skins as well while they are still warm.

Put the chestnuts in a saucepan and just cover with boiling stock. Cook for 35 to 50 minutes or until they are just tender. Drain them thoroughly and toss them in the butter. Stuff the chestnuts into the body cavity of the turkey and secure the opening with a skewer.

Preheat the oven to very hot 450°F (Gas Mark 8, 230°C).

Brush the turkey with the softened butter and season to taste with salt and pepper. Prick the breast skin all over. Then either wrap the bird loosely in aluminium foil and place in a roasting pan or put the bird directly on to the rack in the roasting pan, breast down, and cover with foil, folding the edges over the lip of the pan.

Place the pan in the oven and roast the turkey for 2¼ to 2¾ hours, turning it halfway through cooking. Test for doneness by piercing the thigh with a skewer; the juices that run out should be clear.

When the turkey is cooked, remove the roasting pan from the oven and unwrap the foil. Using two large forks or spoons, carefully transfer the turkey to a large serving platter or a carving board. Set the bird aside and keep it warm.

Meanwhile, prepare the cranberry sauce. Place the cranberries and water in a saucepan and cook over moderate heat until the cranberries 'pop', adding more water if necessary. Rub the fruit through a sieve, sweeten with the sugar and reheat, adding a little sherry or dry vermouth if you wish. Pour into a sauceboat.

Carve the turkey, as illustrated on page 163, and serve the turkey, cut into thin slices or chunks, with the sauce handed round separately.

2. Turkey Divan

225g (8oz) frozen broccoli,
    thawed
3 tablespoons grated Parmesan
    cheese
1 packet savoury white sauce mix
300ml (10fl oz) milk
3 tablespoons dry sherry
2 egg yolks
3 tablespoons double cream
    salt
    freshly ground black pepper
350g (12oz) cooked turkey, thinly
    sliced

Preheat the oven to moderate 350°F (Gas Mark 4, 180°C).

Cook the broccoli according to the instructions on the packet. Drain and arrange on the bottom of an ovenproof casserole. Sprinkle over 1 tablespoon of grated cheese.

Make up the savoury sauce mix according to the instructions on the packet, using the milk. Remove from the heat. In a small bowl, combine the sherry, egg yolks and cream, then stir them into the sauce mix. Add 1 tablespoon of grated cheese and season with salt and pepper to taste.

Spoon half the sauce over the broccoli, arrange the turkey slices on top and cover with the remaining sauce. Sprinkle over the remaining grated cheese.

Place the casserole in the oven and bake for 30 minutes or until the meat is heated through and the sauce is golden and bubbling.

Serve at once.

3. Turkey in Wine Sauce

50g (2oz) butter
25g (1oz) flour
300ml (10fl oz) turkey stock
    salt
    freshly ground black pepper
350g (12oz) sliced cooked turkey
1 small onion, chopped
1 teaspoon dried tarragon
2 tablespoons finely chopped fresh
    parsley
2 tablespoons dry red wine
2 lemon slices

In a saucepan, melt 25 grams (1 ounce) of the butter over moderate heat. Remove the pan from the heat and, using a wooden spoon stir in the flour to form a smooth paste. Gradually add the stock, stirring constantly. Return the pan to the heat and cook the sauce, stirring constantly, for 2 to 3 minutes or until it is thick and smooth. Season to taste with salt and pepper. Set aside.

In a frying-pan, melt the remaining butter over moderate heat. When the foam subsides, fry the turkey for 5 minutes on both sides or until thoroughly heated through. Remove the turkey slices to a heated serving dish and keep warm.

Add the onion to the pan and fry, stirring occasionally, for 5 to 7 minutes or until it is soft and translucent but not brown. Remove the pan from the heat and add the onion to the turkey sauce. Return the sauce to the boil and stir in the tarragon, parsley and wine.

Pour the sauce over the turkey slices, garnish with the lemon slices and serve.

1

2

3

Types of tea

The product of the tea plant which finally reaches the consumer arrives in various forms, which are sold under a variety of confusing names. Although there are several varieties of *camellia sinensis* the difference between the many varieties of tea depends principally on manufacture rather than on the type of bush, soil, locality or additive. The three principal classifications into which tea may be divided are Black Tea, Green Tea and Oolong Tea.

Black Tea is the most common and still the most popular tea in the western world. Its particular characteristic is that the leaves are fully fermented in the process of manufacture, and it is this which makes them black. Black tea is produced principally in Sri Lanka, India and East Africa.

Green Tea is mainly produced in China and Japan, and for that reason is frequently referred to as China tea. The particular characteristic of green tea is that the leaf is dried immediately and does not undergo fermentation, which preserves the green colour of the leaves. Green tea is more astringent in flavour than black tea and tends to be an acquired taste. When brewed, the tea produced tends to be pale and aromatic.

Oolong Tea is only partially fermented before drying and is manufactured in Taiwan and China. The leaves are brown in colour and, when brewed, produce a pale brown tea with a characteristic aroma and flavour.

How to make tea

In order to make perfect tea every time follow this method.

Fill the kettle with freshly-drawn water from the cold tap and place over moderate heat. Just before the water boils, pour a little of it into the teapot to warm the pot and then discard the water. (This enables the tea to infuse better.) Place one teaspoon of tea per person and one 'for the pot' in the teapot. As soon as the water boils,

Tea & coffee

Tea is a beverage made from the leaves of the plant *camellia sinensis*, which is widely cultivated in many tropical and sub-tropical regions throughout the world. The original home of tea is China, although it has also been grown for many centuries in Japan.

bring the teapot to the kettle and pour in the water. Water which is allowed to boil for too long loses any dissolved gases it may contain and consequently gives the tea a flat taste. Place the lid on the teapot and allow the tea to stand for 3 to 5 minutes before using. Tea with fine leaves needs less time to brew than tea with coarser leaves.

The tea is now ready to be served, accompanied by milk, sugar or lemon according to taste.

Coffee

Coffee, believed to be the most popular single beverage on earth, is regularly consumed by about one-third of the world's population. It is made by grinding the roasted beans of the small coffee or *coffea* tree.

Coffee has been known and widely consumed in Arabia for well over 800 years, although some strict Moslems claimed that its caffeine content made

it an intoxicant and therefore forbidden by the Koran. It became popular in Europe during the sixteenth and seventeenth centuries, when coffee houses sprang up in most of the major European cities—Lloyds, the insurance brokers, began life as a coffee shop in Lombard Street, London.

Coffee is now widely produced in many equatorial countries. Brazil is the world's largest producer of coffee, supplying almost 50 percent of the world's requirements.

How to make coffee
Some basic principles apply to coffee-making, no matter what type of coffee you make. The best coffee, for instance, is made from freshly roasted beans ground just before you make the coffee. Ideally, coffee should not be allowed to boil, and although 1 to 2 minutes of boiling is not detrimental to the taste and flavour of the finished coffee, continued boiling will certainly impair its quality.

Basically, western-style coffee-making consists of passing boiling water through coffee grounds, carrying with it the colour and flavour but leaving the grounds behind, usually in a separate section of the coffee pot.

Infused coffee : Pour boiling water on to freshly ground coffee in a warmed jug (about 1 tablespoon of coffee per person). Stir the coffee and leave the jug in a warm place for about 10 minutes. Pour the coffee through a strainer into a heated coffee pot, or straight into coffee cups.

Percolated coffee : Methods vary widely according to the type of percolator used, and it is, therefore, wise to follow the instructions given with your percolator. The principle involved, however, is that the water circulates through the coffee grounds, extracting the flavour and colour and then drips through a strainer, leaving the grounds behind.

Filtered coffee: This is a great favourite in France, and can be produced by placing a perforated filter over a cup or jug and filling the filter with about 1 tablespoon of coffee per person. Then pour boiling water through the filter, to extract flavour and colour as it drips into the cup or jug below.

Cona or suction method: Fill the lower container with water and the upper with coffee grounds. On heating, the water is sucked up the funnel between the two containers, remaining there for about 3 minutes. When it is removed from the heat, the coffee filters down into the lower container, leaving the grounds in the funnel.

Espresso or Italian coffee: This is strong, dark, slightly bitter and is made under pressure in a machine. It can also be made in a drip pot, or *napoletana*, the basket of the inner cylinder being filled with very finely ground coffee and the outer cylinder with water. The spouted vessel is then placed on top of the drip pot, with the spout facing downwards. Over low heat, the water is brought to the boil. The *napoletana* is then reversed so that the spout points upwards and lets the water drip through.

Arabic, Turkish or Greek coffee: This is more complicated—and more wasteful in terms of the amount of coffee grounds used. It is, nevertheless, a most attractive beverage and one that is becoming increasingly popular in western countries. To make Turkish coffee, boil water in a Turkish coffee-maker over moderate heat. Add sugar to taste (usually about 1 teaspoon per cup) and 2½ teaspoons of very finely pulverized coffee grounds to the pot, allowing the coffee grounds to remain on the surface of the water. Bring to the boil again, then remove from the heat to allow the froth to die down. Boil again, then remove from the heat. As the froth dies down, stir the coffee grounds into the liquid. Pour the coffee immediately into small demi-tasse cups, allowing 1 to 2 minutes before drinking to let the sediment sink to the bottom of the cup.

Entertaining

what might seem a complicated procedure much easier.

Timing

Don't rush into organizing your first dinner party, asking guests at 24 hours' notice and then expect to provide them with three courses of sumptuous food. Give yourself at least a week to think about it if you're going to make a special meal. This is important particularly for the first few times you entertain.

It's pleasant, you'll find, to have some time to browse through recipe books and discuss with your husband what you're going to serve, making a comprehensive shopping list at the same time. Shopping for a dinner party is a strenuous business especially if it's a rushed lunch hour or after work task. It's much more enjoyable to gather the ingredients for the dishes at leisure, a few at a time, going to the shops where you get the best quality and value, and to give your butcher or fishmonger an order well in advance for exactly what you want.

Similarly with the cooking. If you're going to take pleasure in preparing for the party you *must* choose dishes which can be prepared up to the very last stage before the party, and which only need either to be finished quickly or heated up in the oven. Doing this is a discipline — it does restrict your choice of menu to some extent—but it's essential for peace of mind. Being panicky, or hot and bothered about a dish that doesn't work out right at the last minute is not the mood with which to greet guests. With experience you'll discover the satisfaction on the day of the party of knowing that everything is ready bar the details, so that you can actually savour the idea of seeing old friends or meeting new people.

The menus on pages 224-239 are designed to help you in this respect: all the dishes require the minimum of attention immediately before the meal. There is a cold menu too (page 230), which you'd be able to put straight on to the table on reaching home, a great asset if you're going out with your friends before eating.

If you're entertaining at the weekend there'll be an opportunity to prepare things on the day, but don't leave so much to do that you're too exhausted to enjoy the guests. If it's a weekday party do leave yourself some time the previous evening or before work that morning. You can do the major work of preparing the food then: make the starter and the dessert, if they're to be

Inviting people into your home for the first time is a special moment. You and your husband are saying, 'This is how we live. Come and share it for a while.' It could be a daunting situation; you wonder what your guests expect, whether they'll enjoy themselves. Remember that entertaining means having fun—and that this applies both to hosts and guests.

The dinner party is probably the most demanding sort of entertaining you can do in your home. You'll be on show and catering for four or six people's needs for food, drink and conversation for several hours at a stretch. But the dinner party is also most rewarding. Being able to provide good food and a convivial atmosphere

The well-organized hostess will try to do as much of the fiddly preparation as she can ahead of time.

for your guests is a skill worth working at, and learning by your minor mistakes can, in this case, be very enjoyable.

You have the opportunity of getting to know people well over a meal table; companionship flourishes when food and wine are served among friends. Don't be put off by the thought of preparing large quantities of food: catering for four or six is only doubling or trebling the amount you and your husband usually eat.

There are some general guide lines to follow which will help to make served cold, and assemble the main dish. In the evening all you'll have to do after coping with the main dish is the last minute details: setting the table, making a salad and garnishing the dishes ready to serve.

If you're lucky enough to have a freezer you could, of course, prepare some of the dishes weeks ahead if you wanted, merely bringing them out to thaw overnight in the fridge.

If you are a working wife allow plenty of time for getting home and changing and doing the last minute organization. Should you get held up at work or on the way home you might find yourself arriving on the doorstep at the same time as the guests. On the other hand, you haven't failed if everything doesn't go like clockwork. Sometimes a casserole will take longer to cook than the recipe says or the potatoes will seem *never* to become tender. Your husband can help out here if the guests have arrived; he can offer them a drink or open a bottle of wine while you complete things in the kitchen.

Choosing the dishes

Costs. You're not aiming to imitate a restaurant when you invite people to dinner, so you don't have to break the bank to feed them, or necessarily serve very expensive dishes. Good cooking makes the best of inexpensive ingredients; it's better to settle for a superbly prepared economical dish than to skimp on the cost of a lavish one beyond your budget.

Extras. Special flavouring ingredients for a new dish might seem an extravagance if you don't use them in your everyday cooking. But a herb or a spice, or additions like nuts or pimentoes, do make the vital difference to a dish. If they'll store in an airtight jar, in the fridge or the freezer, you won't waste what's left over and will have made an investment against dinner parties of the future.

The 'accessories' to a meal, the cheese, the wine and/or liqueurs, the fresh fruit, can add considerably to the expense of it. Take these into consideration from the start because they do play an important part. Likewise with the coffee; it's the finish to a meal and it would be a shame to mar something you've taken trouble over by omitting attention to the small details which complete it.

Flavour, colour and texture. The way the food for a dinner party looks and feels is almost as important as the way it tastes. (Smell is vital too: nothing cheers a cold and tired guest on arrival so much as the aroma of almost-ready food.) With food, the eye often pre-judges for the palate, so when picking the dishes for a menu think through in your mind not only how each one tastes and appears individually but how they are against each other. When you're serving two or three dishes one after the other it's essential that they balance and interplay in all respects. A meal that's all bland, smooth and creamy-white is as unsatisfactory as one that's all rugged, hearty and chewy. Two meat courses, pâté followed by steak for example, are rather an ordeal. Again, it's preferable not to have consecutive dishes that are all very liquid, like soup followed by a juicy casserole and fruit in syrup. The menu on page 238, for a dinner party based round a chicken main course is an example of good menu planning: a fresh flavoured creamy vegetable soup is followed by the drier texture of roast meat and vegetables. An attractive crunchy red and green salad is next, before a refreshing cold fruity dessert.

Alternatively, the meal based around a pork main dish on page 236 starts with light savoury pastry tartlets filled with egg, has a flavourful juicy main dish with mashed potatoes and a succulent green vegetable. Then, a substantial mixed salad and a smooth, sophisticated chocolate dessert.

Obviously you'll be guided by your own tastes in food but it's worth remembering that if you only use one cooking method for a meal, if everything is either grilled, braised or fried for example, there's a danger that it will all taste very same-y.

Presentation: Even with the finest bone china dinner service money could buy, food that is not well presented will look an unappetizing mess. For a dinner party you'll probably want the dishes to look more festive than usual, bringing them to the table and serving them there rather than dishing straight on to a plate. It requires practice to strike the right note with preparing dishes for the table. It's best not to do anything too ambitious at first — fiddly garnishes and last minute complicated sauces are things to be avoided. Lots of oven-to-table ware is very handsome, and a steaming, aromatic dish served like this is

A patchwork table cloth can provide a colourful background to co-ordinated accessories.

always an attractive sight and saves you the problem of transferring cooked food to a serving dish. If you're unsure about your prowess at carving a joint it's a good idea to do this in the kitchen and bring it to the table ready sliced.

Garnishes: Last minute additions to a dish don't necessarily add to the taste very much but they can often transform something ordinary into a visual delight. Lemon and tomato slices with a plate of fish for example, a sprinkle of chopped coriander on top of a tomato salad, parsley on new potatoes, watercress with a grilled chop. These are the sorts of things you'll have time

to do if everything else has been organized to run smoothly.

Equipment

Crockery: If you received a dinner service as a wedding gift you'll be adequately equipped to serve a meal for four to six guests. With luck you'll have been given matching vegetable dishes, sauceboat and meat plate. A table set with all this would look very grand for a formal dinner. Don't despair if you haven't a complete set of anything though: all that's essential is to check in your mind when planning the meal you want to cook that you have enough plates and dishes for the

The cool elegant look of this table makes a perfect setting for a dinner party.

courses you're going to serve. They don't necessarily need to be matching; a random assortment of patterned china, or different patterns all of the same colour combination, like blue and white, can look very pretty on a table. Junk shop finds and relatives' cast-offs come into their own here.

If you're not serving a very formal meal, it's probably better to leave the bone china in the cupboard: hearty peasant soup or good old-fashioned stew look more at home served in everyday dishes or sturdy earthenware.

Glasses: Devotees of wine will drink it from a tooth mug or a cracked china cup, but handsome glasses are a joy to behold on a table and a pleasure to handle. It's worth investing in a set of good goblets if you haven't been given any. For pre-dinner drinking you'll need sherry glasses and tumblers: chunky, squat ones for whisky, long tall ones for gin and tonic. Some liqueur glasses can also be a useful addition. If you drink beer or cider with a meal from time to time, half pint 'pub' beer mugs with handles are attractive to look at and make for relaxed drinking.

Cutlery: A 'canteen' of cutlery contains six or eight place settings and will provide you with all you need to serve a formal dinner. If you're collecting piece by piece or a place setting at a time, that's fine; all you need to keep your guests happy is a knife, fork and spoon each. (It's not unknown for hosts to wash up the soup spoons between courses so that the dessert can be eaten!) Remember extra spoons, preferably large ones, are needed to serve the vegetables.

Fish knives and forks are lovely to look at, but their use is gradually decreasing and they are really not a first priority for you to buy.

Table setting: When you're laying a table the rule is to start from the outside with the cutlery you're going to use for the first course (for example a spoon for soup), then a knife for bread and butter, and the implements for the main course, either meat or fish. At the top of the place setting: a dessert spoon plus a fork if you're likely to need it. The wine glass goes at the top right hand corner of the setting. And the bread and butter plate, possibly with a napkin on it, to the left of the fork.

Tablecloths and napkins: At a dinner party you and your guests spend a large part of the time sitting round the table, so how it looks is a focal part of the evening. You can create a mood by the type of table you lay. Crisp white linen or lace cloth and napkins are perfect against sparkling glasses and fine china for a formal meal; gingham or printed cotton sets off bright coloured plain china or chunky pottery to advantage.

Colour is a mood-maker, too: for light summer meals plain, pale colours or fresh floral cottons are attractive, in winter a deep rich coloured cloth and napkins look warming and welcoming.

Table mats: These save the cloth from disasters, they save the table too.

If it's a highly polished one, putting hot dishes directly on to it or a thin cloth will leave irremovable ring marks. Solid mats made of rush or washable plastic-coated material go directly under the plate so they don't show when you've served the meal.

An alternative idea is to have larger, linen or fabric mats on which you place the whole place setting. These can go straight on to the table or colour co-ordinating them with the cloth can be very effective, two shades of green perhaps, or choose mats in stark contrast, navy ones against a dark red cloth for example.

You can ring the changes with your tablecloths to alter the atmosphere of your dinner parties. It needn't be an expensive business if you buy some yards of fabric and do a simple hem on the unselvedged edge.

Candles and flowers: These are the extras which turn the well-set table into the extra special. Colour co-ordinated to your table and room they are the finishing touch. Try two tall candles at either end of an oblong table with a small posy of flowers at the

base of each. For a round table one fat candle in the centre with some blossoms in full bloom placed round its base looks sensational. Non-drip candles are more expensive but an essential buy to avoid wax on cloth and food.

If your table begins to look crowded when you put on the food, don't feel that it's a waste to remove the candles and flowers. Put them on the mantelpiece or sideboard. The same flattering light will be cast on your guests without their feeling cramped.

Wine

Consult the chart on pages 212–213 if you're uncertain what wine would be most appropriate to serve with your chosen dish. As a general rule, red wine is served with dark meat, white with white meat and fish. These are thought of as combinations which mutually enhance; if you prefer white wine to red there's no reason why you shouldn't drink it regardless of what type of dish is on the table.

There are wine suggestions in the chart for every course of the meal

although it's only at really grand occasions that the wine alters with every dish. At home when you're serving a meal combining fish and meat courses you can either wait until you reach the main course before serving a wine which complements the dish, or alternatively serve a rosé wine or a non-vintage champagne all through the meal. If you have a selection of wines to drink with a meal serve white before red, young wine before mature, dry before sweet.

Red wine should be served 'chambré', at room temperature, so bring it inside and remove the cork half an hour before the meal time. White wine is best chilled and in summer is delicious served straight from the refrigerator. Don't overchill, however; one to two hours in the refrigerator is usually enough.

If you are fortunate enough to have some good vintage claret or Burgundy to drink, decant it first (into a jug if you have no decanter). This is because mature wine can have a heavy sediment in the bottle and you don't want to pour this into a guest's glass.

If you're cooking a dish from one particular country's cuisine it's safe to assume that it will be best enhanced by a wine from that country, for example Osso Buco with a Chianti Classico or a soave or a fiery Hungarian goulash with a bottle of mellow Bull's Blood.

Your wine merchant can be a tremendous ally. If you are able to make a friend of him he'll advise you how to choose from the tremendous range of wines available, steering you clear of both the 'rubbish' and the over-priced.

Of course, to drink wine is not compulsory with food. Cider or beer make a pleasant change and with certain foods, such as simple casseroles or robust-flavoured stews, they are in fact preferable. Lager served with spicy Indian food is another combination where wine is not first choice.

Tea party

An easy way of entertaining a group of mixed ages, parents with children, perhaps relatives out for the day in the car, new neighbours who call in, or friends with young children, is to give a tea party.

Plenty of fresh hot tea, orange juice, lemonade or milk for the kids plus a selection of home-made cakes and biscuits makes a pleasant break in the afternoon. For a more substantial meal, more like the old-fashioned 'high tea' at five o'clock, serve a buttered tea bread (see recipe page), soft boiled eggs, toast or hot buttered scones in winter and add a savoury meat or fish spread before the sweet things.

Drinks party

The cocktail party as such, with alcoholic concoctions as high powered as the conversation, is a thing of the past. But a drinks party can be a useful way of introducing a lot of people to each other where they'll have an opportunity to talk. Sunday morning before lunch is one of the traditional times for drinks; or an early weekend evening may fit in better with your timetable. Serve only tidbits of food: olives, cheese, crisps or some canapés (see the recipes on pages 220–223) assuming that your guests will leave to go and eat later. One kind of drink, such as sherry or wine or a punch, would make for easy serving; you'll only need to take round a bottle or a big jug to make sure that everyone's glass is topped up. Don't forget some soft drinks for teetotallers. Glasses can usually be hired for a small charge from most off-licences.

Dancing Party

Only give this kind of party if you're feeling energetic and prepared for the strenuous work of moving furniture before and clearing up after. It's also perhaps not a good idea if your home has a lot of new light-coloured carpet that can't be taken up, because ash and wine *will* be spilt. Given these disadvantages, dancing parties are the boisterous, celebratory events people remember you for and great fun is had by all. Essentials are: plenty of space, and good, loud, varied music. A tape deck is preferable to a record player because really vigorous dancing in a room can cause the needle to jump on the record. You'll need to provide food later on to sustain the energetic dancers: plenty of French bread and cheese, a dip or a pâté. Bowls of hot soup or baked potatoes with butter go down well on a cold night. If guests are 'bringing a bottle', make sure there are corkscrews around to open them with and plenty of glasses or paper cups. Red and white wine and beer is a selection likely to suit most people's tastes. Again, provide squash or cola for the drivers and non-drinkers. Be prepared to produce hot black coffee last thing, too.

Wine and food chart

Hors d'oeuvre

Pâté, quiche, etc | Fairly strong dry white, such as Traminer, a Rhine wine such as Rüdesheimer, rosé such as Rosé d'Anjou or light red, such as Beaujolais

Salad or cold hors d'oeuvre | Dry white, such as Alsatian Sylvaner or Yugoslavian Zilavka or Riesling

Soups | Dry sherry or a light Madeira is served with consommés, otherwise wine is not usually served with soup

Fish

Grilled or lightly poached fish | Light wine, such as Chablis, Pouilly Fuissé or Moselle

Fish in rich cream sauce | Heavy white, such as white Burgundy (Meursault, Montrachet) or Rhine wine, such as Niersteiner

Shellfish | Light white (Chablis is traditional with oysters), Muscadet, Italian Soave or a slightly flinty Loire, such as Sancerre or Vouvray

Shellfish served as a risotto or with rich sauce | Rosé, such as Tavel, a white Loire wine, such as Pouilly Fumé or a white Burgundy, such as Puligny Montrachet

Smoked Fish | Heavy white, such as white Burgundy, Alsatian Traminer or a spicy Rhine spätlese wine

Dark meat

Beef, roasted or grilled

Beef casseroles and stews

Steaks

Lamb, roasted or grilled

Lamb casseroles, stews and risottos

Game (grouse, partridge, pheasant)

Hare, venison

White meat

Pork

Veal

Ham

Bordeaux, such as Château Montrose or St. Emilion (Any good Bordeaux is perfect with a roast)

Sturdy red Burgundy, such as Beaune, a Rhône wine, such as Châteauneuf-du-Pape, a heavier Italian red, such as Barolo or a Hungarian Egri Bikaver

Bordeaux, such as St. Estephe, a medium red Burgundy, such as Nuits St. Georges, or a Californian Cabernet Sauvignon

Bordeaux, such as a Margaux, a light Burgundy, such as Beaujolais or Macon or a light Italian wine, such as Bardolino

Bordeaux, such as a Médoc, Cabernet Sauvignon, an Italian wine such as Chianti or Valpolicella

Bordeaux, such as St. Emilion or Château Haut-Brion

Strong red, such as Côtes du Rhône or a heavy Burgundy, such as Chambertin

Medium-sweet white, such as Graves or Orvieto or a rosé, such as Côtes de Provence or Mateus

Strong white, such as Montrachet, Pinot Chardonnay or a light red, such as Valpolicella, Zinfandel or Beaujolais

Rosé, such as Tavel or Rosé d'Anjou or a light red, such as Macon

Poultry

Chicken, cooked simply	Heavier white, such as Hungarian Riesling or a white Burgundy
Chicken cooked with red wine or in a very rich vegetable-type stew	Light red, such as Beaujolais or Fleurie
Duck	Heavy white Burgundy, such as Meurseult or a rosé, such as Tavel
Goose	White, such as a Rhine wine or an Alsatian or Hungarian Riesling
Turkey	Heavy white, such as Traminer, a Rhine wine or a rosé, such as Côtes de Provence

Cheese

Soft (Brie, Camembert, etc)	Medium red Burgundy, such as Beaune or a Bordeaux, such as St. Julien
Medium (Port-Salut, Cheddar, etc)	Light, fruity red, such as Fleurie or Beaujolais, or a spicy white, such as Alsatian Gewürztraminer or a Tavel
Cream or Goat's	Medium white, such as Graves, an Alsatian Traminer or a Rhine wine
Blue cheese (Stilton, etc)	Light red such as Bardolino, a medium Burgundy such as Brouilly or a Cabernet Sauvignon

Desserts

Sauternes or Barsac are the traditional dessert wines, but any German wine marked spätlese or auslese would also be suitable. For an extra rich dessert, try a Hungarian Tokay

Generally, wine is not served with desserts containing chocolate

After-dinner

Port, the heavier Madeiras or, for a change, a mature Hungarian Tokay or the 'queen of Sauternes', Château d'Yquem

Tea parties

Chocolate Biscuits

16 BISCUITS

65g (2½oz) dark cooking chocolate,
   broken into pieces
1 tablespoon water
3 egg whites
125g (4oz) castor sugar

Preheat the oven to moderate 350°F
(Gas Mark 4, 180°C).

In a double saucepan or in a small
bowl placed over a pan of hot water,
melt the chocolate with the water,
stirring occasionally. As soon as the
chocolate is melted, remove the pan
from the heat.

In a medium-sized mixing bowl,
beat the egg whites with a wire whisk
or rotary beater until they are almost
stiff. Add 3 teaspoons of the sugar
and beat for 1 more minute. Carefully
fold in the remaining sugar.

Spoon the egg whites into the
saucepan containing the melted chocolate and gently fold the egg whites and
chocolate together.

Put about 2 tablespoonfuls of the
mixture into 16 small paper cases
placed on a baking sheet.

Bake the biscuits in the oven for
20 to 30 minutes. Remove from the
oven and serve cool.

Chocolate Chip Cookies

ABOUT 30 COOKIES

125g (4oz) plus 1 tablespoon butter
125g (4oz) sugar
75g (3oz) soft brown sugar
1 egg
½ teaspoon vanilla essence
175g (6oz) flour
½ teaspoon salt
½ teaspoon bicarbonate of soda
50g (2oz) chopped walnuts
125g (4oz) dark plain chocolate chips

Preheat the oven to fairly hot 375°F
(Gas Mark 5, 190°C). With the 1
tablespoon of butter, grease a baking
sheet and set aside.

In a medium-sized mixing bowl,
cream the remaining butter with a
wooden spoon. Mix the sugars together and add them gradually to the
butter, beating until the mixture is
smooth and fluffy. Beat in the egg and
vanilla essence.

Sift the flour with the salt and soda.
Stir it into the butter-and-sugar mix-

*Devonshire Splits, served warm with
generous helpings of jam and cream,
make appetizing tea-time snacks.*

ture and mix to a smooth batter. Stir
in the nuts and chocolate chips.

Drop teaspoonfuls of the mixture
on to the baking sheet, leaving about
2.5cm (1in) between each cookie.

Bake the cookies for 10 to 15
minutes or until they are lightly
browned. Remove from the oven and
transfer to a wire rack to cool.

Devonshire Splits

16 BUNS

15g (½oz) fresh yeast
1 teaspoon castor sugar
2 tablespoons lukewarm water
450g (1 lb) flour
¼ teaspoon salt
300ml (10fl oz) lukewarm milk
25g (1oz) melted butter

In a small mixing bowl, cream the
yeast and sugar together. Stir in the
lukewarm water and set the bowl aside
in a warm, draught-free place for 15 to
20 minutes, or until the yeast mixture
is puffed up and frothy.

Sift the flour and salt into a large
mixing bowl. Make a well in the
centre and pour in the yeast mixture,
the milk and the melted butter. Mix
the liquid ingredients into the flour
with your hands or a spoon until it
forms a soft dough. Turn the dough

out on to a floured board and knead
it for 5 minutes.

Put the dough in a greased bowl.
Cover with a clean damp cloth and
leave it in a warm, draught-free place
for 1½ hours, or until the dough has
doubled in bulk.

Turn the dough out on to the floured
board and knead for 2 minutes.

Form the dough into 16 round balls.
Place the balls on a floured baking
sheet. Leave them for 20 minutes in a
warm, draught-free place.

Preheat the oven to hot 425°F (Gas
Mark 7, 220°C).

Place the buns in the oven and bake
them for 15 minutes. Serve hot or cold.

Dundee Cake

ONE 20CM (8IN) CAKE

1 tablespoon melted butter
275g (10oz) flour
½ teaspoon baking powder
½ teaspoon ground mixed spice
½ teaspoon ground cinnamon
225g (8oz) butter
225g (8oz) castor sugar
5 eggs
125g (4oz) raisins
125g (4oz) currants
125g (4oz) sultanas
50g (2oz) mixed candied fruit,
   coarsely chopped
50g (2oz) glacé cherries
   grated rind of 1 small orange
   grated rind of 1 small lemon
50g (2oz) blanched almonds, halved

Preheat the oven to warm 325°F (Gas Mark 3, 170°C).

Lightly brush the bottom and sides of a 20cm (8in) cake tin with half of the melted butter. Line the bottom and sides of the tin with greaseproof or waxed paper. Lightly brush the greaseproof or waxed paper with the remaining melted butter. Set the tin aside.

Sift the flour, baking powder, mixed spice and cinnamon into a large bowl.

In a medium-sized mixing bowl, cream the butter with a wooden spoon until it becomes soft and fluffy. Gradually add the sugar, beating until the mixture is pale and drops easily from the spoon when it is tapped against the side of the bowl. Break one egg into the butter-sugar mixture and beat vigorously until the mixture stiffens and becomes fluffy. Add the remaining eggs in the same manner, beating in two tablespoons of the flour before adding the last egg.

Add the raisins, currants, sultanas, candied fruit, cherries and orange and lemon rinds to the flour mixture. Mix together until all the fruits are coated with flour. Using a metal spoon, fold the flour mixture into the butter mixture until they are well blended.

Spoon the cake mixture into the tin, being careful to push the mixture well into the corners. Smooth the top carefully, making it as level as possible. Arrange the halved almonds in concentric circles, their pointed ends towards the centre, on top of the cake.

Bake the cake in the lower part of the oven for 2 hours, or until a skewer inserted into the centre of the cake comes out clean. Cover the top of the cake with brown or waxed paper if it browns too quickly. Turn off the oven heat and leave the cake in the oven for 10 to 15 minutes before removing it from the oven. When it is completely cool remove it from the tin and place it on a wire rack.

Peel off the greaseproof or waxed paper. This cake may be kept for several weeks if it is stored in an airtight tin.

This majestic Dundee Cake provides a perfectly scrumptious centrepiece for any special tea party. It will keep for several weeks if stored in an airtight tin.

Gingerbread

ONE 1 KILO (2 POUND) BREAD

75g (3oz) plus 1 teaspoon butter
225g (8oz) flour
½ teaspoon bicarbonate of soda
1½ teaspoons ground ginger
¼ teaspoon ground cloves
½ teaspoon ground cinnamon
¼ teaspoon salt
125g (4oz) sugar
1 egg
175ml (6fl oz) treacle
225ml (8 fl oz) sour cream
50g (2oz) raisins

Preheat the oven to moderate 350°F (Gas Mark 4, 180°C). Lightly grease a medium-sized loaf tin with the teaspoon of butter. Set aside.

Sift the flour, soda, ginger, cloves, cinnamon and salt into a medium-sized mixing bowl. Set aside.

In a large mixing bowl, cream the remaining butter and the sugar together with a wooden spoon until the mixture is light and fluffy. Add the egg and treacle and beat until the mixture is smooth. Stir in the sour cream.

Gradually incorporate the flour into the butter mixture, beating until the mixture is smooth. Stir in the raisins.

Pour the mixture into the loaf tin and place the tin in the oven. Bake for 1¼ hours, or until a skewer inserted into the centre of the bread comes out clean.

Remove the gingerbread from the oven and allow it to cool a little in the tin. Run a sharp knife lightly around the edge of the gingerbread and gently ease it out of the tin on to a wire cake rack.

Serve the gingerbread warm or cold.

Jam and Coconut Bars

12 BARS

140g (4½oz) butter, softened
125g (4oz) sugar
2 eggs, lightly beaten
225g (8oz) flour
1 teaspoon baking powder
¼ teaspoon salt
50g (2oz) desiccated coconut
350g (12oz) raspberry or strawberry jam

Preheat the oven to fairly hot 400°F (Gas Mark 6, 200°C).

Using a little of the butter, grease a 20cm (8in) square baking tin.

Simple, delicious, easy to eat – that's Jellied Cheesecake.

In a mixing bowl, cream the remaining butter and the sugar together with a wooden spoon until the mixture is light and fluffy. Beat in the eggs.

Sift the flour, baking powder and salt into another mixing bowl. Gradually add the flour mixture and coconut to the egg mixture. Mix well together.

Spread half of the mixture over the bottom of the prepared baking tin and cover it with the jam. Spread the remaining mixture on top of the jam.

Place the tin in the oven and bake for 25 minutes, or until the top is brown and will spring back when lightly pressed with a fingertip.

Remove the tin from the oven and allow to cool. When the mixture is cool, cut it into bars and serve.

Jellied Cheesecake

6-8 SERVINGS

125g (4oz) crushed digestive biscuits
40g (1½oz) butter, melted
1 whole egg
2 egg yolks

140g (4½oz) sugar
¼ teaspoon salt
50ml (2fl oz) milk
15g (½oz) gelatine dissolved in
    4 tablespoons hot water
    juice and grated rind of 1 lemon
350g (12oz) cottage cheese
150ml (5fl oz) double cream, beaten
    until thick but not stiff
2 egg whites

In a medium-sized mixing bowl, combine the crushed biscuits and melted butter with a wooden spoon.

Press the mixture into a 20cm (8in) springform pan, covering it evenly.

In another mixing bowl, beat the egg, egg yolks, 125 grams (4 ounces) sugar, salt and milk with a wire whisk or rotary beater.

Pour the mixture into a saucepan and place it over low heat. Cook, stirring constantly, for 3 to 4 minutes or until the custard thickens. Do not let the custard boil or it will curdle. Remove the pan from the heat and stir in the gelatine.

Set the pan aside until the mixture has cooled to room temperature. Mix in the lemon juice and rind, cottage cheese and the remaining sugar. Fold in the cream.

In a medium-sized mixing bowl, beat the egg whites with a wire whisk or rotary beater until they form stiff peaks.

With a metal spoon, carefully fold the egg whites into the cheese mixture.

Spoon the mixture into the crumb crust and place the pan in the refrigerator. Leave the cheesecake to chill for at least 2 hours, or until it is set.

Remove the cheesecake from the springform pan and place it on a decorative serving plate. Serve immediately.

Meringue Layer Cake

ONE 18CM (7IN) CAKE

125g (4oz) plus 2 teaspoons butter
225g (8oz) icing sugar, sifted
4 egg yolks
125g (4oz) self-raising flour, sifted
⅛ teaspoon salt
½ teaspoon almond essence
2 egg whites
125g (4oz) castor sugar
50g (2oz) silvered almonds, toasted
FILLING
50g (2oz) butter
125g (4oz) icing sugar, sifted
⅛ teaspoon salt
½ teaspoon vanilla essence
2 tablespoons coffee essence

Preheat the oven to moderate 350°F (Gas Mark 4, 180°C). With the 2 teaspoons of butter, lightly grease two 18cm (7in) loose-bottomed sandwich tins.

In a medium-sized mixing bowl, cream the remaining butter and the icing sugar together with a wooden spoon until the mixture is light and fluffy. Beat in the egg yolks, one at a time, adding 1 tablespoon of flour with each yolk.

Fold in the remaining flour and the salt, beating until the ingredients are well blended. Stir in the almond essence. Pour half the batter into each of the tins.

In a second mixing bowl, beat the egg whites with a wire whisk or rotary beater until they form soft peaks. Gradually add the castor sugar, beating constantly, and continue beating until the mixture forms stiff peaks.

Spread the meringue mixture evenly over the batter in one of the sandwich tins. Sprinkle the almonds over the top of the meringue mixture.

Place both tins in the oven and bake for 25 minutes, or until a skewer inserted into the centre of the cakes comes out clean. (The meringue-topped cake may require an extra 10 minutes.)

Remove the tins from the oven and allow the cakes to cool in the tins for 10 minutes. Remove the cakes from the tins and place them on a wire rack to cool.

Meanwhile, make the filling. In a large mixing bowl, cream the butter with the back of a wooden spoon until it is soft. Gradually add half of the sugar and the salt. Cream the butter and sugar together until the mixture is pale and fluffy. Mix in the vanilla and coffee essences and beat in the remaining sugar.

With a flat-bladed knife, generously spread the filling over the cake without the meringue topping. Place the meringue-topped cake on top and serve.

No special tea party is complete without at least one spectacular cake – and this delicious Meringue Layer Cake certainly fits the bill. It not only looks superb, it tastes marvellous, too.

Stollen
GERMAN SWEET BREAD

ONE 1½-KILO (3 POUND) LOAF

125g (4oz) plus 1 teaspoon butter
15g (½oz) fresh yeast
175g (6oz) plus ½ teaspoon sugar
1 tablespoon lukewarm water
175ml (6fl oz) scalded milk
450g (1 lb) flour
1 teaspoon salt
½ teaspoon ground cinnamon
¼ teaspoon ground mace
¼ teaspoon ground cardamom
2 eggs, lightly beaten
175g (6oz) chopped candied peel
75g (3oz) sultanas
75g (3oz) chopped walnuts
ICING
25g (1oz) butter, melted
225g (8oz) icing sugar
2 tablespoons water
¼ teaspoon vanilla essence
8 walnuts, halved

With the teaspoon of butter, grease a large baking sheet and set aside.

Crumble the yeast into a small bowl and mash in ½ teaspoon of sugar with a kitchen fork. Add the water and cream the water and yeast together to form a smooth paste. Set the bowl aside in a warm, draught-free place for 15 to 20 minutes or until the yeast mixture is puffed up and frothy.

Meanwhile, add the remaining butter to the scalded milk, stirring constantly until the butter has melted. Set aside to cool to lukewarm.

Sift the flour, the remaining sugar, the salt, cinnamon, mace and cardamom into a warmed, large mixing bowl. Make a well in the centre of the flour mixture and pour in the yeast, milk and butter mixture and the eggs. Using your fingers or a spatula, gradually draw the flour into the liquid. Continue mixing until all the flour is incorporated and the dough comes away from the sides of the bowl.

Turn the dough out on to a floured board or marble slab and knead for about 10 minutes, reflouring the surface if the dough becomes sticky. The dough should be elastic.

Rinse, thoroughly dry and lightly grease the large mixing bowl. Shape the dough into a ball and return it to the bowl. Dust the top of the dough with a little flour and cover the bowl with a clean, damp cloth. Set the bowl aside in a warm, draught-free place

Rich Stollen simply cries out for lots of butter and tea.

for 1 to 1½ hours or until the dough has risen and has doubled in bulk.

Turn the risen dough out of the bowl on to a floured surface and knead vigorously for about 4 minutes. Knead in the candied peel, sultanas and chopped nuts until they are evenly distributed. Shape the dough into an oval and place it on the prepared baking sheet. Cover with a damp cloth and return the dough to a warm place for 30 to 45 minutes or until the dough has risen slightly.

Preheat the oven to fairly hot 400°F (Gas Mark 6, 200°C). Place the baking sheet in the oven and bake for 15 minutes. Reduce the temperature to moderate 350°F (Gas Mark 4, 180°C) and bake for another 30 minutes.

After removing the bread from the oven, rap the underside of the loaf with your knuckles. If the bread sounds hollow, like a drum, it is cooked. If it does not sound hollow, lower the oven temperature to warm 325°F (Gas Mark 3, 170°C), return the loaf, upside down, to the oven and bake for a further 5 to 10 minutes.

Cool the loaf on a wire rack.

Meanwhile, make the icing. In a medium-sized mixing bowl, beat the butter, sugar and water together until they are well blended. Beat in the vanilla essence.

When the loaf is cool, using a table knife or palette knife, generously spread the icing over the top. Decorate the top of the stollen with the walnut halves and cut it into thick slices.

Shortbread

TWO 15CM (6IN) ROUNDS

225g (8oz) plus 1 teaspoon butter
225g (8oz) flour
125g (4oz) rice flour
125g (4oz) plus 1 tablespoon sugar

Using the teaspoon of butter, lightly grease a large baking sheet and set it aside.

Sift the flour and rice flour into a medium-sized mixing bowl and stir in the 125 grams (4 ounces) of sugar. Add the remaining butter and cut it into small pieces with a knife. With your fingertips, rub the butter into the flour until it resembles breadcrumbs.

Knead the mixture gently until it forms a smooth dough. Turn the dough out on to a floured board and divide the dough in half. Form each piece into a circle about 1.3cm (½in) thick and 15cm (6in) in diameter. Transfer the dough circles on to the

baking sheet, crimping the edges with your fingertips. Prick the top of the dough with a fork. Place the baking sheet in the refrigerator and chill the dough for 20 minutes.

Preheat the oven to moderate 350°F (Gas Mark 4, 180°C).

Place the baking sheet in the centre of the oven and bake the shortbread for 10 minutes. Reduce the oven temperature to cool 300°C (Gas Mark 2, 150°C) and continue to bake the shortbread for a further 30 to 40 minutes or until it is crisp and lightly browned.

Remove the sheet from the oven and, with a knife, cut the circles into triangles. Allow to cool slightly on the baking sheet. Sprinkle the remaining tablespoon of sugar over the triangles.

Transfer the shortbread to a wire rack to cool completely.

Serve immediately or store in an airtight tin.

Scones with Dried Fruit

ABOUT 12 SCONES

225g (8oz) flour
2 teaspoons baking powder
1 teaspoon bicarbonate of soda
¼ teaspoon salt
40g (1½oz) vegetable fat
50g (2oz) castor sugar
50g (2oz) raisins
2 tablespoons currants
1 large egg, beaten with 75ml (3fl oz) milk

Preheat the oven to very hot 450°F (Gas Mark 8, 230°C).

Sift the flour, baking powder, soda and salt into a large mixing bowl. Using your fingertips, rub the fat into the flour until the mixture resembles fine breadcrumbs. Stir in the sugar, raisins and currants. Using a fork, mix in enough of the egg and milk mixture to form a soft dough. Knead the dough slightly.

Turn the dough out on to a lightly floured board and roll it out to approximately 1.3cm (½in) thick. With a 5cm (2in) pastry cutter, cut the dough into circles.

Place the dough circles, well spaced apart, on a greased baking sheet. Place the baking sheet in the centre of the oven and bake for 10 to 15 minutes or until the scones have risen and are golden brown.

Remove the baking sheet from the oven. Transfer the scones to a warmed serving plate and serve at once, if they are to be eaten hot.

Drinks parties

Crab Canapés

18 CANAPÉS

40g (1½oz) butter
1 tablespoon finely chopped onion
1 tablespoon flour
175ml (6fl oz) single cream
225g (8oz) crabmeat, with the bones
    and cartilage removed, flaked
¼ teaspoon salt
⅛ teaspoon white pepper
⅛ teaspoon Tabasco sauce
1 teaspoon fresh lemon juice
6 slices of toast, with the crusts
    removed and each slice cut into
    3 fingers
1 tablespoon cream cheese
½ teaspoon paprika
2 teaspoons chopped capers

In a small saucepan melt 15 grams (½
ounce) of butter over moderate heat.
When the foam subsides, add the
onion and fry for 5 minutes, or until it
is soft and translucent but not brown.

Remove the saucepan from the heat
and stir in the flour. Pour in the cream,
return the pan to the heat and bring
the cream to the boil, stirring constantly with a wooden spoon. Add the
crab, salt, pepper, Tabasco sauce and
lemon juice. Bring the mixture to the
boil again.

Remove the pan from the heat and
spread the toast fingers with the crab
mixture.

Preheat the grill to moderately
high.

In a small bowl, blend the cream
cheese and remaining butter together
with a fork until they form a smooth
paste. Add the paprika. Dot a teaspoonful of the cheese paste over the
crab mixture.

Place the canapés under the grill and
cook for 1 minute. Remove the canapés from the heat and transfer them to
a warmed serving dish. Garnish with
the chopped capers.

Sardine Canapés

16 CANAPÉS

4 slices white bread, crusts removed
50g (2oz) butter
1 medium-sized can of sardines,
    drained
¼ teaspoon freshly ground black
    pepper
½ teaspoon fresh lemon juice
2 teaspoons finely chopped fresh
    parsley

3 hard-boiled eggs, thinly sliced
16 anchovy fillets, rolled

Butter each slice of bread. Cut each
slice into 4 squares.

In a small mixing bowl, mash the
sardines, pepper, lemon juice and
parsley to a paste with a fork.

Spread the mixture on the squares
of bread. Place a slice of hard-boiled
egg on top of the sardine mixture and
garnish with the rolled anchovy fillets.

Shrimp Canapés

12 CANAPÉS

50g (2oz) butter
90g (3½oz) canned small shrimps,
    drained
¼ teaspoon curry powder
⅛ teaspoon cayenne pepper
⅛ teaspoon chilli sauce
¼ teaspoon salt
    juice of ¼ lemon
4 slices of fried bread, with the
    crusts removed and each slice cut
    into 3 ovals
    chopped parsley to garnish

In a small saucepan, melt the butter
over moderately low heat. When the
foam subsides, add the shrimps,
curry powder, cayenne, chilli sauce,
salt and lemon juice and simmer
gently for 4 minutes.

With a slotted spoon, remove the
shrimps from the pan and place them
on the pieces of fried bread.

Garnish each canapé with chopped
parsley.

Spinach and Cheese Canapés

24 CANAPÉS

1 teaspoon salt
675g (1½ lb) spinach, washed and
    stalks removed
50g (2oz) butter
½ teaspoon freshly ground black
    pepper
75g (3oz) Cheddar cheese, grated
1 tablespoon olive oil
24 triangles of day-old white bread
25g (1oz) fine dry white breadcrumbs
25g (1oz) butter, melted

Half-fill a large saucepan with cold
water. Add the salt and bring the
water to the boil over high heat. Put
the spinach in the pan and reduce the
heat to moderate. Cook the spinach
for 7 to 12 minutes or until it is
tender. Remove the pan from the heat.

Drain the spinach in a colander and

squeeze it dry between two plates.
Chop it finely and return it to the
saucepan. Add 25 grams (1 ounce) of
the butter, the pepper and two-thirds
of the cheese and stir to mix. Cover
the pan and set it aside in a warm place.

In a large frying-pan, melt the
remaining butter and the oil over
moderately high heat. When the foam
subsides, add the triangles of bread.

Fry for 10 minutes on each side, or
until lightly browned.

Remove the croûtes from the pan
with a slotted spoon and place them on
kitchen paper towels to drain.

Preheat the grill to high.

Place a tablespoon of the spinach and cheese mixture on each croûte and top with the remaining cheese, breadcrumbs and melted butter.

Place the canapés under the grill and cook them for 2 to 3 minutes or until they are hot and the cheese is lightly browned. Serve at once.

Tabasco Cheese Canapés

24 CANAPÉS

125g (4oz) **cream cheese**

1 **shallot, minced**
1 **egg, lightly beaten**
$\frac{1}{2}$ **teaspoon Tabasco sauce**
6 **slices of toasted bread, crusts removed and quartered**

Preheat the oven to fairly hot 375°F (Gas Mark 5, 190°C).

Put the cheese, shallot, egg and Tabasco into a bowl. Using a wire whisk, beat until creamy.

Spread the mixture on the toast and place the squares on a baking sheet.

Bake the canapés in the oven for 5 to 10 minutes or until they brown.

A colourful and tempting selection of cocktail party canapés, guaranteed to grace the most elegant occasion – from left to right: Crab Canapés (recipe given), thin slices of salami with gherkin fans on rounds of toast, Sardine Canapés, Shrimp Canapés and Spinach and Cheese Canapés (recipes given), slices of tomato piped with a cream cheese, garlic and parsley mixture on crisp, savoury biscuits, small squares of pâté garnished with stuffed green olives on brown bread with lemon butter, and thin slices of smoked salmon garnished with lemon twists and parsley on diamonds of brown bread.

Guacamole
AVOCADO DIP

300 MILLILITRES (12 FLUID OUNCES)

3 medium-sized ripe avocados
3 teaspoons lemon juice
2 teaspoons olive oil
½ teaspoon salt
½ teaspoon black pepper
½ teaspoon ground coriander
1 hard-boiled egg, finely chopped
½ medium-sized green pepper, white
 pith removed, seeded and chopped
1½ green chillis, chopped
2 spring onions, chopped
1 tomato, blanched, peeled, seeded
 and chopped

With a sharp knife, halve the avocados. Slice off the skins and cut out the stones. Discard the stones and skin. Place the flesh in a medium-sized bowl and mash it with a fork.

Add the lemon juice, olive oil, salt, black pepper and coriander, and stir well to blend. Still stirring, add the finely chopped egg, green pepper, chillis, spring onions and tomato. The dip should be fairly thick. It is best used immediately, but if it is to be

Glamorous Guacamole, a creamy avocado dip, may be served with a selection of raw vegetables.

kept, cover the bowl with aluminium foil and store in the refrigerator.

Stir well before serving.

Taramasalata
COD'S ROE PASTE

675 GRAMS (1½ POUNDS)

450g (1 lb) smoked cod's roe, skinned
4 slices white bread, crusts removed
 and soaked in milk for 15 minutes
4 medium-sized garlic cloves, crushed
300ml (10fl oz) olive oil
4 tablespoons lemon juice
½ teaspoon freshly ground black
 pepper
¼ cucumber, thinly sliced
6 firm tomatoes, sliced
6 black olives

Place the smoked cod's roe in a medium-sized mixing bowl and pound it with the end of a rolling pin, or use a pestle and mortar, until the gritty texture of the roe is eliminated.

Squeeze as much moisture out of the bread as possible and add it to the bowl. Stir in the crushed garlic. Continue pounding with the pin or pestle until the mixture is smooth.

Add the oil, a few drops at a time, pounding constantly and adding a little of the lemon juice from time to time. Continue pounding until the mixture forms a soft, smooth paste and is pale pink in colour.

Alternatively, place all the ingredients in the jar of an electric blender and blend at moderately high speed until a soft paste is formed.

Beat the pepper into the mixture and arrange equal quantities of it on individual small serving plates or on one large serving platter. Surround the paste with the cucumber and tomato slices and scatter the olives decoratively over the top. Serve immediately.

Punch I

1¼ LITRES (2½ PINTS)

900ml (30fl oz) red wine
300ml (10fl oz) port
175ml (6fl oz) brandy

juice of 3 oranges
juice of 2 lemons
75g (3oz) castor sugar
pared rind of 1 orange
pared rind of 1 lemon
175ml (6fl oz) soda water
6 ice cubes
1 orange, thinly sliced

In a large punch bowl or mixing bowl, combine the wine, port, brandy and orange and lemon juice. Add the sugar and stir, using a long-handled spoon, until it has completely dissolved. Stir in the orange and lemon rind and pour over the soda water. Place the bowl in the refrigerator to chill for 30 minutes.

Remove the bowl from the refrigerator. Add the ice cubes to the bowl and float the orange slices on the top of the punch. Serve immediately.

Punch II

2¼ litres (4½ pints)

2l (4 pints) dry cider
12 cloves
2 oranges
1 × 2 inch piece cinnamon stick
2 eating apples, peeled, cored and
  sliced

75g (3oz) sugar
75ml (3fl oz) brandy

Pour the cider into a large saucepan and place the pan over low heat. Stick 6 cloves in each orange and add them, the cinnamon stick, apples and sugar to the pan. Using a wooden spoon, stir the mixture until the sugar has dissolved. When the cider begins to boil (this should take about 15 minutes), stir in the brandy and remove the pan from the heat. Remove and discard the cinnamon stick. Remove and reserve the oranges.

Pour the cider mixture into a warmed punch bowl. Place the oranges on a board and cut them into thin thin slices or wedges, discarding the cloves. Add the orange slices or wedges to the punch and serve.

Punch III

ABOUT 2½ litres (5 pints)

225 ml (8fl oz) brandy
175 ml (6fl oz) orange-flavoured
  liqueur
125 ml (4fl oz) kirsch
1.25 l (2½ pints) Champagne, chilled
900ml (1½ pints) soda water, chilled

Pour the brandy, orange-flavoured liqueur and kirsch into a large punch bowl and stir well with a long-handled spoon.

Pour in the Champagne and soda water. Ladle the punch into individual serving glasses and serve at once.

Lemonade

1¼ litres (2½ pints)

grated rind and juice of 6 lemons
225g (8 oz) sugar
1.1 l (2 pints) boiling water

Place the lemon rind and the sugar in a tall jug. Pour in the boiling water and mix thoroughly with a long-handled spoon until the sugar has dissolved.

Place the jug in the refrigerator or a cool place and chill it for 2 hours, or until it is very cold. Remove the jug from the refrigerator and stir in the lemon juice.

Strain the lemonade through a fine strainer into a serving jug. Serve at once.

Cool, refreshing and with a distinctive fruity flavour, Punch I is guaranteed to make your party swing.

Dinner for 4 around Beef

prosciutto roll in each 'vee-shaped' cut. Serve immediately.

Prosciutto with Melon

Oven Braised Beef with Burgundy
Noodles
French Beans

Tomato Salad

Fruit Fool

A selection of cheeses such as
Brie, Cheddar or Stilton

Wine: a full-bodied Burgundy such as
Chambertin; or a Rhône wine
such as Châteauneuf-du-Pape
or Côtes-du-Rhône

Oven Braised Beef with Burgundy

900g (2 lb) lean stewing beef, cut into cubes
50g (2oz) seasoned flour, made with 50g (2oz) flour, 1 teaspoon salt and 1 teaspoon black pepper
75g (3oz) butter
4 medium-sized onions, thinly sliced
4 carrots, scraped and cut into lengths
300ml (10fl oz) red wine (preferably Burgundy)
½ teaspoon salt
½ teaspoon black pepper
bouquet garni, consisting of 4 parsley sprigs, 1 thyme spray and 1 bay leaf tied together
1 teaspoon grated lemon rind
1 teaspoon dried oregano

Roll the beef cubes in the seasoned flour and set aside.

Preheat the oven to warm 325°F (Gas Mark 3, 170°C).

In a large flameproof casserole, melt 50 grams (2 ounces) of the butter over moderate heat. When the foam subsides, add the beef cubes and fry, stirring and turning occasionally, for 5 to 8 minutes or until they are lightly and evenly browned. With a slotted

Prosciutto with Melon

1 small cantaloup or watermelon, halved and seeded
125g (4oz) prosciutto, thinly sliced and halved, lengthways

With a sharp knife, slice the melon, lengthways, into 4 slices. Cut the flesh from the skin, then return the flesh to the skin to form its original shape. Make 4 'vee' shapes at equal distances along the length of each melon slice.

Cut each prosciutto strip in half and roll up each piece neatly. Place 1

Light and cool to taste, Prosciutto with Melon makes a perfect first course to a sturdy stew.

spoon, transfer the cubes to a plate.

Add the remaining butter to the casserole. When the foam subsides, add the onions and cook, stirring occasionally, for 5 to 7 minutes or until they are soft and translucent but not brown. Add the carrots and cook, stirring occasionally, for 3 minutes or until they are lightly browned. Pour over the wine and add the salt, pepper, bouquet garni, lemon rind and oregano. Stir well to mix. Bring the liquid to the boil.

Return the beef to the casserole and mix well. Cover the casserole and place it in the oven. Braise the beef, stirring occasionally, for 2 to 2½ hours or until the meat is very tender when pierced with the point of a sharp knife.

Remove the casserole from the oven. Remove and discard the bouquet garni. Serve at once.

Noodles

450g (1 lb) egg noodles
1 teaspoon salt
25g (1oz) butter

Half-fill a saucepan with water and bring it to the boil over moderate heat. Add the salt and noodles and cook for 5 to 8 minutes or until the noodles are 'al dente' or just tender.

Drain the noodles, then transfer them to a serving bowl. Stir in the butter and serve at once.

French Beans

(see page 171 for how to cook French beans)

Tomato Salad

450g (1 lb) firm tomatoes, thinly sliced
1 tablespoon finely chopped fresh chives
1 teaspoon chopped fresh basil or ½ teaspoon dried basil
DRESSING
3 tablespoons olive oil
1 tablespoon white wine vinegar
½ teaspoon lemon juice
¼ teaspoon prepared French mustard
½ teaspoon salt
½ teaspoon freshly ground black pepper
½ teaspoon chopped fresh basil or ¼ teaspoon dried basil

Arrange the tomato slices decoratively on a salad plate and sprinkle over the

This hearty Oven Braised Beef with Burgundy almost cooks itself!

chives. Set aside.

In a small bowl, combine all the dressing ingredients, beating with a fork until they are well blended. Dribble over the tomato slices.

Sprinkle over the basil and serve at once.

Fruit Fool

900g (2 lb) fresh fruit, such as strawberries, gooseberries, raspberries, blackcurrants or apricots, washed and hulled if necessary
300ml (10fl oz) double cream, lightly whipped

If necessary, poach the fruit first, then drain it. With a wooden spoon, mash the fruit through a strainer or purée it through a food mill into a large mixing bowl. Allow it to cool.

Lightly fold the whipped cream into the purée. Place the bowl in the refrigerator and chill for at least 2 hours.

Pour the fool into a serving dish and serve cold.

Dinner for 4 around Lamb

Corn on the Cob

Lamb Stew
Saffron Rice
Walnut, Artichoke Heart and Cheese Salad

Fresh Fruit

A selection of cheeses such as
Caerphilly, Sage Derby or cream cheese

Wine: a well-chilled white wine,
such as an Eastern European,
German or Alsatian Riesling;
or an Italian Frascati

Corn on the Cob

4 ears of corn
1 teaspoon sugar

Remove the husks and silk threads from the corn ears.

Half-fill a large saucepan with water. Add the sugar. Place the pan over high heat and bring the water to the boil.

When the water is boiling, place the ears of corn in the pan.

Bring the water back to the boil and boil for 10 to 20 minutes depending on the age of the corn, or until the kernels have turned bright yellow.

Drain the corn and serve with plenty of melted butter.

Lamb Stew

75ml (3fl oz) olive oil
1 large onion, chopped

Exotic Lamb Stew with Saffron Rice.

Fresh-tasting Walnut, Cheese and Arti-choke Heart Salad is an unusual combination of ingredients – and tastes absolutely delicious.

2 garlic cloves, crushed
400g (14oz) canned peeled tomatoes, drained and chopped
1 red pepper, white pith removed, seeded and sliced
1 green pepper, white pith removed, seeded and sliced
½ teaspoon hot chilli powder
1 teaspoon coriander seeds, coarsely crushed
1 teaspoon salt
900g (2 lb) boned leg of lamb, cut into cubes
250ml (8fl oz) white wine
2 tablespoons chopped fresh coriander leaves

In a medium-sized saucepan, heat half the oil over moderate heat. Add the onion and garlic and fry them for 6 to 8 minutes, or until the onion is soft and translucent but not brown. Add the tomatoes, red and green peppers, chilli powder, coriander seeds and salt and stir to mix. Reduce the heat to low, cover the pan and simmer for 15 minutes.

In a large frying-pan, heat the re-maining oil over moderate heat. Add the lamb cubes a few at a time and fry them for 6 to 8 minutes, or until they are browned all over. As the meat browns, remove it from the pan with a slotted spoon and transfer it to the pan with the vegetables. Stir in the wine and fresh coriander leaves. Cook, covered, for 45 minutes.

Remove from the heat and serve.

Saffron Rice

50g (2oz) butter
seeds of 4 whole cardamom pods
4 cloves
3 × 1 inch pieces cinnamon stick
1 medium-sized onion, finely chopped
350g (12oz) long-grain rice, washed, soaked in cold water for 30 minutes and drained
750ml (1¼ pints) chicken stock, boiling
1 teaspoon salt
¾ teaspoon crushed saffron threads, soaked in 2 tablespoons boiling water for 20 minutes

In a medium-sized saucepan, melt the butter over moderate heat. When the foam subsides, add the cardamom seeds, cloves and cinnamon sticks and fry, stirring constantly, for 2 minutes.

Add the onion and fry, stirring occasionally, for 8 to 10 minutes or until it is golden brown. Add the rice, reduce the heat to moderately low and fry gently, stirring constantly, for 5 minutes.

Pour the boiling stock over the rice, add the salt and stir in the saffron mixture.

Cover the pan, reduce the heat to low and cook for 15 to 20 minutes or until the rice is tender and all the liquid has been absorbed.

Remove the pan from the heat. Spoon the rice on to a warmed serving platter and serve immediately.

Walnut, Cheese and Artichoke Heart Salad

275g (10oz) cooked long-grain rice
6 spring onions, trimmed and finely chopped
125ml (4fl oz) olive oil
50ml (2fl oz) wine vinegar
125g (4oz) leaf spinach, washed, shaken dry and chopped
175g (6oz) Gruyère cheese, cubed
125g (4oz) walnuts, roughly chopped
4 large artichoke hearts, cooked and cooled
4 tablespoons mayonnaise
2 tablespoons sour cream
½ teaspoon salt
½ teaspoon white pepper
¾ teaspoon cayenne pepper

Place the rice and spring onions in a large bowl, and pour over the oil and vinegar. Using two large spoons, toss the rice mixture until it is well coated with the dressing. Transfer the mixture to a large serving dish.

In a second mixing bowl, combine the spinach, Gruyère cheese and walnuts. Cut two of the artichoke hearts into small dice and add them to the cheese mixture. In a small jug, combine the mayonnaise, sour cream, salt, pepper and cayenne, beating to blend well. Pour the mixture over the cheese and walnut mixture and toss well to blend.

Spoon the mixture over the rice bed. Cut the remaining artichoke hearts into thick slices and arrange them decoratively around the sides of the serving dish. Chill the dish in the refrigerator for 30 minutes before serving.

Fresh Fruit
(of choice)

Dinner for 4 around Pork

Eggs with Tarragon Mayonnaise

Pork and Apple Casserole
French Beans
Watercress, Fennel and Tomato Salad

Apricot Sorbet

A selection of cheeses such as
Lancashire, Sage Derby or Port Salut

Wine : a lightly chilled rosé such as
Côtes de Provence, or a Hungarian Riesling

Eggs with Tarragon Mayonnaise

300ml (10fl oz) mayonnaise
1 teaspoon chopped fresh tarragon
1 teaspoon chopped fresh chives
1½ tablespoons boiling water
8 lettuce leaves
6 hard-boiled eggs, cut in half lengthways
4 anchovies
1 tablespoon chopped fresh parsley

Blend the mayonnaise, tarragon and chives together. Add the boiling water and stir to mix.

To serve, place the lettuce leaves on 4 serving plates. Place 3 egg halves, cut side down, arranged like a 3 petalled flower, on the lettuce. Coat the eggs with the mayonnaise. Put one curled anchovy in the centre of each egg 'flower'. Sprinkle over the parsley and serve.

Pork and Apple Casserole

25g (1oz) butter, softened
2 medium-sized onions, chopped
½ teaspoon dried sage
½ teaspoon salt
½ teaspoon black pepper
900g (2 lb) lean pork fillets, cubed
2 medium-sized cooking apples, peeled, cored and thinly sliced

3 tablespoons cider
675g (1½ lb) potatoes, peeled
2 tablespoons hot milk
15g (½oz) butter, cut into pieces

Preheat the oven to warm 325°F (Gas Mark 3, 170°C). Grease a large oven-proof casserole with half the butter.

Put the onions, sage, salt and pepper in a mixing bowl and stir to mix.

Place about one third of the pork cubes in the casserole. Cover them with one-half of the onion mixture and then with half of the sliced apples. Continue to fill the casserole with the remaining pork, onions and apples, finishing with pork. Add the cider.

Cover the casserole and cook in the oven for 2 to 2½ hours or until the pork is tender.

About 30 minutes before the pork is cooked, boil the potatoes in lightly salted water in a covered saucepan. When tender, drain thoroughly, return to the saucepan and shake over a low heat to dry them. Press the potatoes through a coarse strainer. Return them to the pan and beat in the milk and the remaining butter until the potato is fluffy.

When the pork is cooked, spread the potato over it and dot over the butter. Return to the oven for a further 15 minutes or until the topping is golden. Serve at once.

French Beans
(see page 171 for how to cook French beans)

Watercress, Fennel and Tomato Salad

1 bunch watercress, washed and shaken dry
½ fennel, trimmed and sliced
½ small cucumber, thinly sliced
4 tomatoes, quartered
6 anchovy fillets, halved
1 spring onion, finely chopped
2 tablespoons chopped pimiento
DRESSING
4 tablespoons olive oil
2 tablespoons wine vinegar
½ teaspoon mustard
½ teaspoon salt
½ teaspoon black pepper

In a large, deep serving plate, combine all the salad ingredients.

Pour the dressing ingredients into a small bowl and beat well to blend. Pour the dressing over the mixture and gently toss until the ingredients are coated.

Apricot Sorbet

450g (1 lb) canned apricot halves, drained and juice reserved
50g (2oz) castor sugar
2 tablespoons fresh orange juice
2 tablespoons fresh lemon juice
2 egg whites, stiffly beaten
2 drops vanilla essence

Set the thermostat of the refrigerator to its coldest setting.

Put half the apricots in a blender and purée them at high speed. Pour the purée into a large jug and repeat the process with the remaining apricots. Measure the purée and mix in enough of the reserved can juice to make 425 millilitres (16 fluid ounces).

Transfer the purée to a medium-sized mixing bowl and stir in the sugar, orange juice and lemon juice. Using a wire whisk or rotary beater, whisk the egg whites into the mixture until it is smooth. Stir in the vanilla essence. Pour the mixture into a freezer tray and place the tray in the frozen food storage compartment of the refrigerator. Leave to freeze for 30 minutes or until the mixture has begun to set around the edges.

Remove the tray from the refrigerator and scrape the apricot mixture into a medium-sized mixing bowl. Using a wire whisk or rotary beater, beat the mixture until it is smooth. Return the mixture to the freezer tray and the tray to the storage compartment. Freeze for a further 4 hours or until the sorbet is firm to the touch.

Meanwhile, chill 4 individual serving glasses in the refrigerator for 30 minutes before you serve the sorbet.

Remove the glasses from the refrigerator and the freezer tray from the frozen food storage compartment. Using a tablespoon which has been dipped in hot water, spoon the sorbet into the chilled glasses. Serve immediately.

Colourful Apricot Sorbet makes an elegant end to a rich meal, and can be made well ahead of time.

Dinner for 4 around Chicken

Asparagus Quiche

Chicken Salad with Sour Cream Dressing
Wheat and Tomato Salad

Coffee Cream

A selection of cheeses such as
cream cheese, Wensleydale or Stilton

Wine : a well-chilled Alsatian Traminer ;
or a Rhine wine such as Liebfraumilch

Asparagus Quiche

1 × 23cm (9in) flan case made with
   shortcrust pastry
FILLING
175g (6oz) lean cooked ham, chopped
125ml (4fl oz) single cream
75ml (3fl oz) milk
3 eggs
25g (1oz) Cheddar cheese, finely
   grated
$\frac{1}{4}$ teaspoon salt
$\frac{1}{2}$ teaspoon white pepper
12 asparagus tips, cooked and
   drained

Preheat the oven to fairly hot 400°F
(Gas Mark 6, 200°C). Place the flan
case on a baking sheet.

Cover the bottom of the flan case
with the chopped ham and set aside.

In a medium-sized mixing bowl,
combine the cream, milk, eggs, grated
cheese, salt and pepper and beat well.

Pour the mixture over the ham. Arrange the asparagus tips around the
edge of the filling.

Place the baking sheet in the oven.

Bake the quiche for 35 to 40
minutes or until the filling is firm.

Cool the quiche before serving.

Chicken Salad with Sour Cream Dressing

1 × 2kg (4$\frac{1}{4}$ lb) cold cooked chicken,
   shredded
6 hard-boiled eggs
2 green peppers, white pith removed,
   seeded and shredded
4 tablespoons stuffed olives, sliced
450g (1 lb) grapes, peeled and seeded
125g (4oz) blanched almonds
$\frac{1}{2}$ teaspoon black pepper
FRENCH DRESSING
3 tablespoons white wine vinegar
2 teaspoons prepared mustard
$\frac{1}{2}$ teaspoon salt
6 tablespoons olive oil
SOUR CREAM DRESSING
6 tablespoons white wine vinegar
300ml (10fl oz) sour cream
2 teaspoons sugar
$\frac{1}{2}$ teaspoon salt
$\frac{1}{2}$ teaspoon white pepper

Place the shredded chicken in a salad
bowl. Separate the yolks from the
whites of the hard-boiled eggs. Finely
chop the whites and add to the
chicken. Keep the yolks aside. Add the
peppers, olives, grapes and almonds.

Prepare the French dressing. In a
small mixing bowl, combine all the

*A perfect summer buffet centrepiece –
Chicken Salad with Sour Cream Dressing.*

ingredients. Pour over the ingredients in the bowl.

Press the egg yolks through a fine strainer or push them through a garlic press over the chicken mixture. Toss the salad to mix the ingredients well. Sprinkle the black pepper over the top. Cover the salad bowl and keep it in the refrigerator until you are ready to serve it.

Lastly prepare the sour cream dressing. In a small mixing bowl, slowly beat the vinegar into the sour cream. Add the sugar, salt and pepper and mix well. Taste the dressing and add more salt, sugar or vinegar, if necessary. Pour the dressing into a sauceboat or small bowl.

Wheat and Tomato Salad

225g (8oz) cracked wheat, soaked in
    cold water for 20 minutes and
    drained
4 tablespoons chopped fresh parsley
2 tablespoons chopped fresh mint
1 onion, finely chopped
3 spring onions, finely chopped
450g (1 lb) tomatoes, coarsely
    chopped
1 teaspoon salt
2 teaspoons black pepper
50ml (2fl oz) lemon juice

75ml (3fl oz) olive oil
10 lettuce leaves, washed and
    shaken dry
4 tomatoes, quartered

In a mixing bowl, mix together the wheat, 3 tablespoons of the parsley, the mint, onion, spring onions and chopped tomatoes until they are combined.

In a small mixing bowl, combine the salt, pepper, lemon juice and oil, beating well with a fork. Pour the dressing over the salad and toss well.

Line a salad bowl with the lettuce leaves and arrange the salad in the middle. Garnish with the tomato quarters and remaining parsley before serving.

Coffee Cream

1 teaspoon vegetable oil
5 egg yolks
3 tablespoons sugar
600ml (1 pint) hot strong black coffee
15g ($\frac{1}{2}$oz) gelatine dissolved in
    3 tablespoons hot water
150ml (5fl oz) double cream, whipped
    until thick

Using a pastry brush, grease the inside of a 1-litre (2-pint) mould with

Melt-in-the-mouth Coffee Cream is the dessert which ends this superb dinner.

the oil. Place the mould upside down on kitchen paper towels to drain off any excess.

In a heatproof mixing bowl, beat together the egg yolks and sugar using a wire whisk or rotary beater. Beating constantly, gradually pour the coffee in a thin stream on to the egg mixture.

Place the bowl over a saucepan one third full of hot water set over low heat. Stirring constantly with a wooden spoon, cook the custard for 5 minutes, or until it is thick enough to coat the back of the spoon. Remove the bowl from the heat.

Stir the dissolved gelatine into the custard.

Strain the coffee mixture into a medium-sized mixing bowl. Place the bowl over ice in another bowl. Stir until the mixture thickens.

Fold the cream into the custard, then spoon the mixture into the mould.

Cover the mould and place it in the refrigerator to chill for 6 hours or until the cream is firm and set.

To serve, quickly dip the bottom of the mould into hot water. Run a knife around the edge of the cream and turn it out on to a chilled serving dish.

Dinner for 6 around Beef

Prawn or Shrimp Cocktail

Beef Pot Roast
Boiled Potatoes with Parsley
Carrots with Onions

Lettuce Salad with French Dressing

Lemon Pudding

A selection of cheeses such as
Brie or Camembert,
St. Paulin or Dolcelatte

Wine: a claret such as St. Emilion;
or a light Burgundy such as Fleurie

Prawn or Shrimp Cocktail

6 large lettuce leaves, washed,
  shaken dry and very finely
  shredded
175ml (6fl oz) mayonnaise
6 tablespoons double cream
3 teaspoons Worcestershire sauce
3 teaspoons lemon juice
3 teaspoons tomato ketchup
$\frac{1}{4}$ teaspoon cayenne pepper
$\frac{1}{2}$ teaspoon salt
$\frac{1}{2}$ teaspoon black pepper
450g (1 lb) prawns or shrimps,
  shelled
1 teaspoon paprika
6 thin cucumber slices
$\frac{1}{2}$ lemon, sliced

Stand 6 individual serving glasses on 6 small plates. Divide the shredded lettuce equally among the glasses and set aside.

In a medium-sized mixing bowl, combine the mayonnaise, cream, Worcestershire sauce, lemon juice, tomato ketchup, cayenne, salt and pepper, beating with a wooden spoon until the mixture is smooth and evenly coloured. Stir in the prawns or shrimps.

Spoon the mixture equally over the lettuce in the glasses and sprinkle over the paprika.

Garnish with the cucumber and lemon slices and serve immediately.

Beef Pot Roast

1 × 2kg (4$\frac{1}{4}$ lb) top rump of beef
1 teaspoon salt
$\frac{1}{2}$ teaspoon black pepper
50ml (2fl oz) vegetable oil
2 large onions, thinly sliced
2 large carrots, scraped and thinly
  sliced
350ml (12fl oz) red wine
175ml (6fl oz) wine vinegar
50g (2oz) sugar
  bouquet garni, consisting of 4

parsley sprigs, 1 thyme spray and
  1 bay leaf tied together
½ teaspoon finely grated lemon rind
175g (6oz) stoned prunes, chopped
1 tablespoon butter blended with
  1 tablespoon flour
12 canned prunes, drained

Rub the meat all over with the salt and
pepper and set aside.

In a large, flameproof casserole,
heat the vegetable oil over moderate
heat. When the oil is hot, add the
beef to the casserole and, turning
frequently, cook for 10 to 12 minutes
or until it is evenly browned on all
sides. Place the onions and carrots
around the meat and cook, stirring
occasionally, for 5 to 7 minutes or
until the onions are soft and translucent but not brown.

Pour in the wine, vinegar and sugar
and bring the liquid to the boil. Add
the bouquet garni and lemon rind.
Cover the casserole, reduce the heat
to low and cook for 2 hours. Add the
chopped prunes to the casserole and
cook for a further 40 minutes to
1¼ hours or until the meat is very
tender when pierced with the point of
a sharp knife.

Preheat the oven to cool 300°F
(Gas Mark 2, 150°C).

Remove the casserole from the heat.
Using two large forks, remove the
meat from the casserole and transfer
it to a warmed, ovenproof plate.
Cover with aluminium foil and put in
the oven to keep hot.

With a metal spoon, skim off any
fat from the liquid in the casserole.
Pour the liquid through a fine strainer
held over a medium-sized saucepan,
pressing down on the vegetables and
prunes to extract all of their liquid.
Discard the contents of the strainer.

Place the pan over moderately high
heat and boil the liquid for 10 to 15
minutes or until it has reduced by
about one-third. Reduce the heat to
low and stir in the butter mixture, a
little at a time, until the sauce is
thick and smooth. Remove the pan
from the heat and keep warm.

Remove the meat from the oven and
remove and discard the foil. Place
the meat on a carving board. Carve it
into thick slices and transfer the
slices to a warmed serving dish.

Pour over the sauce and garnish
with the whole prunes. Serve at once.

*A warming Beef Pot Roast, followed by
the cooling, slightly tangy flavour of
Lemon Pudding, provides a perfect complement of taste and texture to this meal.*

Boiled Potatoes with Parsley
(see page 172 for how to boil potatoes)

Carrots with Onions

450g (1 lb) carrots, scraped and
  thinly sliced
450g (1 lb) small white onions, peeled
  and left whole
1 bay leaf
2 thyme sprays
600ml (1 pint) chicken stock
25g (1oz) butter
½ teaspoon salt
¼ teaspoon freshly ground black
  pepper
2 tablespoons finely chopped fresh
  parsley

In a medium-sized saucepan, cook the
carrots and onions with the bay leaf
and thyme in the chicken stock over
moderate heat for 15 minutes, or until
they are tender. Remove and discard
the bay leaf and thyme sprays. Drain
the vegetables in a colander and
discard the cooking liquid.

Return the carrots and onions to
the saucepan. Add the butter, salt and
pepper. Place the pan over low heat
and toss the vegetables in the butter
until they are well coated. Carefully
turn the vegetables into a warmed

serving dish.

Sprinkle with the chopped parsley
and serve immediately.

Lettuce Salad
with French Dressing

(to make the dressing, in a small bowl,
beat 4 tablespoons olive oil, 2 tablespoons wine vinegar, ¼ teaspoon dry
mustard, salt and pepper to taste).

Lemon Pudding

1 package lemon-flavoured jelly
300ml (10fl oz) boiling water
400g (14oz) canned condensed milk
1 teaspoon finely grated lemon rind
2 lemons, thinly sliced

Place the jelly in a large serving
bowl and pour over the boiling water.
Using a wooden spoon, stir briskly
until the jelly has dissolved. Stir in
the condensed milk and lemon rind
and, using a wire whisk or rotary
beater, beat until the mixture becomes
light and frothy.

Place the bowl in the refrigerator
and chill for 3 to 5 hours or until the
pudding sets. Remove from the refrigerator and garnish with the lemon.

Dinner for 6 around Lamb

50g (2oz) stuffed olives, thinly sliced

In a large saucepan, bring the water to the boil over high heat. When the water is boiling, add ½ teaspoon salt, the celery, parsley and peppercorns. Reduce the heat to moderate and simmer for 10 minutes. Add the chicken livers, cover the pan and cook for 10 minutes.

Drain the livers through a strainer and mince them in a food mill or, a few at a time, in an electric blender. Add the remaining salt, Tabasco sauce, butter, nutmeg, mustard, cloves, onion, garlic and brandy or sherry. Blend the ingredients thoroughly together.

Put the pâté into a medium-sized terrine or dish, smooth the top and decorate with the olives. Place in the refrigerator to chill for at least 6 hours before serving.

Chicken Liver Pâté

Leg of Lamb with Rosemary and Garlic
Roast Potatoes
Petits Pois, French-Style

Ratafia Trifle

A selection of cheeses such as
Stilton, Cheshire or marc de raisin

Wine : a claret such as St. Julien ;
or Californian or Australian
Cabernet Sauvignon

Chicken Liver Pâté

1.2 l (2 pints) water
2 teaspoons salt
1 celery stalk, trimmed and halved
3 parsley sprigs
8 peppercorns
450g (1 lb) chicken livers

½ teaspoon Tabasco sauce
225g (8oz) butter
¼ teaspoon grated nutmeg
2 teaspoons dry mustard
¼ teaspoon ground cloves
1 medium-sized onion, finely minced
1 garlic clove, finely minced
2 tablespoons brandy or dry sherry

Leg of Lamb with Rosemary and Garlic

1 × 2kg (4¼ lb) leg of lamb
6 garlic cloves
6 small rosemary sprigs
1 teaspoon salt

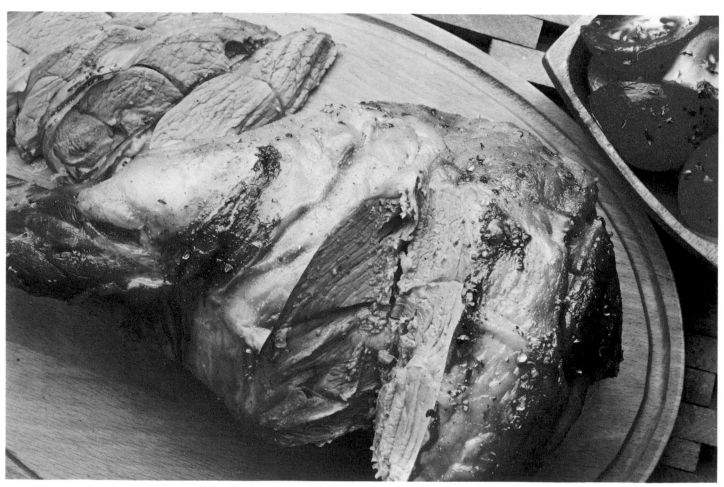

½ teaspoon freshly ground black
    pepper
50g (2oz) butter

Preheat the oven to fairly hot 375°F
(Gas Mark 5, 190°C).

With the tip of a sharp knife, make
six incisions in the leg of lamb, near
the bone. Press the garlic cloves and
the rosemary into the incisions. Rub
the lamb with the salt and pepper.
Place the meat in a medium-sized
roasting tin. Cut the butter into small
pieces and carefully dot it all over the
meat.

Place the tin in the oven and roast
the meat for 2 to 2½ hours, or until the
juices run out faintly rosy when the
meat is pierced with the point of a
sharp knife.

Remove the tin from the oven and
transfer the meat to a carving board.
Serve hot, carved into thick slices. Or
leave the meat to cool thoroughly
before carving and serve cold.

Roast Potatoes
(see page 173 for how to roast potatoes)

Petits Pois, French-Style

675g (1½ lb) small fresh garden peas,
    weighed after shelling or 675g
    (1½ lb) frozen petits pois,
    thawed
1 teaspoon salt
½ teaspoon freshly ground black
    pepper
1 teaspoon sugar
1 medium-sized onion, thinly
    sliced
4 lettuce leaves, washed, shaken dry
    and shredded
1 tablespoon butter blended with
    1 tablespoon flour

Place the peas, salt, pepper, sugar,
onion and lettuce in a large saucepan.
Pour over enough hot water to cover
the peas and set the pan over moderately high heat. Bring the water to the
boil.

Reduce the heat to very low, cover
the pan and simmer the pea mixture
for 20 to 30 minutes or until the onion
is soft and translucent and the peas
are very tender. Stir in the butter
mixture, a little at a time, stirring

A classic French recipe for Petits Pois
French Style is teamed in this menu with
simple, traditional goodness of roasted
Leg of Lamb with Rosemary and Garlic.
The overall effect will be fairly light,
hence the inclusion of a fairly sustaining
first course (Chicken Liver Pâté) and of a
gorgeously rich and filling dessert (Ratafia
Trifle). The end result – a superbly
satisfying meal.

constantly. Simmer the mixture for a
further 2 minutes or until it has
thickened.

Remove the pan from the heat.
Spoon the mixture into a warmed
large serving dish and serve immediately.

Ratafia Trifle

3 tablespoons apricot jam,
    warmed
1 bought sponge flan case
56 ratafia biscuits
225ml (8fl oz) sweet sherry
1 tablespoon apricot brandy
450g (1 lb) canned apricot halves,
    drained
750ml (1¼ pints) thick custard
400ml (15fl oz) double cream
50g (2oz) castor sugar
1 egg white, stiffly beaten
50g (2oz) slivered almonds
1 × 2-inch piece candied angelica,
    chopped

Using a flat-bladed knife, spread the
jam evenly over the base of the sponge
case. Press the sponge into the bottom
of a large serving bowl, being careful
not to break the sponge. Arrange the
ratafia biscuits over the jam, completely covering the surface. Pour over
the sherry and apricot brandy, and set
aside to soak for 1 hour.

Arrange the apricot halves over the
ratafias, to completely cover them.
Using a flat-bladed knife, spread the
thick custard over the top, smoothing
it over with the knife.

Place the cream and sugar in a
medium-sized mixing bowl. Using a
wire whisk or rotary beater, beat the
mixture until it forms stiff peaks.
With a metal spoon, fold in the egg
white. Spread the cream mixture over
the thick custard. Sprinkle over the
slivered almonds and chopped candied
angelica.

Cover the bowl with aluminium foil
and place it in the refrigerator to chill
for 30 minutes. Remove the bowl
from the refrigerator, remove and discard the foil and serve.

Dinner for 6 around Pork

Egg Tartlets

Fruit and Pork Casserole
Mashed Potatoes
Grilled Courgettes

Rum Chocolate Mousse

A selection of cheeses such as
Cheddar, Edam or Camembert

Wine : a lightly chilled rosé
such as Tavel or Rosé d'Anjou ;
or a heavier white such as a
white Burgundy

Egg Tartlets

PASTRY
175g (6oz) flour
⅛ teaspoon salt
40g (1½oz) plus 2 teaspoons butter
40g (1½oz) vegetable fat
1 to 2 tablespoons iced water
FILLING
300ml (10fl oz) mayonnaise
1 large garlic clove, crushed
4 tablespoons chopped fresh basil
4 hard-boiled eggs, finely chopped
GARNISH
6 slices hard-boiled egg
6 small basil sprigs

Preheat the oven to fairly hot 400°F
(Gas Mark 6, 200°C).

First make the pastry. Sift the flour
and salt into a medium-sized mixing
bowl. Add 40 grams (1½ ounces) of
the butter and the vegetable fat and
cut them into small pieces with a table
knife. With your fingertips, rub the
fat into the flour until the mixture
resembles fine breadcrumbs.

Add 1 tablespoon of iced water and,
using the knife, mix it into the flour
mixture. With your hands, mix and
knead the dough until it is smooth.
Add more water if the dough is too
dry. Chill the dough in the refrigerator
for 30 minutes.

Using the remaining butter, grease
six 7.5cm (3in) fluted tartlet tins.

To make the filling, combine the
mayonnaise, garlic and chopped basil.

On a lightly floured surface, roll
out the dough to 0.6cm (¼in) thick.

*Creamy Egg Tartlets are a light but filling
first course.*

Using a 10cm (4in) round pastry
cutter, cut the dough into 6 circles.
Line the tartlet tins with the dough
circles, easing the dough in carefully.
With a knife, trim off the excess
dough. Fill the pastry cases with
crumpled greaseproof or waxed paper
and place them in the oven. Bake blind
for 15 minutes, removing the paper 5
minutes before baking is completed to
allow the pastry to brown.

Remove the tins from the oven and
leave to cool for 30 minutes. Turn the
pastry cases out of the tins.

Half-fill the pastry cases with
chopped hard-boiled eggs. Pour enough
of the mayonnaise mixture over the
eggs just to fill the pastry cases.

Decorate with hard-boiled egg and

Fruit and Pork Casserole

16 dried stoned prunes
16 dried apricot halves
½ teaspoon mixed spice
    juice and grated rind of ½ orange
    juice and grated rind of ½ lemon
600ml (1 pint) dry white wine
1 × 2½kg (5 lb) loin of pork, boned
    and rolled
1 teaspoon salt
½ teaspoon black pepper
1 teaspoon dried sage
25g (1oz) butter
1 tablespoon soft brown sugar
1 garlic clove, crushed
2 large cooking apples, peeled,
    cored and roughly sliced
3 teaspoons cornflour dissolved in
    1 tablespoon wine

Place the dried prunes and apricots in
a medium-sized mixing bowl. Sprinkle
the mixed spice, the orange and lemon
rinds and juices on top and pour over
300 millilitres (10 fluid ounces) of the
wine. Cover and soak overnight.

Rub the pork all over with the salt,
pepper and sage and set aside.

In a large, heavy, flameproof casserole, melt the butter over moderate
heat. When the foam subsides, add the
pork. Cook it, turning frequently,
until it is lightly browned all over.

Pour the soaked fruit and wine over
the pork. Sprinkle on the sugar and
garlic. Pour over the remaining wine.

Reduce the heat to very low, cover
the casserole and cook for 2½ hours.

After two hours, skim off and discard any fat on the surface with a spoon. Add the apples, and cook, uncovered, for a further 30 minutes.

Using two large forks, lift the meat out of the casserole and place it on a carving board. Carve the meat into thick slices and place the slices on a warmed serving dish. Keep hot.

Stir the cornflour into the juices in the casserole. Cook the sauce for 5 minutes, stirring occasionally, or until it thickens. Pour the sauce over the meat and serve.

Mashed Potatoes
(see page 172 for how to cook and mash potatoes)

Grilled Courgettes

1 tablespoon butter
10 courgettes, trimmed and blanched
2 garlic cloves, crushed
2 teaspoons sugar

1 teaspoon salt
1½ teaspoons dried dill
1 large onion, sliced into rings
75g (3oz) Parmesan cheese, grated

Preheat the oven to moderate 350°F (Gas Mark 4, 180°C). Grease a flameproof dish with the butter.

With a sharp knife, slice the courgettes in half lengthways, and arrange them in the bottom of the baking dish, skin side down. Sprinkle them with the garlic, sugar, salt and dill and arrange the onion rings over the top. Spread the cheese on top of the mixture and bake in the upper part of the oven for 15 minutes.

Preheat the grill to moderate.

Remove the courgettes from the oven and place them under the grill for 4 minutes, or until the cheese is bubbly and brown. Serve immediately.

Rum Chocolate Mousse

350g (12oz) dark cooking chocolate

Colourful Fruit and Pork Casserole.

6 tablespoons rum
400ml (15fl oz) double cream
4 egg whites
3 tablespoons chocolate vermicelli

In a small saucepan, melt the chocolate with the rum over low heat, stirring constantly. Remove the pan from the heat and stir in 2 tablespoons of the cream. Set aside to cool.

In a large mixing bowl, whisk the egg whites with a wire whisk or rotary beater until they form stiff peaks.

In a medium-sized bowl, beat the remaining cream until it is thick.

Pour the chocolate mixture into the large mixing bowl and, using a metal spoon, fold it into the egg whites. Fold the cream into the chocolate and egg white mixture. Spoon the chocolate mixture into a medium-sized soufflé or glass dish. Cover the dish and chill it in the refrigerator for at least 3 hours. Sprinkle over the chocolate vermicelli before serving.

Dinner for 6 around Chicken

Mushroom Soup

Roast Chicken with Chicken Liver Stuffing
Boiled Potatoes with Parsley
Tomato and French Bean Salad

Pavlova

A selection of cheeses such as Sage Derby,
Caerphilly or garlic-flavoured cream cheese

**Wine : a well-chilled Rhine wine such as Liebfraumilch ;
or a white Loire wine such as Pouilly Fumé**

Mushroom Soup

25g (1oz) butter
1 small onion, finely chopped
3 tablespoons flour
1 teaspoon salt
$\frac{1}{2}$ teaspoon black pepper
$\frac{1}{4}$ teaspoon dried oregano
$\frac{1}{8}$ teaspoon cayenne pepper
900ml (1$\frac{1}{2}$ pints) chicken stock
450g (1 lb) mushrooms, stalks
  removed, wiped clean and sliced
1 bay leaf
150ml (5fl oz) double cream

In a large saucepan, melt the butter over moderate heat. When the foam

Roast Chicken with Chicken Liver Stuffing and Boiled Potatoes.

subsides, add the onion and fry, stirring occasionally, for 5 to 7 minutes, or until the onion is soft and translucent but not brown.

Remove the pan from the heat. With a wooden spoon, stir in the flour, salt, pepper, oregano and cayenne to make a smooth paste. Gradually stir in the chicken stock, being careful to avoid lumps. Stir in the mushrooms and bay leaf.

Return the pan to the heat and bring the soup to the boil, stirring constantly. Reduce the heat to low, cover the pan and simmer for 30 minutes.

Uncover the pan and stir in the cream. Cook the soup, stirring constantly, for 2 to 3 minutes or until it is hot.

Remove the pan from the heat. Remove and discard the bay leaf. Pour the soup into a warmed soup tureen or individual soup bowls and serve immediately.

Roast Chicken with Chicken Liver Stuffing

75g (3oz) butter, softened
1 large onion, finely chopped
1 × 2½kg (5 lb) chicken, giblets reserved and finely chopped
4 chicken livers, finely chopped
½ teaspoon dried mixed herbs
1 tablespoon finely chopped fresh basil
1 tablespoon finely chopped fresh parsley
125g (4oz) cream cheese
50g (2oz) fine dry breadcrumbs
1 teaspoon salt
1 teaspoon black pepper
SAUCE
150ml (5fl oz) white wine
150ml (5fl oz) chicken stock
150ml (5fl oz) single cream
½ teaspoon salt
½ teaspoon black pepper

Preheat the oven to hot 425°F (Gas Mark 7, 220°C).

In a small frying-pan, melt 25 grams (1 ounce) of the butter over moderate heat. When the foam subsides, add the onion, chicken giblets, livers, mixed herbs, basil and parsley and fry, stirring occasionally, for 5 to 7 minutes or until the onion is soft and translucent but not brown.

Remove the pan from the heat. Place the onion mixture in a medium-sized mixing bowl and leave to cool for 10 minutes. Add the cheese, breadcrumbs and half the salt and pepper.

Stir the ingredients with a fork until they are thoroughly combined.

Place the chicken in a large roasting tin. Spoon the stuffing into the cavity and secure with a trussing needle and string or thread. Rub the chicken all over with the remaining salt and pepper. Using a palette knife, spread the remaining butter all over the chicken.

Place the roasting tin in the oven and roast the chicken for 20 minutes. Reduce the temperature to moderate 350°F (Gas Mark 4, 180°C) and continue roasting the bird for a further 1 hour.

Meanwhile, prepare the sauce. In a large mixing bowl, combine the wine, stock, cream, salt and pepper and stir well. Remove the roasting tin from the oven and pour the mixture into the tin. Return the tin to the oven and cook for a further 30 minutes or until the chicken is cooked and tender and the juices run clear when the thigh is pierced with the point of a sharp knife.

Remove the roasting tin from the oven. Transfer the chicken to a warmed serving dish. Remove the string or thread.

With a metal spoon, skim off any fat from the surface of the juices. Pour the sauce into a warmed sauceboat and serve at once, with the chicken.

Boiled Potatoes with Parsley

(see page 172 for how to cook potatoes)

Tomato and French Bean Salad

450g (1 lb) tomatoes, very thinly sliced and seeded
450g (1 lb) French beans, trimmed, cooked and drained
DRESSING
3 tablespoons wine vinegar
6 tablespoons olive oil
¼ teaspoon salt
¼ teaspoon black pepper
½ teaspoon prepared mustard
½ teaspoon sugar
1 garlic clove, crushed

Place all the dressing ingredients in a screw-top jar and shake vigorously until they are well mixed. Set the dressing aside.

Place the tomatoes and beans in a large serving dish and pour over the dressing. Using two large spoons, toss the salad until the vegetables are thoroughly coated with the dressing.

Chill the salad in the refrigerator before serving.

Pavlova
FRUIT-FILLED MERINGUE CASE

5 egg whites
275g (10oz) plus 1 tablespoon castor sugar
2 teaspoons cornflour, sifted
½ teaspoon vanilla essence
1 teaspoon malt vinegar
1 teaspoon orange-flavoured liqueur (optional)
300ml (10fl oz) double cream, stiffly whipped
450g (1 lb) fresh or canned and drained fruit

Preheat the oven to cool 300°F (Gas Mark 2, 150°C). With a pencil draw a 23cm (9in) circle (use a plate as a guide) on a piece of non-stick silicone paper and place this on a baking sheet. Set aside.

In a large mixing bowl, beat the egg whites with a wire whisk or rotary beater until they form stiff peaks. Beat in 125 grams (4 ounces) of the sugar and continue beating for 1 minute or until the mixture is very stiff and glossy. Using a metal spoon, fold in all but 1 tablespoon of the remaining sugar, the cornflour, vanilla essence and vinegar.

Spoon one-third of the mixture on to the circle of paper to make a base about 0.6cm (¼in) thick. Fill a forcing bag, fitted with a 2.5cm (1in) nozzle, with the remaining mixture and pipe it round the edge of the circle in decorative swirls, to form a case to hold the filling.

Carefully transfer the baking sheet to the centre part of the oven and bake the meringue case for 1 hour. Then turn off the oven heat and leave the meringue case in the oven, with the doors closed, for a further 30 to 35 minutes, or until it is slightly crisp on the outside but still soft in the centre.

Remove the baking sheet from the oven. Leave the meringue to cool completely. When it is cold, lift it off the baking sheet and carefully remove and discard the silicone paper from the bottom.

Place the meringue case on a large, decorative serving plate. With a metal spoon, quickly fold the orange-flavoured liqueur (if you are using it) and the remaining sugar into the whipped cream. Then spoon the cream mixture into the centre of the meringue case and arrange the fruit on top of the cream.

Serve at once.

239

Practical
hints on
practical
matters

Entering marriage

Imagine a Victorian wedding: garden party, splendid banquet, masses of gifts—the lot. In fact, that day meant for the bride a great deal more than gaining a husband, a home and lots of lovely presents. It also meant that all she owned before her marriage and all that she would own after suddenly became the property of her husband. She lost the right to sell, leave or give away any of her money or possessions. She herself became, in fact, part of her new husband's total 'property'. Times have changed since then, of course, and so has the law, but it is perhaps fitting to remember that it was not until just before the Second World War that married women were finally given the legal right to handle their own affairs.

Although it is now recognized that a husband and wife are two distinct individuals, the law still imposes many restrictions on a couple who marry. Luckily, though, these restrictions now apply equally to both partners: marriage these days is regarded as an agreement or contract through which the husband and wife create a legal, as well as emotional, relationship. This legal relationship means that each one has rights and duties towards the other and the marriage which are regulated by law.

Even before entering into the 'contract', the law says that certain conditions must be fulfilled. Not everyone can marry anybody at any time or place they choose, for instance. The conditions you have to meet in order to be legally wed in Great Britain are as follows:

That both participants intend the marriage to last for life: Of course marriage can be dissolved by divorce, but the courts do make it difficult to do this, especially during the first three years of marriage. Basically, it's a sincerity of intention that's required.

That the marriage be monogamous: Once married, you can't go through a marriage ceremony with someone other than your husband unless your first marriage has been dissolved or annulled, or your husband has died. This may seem a bit obvious, and most people born and brought up in Britain are well aware where bigamy can get them, but there are cases of bigamy or even polygamy in England, particularly where one or more of the partners was born in another country where multiple marriages are, in fact, perfectly acceptable.

That the marriage is voluntary: This also probably appears to state the very obvious since most marriages today are happily entered into with love and by the independent choice of both partners. There is the occasional case, though, where it is later proved that a marriage was entered into upon threat of blackmail—and in such a case the courts would declare the marriage invalid and therefore annulled.

That both partners are over 16 years of age: This particular minimum is a recent innovation—until the twentieth century marriage was permitted at the legal age of puberty which was 14 for a boy and 12 for a girl. Today, if you tried—and succeeded—in going through a marriage ceremony at these ages it would be considered illegal and would be annulled. If you marry between the ages of 16 and 18, the consent of your parent or guardian is compulsory. (This is not the case in Scotland, although you have to live there for at least 24 days before the ceremony takes place.)

That the marriage will not occur with a prohibited member of the family: In other words, who can you absolutely NOT marry? If you are a woman, included in the forbidden list is—not surprisingly—your father, son, grandfather, grandson, brother, father-in-law, stepson, stepfather, son-in-law, step-grandfather, mother-in-law's father, father-in-law's father, step-daughter's son, stepson's son, granddaughter's husband, uncle or nephew. The same is true for a man with the sexes reversed.

That the marriage is permitted according to the law of your domicil: Domicil is different from nationality and basically means the country with which you have the greatest connection. (This is very important when we come to consider making wills.) For example, you may have a British passport or British nationality but have lived most of your life and wish to remain in, say, France. Then you'd be domiciled in France, which means that French law would govern your marriage.

That the marriage occurs in the place of residence: This is not so complicated as domicil and simply means that both of you must be resident in the place where you intend to marry for at least 15 days before the ceremony takes place.

Formalities of marriage

Before Elizabethan times, a marriage was valid by simple declaration: that is, each party declared to the other that they consented to be married immediately. Nothing else was necessary. (The Scots obviously approved of this —such ceremonies were considered perfectly legal there until 1940!)

Then the law was changed and it all became a bit more complicated: you had to be married before a priest, minister or rabbi. That gave rise to the Romeo and Juliet situation where many young people were married clandestinely to avoid parental disapproval. The law was therefore further amended to include the publication of Banns in order to stop these secret marriages.

Church of England Marriages: English law distinguishes between marriages according to its 'official' church, the Church of England, and other marriages. There are four main ways to go about getting married according to the rites of the Church of England:

Marriage by Banns is the most common. The Banns are published in the parish church of the parish in which one or both of you reside (if you live in different parishes, they are published in both); marriage by Common Licence is the main alternative to Banns and involves obtaining a licence to marry which is granted by the office of the Registrar for the Bishop of your Diocese; a Superintendent Registrar's Certificate can be obtained from your local Registry Office and enables your clergyman to perform the marriage ceremony in church without Banns or a licence; the fourth, the Special Licence, can only be granted by the Archbishop of Canterbury and is very rare; you do, however, need one if you wish to marry according to rites of the Church of England in a private chapel or house.

Non-Church of England Marriages: If you do not wish to participate in a religious ceremony when you marry or if you wish to be married in a non-Christian church or a church of a different denomination, then the procedure is slightly different, and is carried out in one of two ways:

By Superintendent Registrar's Certificate without Licence (similar to publishing Banns)—the notice of intention to marry is open to public inspection for 21 days, after which a certificate is issued and the marriage can take place; and by Superintendent Registrar's Certificate with Licence—this is much quicker since there is no

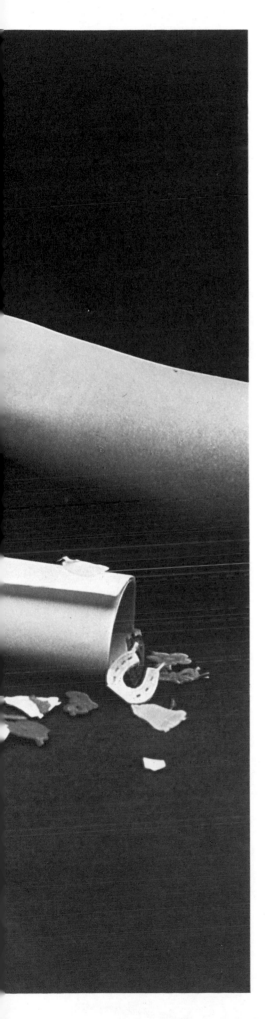

21-day public inspection. The only requirement is that one of you must have lived in the district before giving notice of intent to marry.

Other Requirements: In addition to the above specific requirements, there are a few general, legal requirements, too: the marriage must take place within three months of the licence to marry being granted; a priest, minister or rabbi or some other such person able to perform marriages, and at least two witnesses must be present; and the ceremony must take place between the hours of 8am and 6pm.

Duties of Marriage

Until recently, the consequence of marriage was to fuse the wife into the legal existence of her husband. All the wife's property belonged to her husband and he was responsible for her behaviour, be it merely indiscreet or downright criminal. Blackstone, the first professor of law at Oxford, said in the eighteenth century: 'The husband and wife are one person in law . . . the very being or legal existence of the woman is suspended during marriage or incorporated or consolidated into that of the husband.' Today, thankfully, things are a bit different. A married woman is considered to be a separate individual in law, and is no longer seen merely as a 'chattel' under the protection of her husband.

The effect of this modern role is that neither partner is legally responsible (or liable) for the other's civil or criminal wrongdoings. If you commit a criminal offence your husband is not liable for the consequences unless the offence was committed through his 'force'. Neither of you can be ordered to give evidence for the prosecution in a criminal trial against the other although, if requested, you may give evidence for the defence. (This privilege doesn't extend to civil cases, however.) On the other hand, if one of you takes away the other's property, this will not amount to theft in criminal law so long as you are not legally separated or divorced.

In the same way, if you are involved in a car accident which is shown to be your fault, it is you who must be sued; your husband is not responsible.

Still, the law does impose certain duties on both husband and wife which they are bound to obey.

Consortium: Until the nineteenth century, it was the husband's right to

Marriage is a promise between the two of you to love and cherish each other.

confine his wife and administer what was politely called 'bodily punishment' if he saw fit. Today, however, this right to consortium means only the mutual duty of cohabiting, and sharing a common home and domestic life. Definitely *no* 'bodily punishment' is included in the package! The right to consortium does include a mutual right to sexual intercourse, however, although a husband cannot demand sexual intercourse from his wife whenever he feels like it, or insist on the use of contraception against her will. On the other hand, a wife can't withdraw her husband's sexual privilege completely.

Maintenance: The most basic of the husband's traditional duties in marriage which still survives is to 'provide' for his wife—at least all the necessities commensurate with the family's life style.

Change of name: Strangely, it is only a matter of custom that a wife, upon marriage, assumes her husband's surname; it is not, and never has been, legally necessary. So you may keep your maiden name if you prefer—increasingly, in fact, professional or career women are doing just that, or compromising by continuing to use their maiden name for work purposes and their 'married' name socially.

In fact, if you want to change your name with or without marriage, it's surprisingly uncomplicated to do. There isn't anything sacred or legal about your name; it's merely a convenient means to ease of identification. On the other hand, if you've been known as Mr and Mrs Jones for years, the difficulty of informing everyone—tax collector, rates officer, friends, relatives, bank manager and bill collector—that you now wish to be known as Mr and Mrs Smith is mammoth. The easiest way to do it, in fact, is to provide official evidence of your change of name and this can best be done by changing your name by Deed Poll. A solicitor could be helpful here because he could prepare the necessary document for you.

A change of Christian name (that is, the name given to you at christening or baptism) is, believe it or not, more difficult. In law, in fact, it can only be effected by the Church which gave you the name in the first place. But you can avoid this complicated step by simply using whatever name you choose and also keeping your original name. If you have never been christened then a change of first name is the same as changing your surname.

Acquiring your home

It is probably the dream of every young couple who marry to buy their own home—if not immediately then as soon as possible in the future. Not only does it make economic sense (paying out large amounts of money in rent can ruin the most generous budget and of course at the end of the day you still have nothing to 'show' for it), but it also in a sense symbolizes the commitment that marriage ideally is.

Mortgages

Even before you decide on which house you want to buy, you should investigate the various lending possibilities open to you. Mortgage is the name usually given to the type of loan which has, as its security, a house, and what kind of mortgage you arrange will of course depend on your financial state of affairs. This generally means your salary as lenders don't usually take account of your other assets or of overtime pay and bonuses. The general economic climate is important, too, for if money is 'tight', lenders are not so willing to lend, and if interest rates have gone up it may be harder to finance the mortgage. At the time of writing, lenders are willing to offer mortgages at the sum of about three times your income; in arriving at their estimate of this income, most lenders will take two to two and a half times the husband's plus one times the wife's salary.

The following types of mortgage are generally available:

Building societies . . . the most common for those paying standard rate income tax or above. Most building societies are more ready to grant you a mortgage if you have some money on deposit with them. Repayments are made monthly and represent part-capital, part-interest, spread over a predetermined number of years. Tax relief can be claimed on that part which represents interest.

Insurance Companies . . . available most often if your employer or professional association has a scheme to help employees find a mortgage. Otherwise the company will require you to take out an endowment policy for a term of years which is then given over to the company as security. When the policy comes to an end or 'matures', the money is used to pay back the company for lending you the sum. You will pay both the instalments due on the policy and the monthly instalments due on the interest of the loan. Tax relief is available on the policy and the instalments of interest.

Building Society and Endowment Policy . . . basically the same as an insurance company loan with an endowment policy (see above), except that the insurance company only receives instalments representing the policy and the building society actually loans you the sum. Tax relief is available on both the policy and repayments of interest on the loan. This is perhaps the best scheme as it affords the greatest tax relief, particularly for those paying a high rate of tax.

Bank Loans . . . most often used for those selling one house to buy another, or for those who will be able to pay for the house in cash. Usually only a very short term advance called a 'bridging loan' until you are able to receive the cash for payment. Very high interest repayments.

Local Authorities . . . used for borrowing on inexpensive or older housing. Otherwise similar to building society loans.

Private Mortgages . . . sometimes arranged by a solicitor or through personal means whereby a trustee of a fund or individual invests in the security of housing. Tax relief on interest repayments.

The lender does, by the way, have a statutory right to foreclose or sell your house and take what remains due to him out of the selling price. Having said that, however, it ought also to be stressed that most lending organizations will react sympathetically to genuine cases of temporary difficulty with repayments (for instance, if your husband is unlucky enough to be put on short-time working or if one of you loses your job). If you know in advance that such difficulties may occur, you should get in touch with your lending agency and ask for their help.

Solicitors: You should consult a solicitor at an early stage of the negotiations. In fact, if you're having difficulty obtaining finance, your solicitor may be able to help, although he may

It's always a good idea to know exactly how much your dream house will cost you month by month, year by year. And of course the amounts listed below are payments due before income tax allowances.

	Sample Mortgage Monthly Repayments*					
Advance	15-year period (approximate)		20-year period (approximate)		25-year period (approximate)	
	11%	7.40%	11%	7.40%	11%	7.40%
	£ p	£ p	£ p	£ p	£ p	£ p
1000	11.59	9.38	10.47	8.11	9.90	7.41
1100	12.75	10.32	11.52	8.92	10.89	8.15
1200	13.91	11.26	12.56	9.73	11.88	8.89
1300	15.07	12.20	13.61	10.55	12.87	9.63
1400	16.23	13.13	14.66	11.36	13.86	10.37
1500	17.39	14.07	15.70	12.17	14.85	11.12
2000	23.18	18.76	20.93	16.22	19.80	14.82
3000	34.77	28.15	31.40	24.34	29.69	22.23
4000	46.36	37.53	41.86	32.45	39.59	29.64
5000	57.95	46.91	52.33	40.56	49.48	37.05
6000	69.54	56.29	62.79	48.67	59.38	44.46
7000	81.13	65.67	73.26	56.78	69.27	51.87
8000	92.72	75.06	83.72	64.90	79.18	59.28
9000	104.31	84.44	94.19	73.01	89.07	66.69
10,000	115.90	93.82	104.66	81.12	98.96	74.10

* rates operative at time of writing; check with your building society for details of possible changes

well charge a fee for it. He will act for you alone and must look after *your* interests and not those of the vendor or estate agent, if one is involved in the purchase. He will find out if the title to the property is clear and that no one, apart from the vendor, is entitled to the house or any part of it. He will also check to make sure that the Local Authority has no plans which would affect the value of the property you are about to buy. Finally, he will look over all the contracts drawn up to legalize the transaction to make sure that they are in order.

Surveyors: Often the bank, building society or insurance company which lends you the purchase money will insist on having the property inspected by a surveyor. This surveyor will be liable to the lending agency and will usually consider only the value of the house and not its state of repair. It is therefore very important that you also employ a surveyor to examine the property you are interested in from *your* point of view; if you don't know of one, your solicitor should be able to help. The vendor of the house is under no obligation to inform you of any

problems or defects and some, such as dry rot, woodworm, faulty electrical wiring and damp, are often concealed; hence the need for a surveyor 'on your side' who can tell you just how much repair work needs to be done and how much it should cost. He should also be able to tell you what he considers to be the true value of the house. The surveyor will be as thorough as possible because if he is negligent and faults are discovered later, you have the right to sue him. Your solicitor will tell you when he thinks you should arrange for your survey to be done.

Estate Agents: If you find that the house you wish to purchase has been advertised by, or is on the books of, an estate agent, be warned: an estate agent acts *only* for the vendor and it is therefore in his interest to sell the house for the best price obtainable. Do not sign any agreements or pay any deposits until you have consulted your solicitor and surveyor. If you do sign an agreement which states the parties, the property and the price, then you may be unable to get out of it.

In these circumstances, much the best course to pursue is to instruct your solicitor to make the estate agent an offer on your behalf and, if the owner accepts your offer, you may then be asked to pay a preliminary deposit to the estate agent. It is advisable to pay not more than one percent or, say, £100 at this time, and certainly you should not pay out any further sums without your solicitor's advice. The object of such a preliminary deposit is merely to show serious intent to purchase and if you subsequently decide to withdraw from purchase, this money will be returned to you by the estate agent.

It's one of the most exciting things that the two of you can do together when you're newly married – to 'shop around' new housing estates, or buildings under construction, in the hope of finding that house of your dreams – and preferably at a price you can afford.

The Fees Involved: Be prepared! In addition to the purchase price of your new home, there will be some 'extras' —the fees of your solicitor and surveyor, for instance. In addition to these, you may also have to pay stamp duty (if the cost of your house is over

£15,000), and, when buying certain houses, mainly in major residential areas, some fees may also be due to the Government Land Registry.

Costs and fees chargeable will, of course, vary according to the amount you are paying for your house, but to give just one example, on a house where the purchase price is £14,000 the total fees would probably be between £200 and £250.

The Contract of Sale and Title : When the initial formalities of purchasing your house (engaging a solicitor, arranging finance, etc) are decided, the contract of sale is prepared. Both the vendor and buyer sign similar contracts. To protect both of you, by the way, it's a good idea to have the documents (and therefore ownership) drawn up in joint names—this means, essentially, that one of you can't sell the house without the consent of the other; your solicitor will be able to explain how best to do this and also the effect of placing the property in both your names, since there are a number of rather complicated legal consequences that are not readily apparent to the innocent layman!

(If you've already bought your home, and it's in your husband's name you may still have legal rights to the property, even though you may not be working and contributing to the mortgage repayments. You can, at any time, approach a solicitor and ask him to register a note of your interest with the Government Land Registry. This means that any person intending to buy the property will find this note and will not proceed with the purchase until such time as your rights have been properly safeguarded. You ought to tell your husband you're doing this of course so that he's aware of the situation before signing legally binding contracts to sell the property.)

When the contracts are exchanged you will be asked to pay ten per cent of the purchase price to the vendor by way of a deposit. Normally this deposit will be held by the vendor's solicitor until such time as the purchase is finally completed.

The final completion of the transaction occurs when a Deed of Conveyance or a Deed of Transfer is handed over in return for the balance of the sale price. The final completion will take place approximately one month after the exchange of contracts. Once 'completion' has taken place, incidentally, the title to the house passes to you as buyer, although the lender of the purchase money will keep the title deed as security on his mortgage. If at any time between the exchange of contracts and final 'completion' the house is destroyed, for example by fire, you would still be bound to pay for it and should therefore make sure that the house is insured in your own names as soon as the contracts have been exchanged.

Freehold and Leasehold
The major difference between freehold and leasehold purchase is that when you obtain a freehold you own the property for ever, that is your ownership is absolute; with leasehold property you will own it only for a fixed term of years, although if the fixed term is 99 years then obviously the difference is somewhat academic. It's important to note, though, that if you own the leasehold of a house for a period in excess of 21 years, then when you have lived in the house for more than five years, you automatically have the right to purchase the freehold. The valuation of the freehold is fixed by statute and will depend on its original cost and how many years remain unexpired on the lease. Unfortunately, you don't have this right where you own the lease of a flat.

Flats and Houses
There's no real difference between purchasing a flat rather than a house, although you'll probably find that the title to a flat is normally leasehold while a house is normally freehold. There will be legal conditions attaching to the leasehold to provide for payment of maintenance and repair of the common parts of a block of flats or house, plus the payment of a small annual ground rent. There may also be an annual service charge to pay for insurance premiums, common maintenance of lifts, etc.

Rented Accommodation
If you are postponing purchasing a house for one reason or another, then you'll probably rent a flat, either furnished or unfurnished. The law concerning rented housing is complex but the most important thing for you to appreciate when renting is that you are bound by the terms and conditions in your tenancy; if you are in breach of these conditions then the landlord has the right to repossess the premises by taking you to court. However, it's often possible to show the court valid reasons for the breach and in such cases you may be given a chance to remedy the problem.

If you continue to occupy premises after the expiry date of your contract or lease, you are considered to be a 'statutory tenant'. As long as you continue to reside there personally, you are bound by the conditions of the original lease but at the same time the landlord cannot evict you unless the 'rent has not been paid or you have committed a nuisance, breach of conditions, assigned or sublet without the owner's consent or if the landlord needs the accommodation for himself, his children or his parents.'

The situation is different, however, where an owner/occupier lets his accommodation to you, for example, if he goes abroad for a couple of years. As long as the owner has given you notice in writing before the commencement of your tenancy, you are bound by law to allow him to repossess upon his return.

Basically all tenancies, unfurnished or furnished, are now covered by the various Rent Acts and are called (with some exceptions) 'regulated tenancies'. Should either you or your landlord think that the rent you're paying is too high or too low, both of you have the right to make application to your local rent officer to fix what he considers to be a 'fair rent'. The law on this subject can be complicated, so do seek professional advice if you run into difficulties. And if something has to be done in a hurry, go and see your rent officer—he should be able to advise you.

Identifying the house (or flat) of your dreams can be quite a long, drawn-out process, and you could look at literally hundreds of properties before making that final, important decision. The main thing is to try to enjoy it as much as you can. Apart from anything else, you'll get to know what you can expect for the price you can afford.

Income tax

Any income received by a person resident in this country is subject to taxation. Tax law is very complicated indeed, so if you have any specific queries relating to your particular tax situation, then you really ought to see your bank manager, accountant or solicitor. Parliament can, and frequently does, change the rate of tax charged, but the information given below will give you some idea of the basic rates and allowances operative at the time of writing.

When a couple marry, the wife's income is then normally considered to be that of her husband's for the purposes of taxation. Where your joint income is considerable it may be beneficial for the two of you to be taxed separately, but this will only affect your 'earned income', that is, wages, etc as opposed to investment income (such as dividends or interest) which will continue to be lumped with your husband's income for tax purposes. Therefore, if your husband is earning £2500 per year and you are earning £2000, then you'll be liable to pay income tax on the sum of £4500. Your husband can, however, deduct a 'married man's allowance' from this sum and you (so long as you continue to work) can deduct a 'wife's earned income allowance'. These allowances are currently £955 and £675 respectively, so out of your total earnings of £4500, £1630 will not be subject to tax. You will be liable for tax on the remaining £2870 and at the current rate that works out at approximately £1005 tax.

Assuming that you can claim no other relief apart from the two mentioned above and that you have no other income (from investments etc), then it's best for you to be taxed together. When the total amount of your taxable income (income following deduction of all allowances) exceeds £4500, tax becomes payable at a higher rate than the standard one—the rates increase as the income increases. Therefore, if you were taxed as two single people, you could each earn £5175 before being liable for tax at higher rates (£4500 plus personal allowances of £675). Your husband can't claim a 'married man's allowance' if you've opted to be taxed separately, however.

If you continue to be taxed together you would start paying tax at a higher rate once your total income exceeded £7360 (at this point the extra benefit which the married couple obtain by claiming the 'married man's allowance' exactly balances the tax at higher rates that must be paid by them as soon as their income exceeds £6130). If your income was as high as your husband's, and you were taxed separately, it would be possible for you and your husband to earn a maximum of £10,350 before being taxed at a higher rate.

Therefore, if your joint earnings exceed £7360, it's obviously beneficial for you to opt to be taxed separately.

Allowances
No matter how you're taxed—through your employer or individually—these are the new important personal reliefs deductible at present:

1. **Married man** (available where husband and wife opt to be taxed together; it cannot be claimed in addition to a single person's allowance) **£955**
2. **Single person** (available to all who are not married and to husbands whose wives opt to be taxed separately) **£675**
3. **Wife's earned income** (available to all wives who are earning) **£675**
4. **Children**
   over 16 (and in full time education or training) **£305**
   ages 11-16 **£275**
   under 11 **£240**
5. **Widow or widower's housekeeper** **£100**
6. **Additional children which you look after** **£200**
7. **Dependent relative** (if you maintain a relative of old age or who is infirm) **£100-145**
8. **If either spouse is blind** **£180**
9. **Relief on life assurance policies, mortgages, etc** depends on amount of premium or interest payable.

When to get married
When you get married, your husband's 'personal allowance' of £675 is replaced by a 'married man's allowance' of £955. Assuming that you continue to work, your personal allowance of £675 is replaced by a 'wife's earned income allowance' of the same amount. These two allowances are not the same, however—and both can be claimed during the financial year in which the marriage takes place. You should therefore try to ensure that you receive maximum benefit from all these allowances. So far as the 'married man's allowance' is concerned, the extra benefit of this over and above the husband's former 'personal allowance' reduces as the financial year (which begins on April 6) proceeds.

If you continue working (and a 'wife's earned income allowance' is only available to you if you do), it is advisable for you to take full advantage of your personal allowance before being married, and this means that you must earn £675 from the start of the tax year and before the date of the marriage. Therefore, assuming that you earn, say, £30 a week, you will have used up your personal allowance by the end of August. If you marry at that time and continue working, you then obtain the benefit of the 'wife's earned income allowance', which means that you may earn a further £675 during the remainder of the tax year free of tax.

If you do marry at the end of August, then the benefit of the 'married man's allowance' would have reduced somewhat but it is still better for you to make use of both of *your* allowances available to you during the year.

If you don't intend to continue working after your marriage, then maximum benefit must be taken of your husband's 'married man's allowance' and your own 'personal allowance', the marriage taking place as soon as your personal allowance for the year has been used up. If you were not working prior to your marriage and don't intend working after it, then you should marry as early as possible in the financial year so that you can both take full advantage of the 'married man's allowance'.

There isn't a soul alive who actually WANTS to pay too much income tax – but unfortunately some people do, and usually because they don't realize that their tax positions change on marriage. For instance, there's a special allowance for married men, sometimes it's better to be taxed together, sometimes separately – there's lots to know to make sure that you are getting all that you're entitled to. And because it's so complicated, it's probably better to seek the advice of a specialist, such as a solicitor or an accountant right at the beginning. He could even tell you what would be the best day for you to get married!

Banks insurances wills and intestacy

Bank Accounts

The other type of 'property' most likely to be owned by any young couple is a bank account, and whether to open a joint account after your wedding, keep separate personal ones, or have several different accounts for specific purposes, is probably one of the most pressing decisions awaiting any newly-wed.

Problems can arise if you have a joint account. One of you may be 'good' with money, the other may well not be so. Legally, if both of you contribute equally to such an account then your interest is considered to be joint and equal; if only your husband contributes then the law rather kindly assumes a gift to you of half the fund; on the other hand, men's lib has not yet arrived and if *you* contribute solely to the joint account then the courts consider you to be the sole owner. One of the main advantages of this type of account undoubtedly is that, upon the death of one of you, the balance will pass to the other upon reproduction to the bank of the deceased holder's death certificate.

What kind of accounts you choose will probably depend on you, and on your circumstances, but it is an important decision and one that should be gone into carefully before any final commitments are made.

Life assurance policies

A life assurance policy can be a valuable asset—apart from its obvious advantage, it can also be used as security for loans, etc. Insurance companies offer lots of different types of policies these days, so it's a sensible idea to discuss the pros and cons of them all with your insurance agent before coming to any decision. There are, however, four basic types:

1. Whole life insurance: For the payment of instalments (called premiums) over the period of your life, the company agrees to pay, on your death, a fixed sum to your surviving dependants.

2. Endowment insurance: Where a young person agrees to pay premiums for a fixed period and the company agrees to pay a lump sum at the end of the period or upon death, if this occurs first. So if at 25 you take out an endowment policy which matures when you are 50, when you reach 50 the whole of the endowment policy is payable to you. If you die at any time before reaching 50, the whole of the policy is payable to your surviving dependants.

3. Term life policies: This is an insurance policy which you take out for a fixed term of, say, five or ten years. If you die within this period, the insurance is payable to your surviving dependants but if you survive the five or ten years you receive nothing. It may seem absurd to pay premiums which may amount to nothing in the end, but it does have advantages. For instance if you want to open a shop and sink all your money into it, not knowing whether it will be successful or not, a term life policy will provide you with the security you need. If you die within this period while owing large sums of money, the policy will enable your dependants to cover your debts. Furthermore, owning the policy will serve as collateral and security for any bank manager who might consider lending you money for the business.

4. Annuities: These are usually purchased towards retirement age, whereby for the payment of a lump sum, an insurance company agrees to pay a certain income for the remainder of life. The advantages are that the purchaser can be assured of a guaranteed income, and that repayments of capital under the annuity are not subject to tax.

Other Insurance Policies

It is wise to insure yourself against theft and or damage to your home. Some people also like to take out special insurances against specific events, a plane journey for instance; others may wish to insure against personal injury, such as accidents or chronic illness. For this latter type of coverage, you will probably be required to give exhaustive details of your occupation, medical and physical history, and the older you are the more difficult it will probably be for you to obtain such insurance without a thorough medical examination.

Wills

It seems a bit depressing to think about making wills and provision for after death just as you're embarking upon married life. But it is one area where it's definitely best to be prepared and aware. If you die without making a will (intestate), then potentially a great deal of your property and other assets could end up being heavily taxed and, more important, going to someone other than the person or persons you intend to receive it. Even if you have made a will in the dim and distant past, remember that such a will is automatically invalidated by marriage, unless made expressly 'in

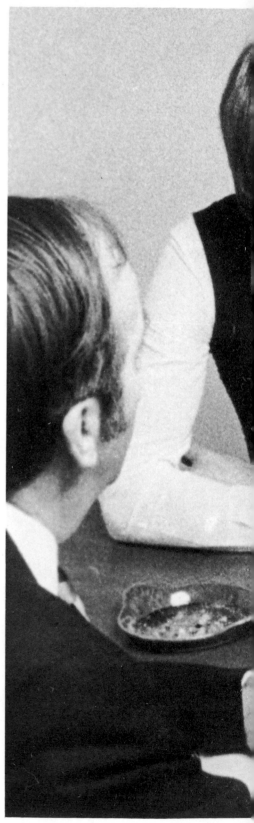

contemplation' of it (this doesn't apply in Scotland, by the way; marriage doesn't revoke a will made previously but the birth of your first child does).

These are the most important things to remember when making a will:

1. A will must be written, not spoken.
2. It must be signed by the 'testator' (you, if you're making the will) and, if it's longer than one page, it's advisable to sign it on each page.
3. The signature must come at the end of the will.
4. The will must be signed in the presence of two witnesses, who must in turn sign the will.

The making of a will is important and is something you should ideally do through your solicitor, who will be able to ensure that the wording and completion are correct in law.

There's lots of ways you can protect and provide for one another's future right at the start of your marriage – by opening joint bank accounts, by taking out sensible life and house insurance coverage and by making a will.

Index